IMPALER ™

VOLUME 2

written and created by:
William Harms

art by:
Matt Timson

lettered by:
Troy Peteri

published by
Top Cow Productions, Inc.
Los Angeles

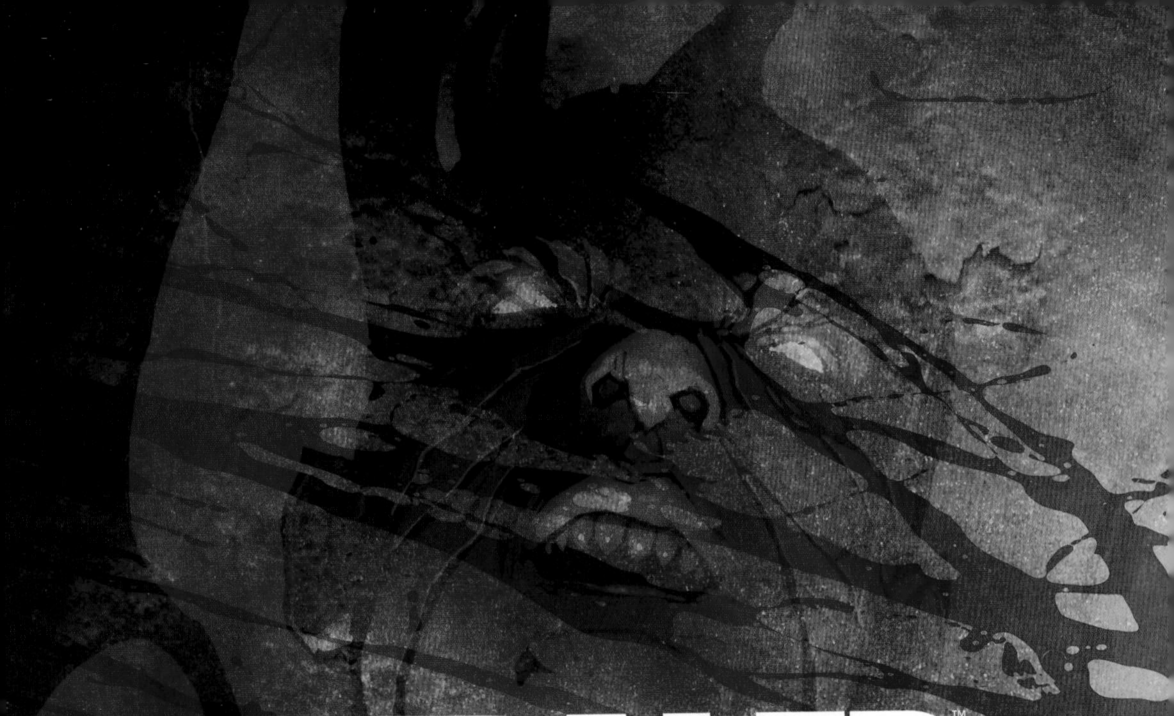

IMPALER

VOLUME 2

For Top Cow Productions, Inc.:
Marc Silvestri - Chief Executive Officer
Matt Hawkins - President and Chief Operating Officer
Filip Sablik - Publisher
Phil Smith - Managing Editor
Bryan Rountree - Assistant to the Publisher
Christine Dinh - Marketing Assistant
Mark Haynes - Webmaster
Anthony McAfee and **Ernesto Gomez** - Interns

 for *image* comics
publisher:
Eric Stephenson

 to find the comic shop
nearest you call:
888-COMIC-BOOK   1-888-COMICBOOK

Want more info? check out:
www.topcow.com and **www.thetopcowstore.com**
for news and exclusive Top Cow merchandise!

For this edition
Cover Art by:
Matt Timson

For this edition
Book Design and Layout by:
Phil Smith

Original editions edited by:
Rob Levin, Filip Sablik and **Phil Smith**
Original editions Book Design and Layout by:
Scott Newman and **Chaz Riggs**

Impaler volume 2 Trade Paperback, July 2010. FIRST PRINTING. ISBN: 978-1-60706-101-4.
Published by Image Comics Inc. Office of Publication: 2134 Allston Way, 2nd Floor Berkeley, CA 94704. $14.99 U.S.D.
Originally published in single magazine form as Impaler volume 2 #1-5. Impaler. © 2010 William Harms and Top Cow
Productions, Inc. All rights reserved. "Impaler," the Impaler logos, and the likeness of all characters (human or
otherwise) featured herein are trademarks of William Harms and Top Cow Productions, Inc. Image Comics and the
Image Comics logo are trademarks of Image Comics, Inc. The characters, events, and stories in this publication are
entirely fictional. Any resemblance to actual persons (living or dead), events, institutions, or locales, without satiric intent,
is coincidental. No portion of this publication may be reproduced or transmitted, in any form or by any means, without the
express written permission of Top Cow Productions, Inc. **PRINTED IN KOREA.**

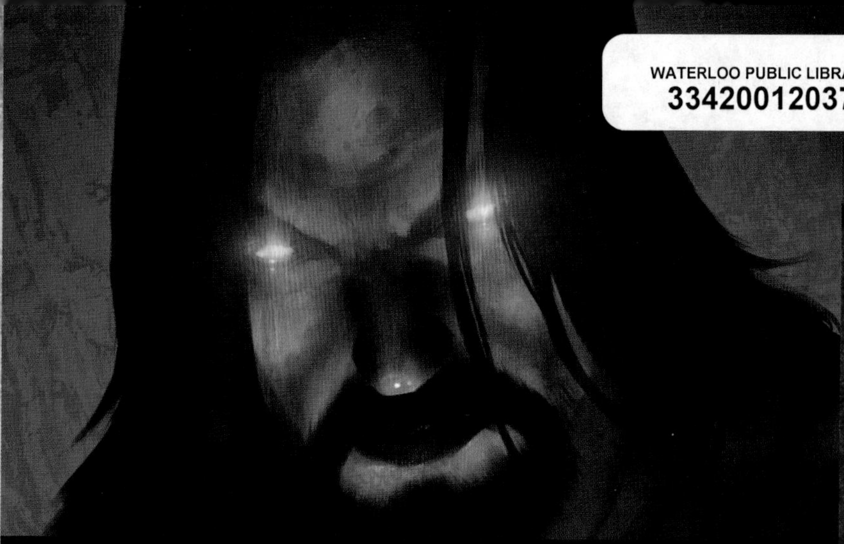

TABLE OF CONTENTS

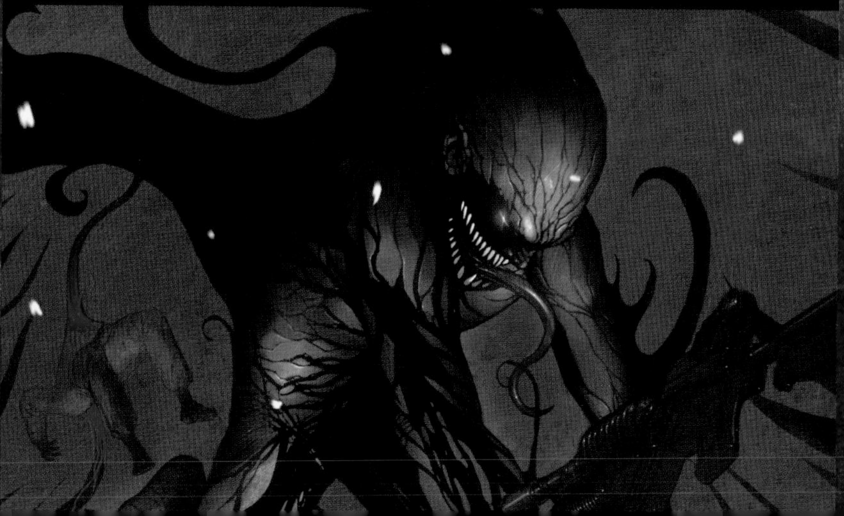

I've written a lot about folkloric and pop culture vampires in my books, *Vampire Universe*, *They Bite* and *Wanted Undead or Alive* (Citadel Press, respectively 2006, 2009 and 2010). I've also built novels around them, relying more on the folkloric monsters rather than riffing off of the sanitized pop culture versions. I love a good horror story, but damn it I want it to be built on a strong foundation that blends beliefs in the supernatural, science, history and solid storytelling.

With *Impaler*, Harms twists the genre to present the historical Vlad as both a vampire and a hero. That's hard as hell to pull off, but Harms does it with power and style. The stunning and moody artwork by Matt Timson is a perfect (if chilling) compliment to the gritty in-your-face writing.

The vampires of *Impaler* are nasty and evil and very frightening. They don't want to bond with a teenage girl or take over a small town–they are an invading force bent on global domination. They want to see humanity drown in an ocean of blood. The very viciousness of their campaign sets the dark and urgent tone for this series. What gives all this a heroic spin are the individuals who stand between the bloodthirsty horde and us. One of them is a human and the other is Vlad Dracula himself, who doesn't want the world to fall. Their partnering is a devil's deal that is explored through many psychological and philosophical layers.

If you are coming to this collection because you've read the individual comics and want to re-visit this dark and dangerous territory, then welcome back.

If this is your first visit to the world of *Impaler*, then wow, are you in for a treat. I won't recommend for you to lock the doors or turn on all the lights. It won't help. This book is going to be scary no matter where you read it.

Yeah…vampires are scary.

-**Jonathan Maberry**
NY Times bestseller and multiple Bram Stoker Award winning
author of *The Dragon Factory*, *The Wolfman* and *Rot & Ruin*

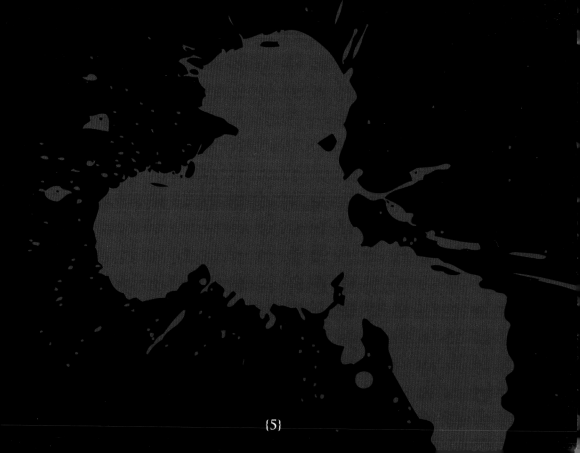

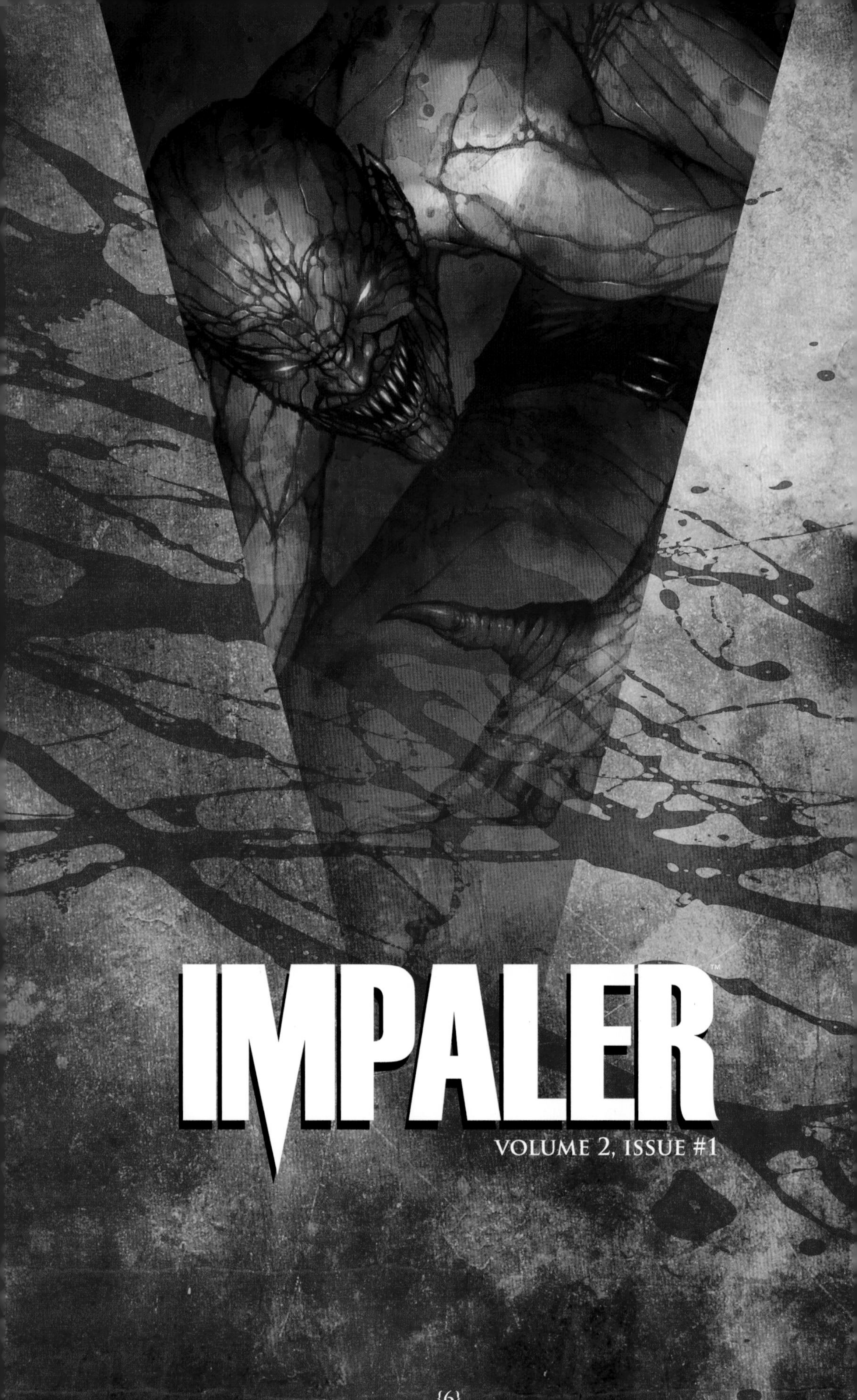
IMPALER™
VOLUME 2, ISSUE #1

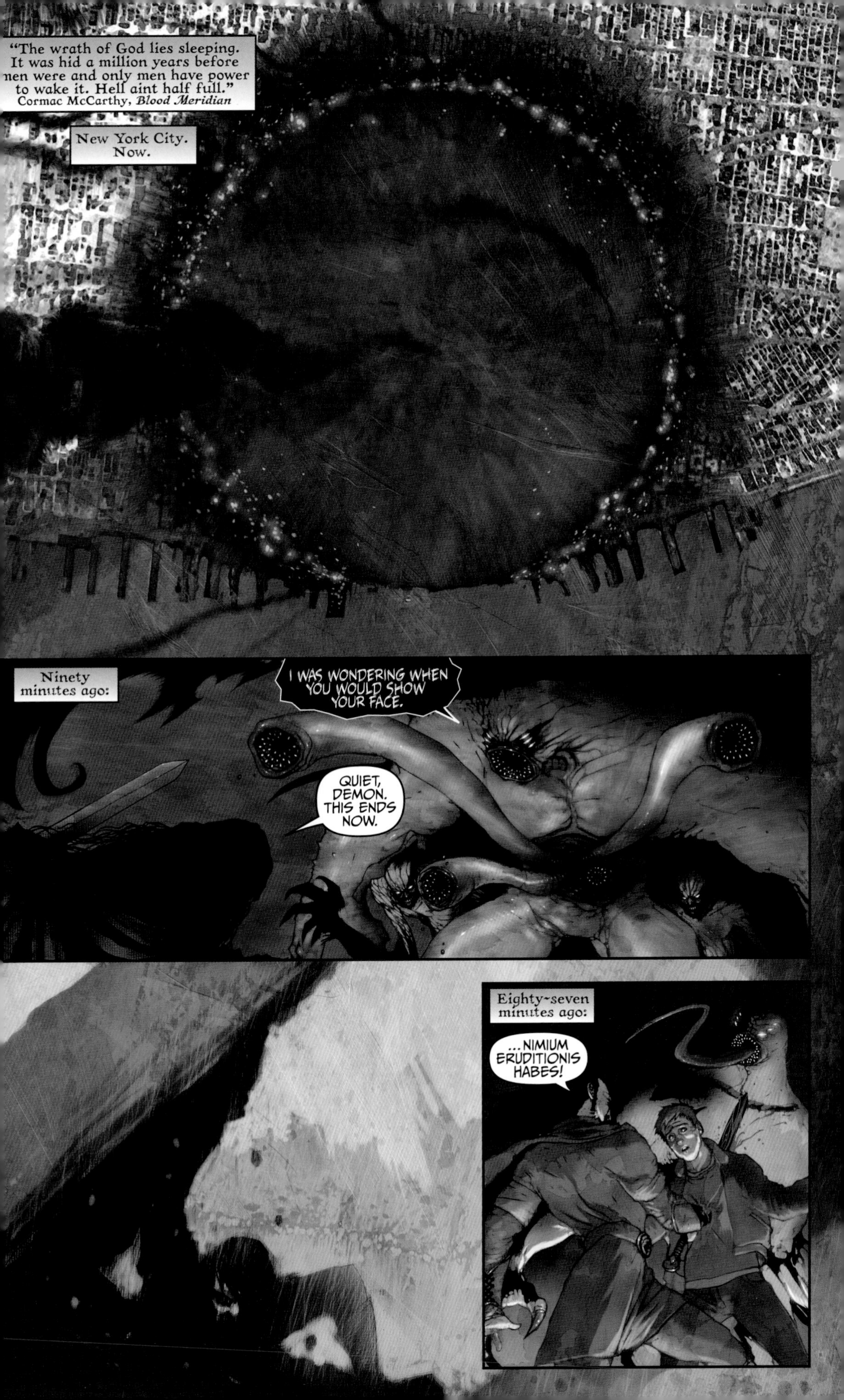
"The wrath of God lies sleeping. It was hid a million years before men were and only men have power to wake it. Hell aint half full."
Cormac McCarthy, *Blood Meridian*
New York City. Now.
Ninety minutes ago:
I WAS WONDERING WHEN YOU WOULD SHOW YOUR FACE.
QUIET, DEMON. THIS ENDS NOW.
Eighty-seven minutes ago:
...NIMIUM ERUDITIONIS HABES!

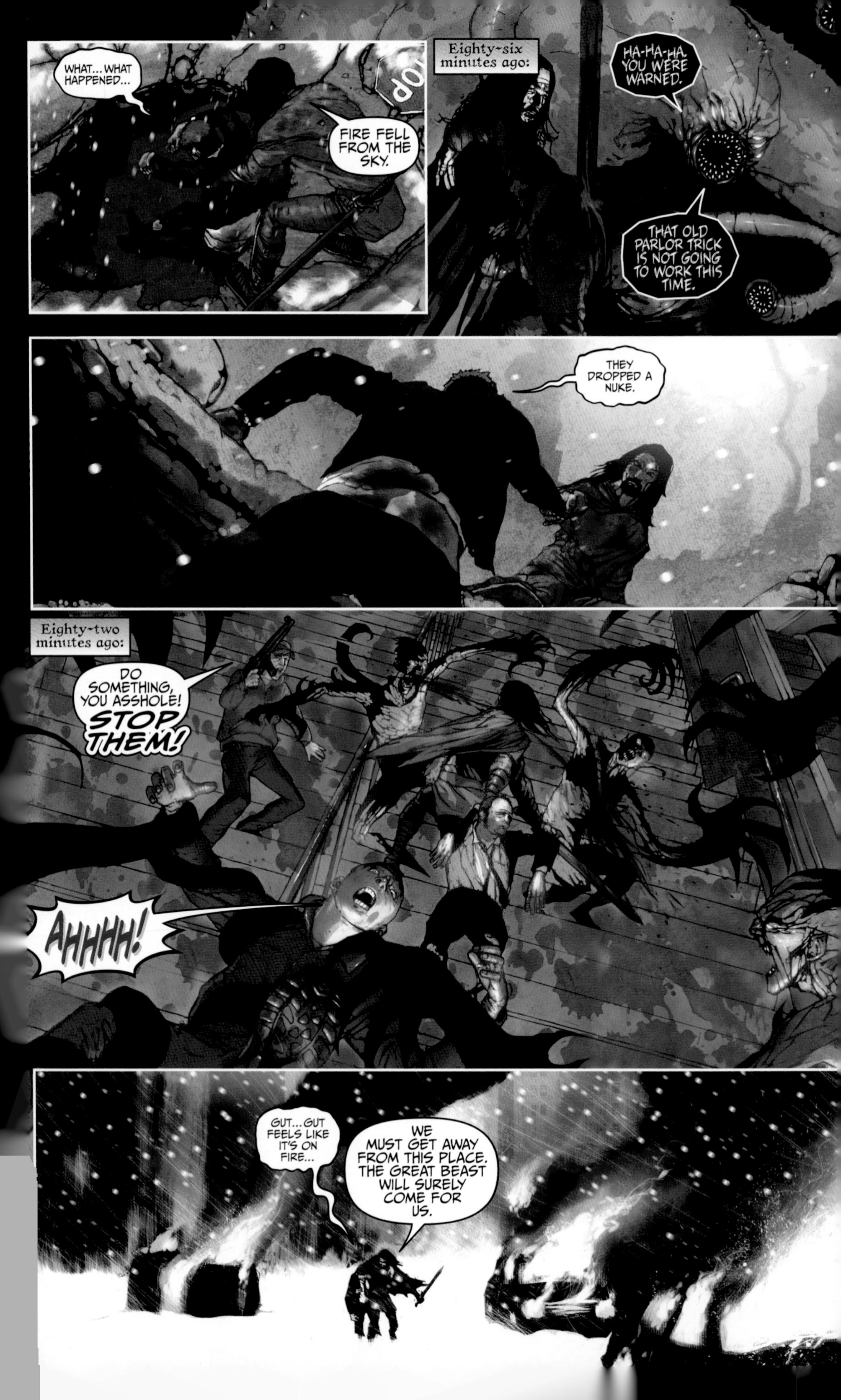
WHAT...WHAT HAPPENED...
FIRE FELL FROM THE SKY.
Eighty-six minutes ago:
HA-HA-HA. YOU WERE WARNED.
THAT OLD PARLOR TRICK IS NOT GOING TO WORK THIS TIME.
THEY DROPPED A NUKE.
Eighty-two minutes ago:
DO SOMETHING, YOU ASSHOLE! STOP THEM!
AHHHH!
GUT...GUT FEELS LIKE IT'S ON FIRE...
WE MUST GET AWAY FROM THIS PLACE. THE GREAT BEAST WILL SURELY COME FOR US.

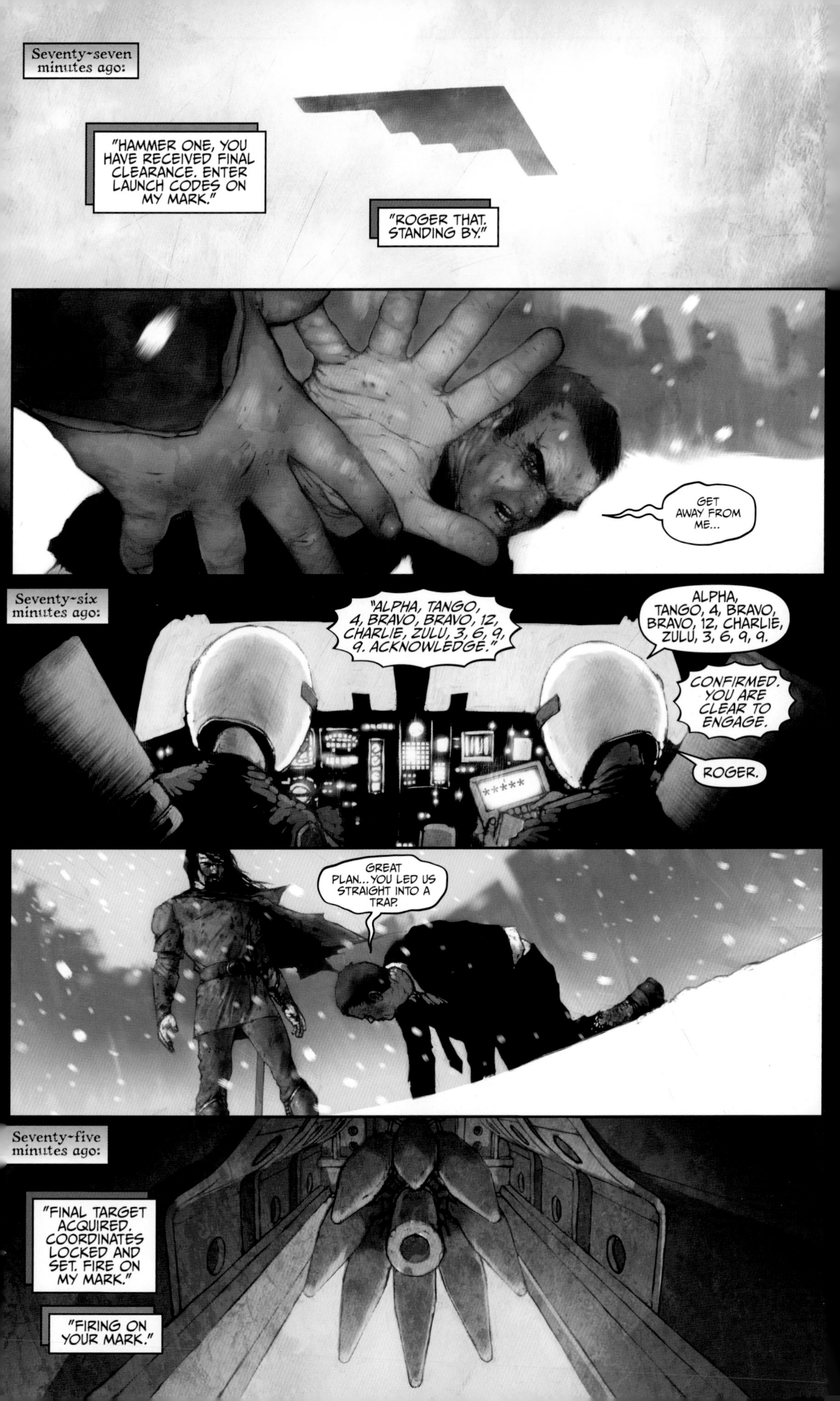
Seventy-seven minutes ago:
"HAMMER ONE, YOU HAVE RECEIVED FINAL CLEARANCE. ENTER LAUNCH CODES ON MY MARK."
"ROGER THAT. STANDING BY."
GET AWAY FROM ME...
Seventy-six minutes ago:
"ALPHA, TANGO, 4, BRAVO, BRAVO, 12, CHARLIE, ZULU, 3, 6, 9, 9. ACKNOWLEDGE."
ALPHA, TANGO, 4, BRAVO, BRAVO, 12, CHARLIE, ZULU, 3, 6, 9, 9.
CONFIRMED. YOU ARE CLEAR TO ENGAGE.
ROGER.
*****
GREAT PLAN... YOU LED US STRAIGHT INTO A TRAP.
Seventy-five minutes ago:
"FINAL TARGET ACQUIRED. COORDINATES LOCKED AND SET. FIRE ON MY MARK."
"FIRING ON YOUR MARK."

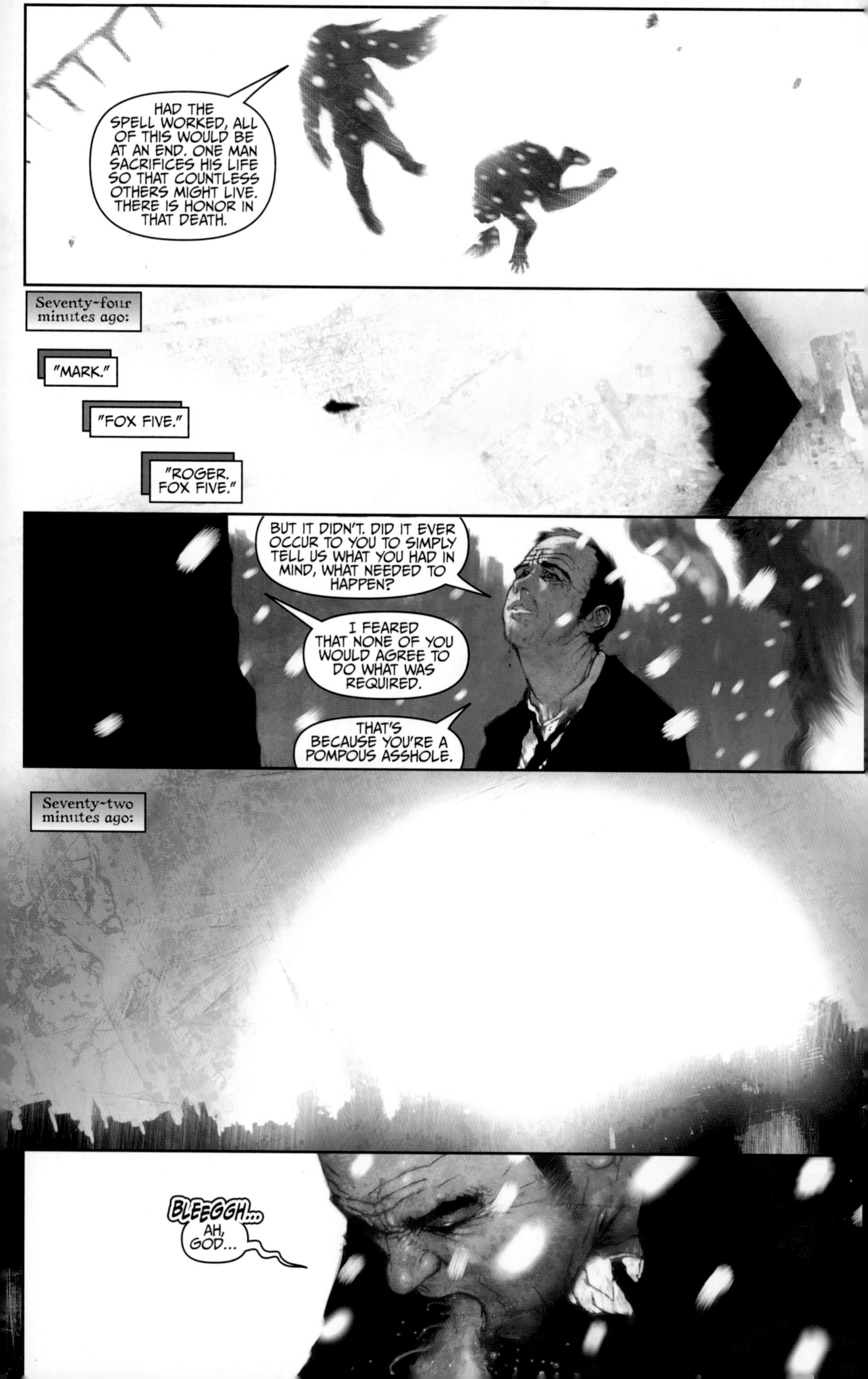
HAD THE SPELL WORKED, ALL OF THIS WOULD BE AT AN END. ONE MAN SACRIFICES HIS LIFE SO THAT COUNTLESS OTHERS MIGHT LIVE. THERE IS HONOR IN THAT DEATH.
Seventy-four minutes ago:
"MARK."
"FOX FIVE."
"ROGER. FOX FIVE."
BUT IT DIDN'T. DID IT EVER OCCUR TO YOU TO SIMPLY TELL US WHAT YOU HAD IN MIND, WHAT NEEDED TO HAPPEN?
I FEARED THAT NONE OF YOU WOULD AGREE TO DO WHAT WAS REQUIRED.
THAT'S BECAUSE YOU'RE A POMPOUS ASSHOLE.
Seventy-two minutes ago:
BLEEGGH... AH, GOD...

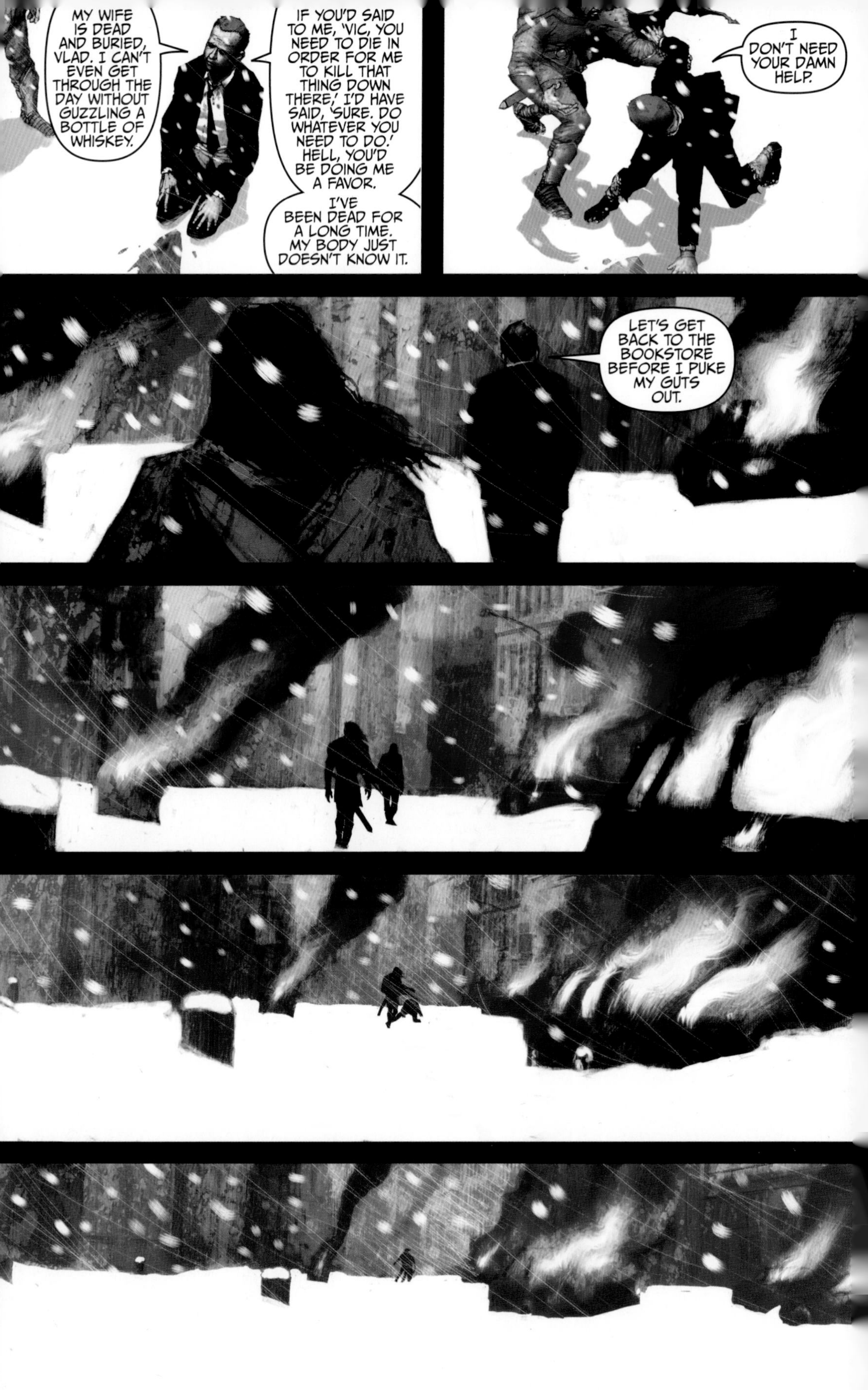
MY WIFE IS DEAD AND BURIED, VLAD. I CAN'T EVEN GET THROUGH THE DAY WITHOUT GUZZLING A BOTTLE OF WHISKEY.
IF YOU'D SAID TO ME, 'VIC, YOU NEED TO DIE IN ORDER FOR ME TO KILL THAT THING DOWN THERE,' I'D HAVE SAID, 'SURE. DO WHATEVER YOU NEED TO DO.' HELL, YOU'D BE DOING ME A FAVOR.
I'VE BEEN DEAD FOR A LONG TIME. MY BODY JUST DOESN'T KNOW IT.
I DON'T NEED YOUR DAMN HELP.
LET'S GET BACK TO THE BOOKSTORE BEFORE I PUKE MY GUTS OUT.

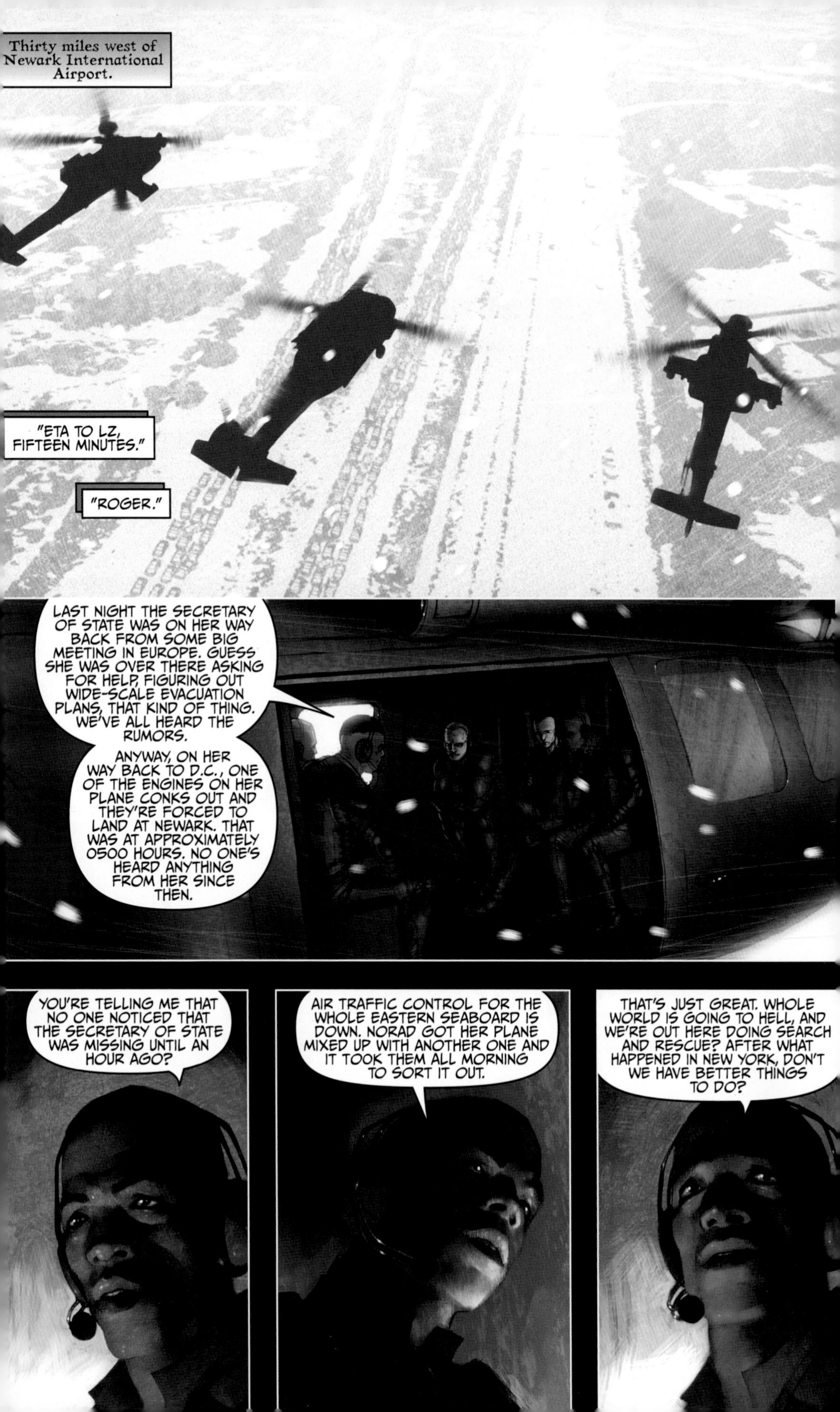
Thirty miles west of Newark International Airport.
"ETA TO LZ, FIFTEEN MINUTES."
"ROGER."
LAST NIGHT THE SECRETARY OF STATE WAS ON HER WAY BACK FROM SOME BIG MEETING IN EUROPE. GUESS SHE WAS OVER THERE ASKING FOR HELP, FIGURING OUT WIDE-SCALE EVACUATION PLANS, THAT KIND OF THING. WE'VE ALL HEARD THE RUMORS.
ANYWAY, ON HER WAY BACK TO D.C., ONE OF THE ENGINES ON HER PLANE CONKS OUT AND THEY'RE FORCED TO LAND AT NEWARK. THAT WAS AT APPROXIMATELY 0500 HOURS. NO ONE'S HEARD ANYTHING FROM HER SINCE THEN.
YOU'RE TELLING ME THAT NO ONE NOTICED THAT THE SECRETARY OF STATE WAS MISSING UNTIL AN HOUR AGO?
AIR TRAFFIC CONTROL FOR THE WHOLE EASTERN SEABOARD IS DOWN. NORAD GOT HER PLANE MIXED UP WITH ANOTHER ONE AND IT TOOK THEM ALL MORNING TO SORT IT OUT.
THAT'S JUST GREAT. WHOLE WORLD IS GOING TO HELL, AND WE'RE OUT HERE DOING SEARCH AND RESCUE? AFTER WHAT HAPPENED IN NEW YORK, DON'T WE HAVE BETTER THINGS TO DO?

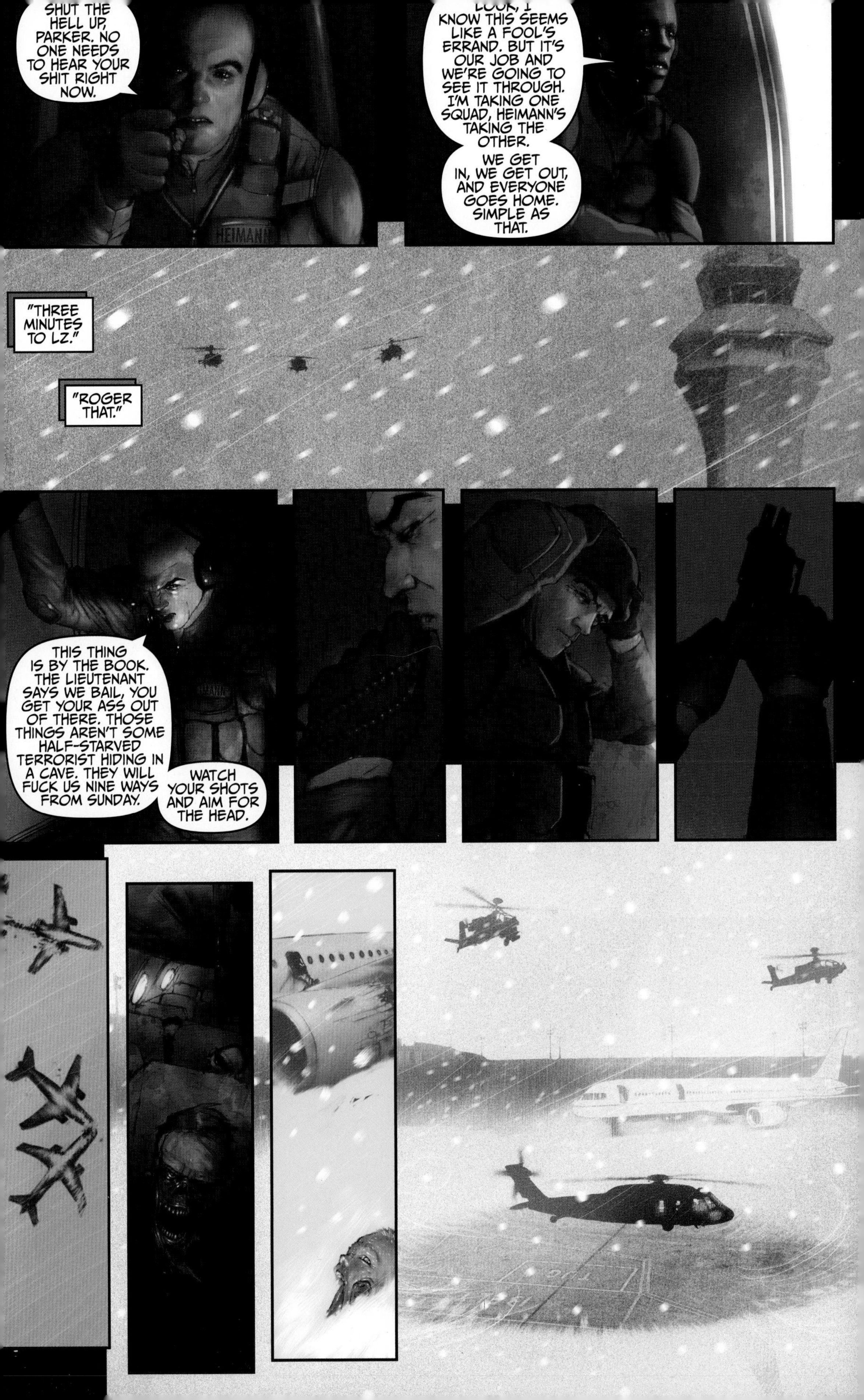
SHUT THE HELL UP, PARKER. NO ONE NEEDS TO HEAR YOUR SHIT RIGHT NOW.
LOOK, I KNOW THIS SEEMS LIKE A FOOL'S ERRAND. BUT IT'S OUR JOB AND WE'RE GOING TO SEE IT THROUGH. I'M TAKING ONE SQUAD, HEIMANN'S TAKING THE OTHER.
WE GET IN, WE GET OUT, AND EVERYONE GOES HOME. SIMPLE AS THAT.
HEIMANN
"THREE MINUTES TO LZ."
"ROGER THAT."
THIS THING IS BY THE BOOK. THE LIEUTENANT SAYS WE BAIL, YOU GET YOUR ASS OUT OF THERE. THOSE THINGS AREN'T SOME HALF-STARVED TERRORIST HIDING IN A CAVE. THEY WILL FUCK US NINE WAYS FROM SUNDAY.
WATCH YOUR SHOTS AND AIM FOR THE HEAD.

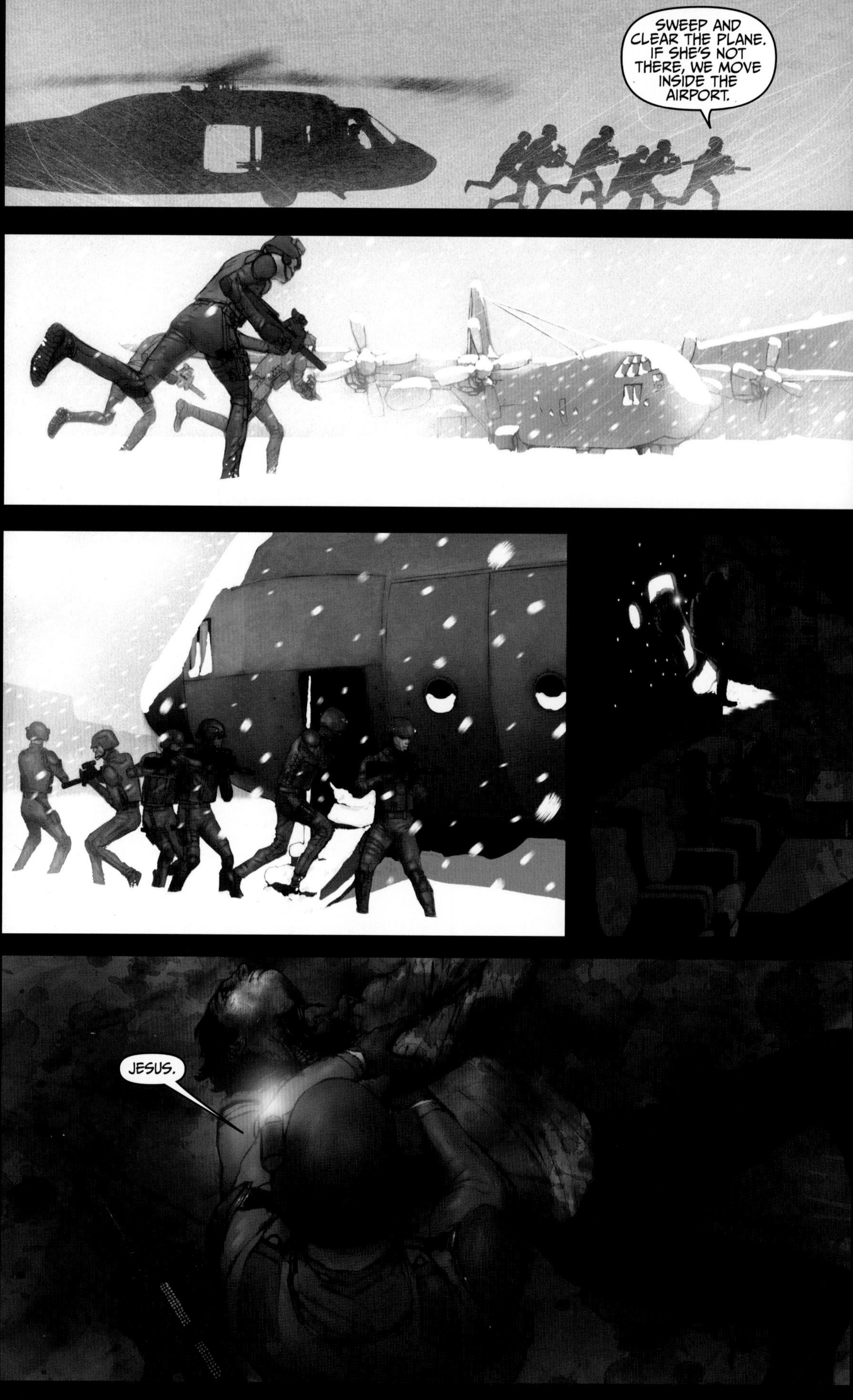
SWEEP AND CLEAR THE PLANE. IF SHE'S NOT THERE, WE MOVE INSIDE THE AIRPORT.
JESUS.

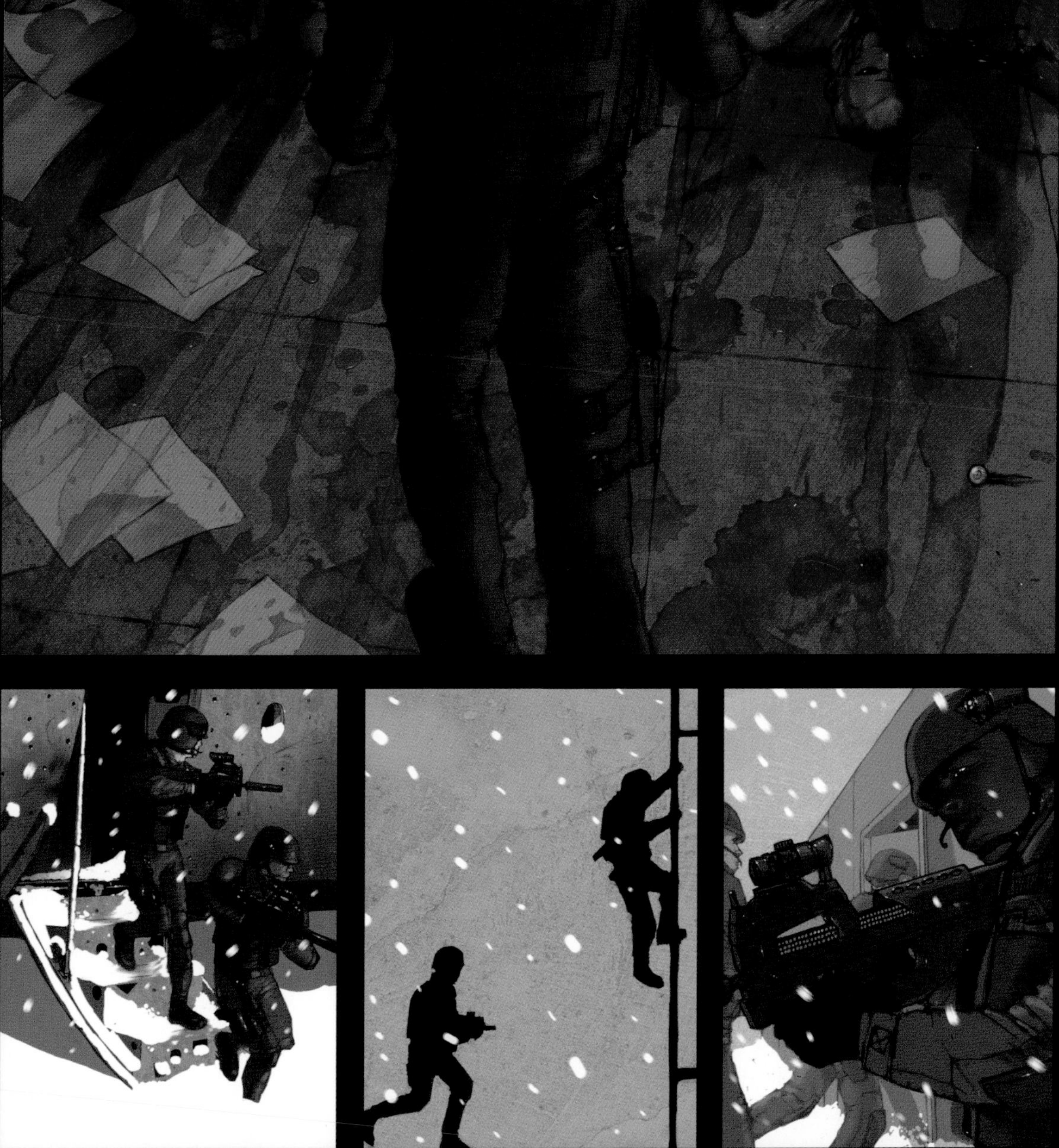

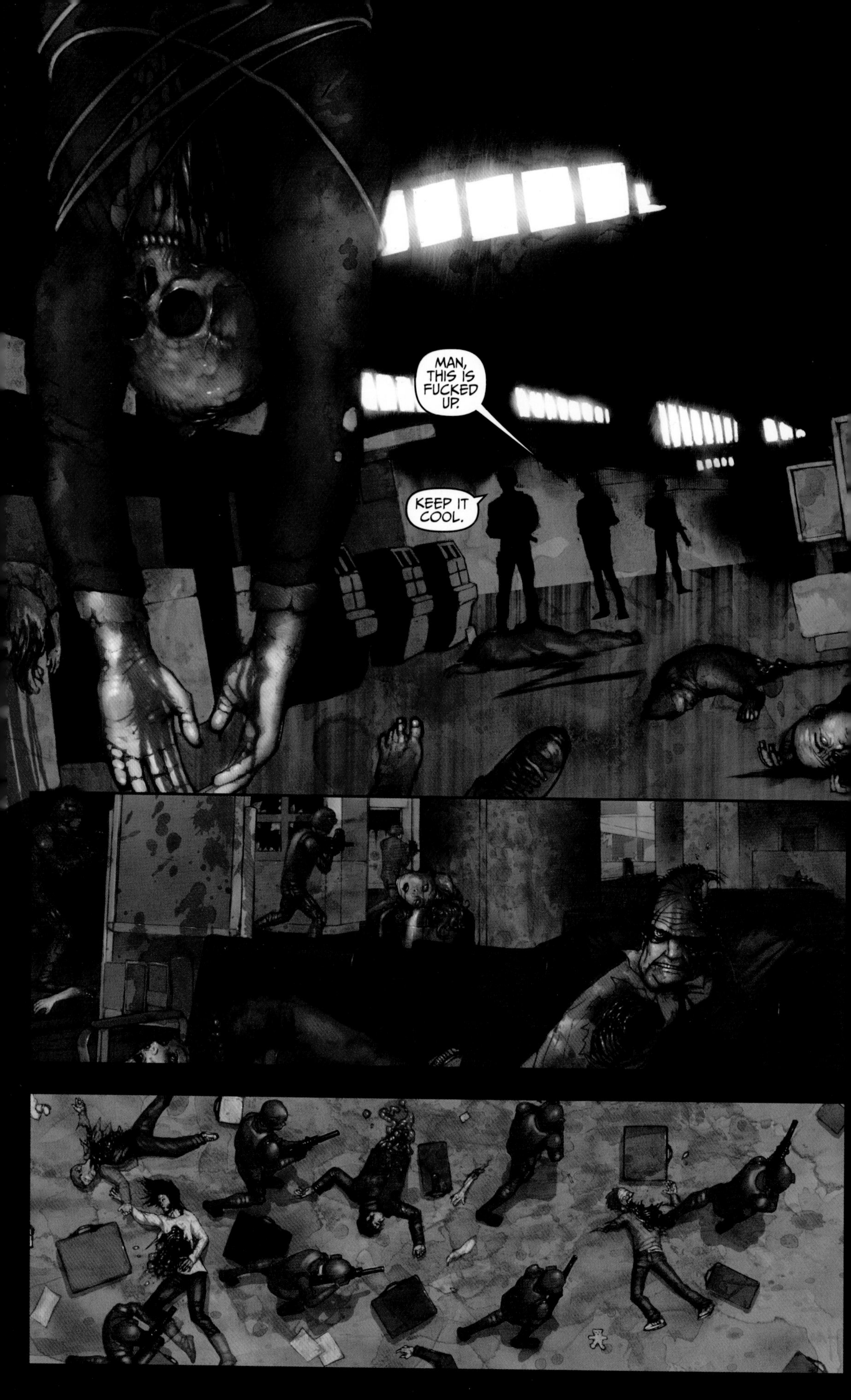
MAN, THIS IS FUCKED UP.
KEEP IT COOL.

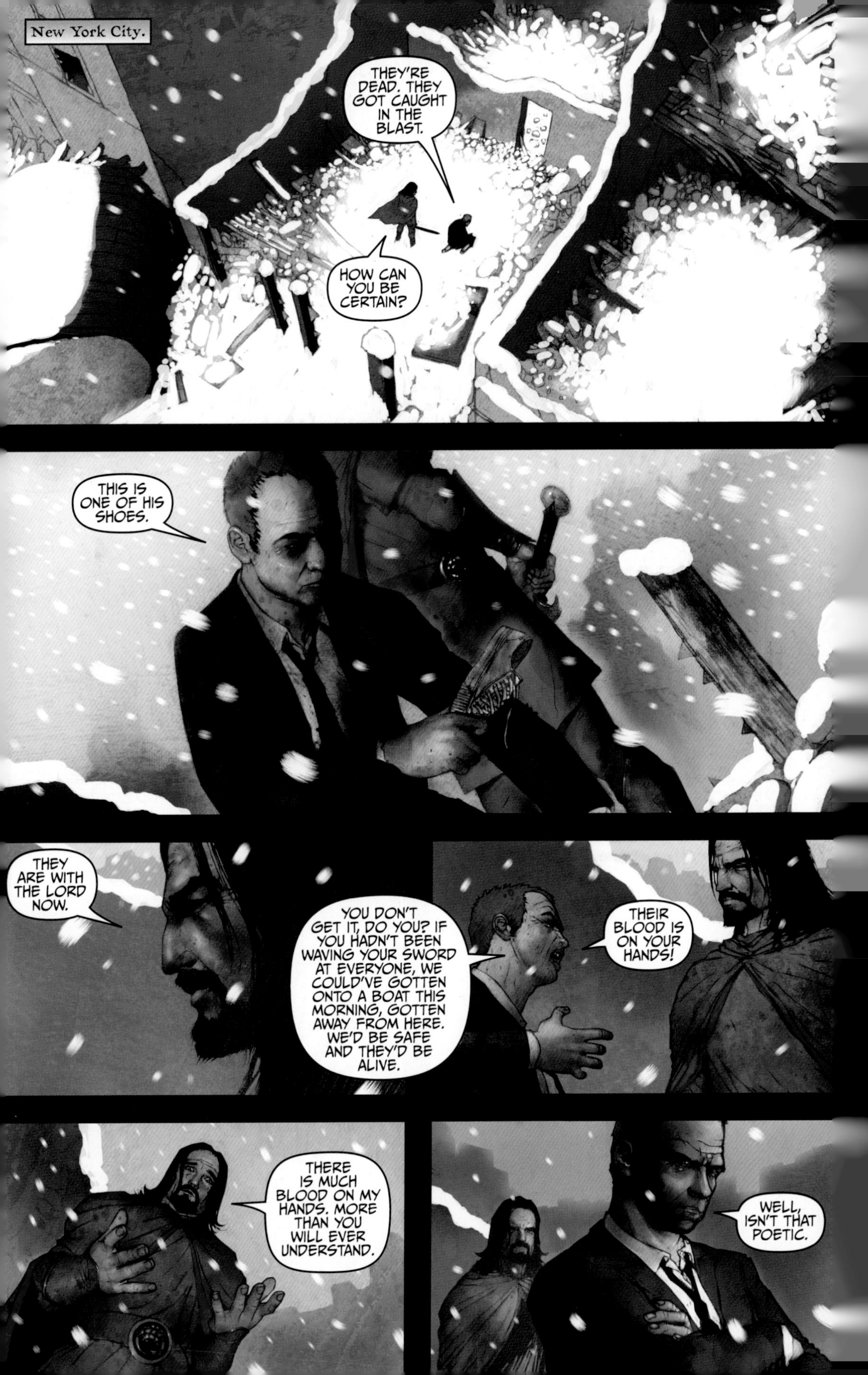

New York City.
THEY'RE DEAD. THEY GOT CAUGHT IN THE BLAST.
HOW CAN YOU BE CERTAIN?
THIS IS ONE OF HIS SHOES.
THEY ARE WITH THE LORD NOW.
YOU DON'T GET IT, DO YOU? IF YOU HADN'T BEEN WAVING YOUR SWORD AT EVERYONE, WE COULD'VE GOTTEN ONTO A BOAT THIS MORNING, GOTTEN AWAY FROM HERE. WE'D BE SAFE AND THEY'D BE ALIVE.
THEIR BLOOD IS ON YOUR HANDS!
THERE IS MUCH BLOOD ON MY HANDS. MORE THAN YOU WILL EVER UNDERSTAND.
WELL, ISN'T THAT POETIC.

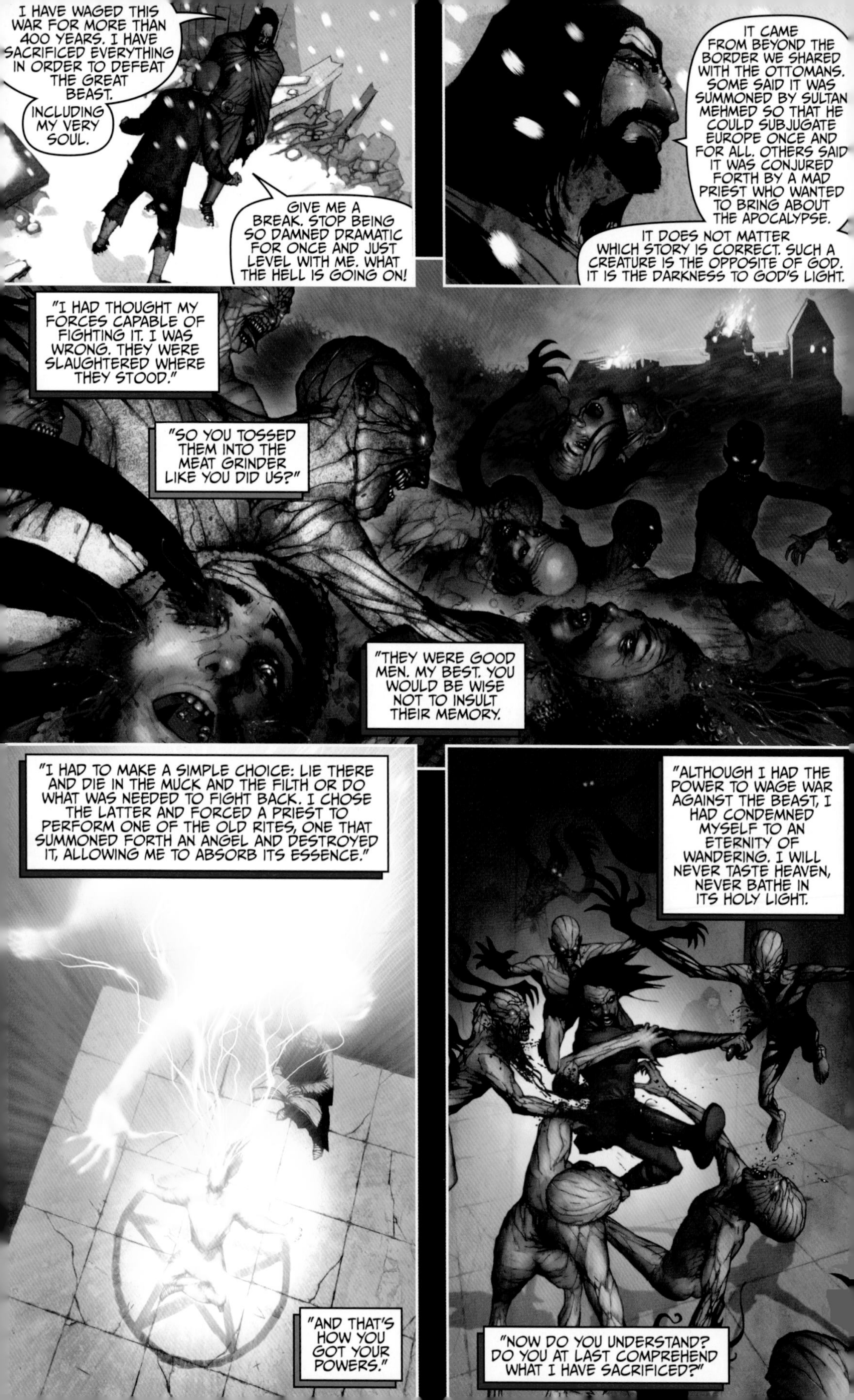
I HAVE WAGED THIS WAR FOR MORE THAN 400 YEARS. I HAVE SACRIFICED EVERYTHING IN ORDER TO DEFEAT THE GREAT BEAST.
INCLUDING MY VERY SOUL.
GIVE ME A BREAK. STOP BEING SO DAMNED DRAMATIC FOR ONCE AND JUST LEVEL WITH ME. WHAT THE HELL IS GOING ON!
IT CAME FROM BEYOND THE BORDER WE SHARED WITH THE OTTOMANS. SOME SAID IT WAS SUMMONED BY SULTAN MEHMED SO THAT HE COULD SUBJUGATE EUROPE ONCE AND FOR ALL. OTHERS SAID IT WAS CONJURED FORTH BY A MAD PRIEST WHO WANTED TO BRING ABOUT THE APOCALYPSE.
IT DOES NOT MATTER WHICH STORY IS CORRECT. SUCH A CREATURE IS THE OPPOSITE OF GOD. IT IS THE DARKNESS TO GOD'S LIGHT.
"I HAD THOUGHT MY FORCES CAPABLE OF FIGHTING IT. I WAS WRONG. THEY WERE SLAUGHTERED WHERE THEY STOOD."
"SO YOU TOSSED THEM INTO THE MEAT GRINDER LIKE YOU DID US?"
"THEY WERE GOOD MEN. MY BEST. YOU WOULD BE WISE NOT TO INSULT THEIR MEMORY.
"I HAD TO MAKE A SIMPLE CHOICE: LIE THERE AND DIE IN THE MUCK AND THE FILTH OR DO WHAT WAS NEEDED TO FIGHT BACK. I CHOSE THE LATTER AND FORCED A PRIEST TO PERFORM ONE OF THE OLD RITES, ONE THAT SUMMONED FORTH AN ANGEL AND DESTROYED IT, ALLOWING ME TO ABSORB ITS ESSENCE."
"AND THAT'S HOW YOU GOT YOUR POWERS."
"ALTHOUGH I HAD THE POWER TO WAGE WAR AGAINST THE BEAST, I HAD CONDEMNED MYSELF TO AN ETERNITY OF WANDERING. I WILL NEVER TASTE HEAVEN, NEVER BATHE IN ITS HOLY LIGHT.
"NOW DO YOU UNDERSTAND? DO YOU AT LAST COMPREHEND WHAT I HAVE SACRIFICED?"

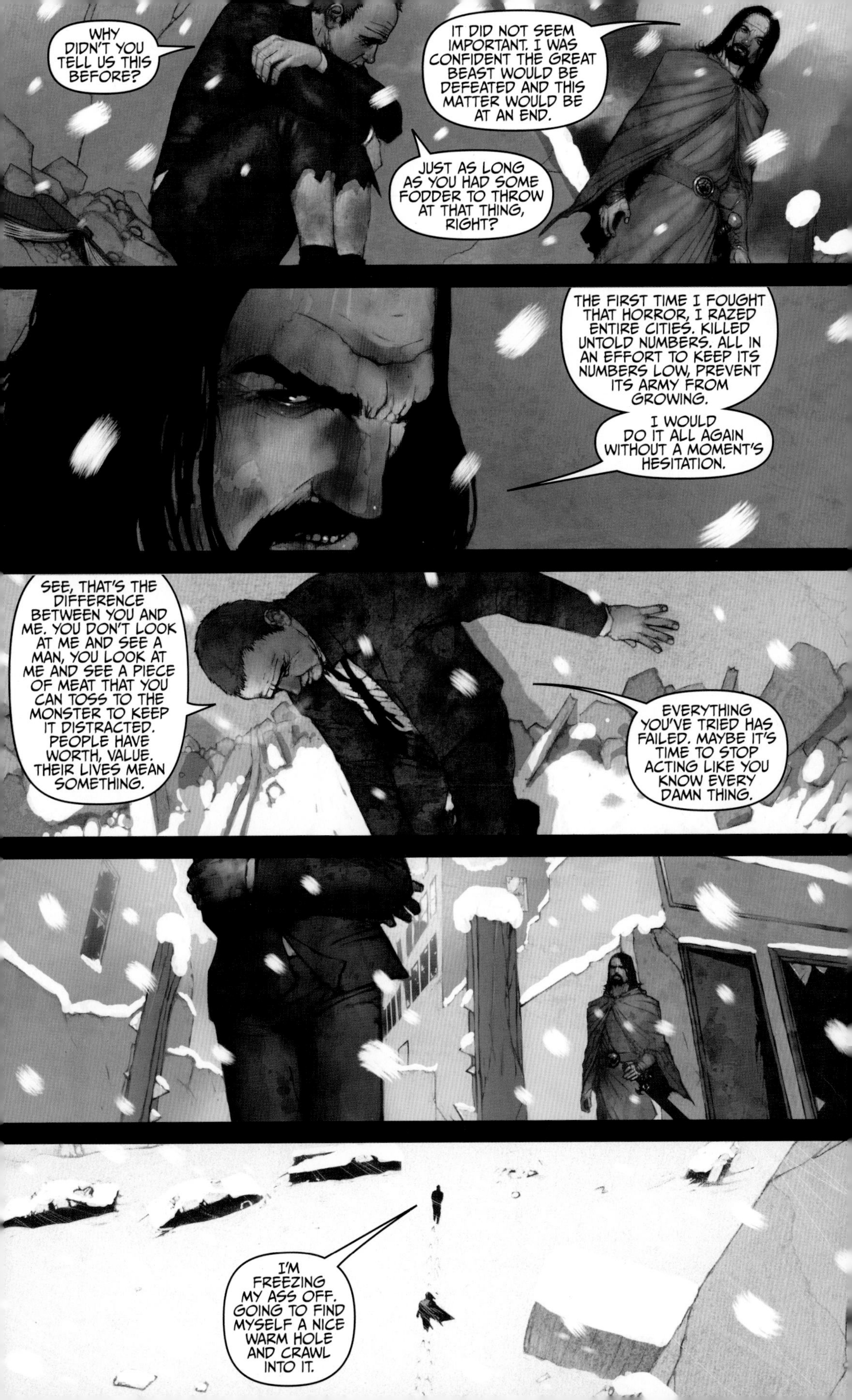
WHY DIDN'T YOU TELL US THIS BEFORE?
IT DID NOT SEEM IMPORTANT. I WAS CONFIDENT THE GREAT BEAST WOULD BE DEFEATED AND THIS MATTER WOULD BE AT AN END.
JUST AS LONG AS YOU HAD SOME FODDER TO THROW AT THAT THING, RIGHT?
THE FIRST TIME I FOUGHT THAT HORROR, I RAZED ENTIRE CITIES. KILLED UNTOLD NUMBERS. ALL IN AN EFFORT TO KEEP ITS NUMBERS LOW, PREVENT ITS ARMY FROM GROWING.
I WOULD DO IT ALL AGAIN WITHOUT A MOMENT'S HESITATION.
SEE, THAT'S THE DIFFERENCE BETWEEN YOU AND ME. YOU DON'T LOOK AT ME AND SEE A MAN, YOU LOOK AT ME AND SEE A PIECE OF MEAT THAT YOU CAN TOSS TO THE MONSTER TO KEEP IT DISTRACTED. PEOPLE HAVE WORTH, VALUE. THEIR LIVES MEAN SOMETHING.
EVERYTHING YOU'VE TRIED HAS FAILED. MAYBE IT'S TIME TO STOP ACTING LIKE YOU KNOW EVERY DAMN THING.
I'M FREEZING MY ASS OFF. GOING TO FIND MYSELF A NICE WARM HOLE AND CRAWL INTO IT.

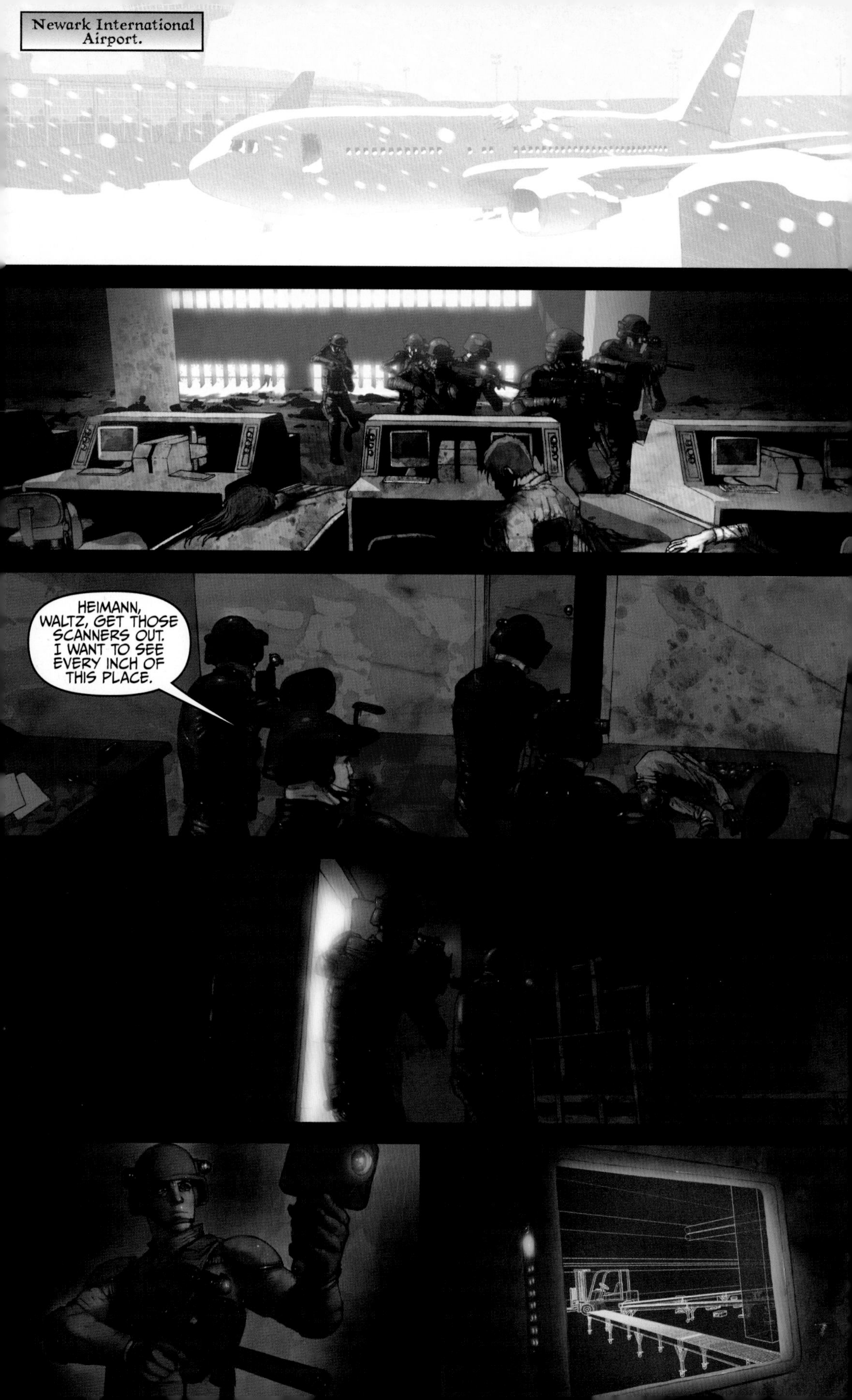
Newark International Airport.
HEIMANN, WALTZ, GET THOSE SCANNERS OUT. I WANT TO SEE EVERY INCH OF THIS PLACE.

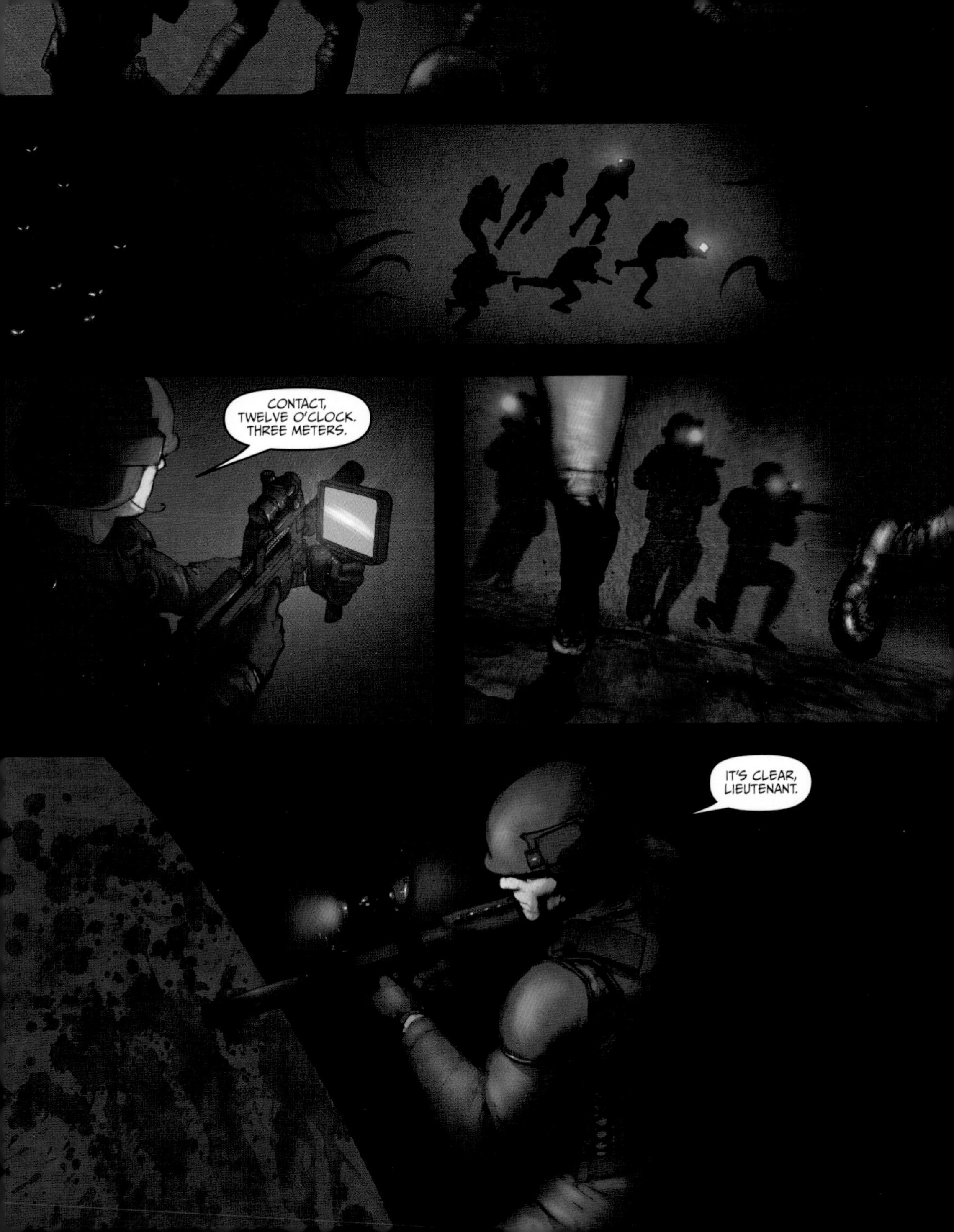
CONTACT, TWELVE O'CLOCK. THREE METERS.
IT'S CLEAR, LIEUTENANT.

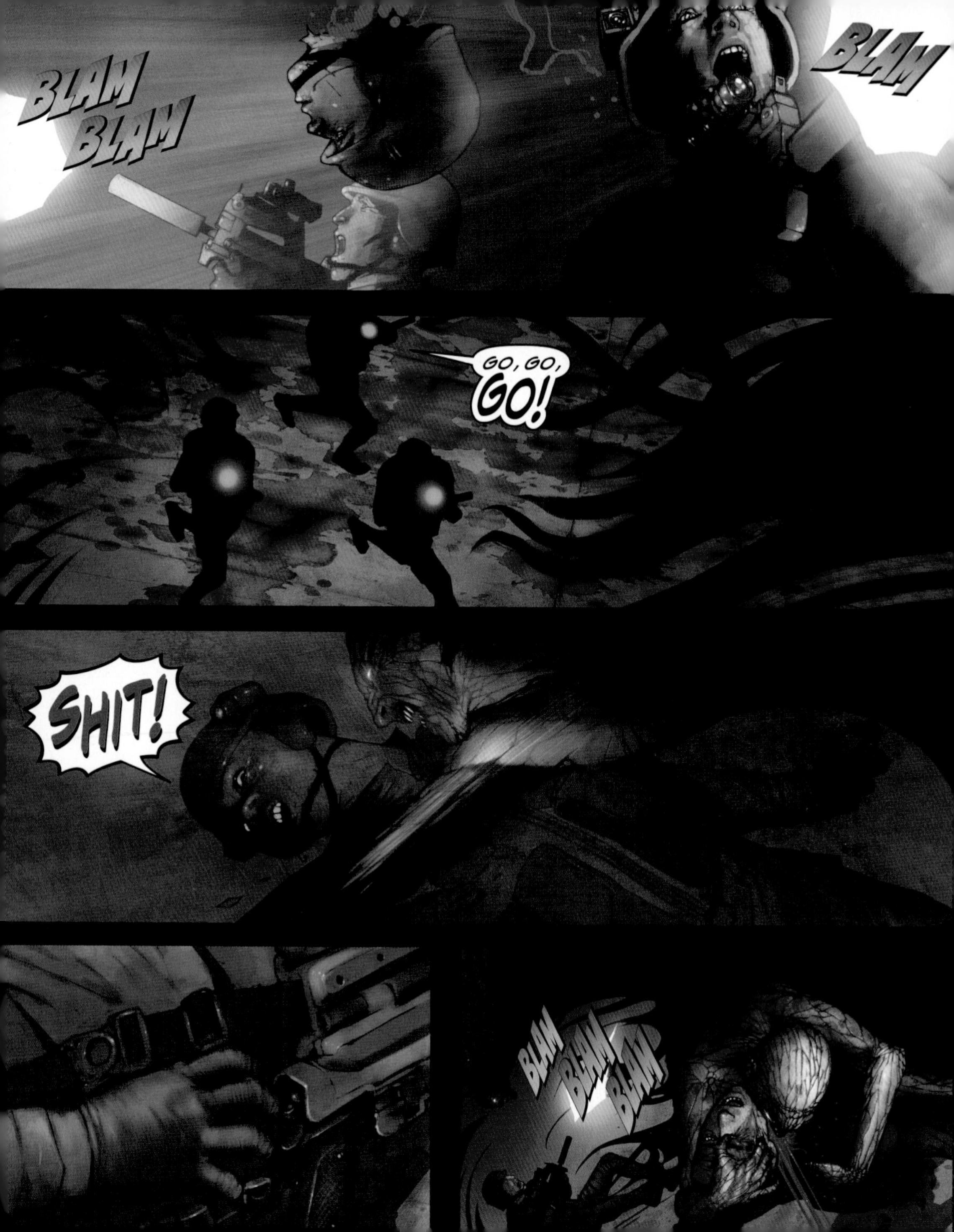
BLAM
BLAM
BLAM
GO, GO, GO!
SHIT!
BLAM
BLAM
BLAM

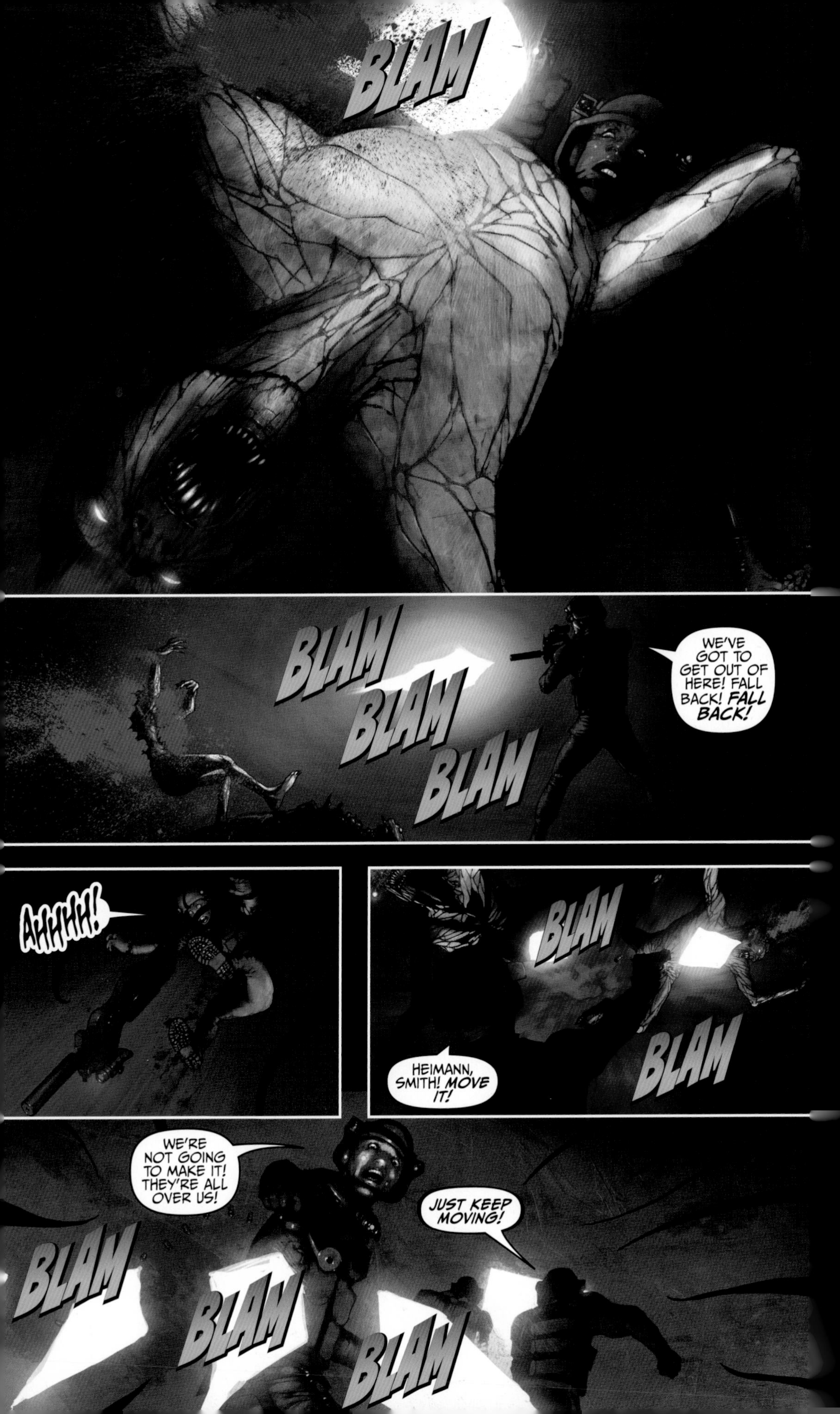
BLAM
BLAM
BLAM
BLAM
WE'VE GOT TO GET OUT OF HERE! FALL BACK! FALL BACK!
AHHHH!
BLAM
BLAM
HEIMANN, SMITH! MOVE IT!
WE'RE NOT GOING TO MAKE IT! THEY'RE ALL OVER US!
JUST KEEP MOVING!
BLAM
BLAM
BLAM

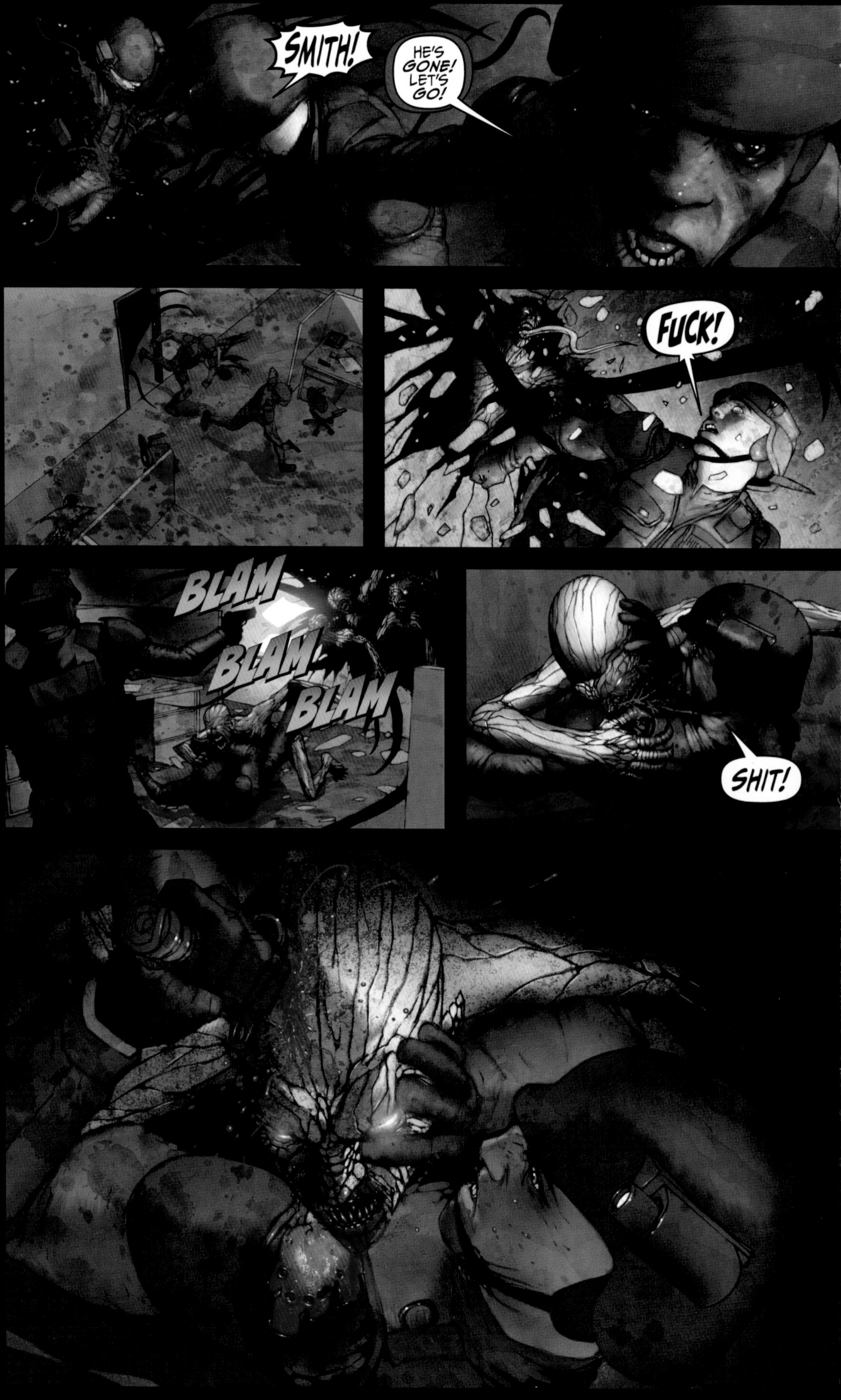
SMITH!
HE'S GONE! LET'S GO!
FUCK!
BLAM
BLAM
BLAM
SHIT!

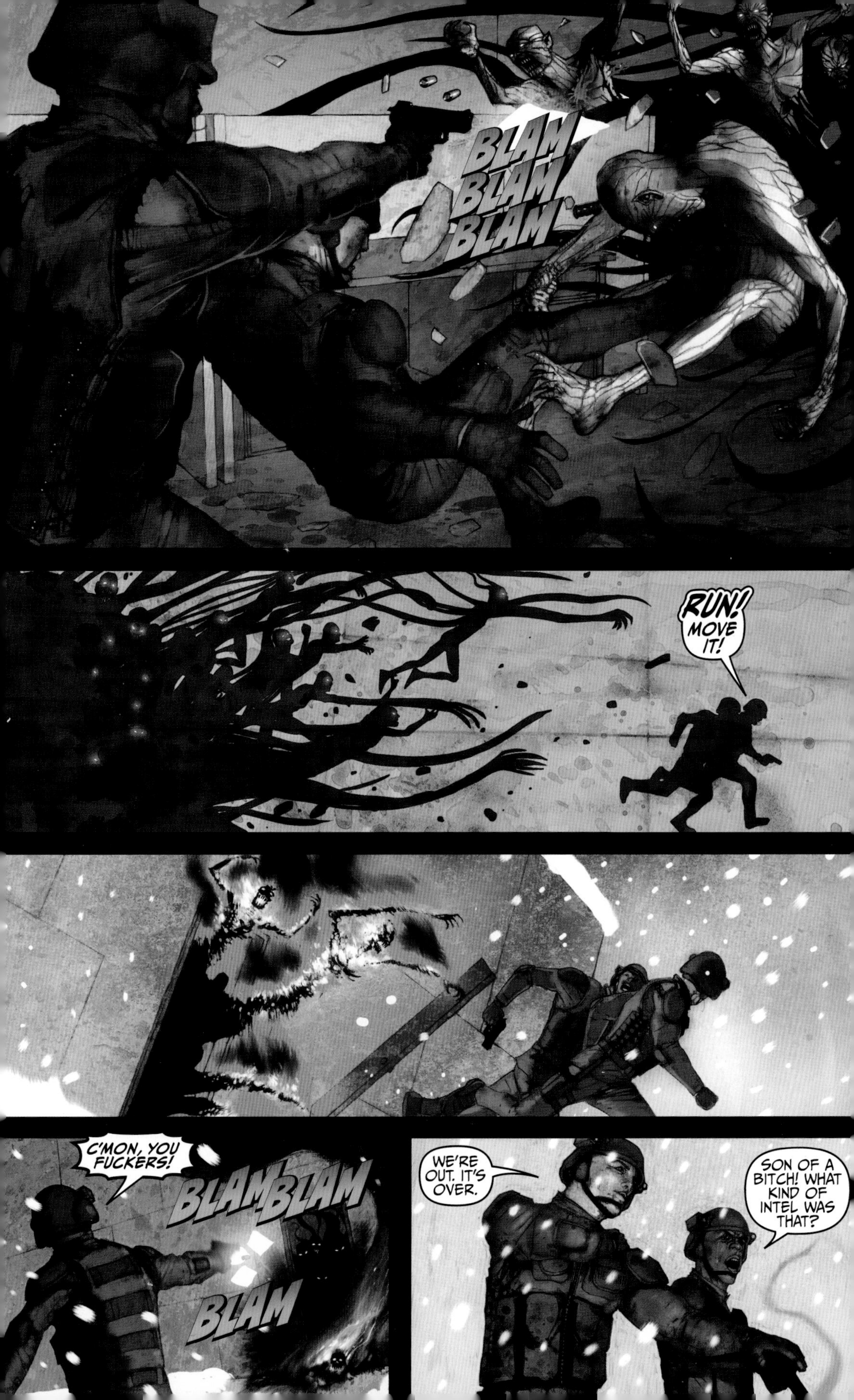
BLAM BLAM BLAM
RUN! MOVE IT!
C'MON, YOU FUCKERS!
BLAMBLAM
BLAM
WE'RE OUT. IT'S OVER.
SON OF A BITCH! WHAT KIND OF INTEL WAS THAT?

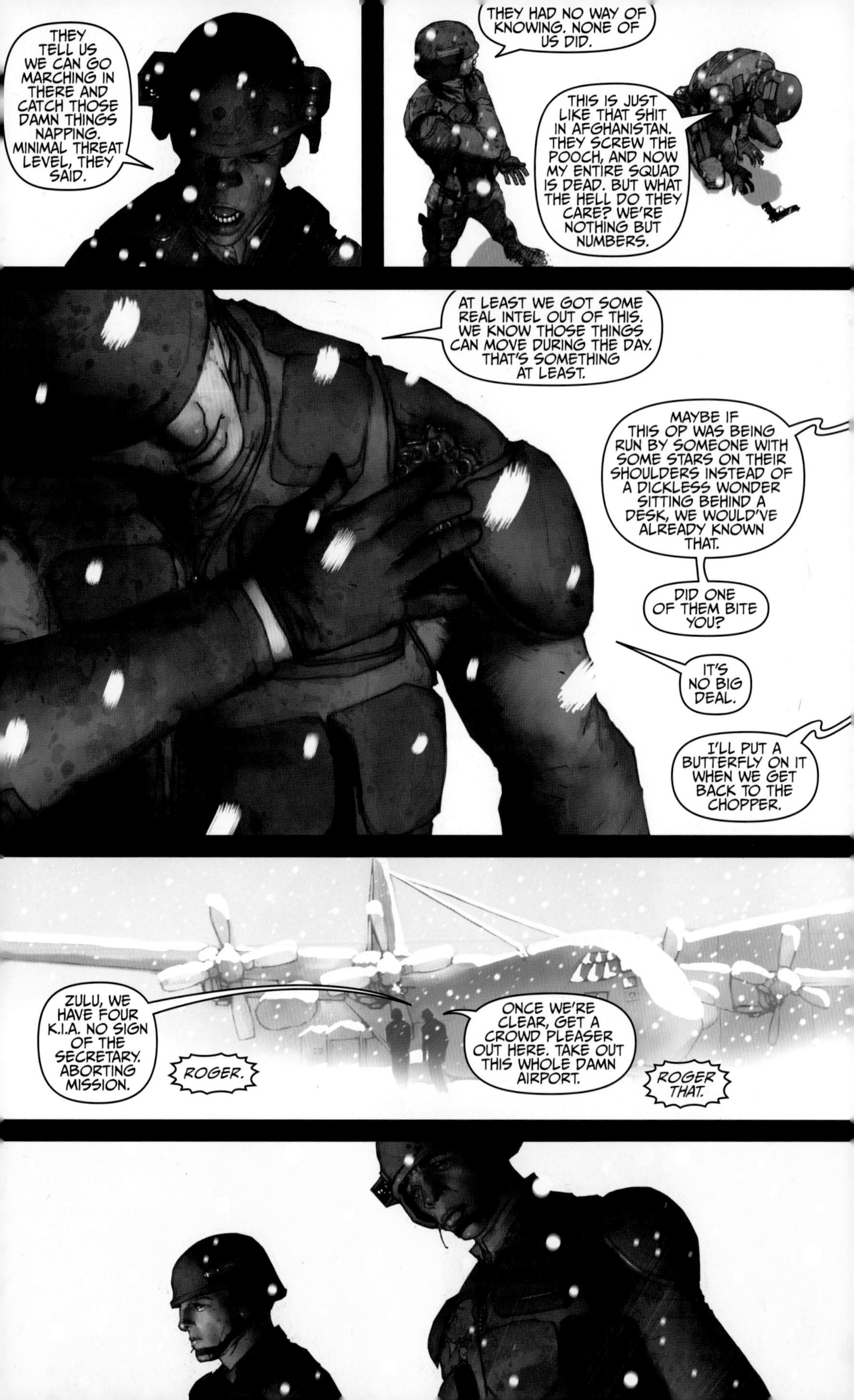
THEY TELL US WE CAN GO MARCHING IN THERE AND CATCH THOSE DAMN THINGS NAPPING. MINIMAL THREAT LEVEL, THEY SAID.
THEY HAD NO WAY OF KNOWING. NONE OF US DID.
THIS IS JUST LIKE THAT SHIT IN AFGHANISTAN. THEY SCREW THE POOCH, AND NOW MY ENTIRE SQUAD IS DEAD. BUT WHAT THE HELL DO THEY CARE? WE'RE NOTHING BUT NUMBERS.
AT LEAST WE GOT SOME REAL INTEL OUT OF THIS. WE KNOW THOSE THINGS CAN MOVE DURING THE DAY. THAT'S SOMETHING AT LEAST.
MAYBE IF THIS OP WAS BEING RUN BY SOMEONE WITH SOME STARS ON THEIR SHOULDERS INSTEAD OF A DICKLESS WONDER SITTING BEHIND A DESK, WE WOULD'VE ALREADY KNOWN THAT.
DID ONE OF THEM BITE YOU?
IT'S NO BIG DEAL.
I'LL PUT A BUTTERFLY ON IT WHEN WE GET BACK TO THE CHOPPER.
ZULU, WE HAVE FOUR K.I.A. NO SIGN OF THE SECRETARY. ABORTING MISSION.
ROGER.
ONCE WE'RE CLEAR, GET A CROWD PLEASER OUT HERE. TAKE OUT THIS WHOLE DAMN AIRPORT.
ROGER THAT.

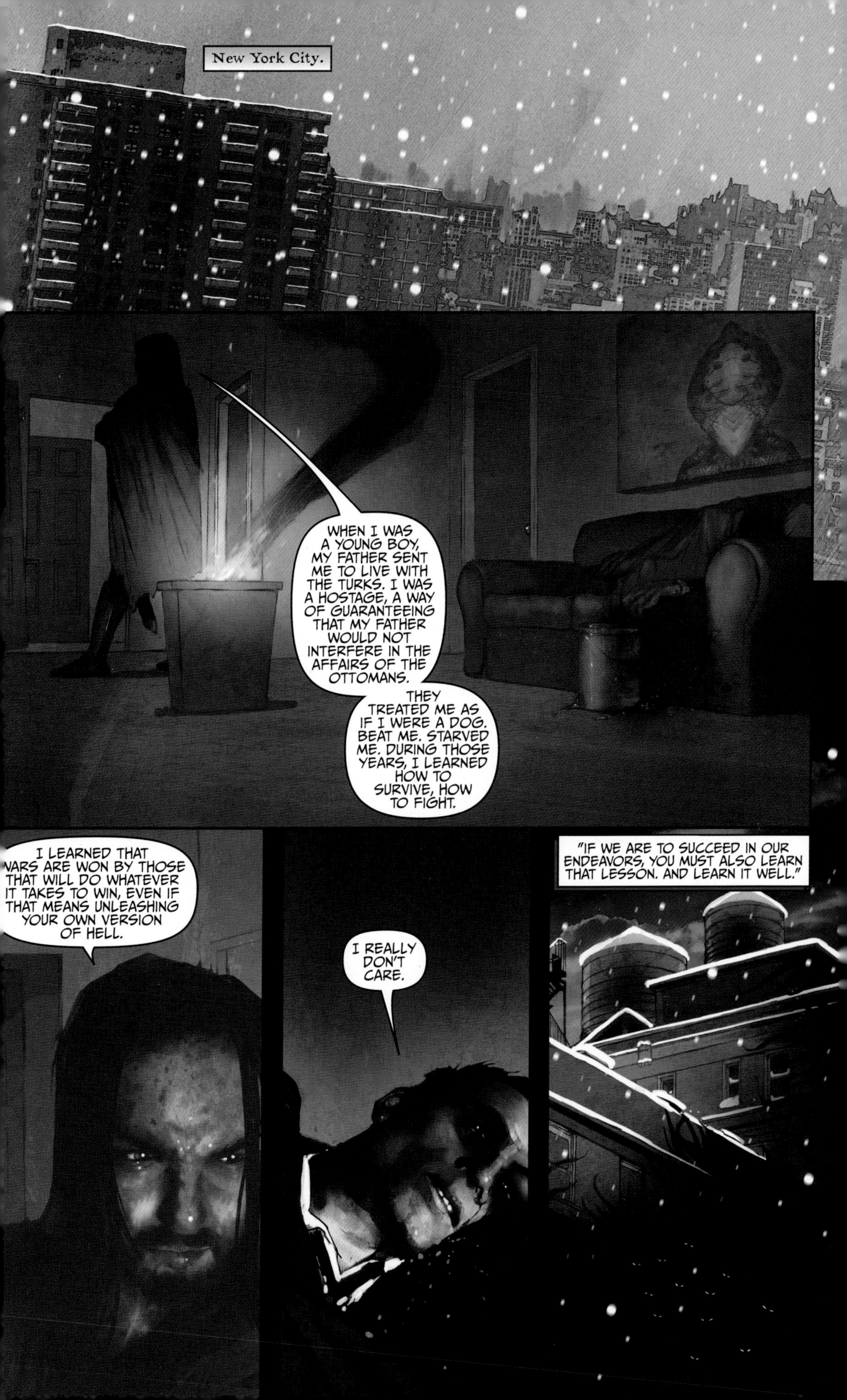
New York City.
WHEN I WAS A YOUNG BOY, MY FATHER SENT ME TO LIVE WITH THE TURKS. I WAS A HOSTAGE, A WAY OF GUARANTEEING THAT MY FATHER WOULD NOT INTERFERE IN THE AFFAIRS OF THE OTTOMANS.
THEY TREATED ME AS IF I WERE A DOG. BEAT ME. STARVED ME. DURING THOSE YEARS, I LEARNED HOW TO SURVIVE, HOW TO FIGHT.
I LEARNED THAT WARS ARE WON BY THOSE THAT WILL DO WHATEVER IT TAKES TO WIN, EVEN IF THAT MEANS UNLEASHING YOUR OWN VERSION OF HELL.
I REALLY DON'T CARE.
"IF WE ARE TO SUCCEED IN OUR ENDEAVORS, YOU MUST ALSO LEARN THAT LESSON. AND LEARN IT WELL."

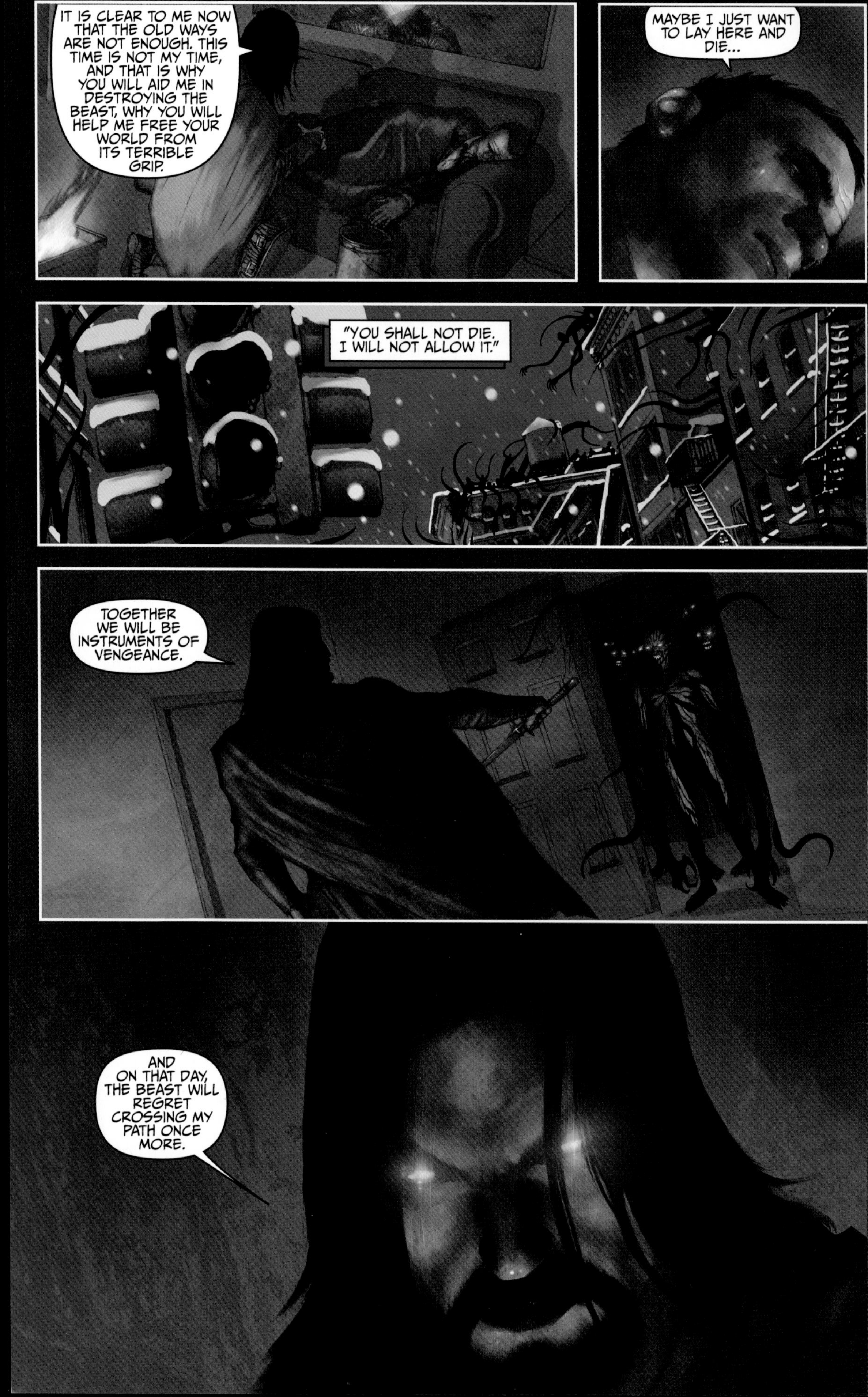
IT IS CLEAR TO ME NOW THAT THE OLD WAYS ARE NOT ENOUGH. THIS TIME IS NOT MY TIME, AND THAT IS WHY YOU WILL AID ME IN DESTROYING THE BEAST, WHY YOU WILL HELP ME FREE YOUR WORLD FROM ITS TERRIBLE GRIP.
MAYBE I JUST WANT TO LAY HERE AND DIE...
"YOU SHALL NOT DIE. I WILL NOT ALLOW IT."
TOGETHER WE WILL BE INSTRUMENTS OF VENGEANCE.
AND ON THAT DAY, THE BEAST WILL REGRET CROSSING MY PATH ONCE MORE.

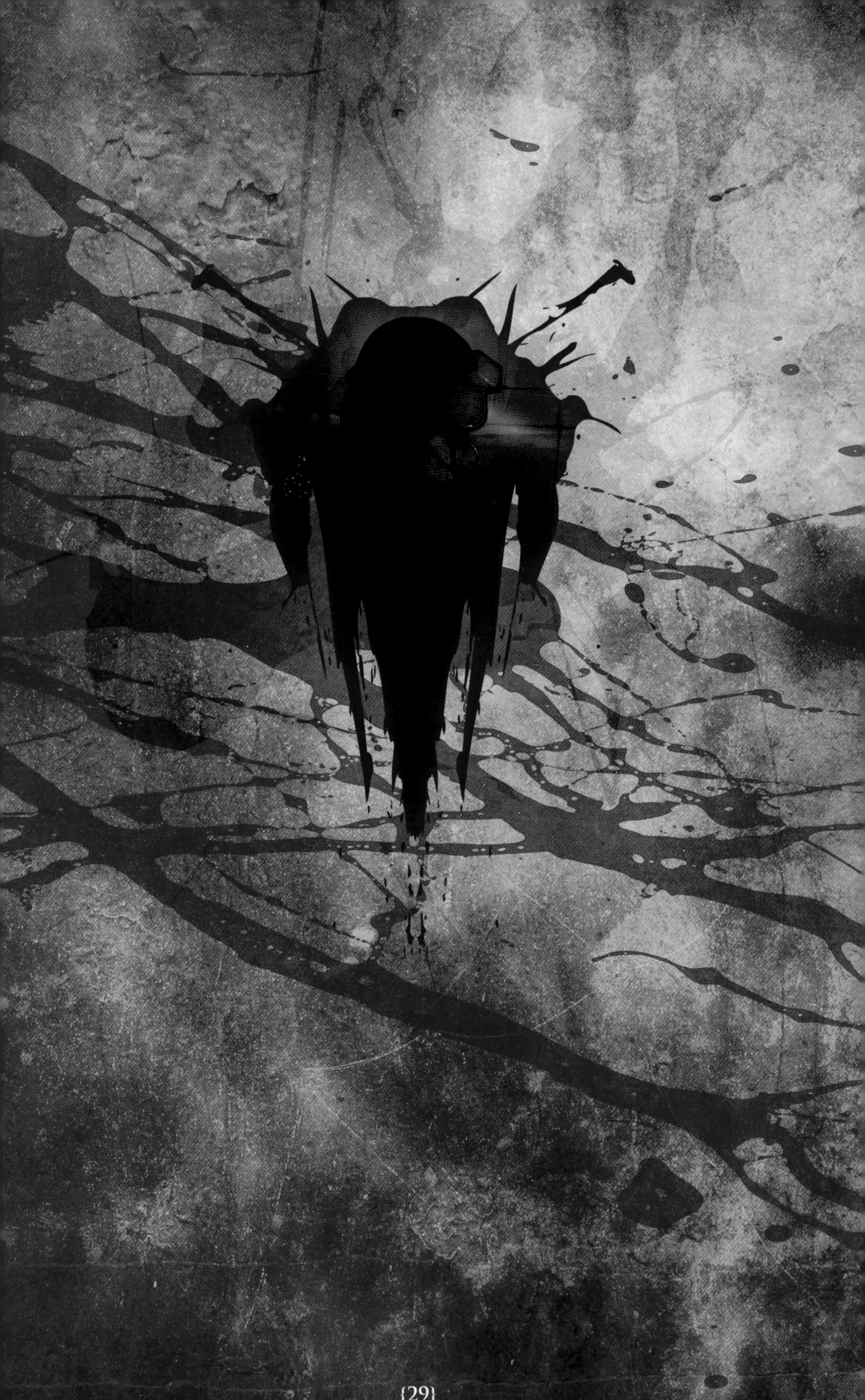

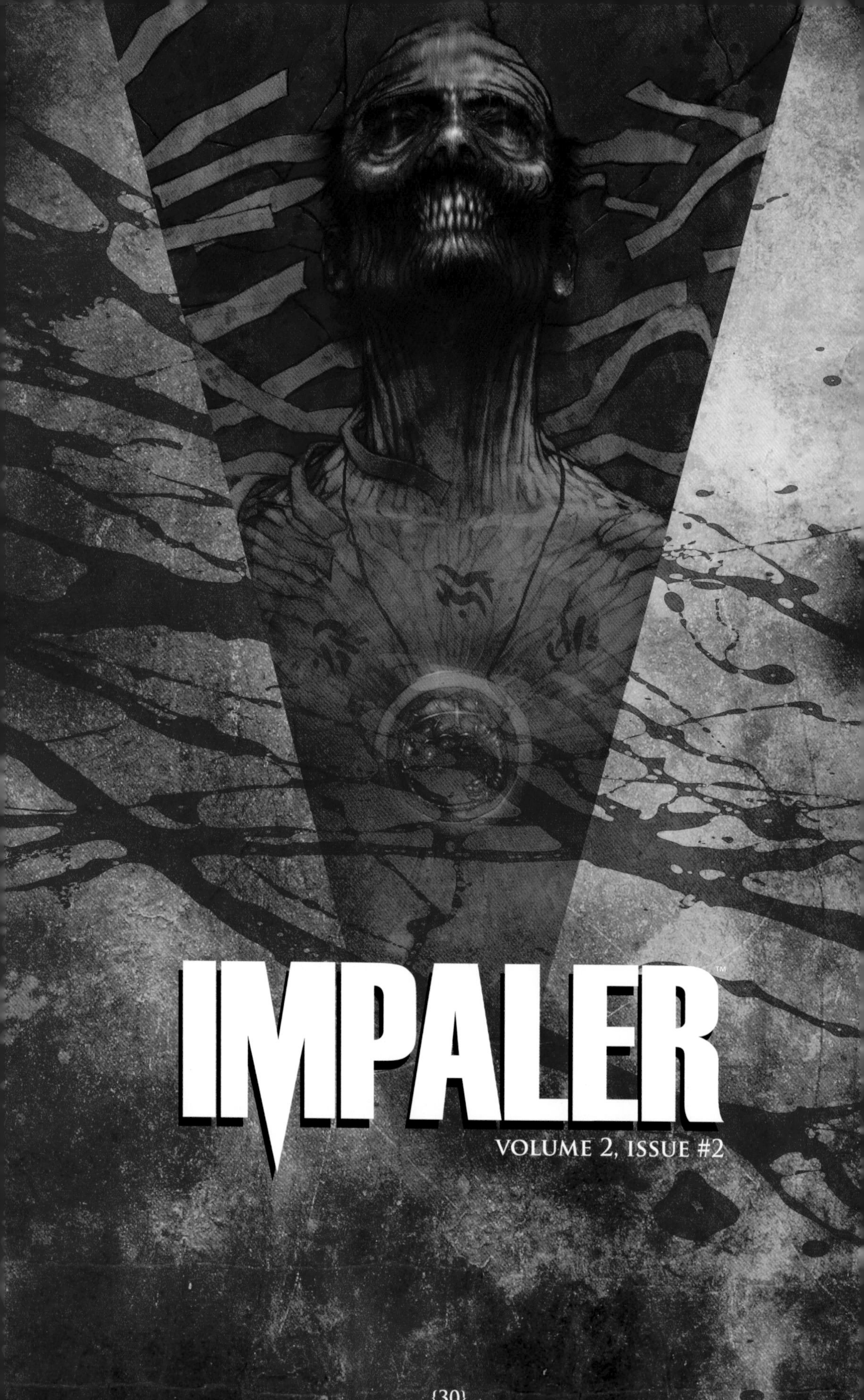
IMPALER™
VOLUME 2, ISSUE #2

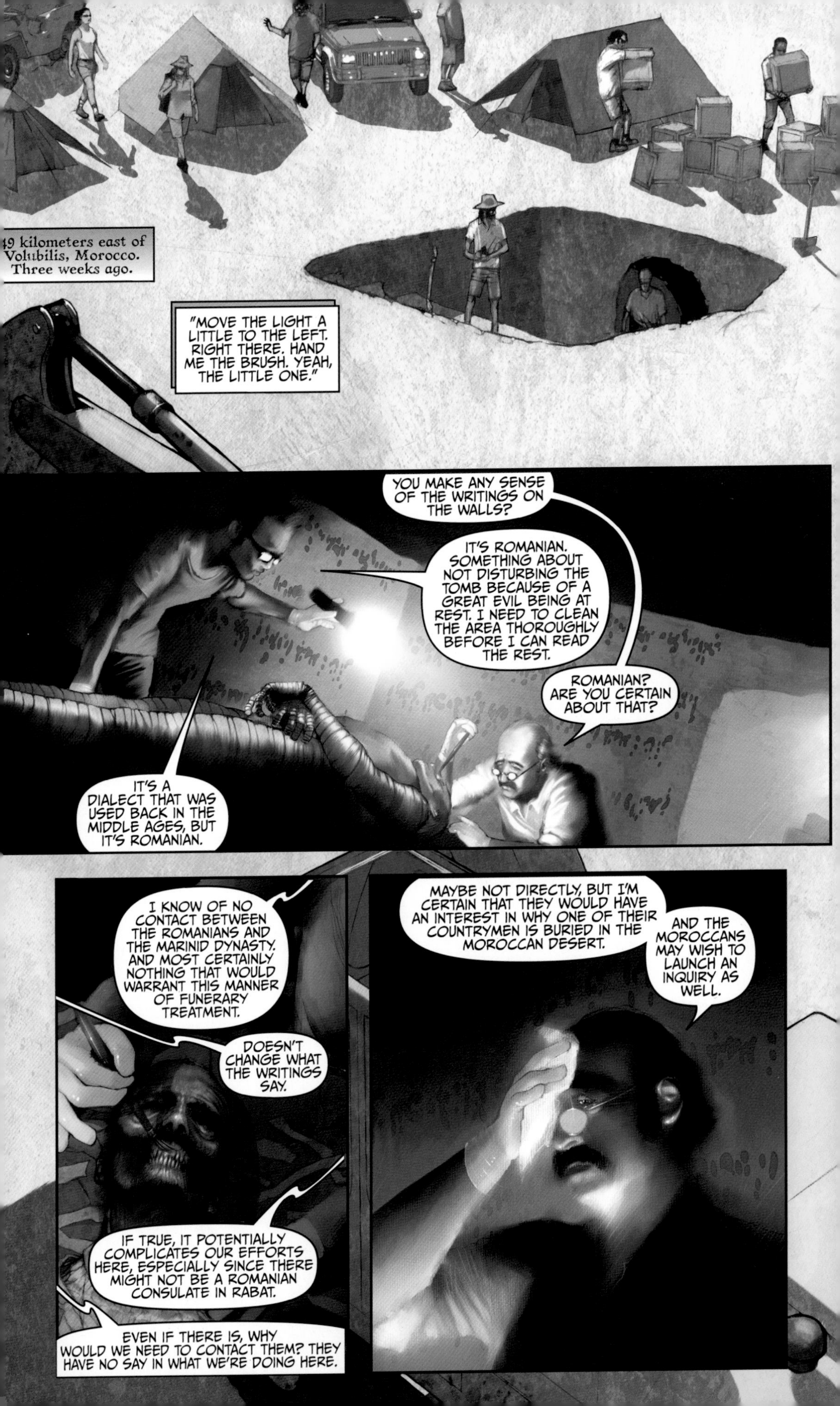
49 kilometers east of Volubilis, Morocco. Three weeks ago.
"MOVE THE LIGHT A LITTLE TO THE LEFT. RIGHT THERE. HAND ME THE BRUSH. YEAH, THE LITTLE ONE."
YOU MAKE ANY SENSE OF THE WRITINGS ON THE WALLS?
IT'S ROMANIAN. SOMETHING ABOUT NOT DISTURBING THE TOMB BECAUSE OF A GREAT EVIL BEING AT REST. I NEED TO CLEAN THE AREA THOROUGHLY BEFORE I CAN READ THE REST.
ROMANIAN? ARE YOU CERTAIN ABOUT THAT?
IT'S A DIALECT THAT WAS USED BACK IN THE MIDDLE AGES, BUT IT'S ROMANIAN.
I KNOW OF NO CONTACT BETWEEN THE ROMANIANS AND THE MARINID DYNASTY. AND MOST CERTAINLY NOTHING THAT WOULD WARRANT THIS MANNER OF FUNERARY TREATMENT.
DOESN'T CHANGE WHAT THE WRITINGS SAY.
IF TRUE, IT POTENTIALLY COMPLICATES OUR EFFORTS HERE, ESPECIALLY SINCE THERE MIGHT NOT BE A ROMANIAN CONSULATE IN RABAT.
EVEN IF THERE IS, WHY WOULD WE NEED TO CONTACT THEM? THEY HAVE NO SAY IN WHAT WE'RE DOING HERE.
MAYBE NOT DIRECTLY, BUT I'M CERTAIN THAT THEY WOULD HAVE AN INTEREST IN WHY ONE OF THEIR COUNTRYMEN IS BURIED IN THE MOROCCAN DESERT.
AND THE MOROCCANS MAY WISH TO LAUNCH AN INQUIRY AS WELL.

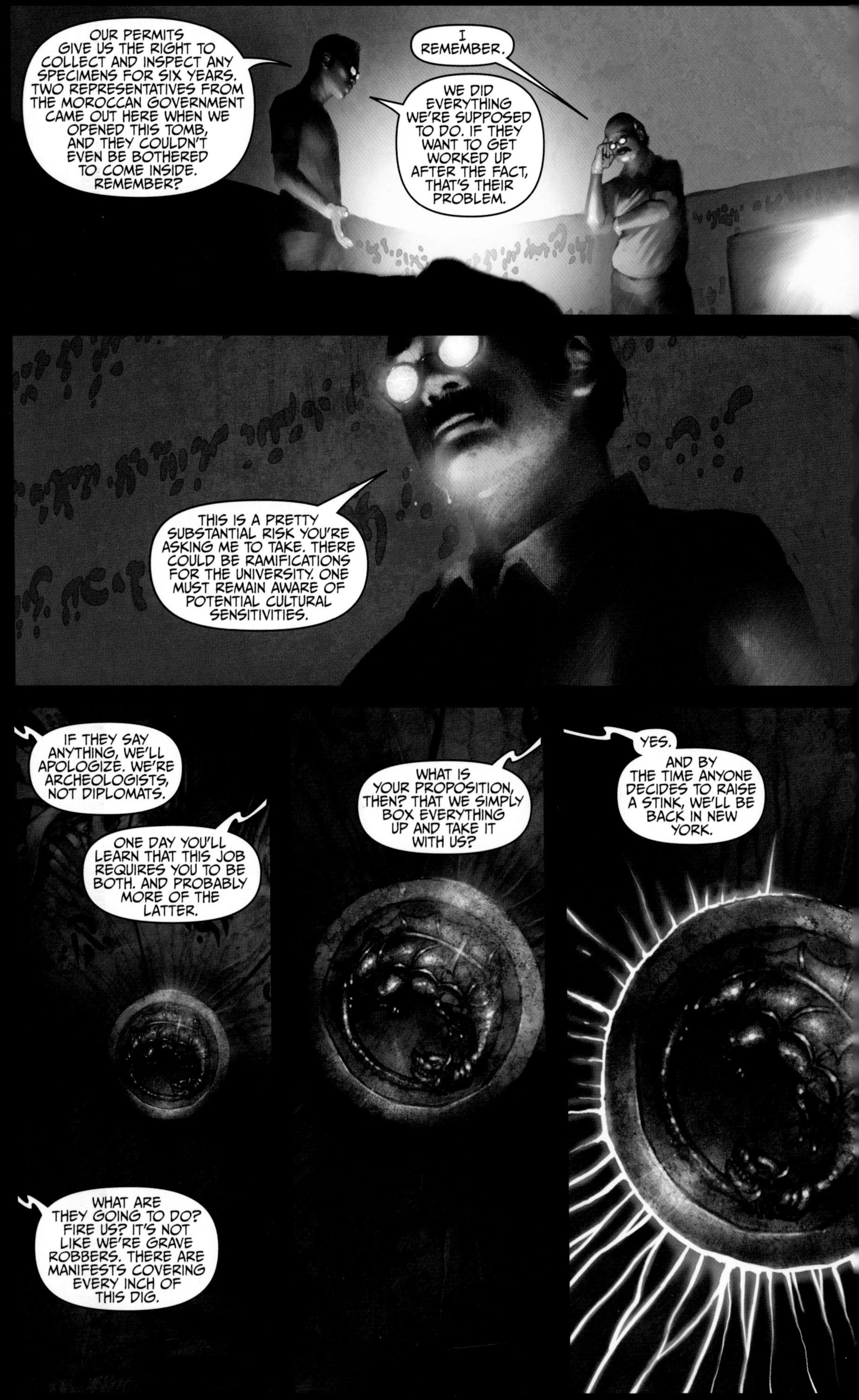
OUR PERMITS GIVE US THE RIGHT TO COLLECT AND INSPECT ANY SPECIMENS FOR SIX YEARS. TWO REPRESENTATIVES FROM THE MOROCCAN GOVERNMENT CAME OUT HERE WHEN WE OPENED THIS TOMB, AND THEY COULDN'T EVEN BE BOTHERED TO COME INSIDE. REMEMBER?
I REMEMBER.
WE DID EVERYTHING WE'RE SUPPOSED TO DO. IF THEY WANT TO GET WORKED UP AFTER THE FACT, THAT'S THEIR PROBLEM.
THIS IS A PRETTY SUBSTANTIAL RISK YOU'RE ASKING ME TO TAKE. THERE COULD BE RAMIFICATIONS FOR THE UNIVERSITY. ONE MUST REMAIN AWARE OF POTENTIAL CULTURAL SENSITIVITIES.
IF THEY SAY ANYTHING, WE'LL APOLOGIZE. WE'RE ARCHEOLOGISTS, NOT DIPLOMATS.
ONE DAY YOU'LL LEARN THAT THIS JOB REQUIRES YOU TO BE BOTH. AND PROBABLY MORE OF THE LATTER.
WHAT ARE THEY GOING TO DO? FIRE US? IT'S NOT LIKE WE'RE GRAVE ROBBERS. THERE ARE MANIFESTS COVERING EVERY INCH OF THIS DIG.
WHAT IS YOUR PROPOSITION, THEN? THAT WE SIMPLY BOX EVERYTHING UP AND TAKE IT WITH US?
YES.
AND BY THE TIME ANYONE DECIDES TO RAISE A STINK, WE'LL BE BACK IN NEW YORK.

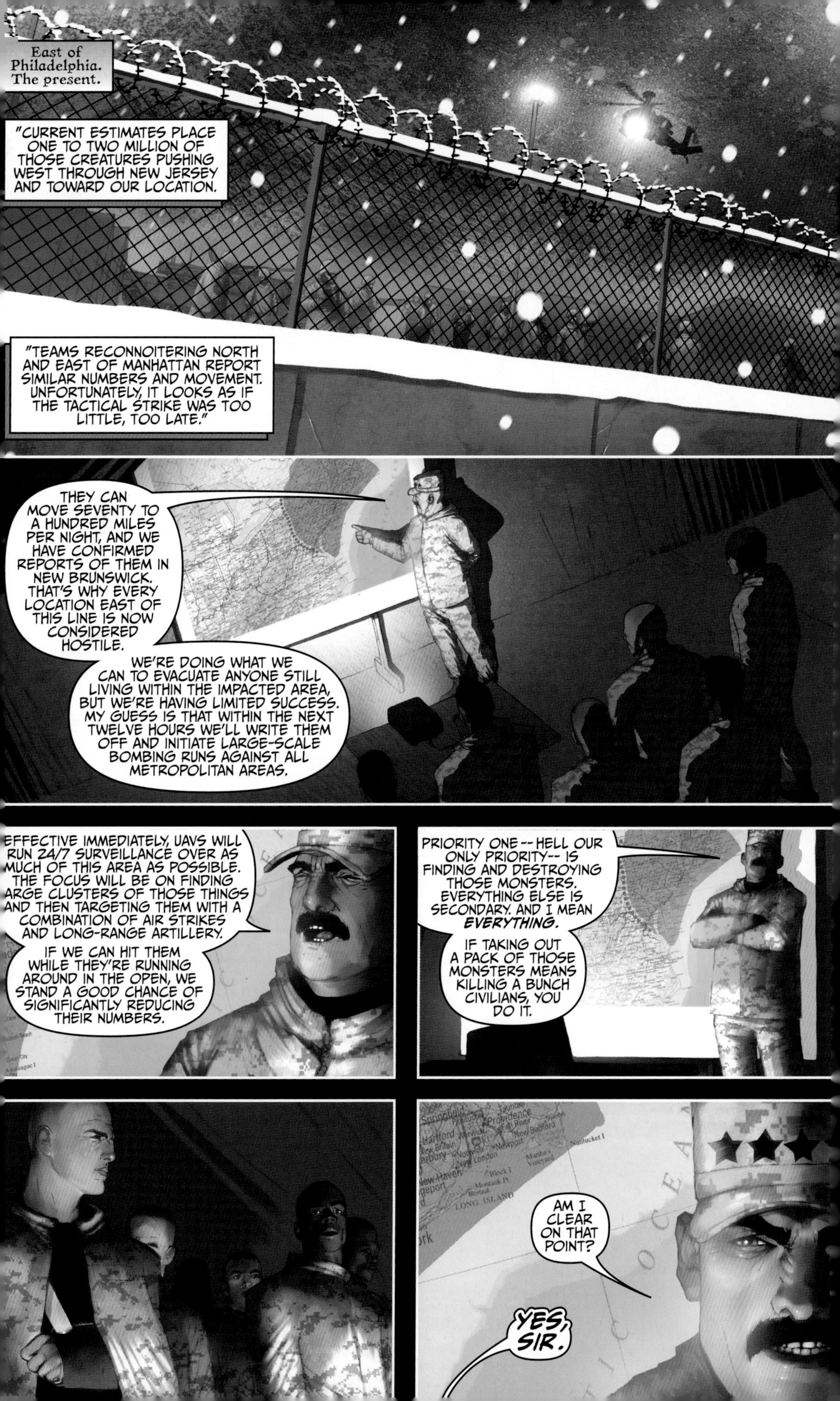
East of Philadelphia. The present.
"CURRENT ESTIMATES PLACE ONE TO TWO MILLION OF THOSE CREATURES PUSHING WEST THROUGH NEW JERSEY AND TOWARD OUR LOCATION.
"TEAMS RECONNOITERING NORTH AND EAST OF MANHATTAN REPORT SIMILAR NUMBERS AND MOVEMENT. UNFORTUNATELY, IT LOOKS AS IF THE TACTICAL STRIKE WAS TOO LITTLE, TOO LATE."
THEY CAN MOVE SEVENTY TO A HUNDRED MILES PER NIGHT, AND WE HAVE CONFIRMED REPORTS OF THEM IN NEW BRUNSWICK. THAT'S WHY EVERY LOCATION EAST OF THIS LINE IS NOW CONSIDERED HOSTILE.
WE'RE DOING WHAT WE CAN TO EVACUATE ANYONE STILL LIVING WITHIN THE IMPACTED AREA, BUT WE'RE HAVING LIMITED SUCCESS. MY GUESS IS THAT WITHIN THE NEXT TWELVE HOURS WE'LL WRITE THEM OFF AND INITIATE LARGE-SCALE BOMBING RUNS AGAINST ALL METROPOLITAN AREAS.
EFFECTIVE IMMEDIATELY, UAVS WILL RUN 24/7 SURVEILLANCE OVER AS MUCH OF THIS AREA AS POSSIBLE. THE FOCUS WILL BE ON FINDING LARGE CLUSTERS OF THOSE THINGS AND THEN TARGETING THEM WITH A COMBINATION OF AIR STRIKES AND LONG-RANGE ARTILLERY.
IF WE CAN HIT THEM WHILE THEY'RE RUNNING AROUND IN THE OPEN, WE STAND A GOOD CHANCE OF SIGNIFICANTLY REDUCING THEIR NUMBERS.
PRIORITY ONE -- HELL OUR ONLY PRIORITY-- IS FINDING AND DESTROYING THOSE MONSTERS. EVERYTHING ELSE IS SECONDARY. AND I MEAN *EVERYTHING.*
IF TAKING OUT A PACK OF THOSE MONSTERS MEANS KILLING A BUNCH CIVILIANS, YOU DO IT.
AM I CLEAR ON THAT POINT?
YES, SIR.

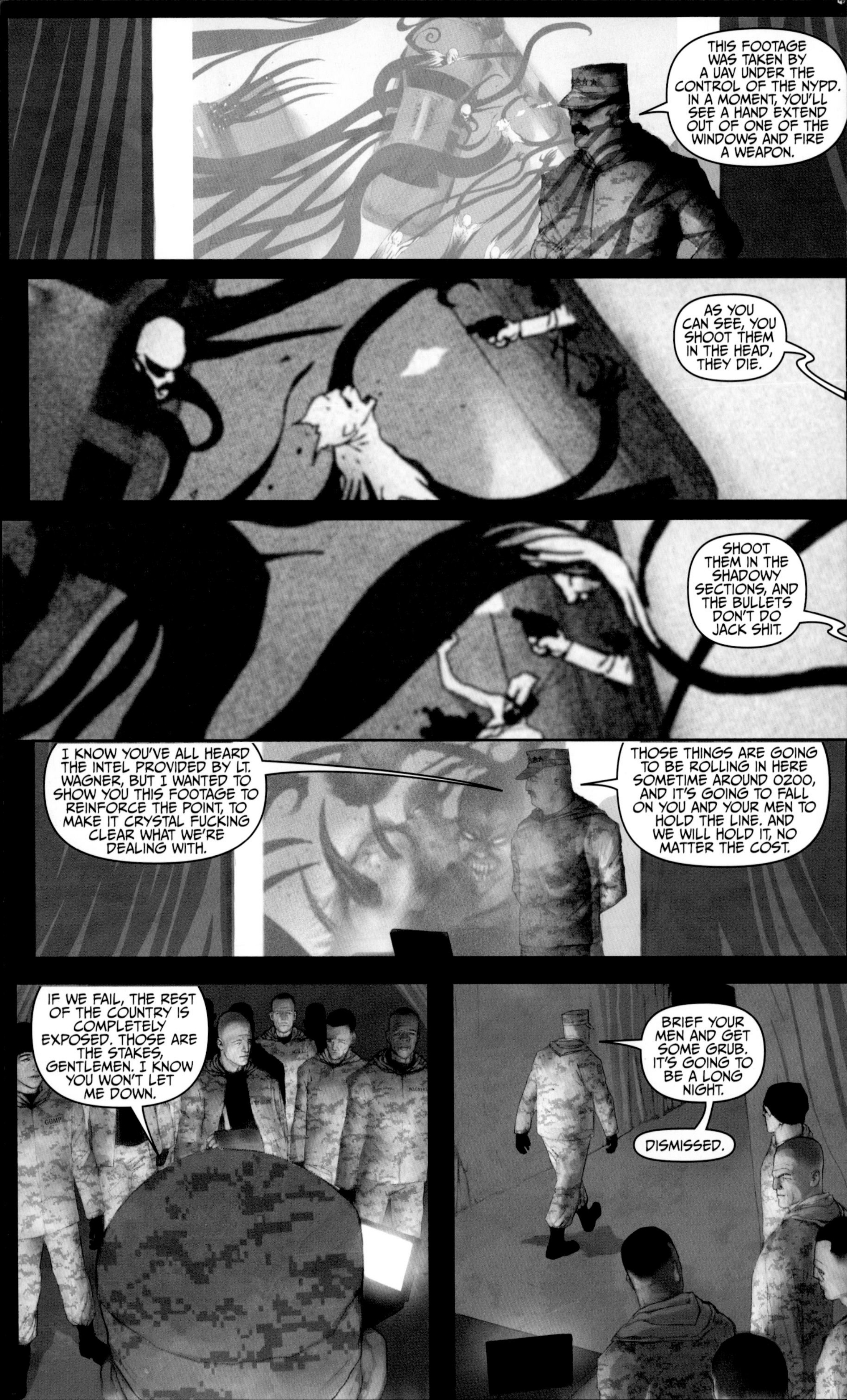
THIS FOOTAGE WAS TAKEN BY A UAV UNDER THE CONTROL OF THE NYPD. IN A MOMENT, YOU'LL SEE A HAND EXTEND OUT OF ONE OF THE WINDOWS AND FIRE A WEAPON.
AS YOU CAN SEE, YOU SHOOT THEM IN THE HEAD, THEY DIE.
SHOOT THEM IN THE SHADOWY SECTIONS, AND THE BULLETS DON'T DO JACK SHIT.
I KNOW YOU'VE ALL HEARD THE INTEL PROVIDED BY LT. WAGNER, BUT I WANTED TO SHOW YOU THIS FOOTAGE TO REINFORCE THE POINT, TO MAKE IT CRYSTAL FUCKING CLEAR WHAT WE'RE DEALING WITH.
THOSE THINGS ARE GOING TO BE ROLLING IN HERE SOMETIME AROUND 0200, AND IT'S GOING TO FALL ON YOU AND YOUR MEN TO HOLD THE LINE. AND WE WILL HOLD IT, NO MATTER THE COST.
IF WE FAIL, THE REST OF THE COUNTRY IS COMPLETELY EXPOSED. THOSE ARE THE STAKES, GENTLEMEN. I KNOW YOU WON'T LET ME DOWN.
BRIEF YOUR MEN AND GET SOME GRUB. IT'S GOING TO BE A LONG NIGHT.
DISMISSED.

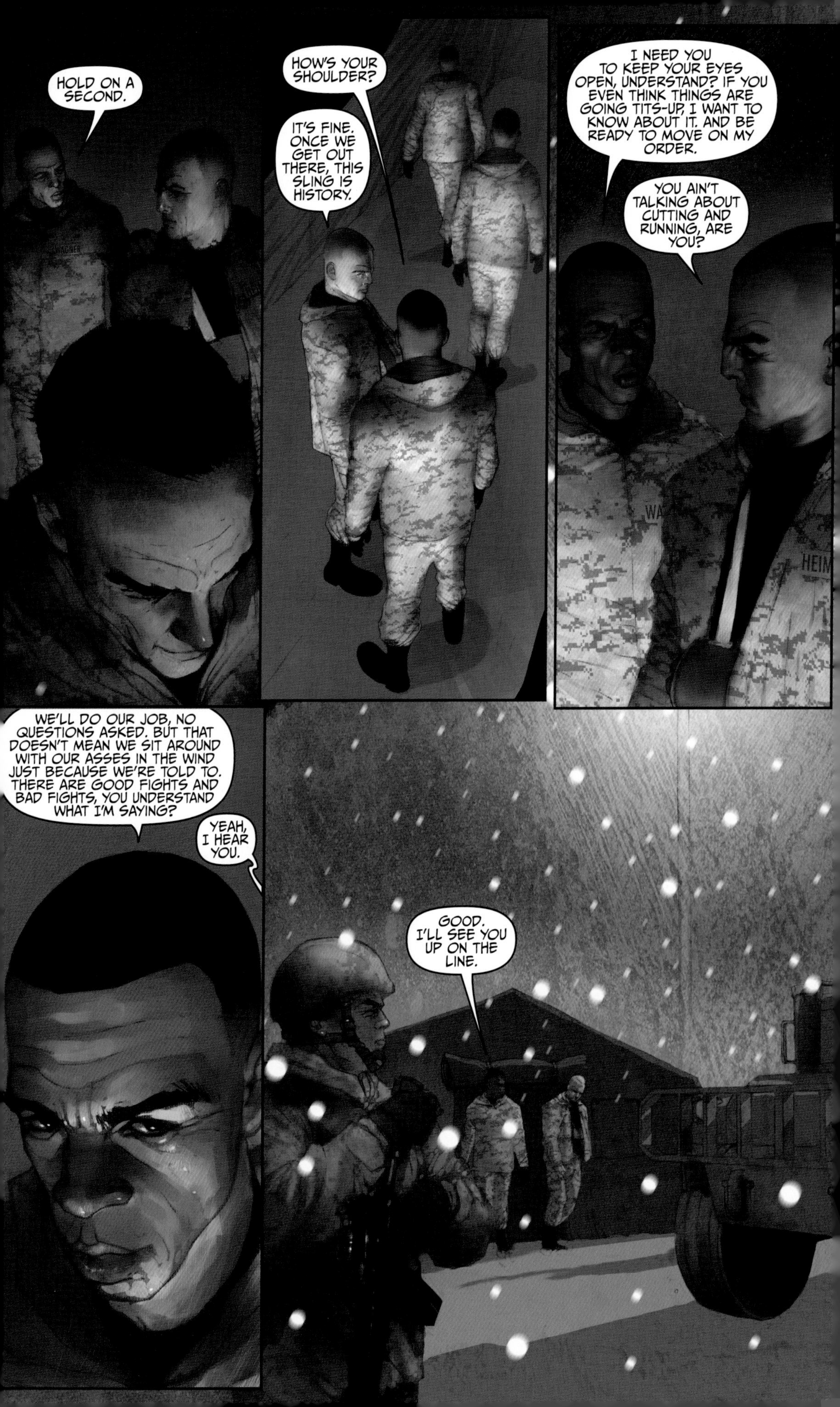
HOLD ON A SECOND.
HOW'S YOUR SHOULDER?
IT'S FINE. ONCE WE GET OUT THERE, THIS SLING IS HISTORY.
I NEED YOU TO KEEP YOUR EYES OPEN, UNDERSTAND? IF YOU EVEN THINK THINGS ARE GOING TITS-UP, I WANT TO KNOW ABOUT IT. AND BE READY TO MOVE ON MY ORDER.
YOU AIN'T TALKING ABOUT CUTTING AND RUNNING, ARE YOU?
WA
HEIM
WE'LL DO OUR JOB, NO QUESTIONS ASKED. BUT THAT DOESN'T MEAN WE SIT AROUND WITH OUR ASSES IN THE WIND JUST BECAUSE WE'RE TOLD TO. THERE ARE GOOD FIGHTS AND BAD FIGHTS, YOU UNDERSTAND WHAT I'M SAYING?
YEAH, I HEAR YOU.
GOOD. I'LL SEE YOU UP ON THE LINE.

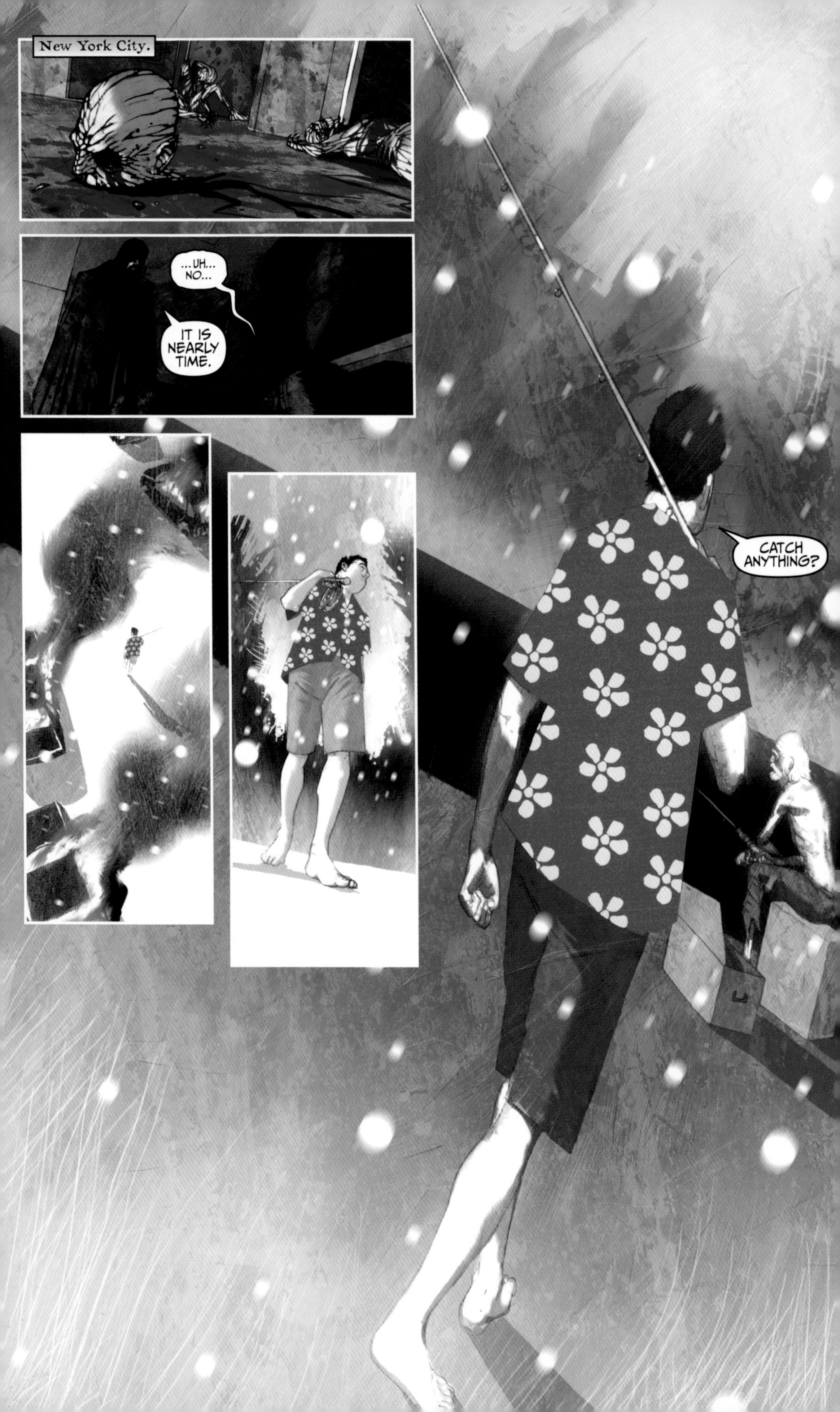
New York City.
...UH... NO...
IT IS NEARLY TIME.
CATCH ANYTHING?

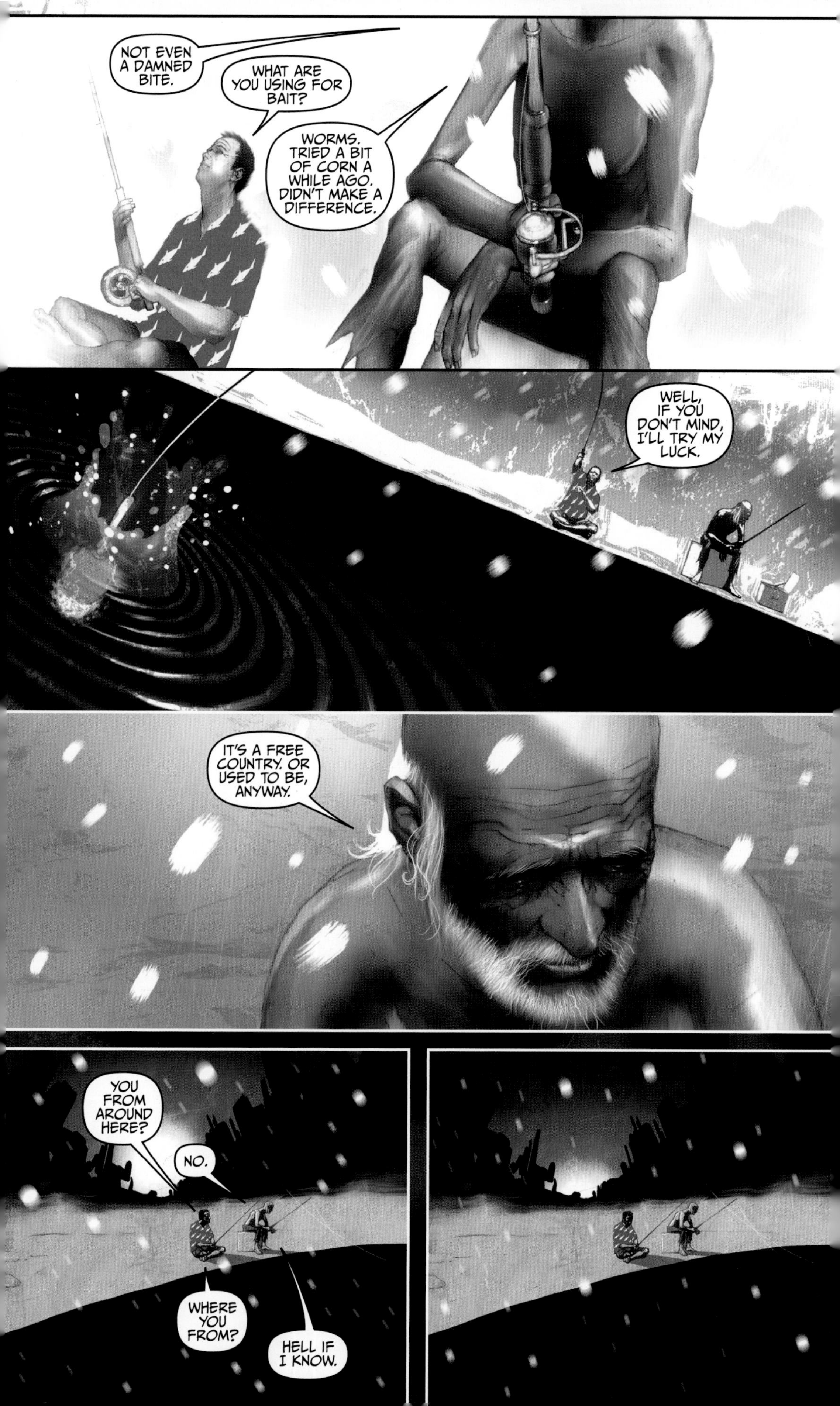
NOT EVEN A DAMNED BITE.
WHAT ARE YOU USING FOR BAIT?
WORMS. TRIED A BIT OF CORN A WHILE AGO. DIDN'T MAKE A DIFFERENCE.
WELL, IF YOU DON'T MIND, I'LL TRY MY LUCK.
IT'S A FREE COUNTRY. OR USED TO BE, ANYWAY.
YOU FROM AROUND HERE?
NO.
WHERE YOU FROM?
HELL IF I KNOW.

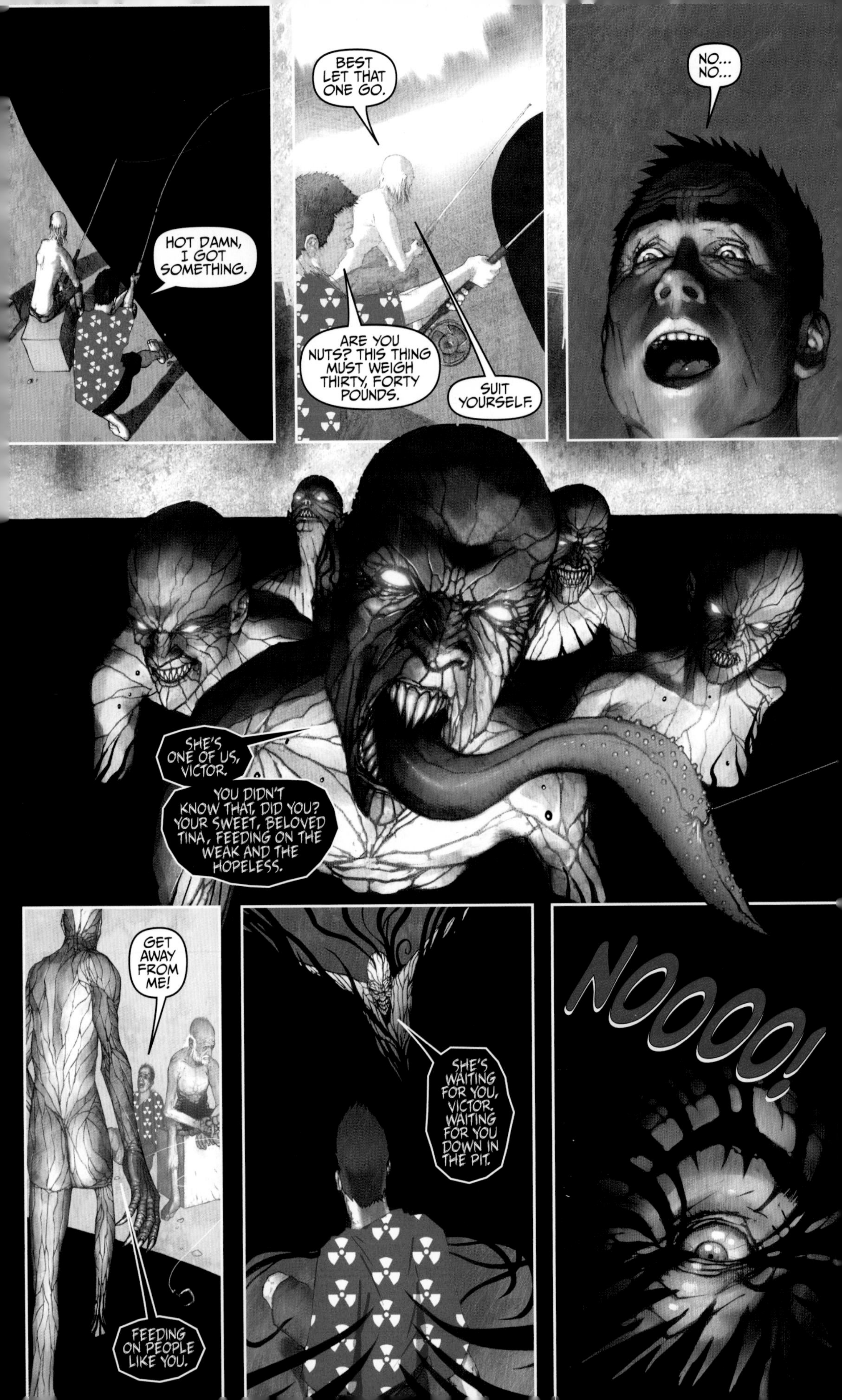
HOT DAMN, I GOT SOMETHING.
BEST LET THAT ONE GO.
ARE YOU NUTS? THIS THING MUST WEIGH THIRTY, FORTY POUNDS.
SUIT YOURSELF.
NO... NO...
SHE'S ONE OF US, VICTOR.
YOU DIDN'T KNOW THAT, DID YOU? YOUR SWEET, BELOVED TINA, FEEDING ON THE WEAK AND THE HOPELESS.
GET AWAY FROM ME!
FEEDING ON PEOPLE LIKE YOU.
SHE'S WAITING FOR YOU, VICTOR. WAITING FOR YOU DOWN IN THE PIT.
NOOOO!

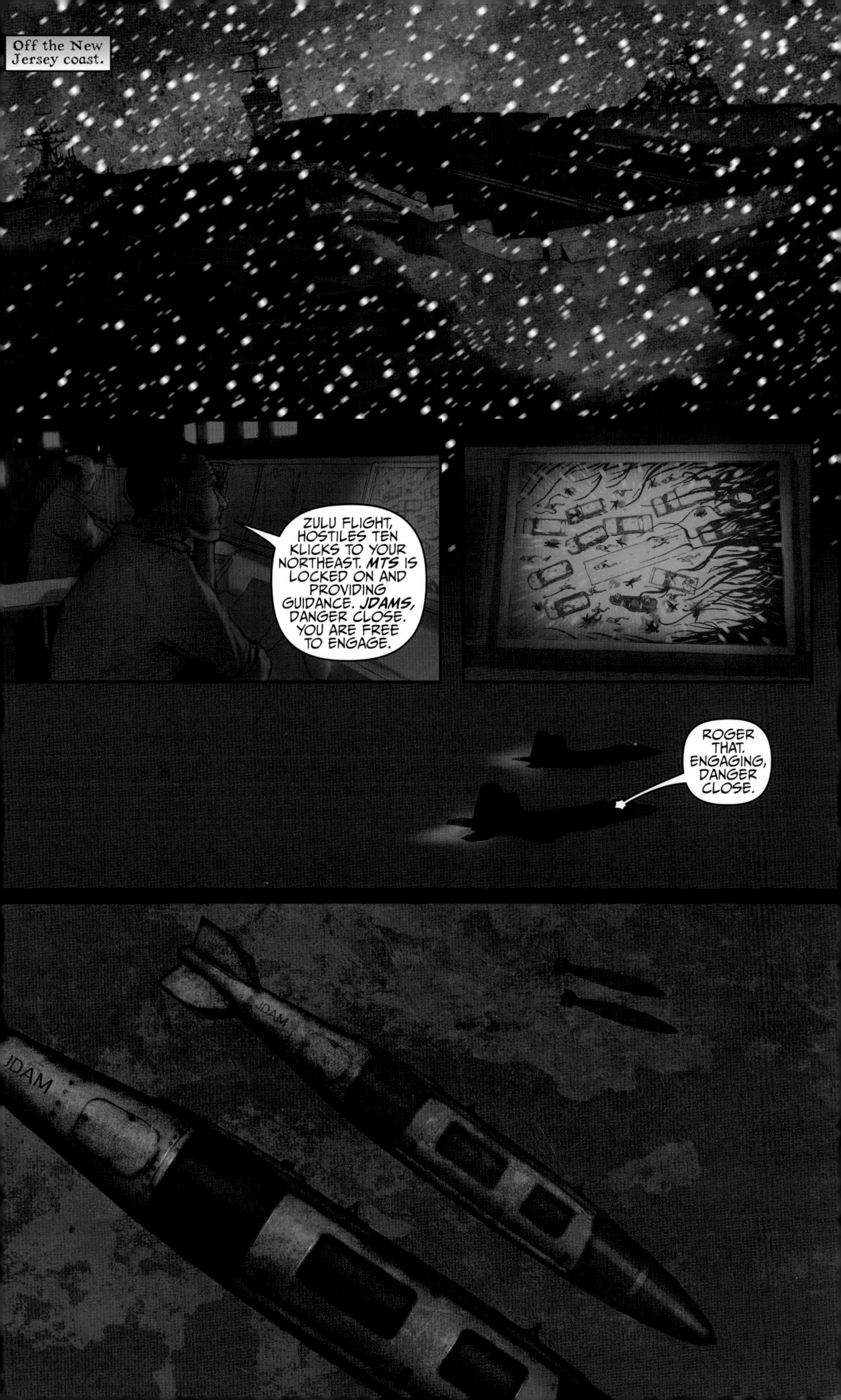
Off the New Jersey coast.
ZULU FLIGHT, HOSTILES TEN KLICKS TO YOUR NORTHEAST. MTS IS LOCKED ON AND PROVIDING GUIDANCE. JDAMS, DANGER CLOSE. YOU ARE FREE TO ENGAGE.
ROGER THAT. ENGAGING, DANGER CLOSE.
JDAM
JDAM

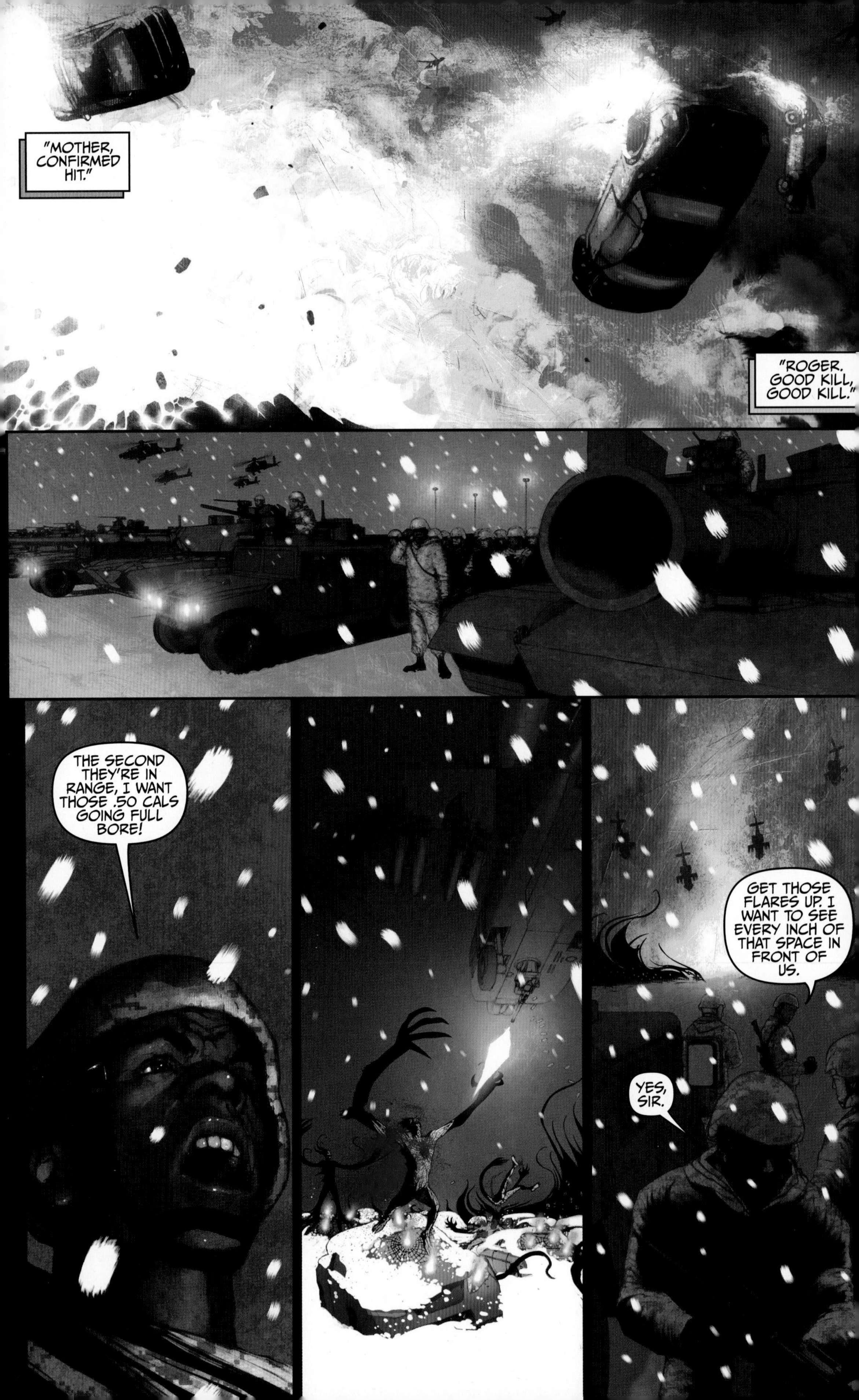
"MOTHER, CONFIRMED HIT."
"ROGER. GOOD KILL, GOOD KILL."
THE SECOND THEY'RE IN RANGE, I WANT THOSE .50 CALS GOING FULL BORE!
GET THOSE FLARES UP. I WANT TO SEE EVERY INCH OF THAT SPACE IN FRONT OF US.
YES, SIR.

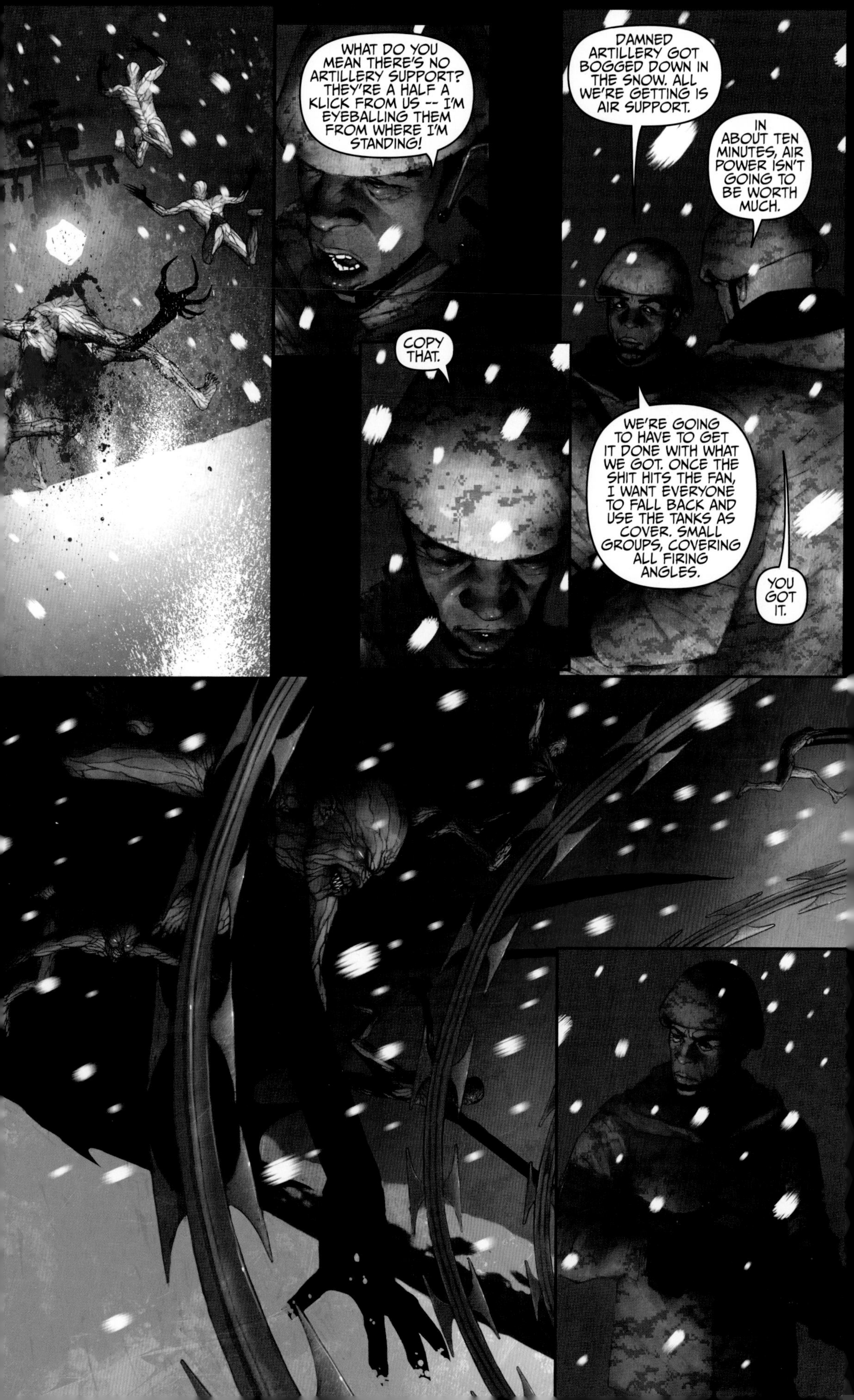
WHAT DO YOU MEAN THERE'S NO ARTILLERY SUPPORT? THEY'RE A HALF A KLICK FROM US -- I'M EYEBALLING THEM FROM WHERE I'M STANDING!
DAMNED ARTILLERY GOT BOGGED DOWN IN THE SNOW. ALL WE'RE GETTING IS AIR SUPPORT.
IN ABOUT TEN MINUTES, AIR POWER ISN'T GOING TO BE WORTH MUCH.
COPY THAT.
WE'RE GOING TO HAVE TO GET IT DONE WITH WHAT WE GOT. ONCE THE SHIT HITS THE FAN, I WANT EVERYONE TO FALL BACK AND USE THE TANKS AS COVER. SMALL GROUPS, COVERING ALL FIRING ANGLES.
YOU GOT IT.

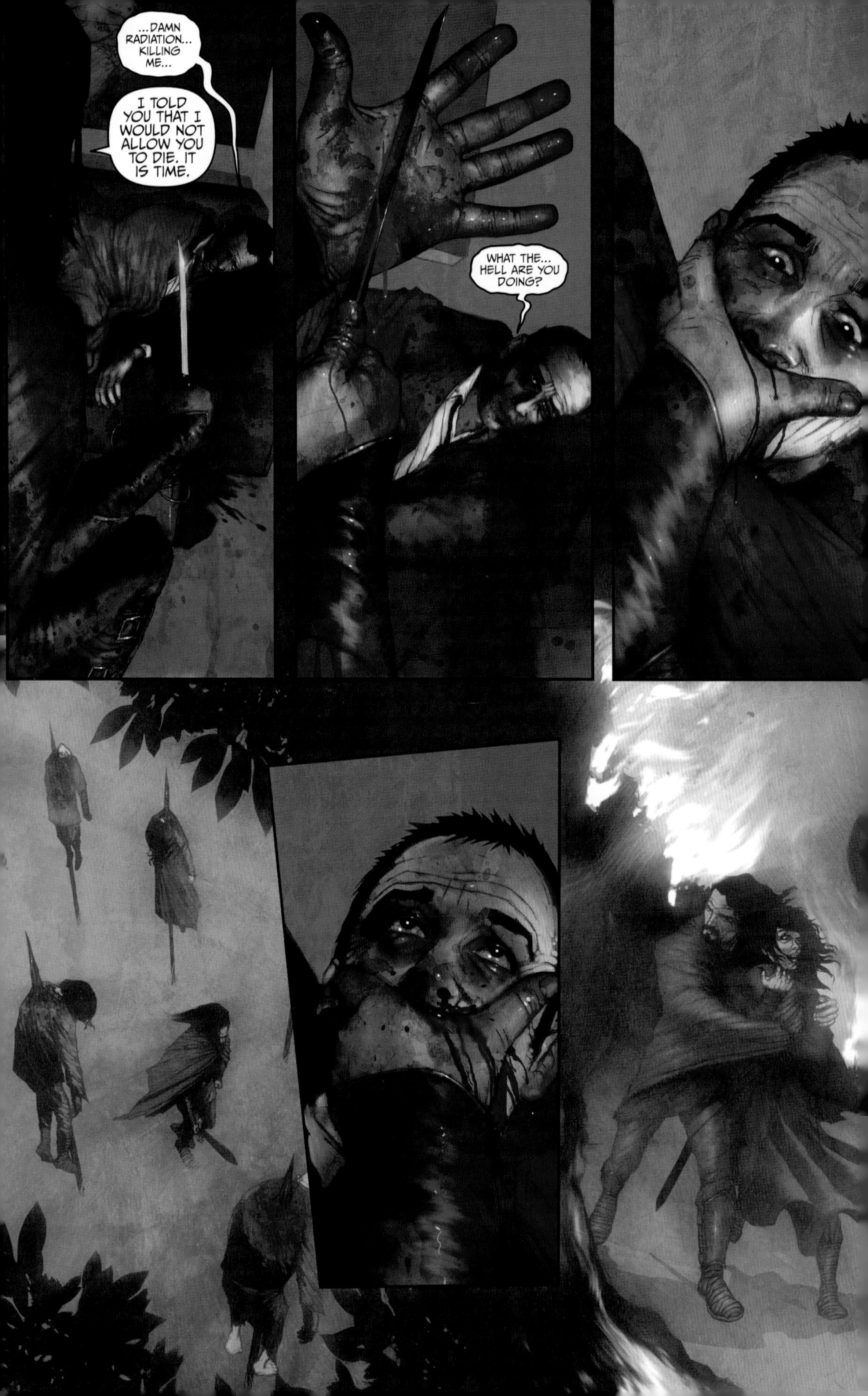
...DAMN RADIATION... KILLING ME...
I TOLD YOU THAT I WOULD NOT ALLOW YOU TO DIE. IT IS TIME.
WHAT THE... HELL ARE YOU DOING?

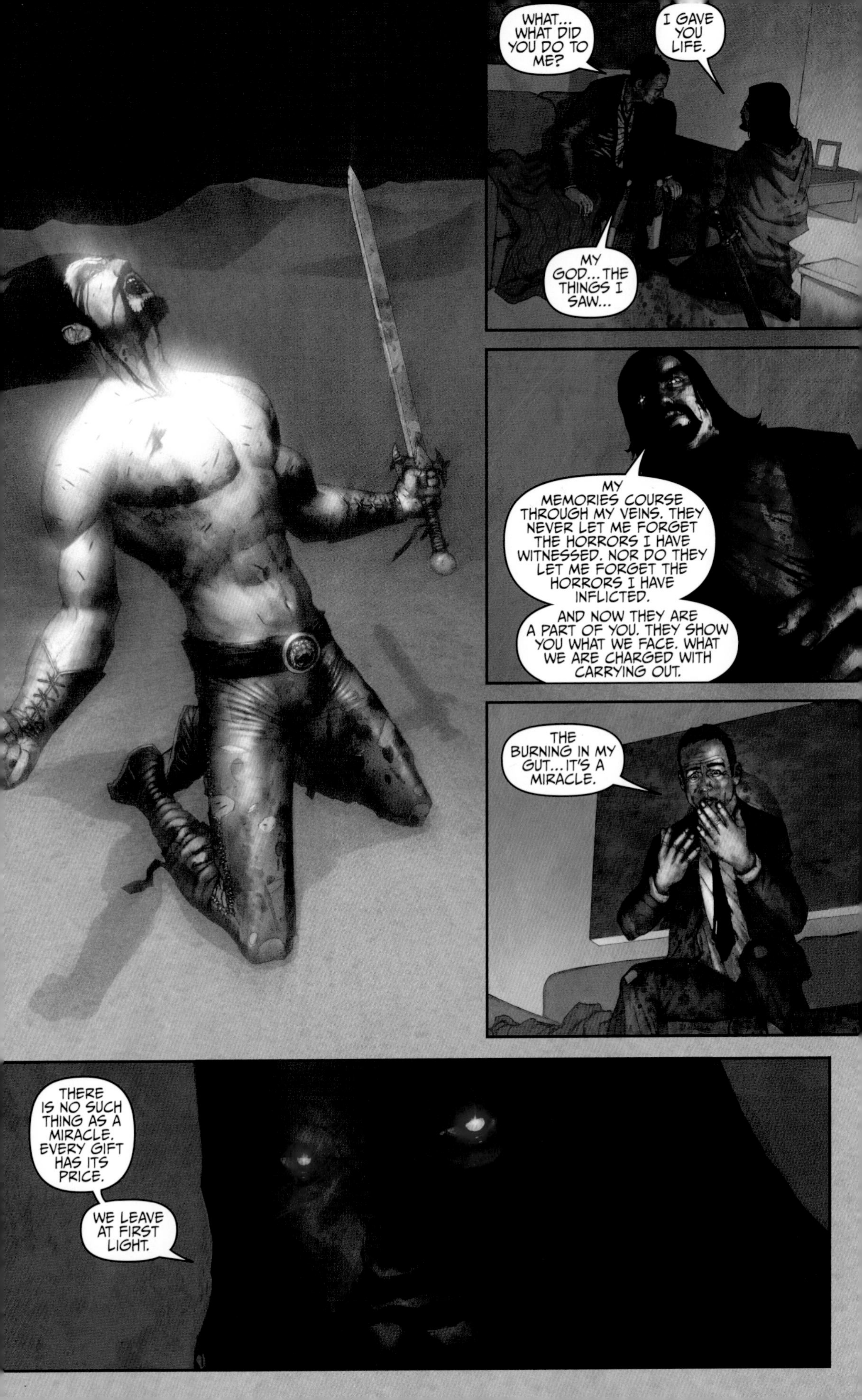
WHAT... WHAT DID YOU DO TO ME?
I GAVE YOU LIFE.
MY GOD... THE THINGS I SAW...
MY MEMORIES COURSE THROUGH MY VEINS. THEY NEVER LET ME FORGET THE HORRORS I HAVE WITNESSED. NOR DO THEY LET ME FORGET THE HORRORS I HAVE INFLICTED.
AND NOW THEY ARE A PART OF YOU. THEY SHOW YOU WHAT WE FACE. WHAT WE ARE CHARGED WITH CARRYING OUT.
THE BURNING IN MY GUT... IT'S A MIRACLE.
THERE IS NO SUCH THING AS A MIRACLE. EVERY GIFT HAS ITS PRICE.
WE LEAVE AT FIRST LIGHT.

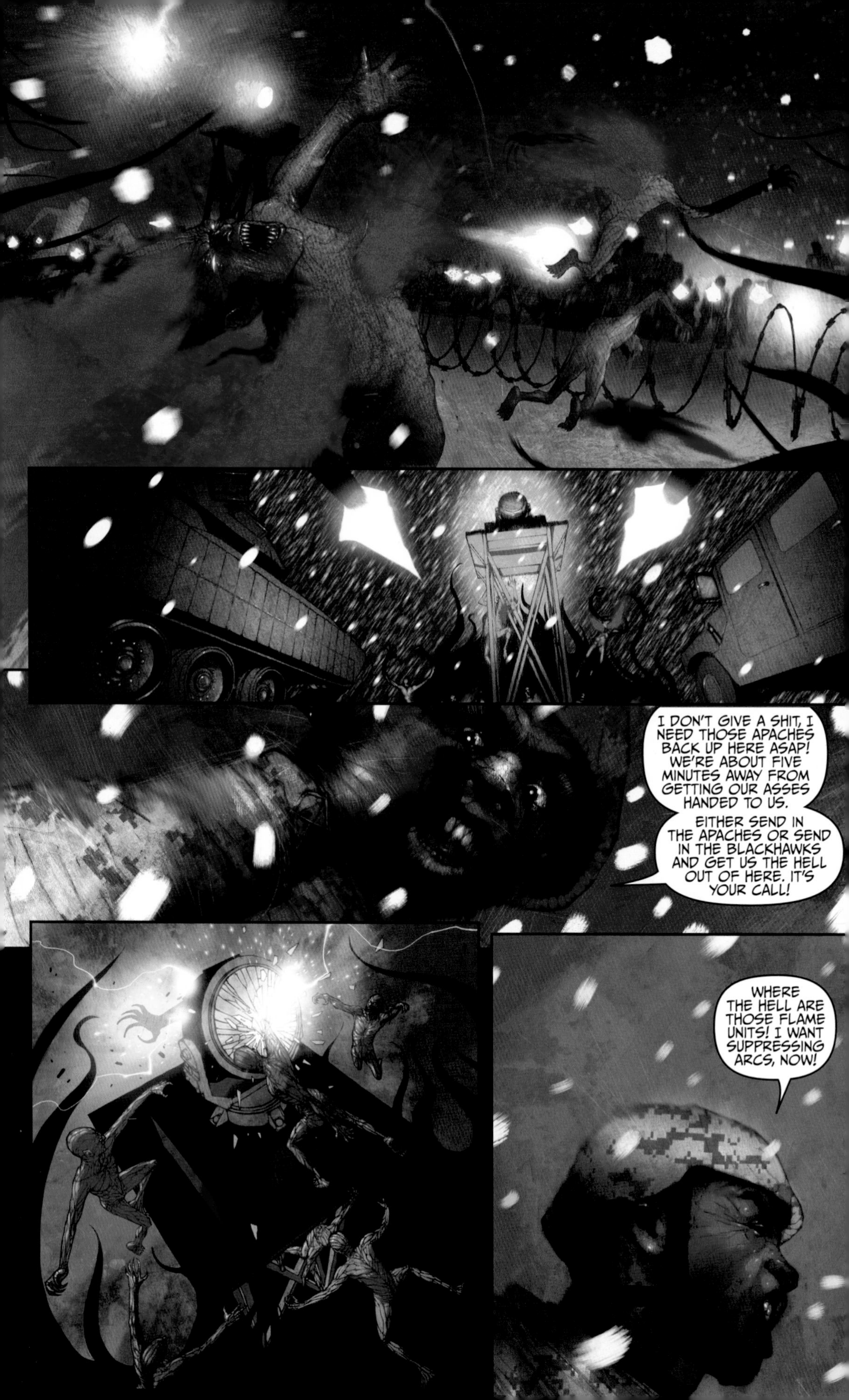
I DON'T GIVE A SHIT, I NEED THOSE APACHES BACK UP HERE ASAP! WE'RE ABOUT FIVE MINUTES AWAY FROM GETTING OUR ASSES HANDED TO US.
EITHER SEND IN THE APACHES OR SEND IN THE BLACKHAWKS AND GET US THE HELL OUT OF HERE. IT'S YOUR CALL!
WHERE THE HELL ARE THOSE FLAME UNITS! I WANT SUPPRESSING ARCS, NOW!

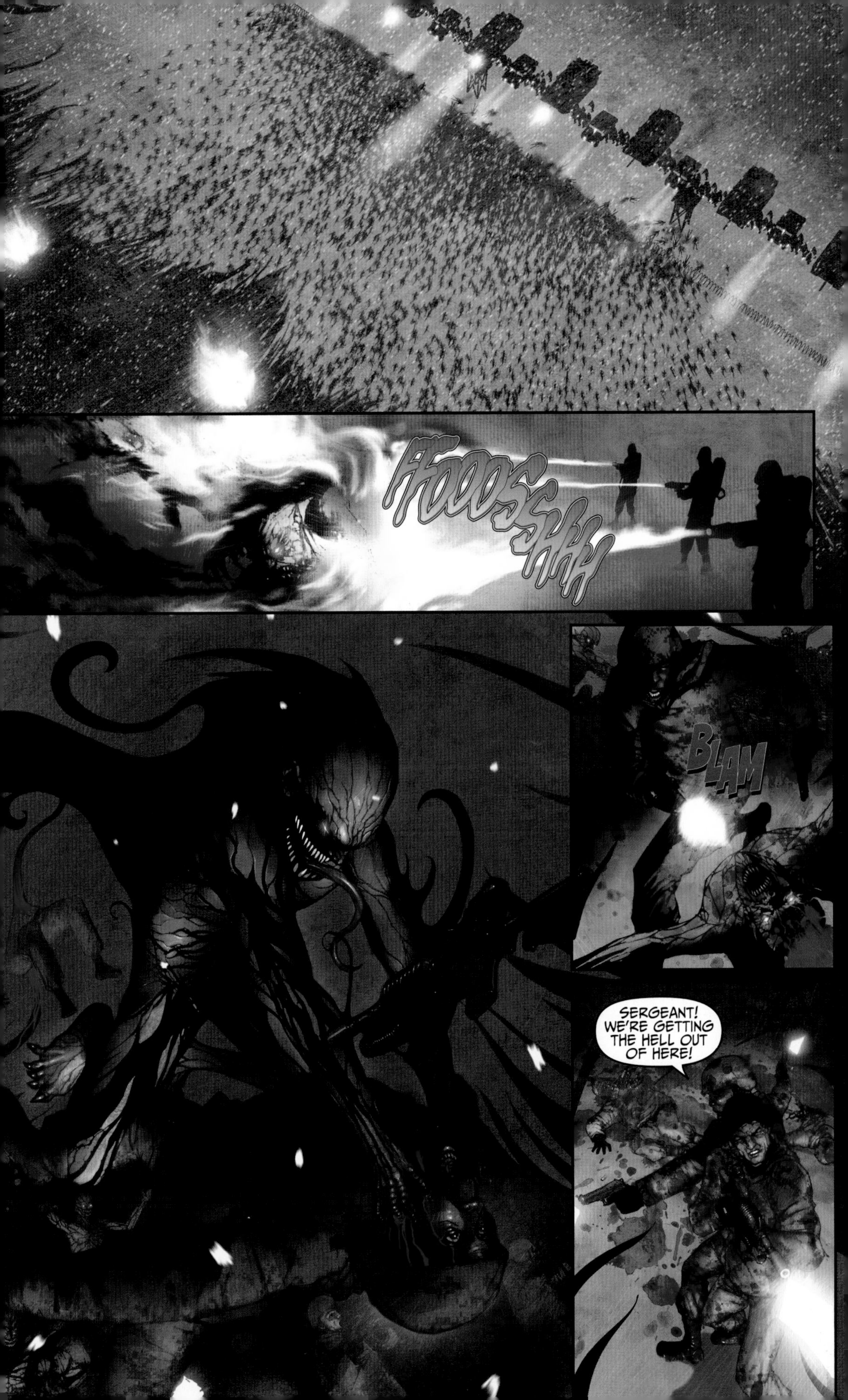
FFOOOSSHHH
BLAM
SERGEANT! WE'RE GETTING THE HELL OUT OF HERE!

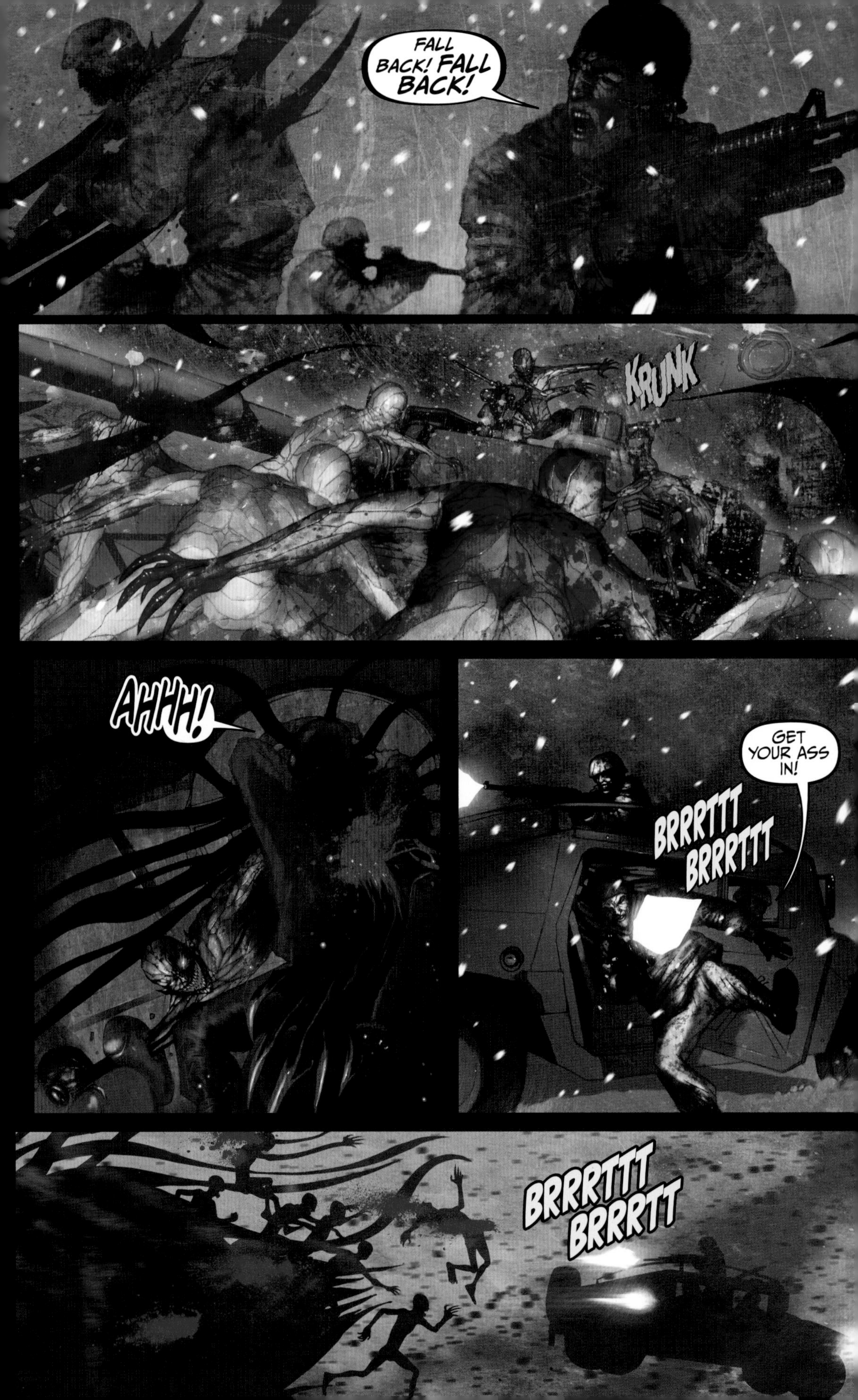
FALL BACK! FALL BACK!
KRUNK
AHHH!
GET YOUR ASS IN!
BRRRTTT BRRRTTT
BRRRTTT BRRRTT

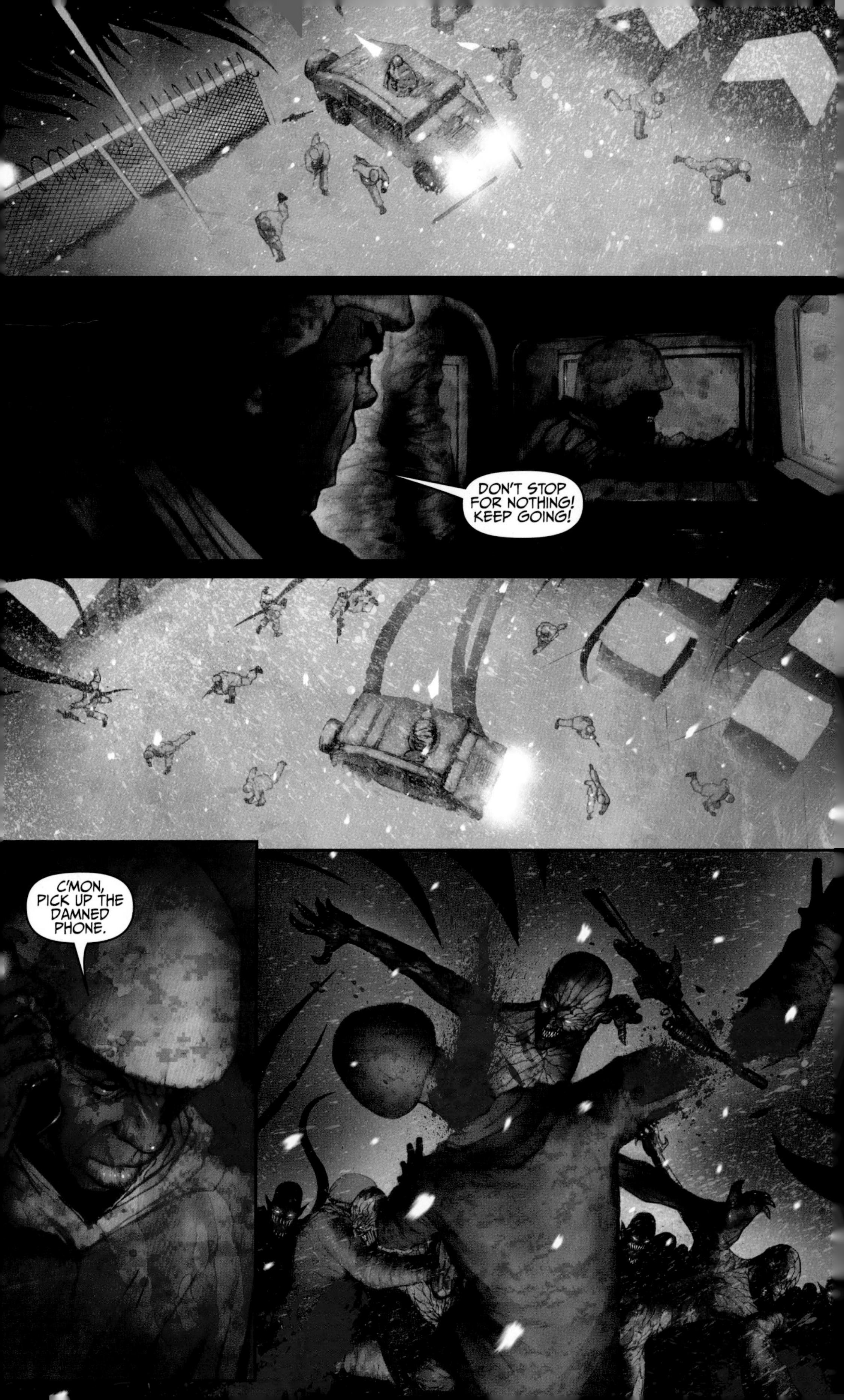
DON'T STOP FOR NOTHING! KEEP GOING!
C'MON, PICK UP THE DAMNED PHONE.

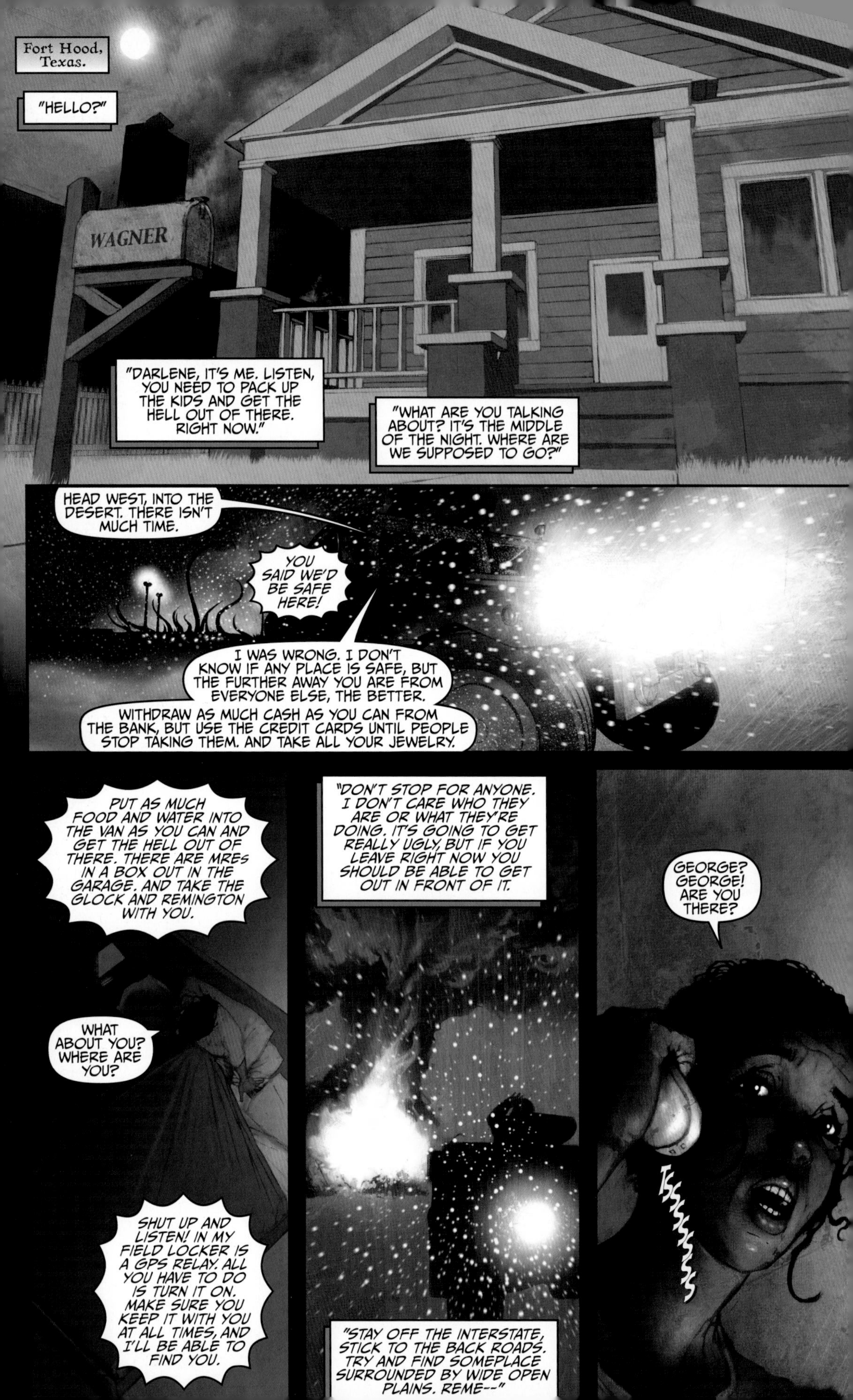
Fort Hood, Texas.
"HELLO?"
WAGNER
"DARLENE, IT'S ME. LISTEN, YOU NEED TO PACK UP THE KIDS AND GET THE HELL OUT OF THERE. RIGHT NOW."
"WHAT ARE YOU TALKING ABOUT? IT'S THE MIDDLE OF THE NIGHT. WHERE ARE WE SUPPOSED TO GO?"
HEAD WEST, INTO THE DESERT. THERE ISN'T MUCH TIME.
YOU SAID WE'D BE SAFE HERE!
I WAS WRONG. I DON'T KNOW IF ANY PLACE IS SAFE, BUT THE FURTHER AWAY YOU ARE FROM EVERYONE ELSE, THE BETTER.
WITHDRAW AS MUCH CASH AS YOU CAN FROM THE BANK, BUT USE THE CREDIT CARDS UNTIL PEOPLE STOP TAKING THEM. AND TAKE ALL YOUR JEWELRY.
PUT AS MUCH FOOD AND WATER INTO THE VAN AS YOU CAN AND GET THE HELL OUT OF THERE. THERE ARE MREs IN A BOX OUT IN THE GARAGE. AND TAKE THE GLOCK AND REMINGTON WITH YOU.
WHAT ABOUT YOU? WHERE ARE YOU?
SHUT UP AND LISTEN! IN MY FIELD LOCKER IS A GPS RELAY. ALL YOU HAVE TO DO IS TURN IT ON. MAKE SURE YOU KEEP IT WITH YOU AT ALL TIMES, AND I'LL BE ABLE TO FIND YOU.
"DON'T STOP FOR ANYONE. I DON'T CARE WHO THEY ARE OR WHAT THEY'RE DOING. IT'S GOING TO GET REALLY UGLY, BUT IF YOU LEAVE RIGHT NOW YOU SHOULD BE ABLE TO GET OUT IN FRONT OF IT.
"STAY OFF THE INTERSTATE, STICK TO THE BACK ROADS. TRY AND FIND SOMEPLACE SURROUNDED BY WIDE OPEN PLAINS. REME--"
GEORGE? GEORGE! ARE YOU THERE?
TSSSSSSS

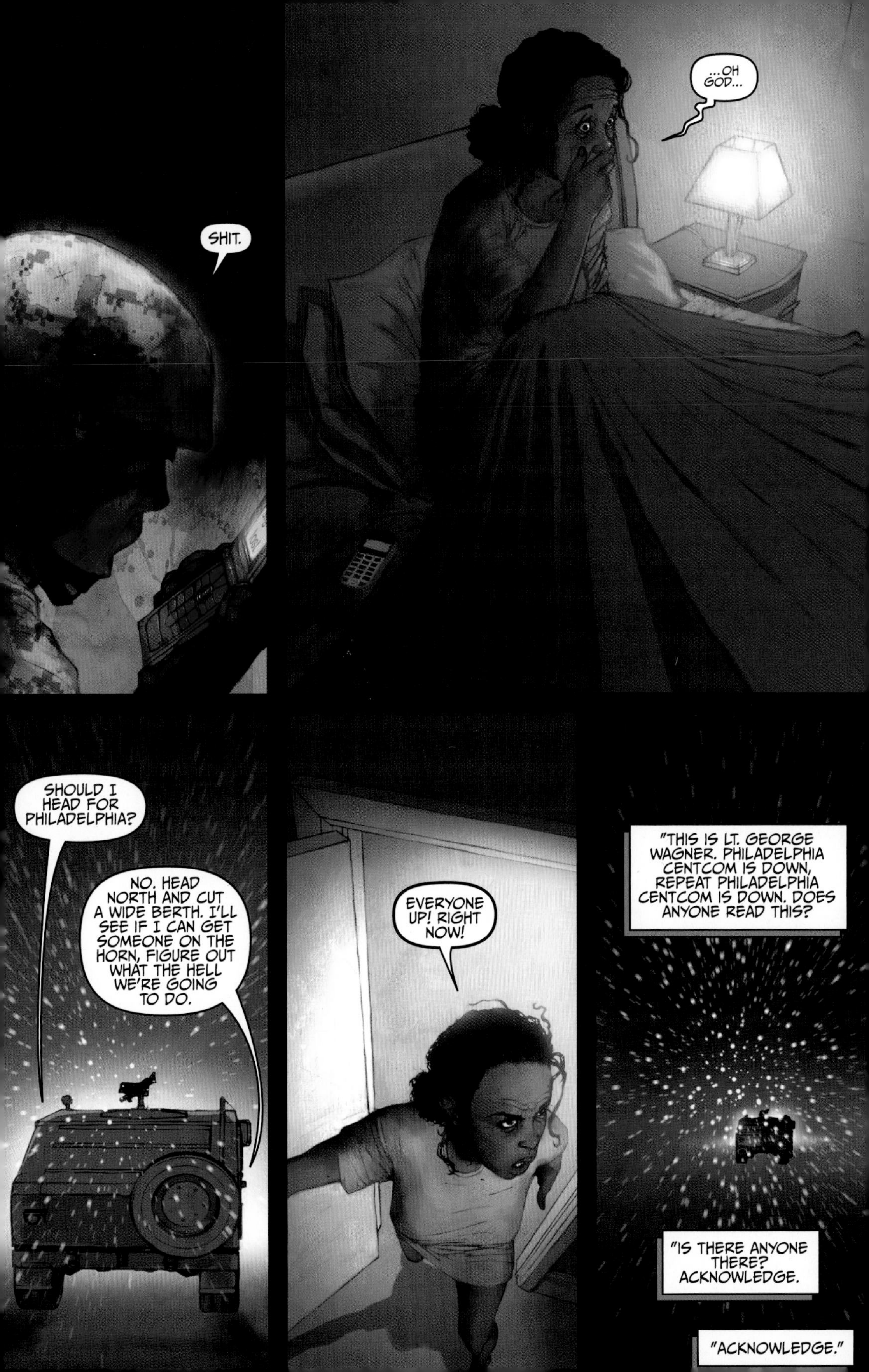
SHIT.
...OH GOD...
SHOULD I HEAD FOR PHILADELPHIA?
NO. HEAD NORTH AND CUT A WIDE BERTH. I'LL SEE IF I CAN GET SOMEONE ON THE HORN, FIGURE OUT WHAT THE HELL WE'RE GOING TO DO.
EVERYONE UP! RIGHT NOW!
"THIS IS LT. GEORGE WAGNER. PHILADELPHIA CENTCOM IS DOWN, REPEAT PHILADELPHIA CENTCOM IS DOWN. DOES ANYONE READ THIS?
"IS THERE ANYONE THERE? ACKNOWLEDGE.
"ACKNOWLEDGE."

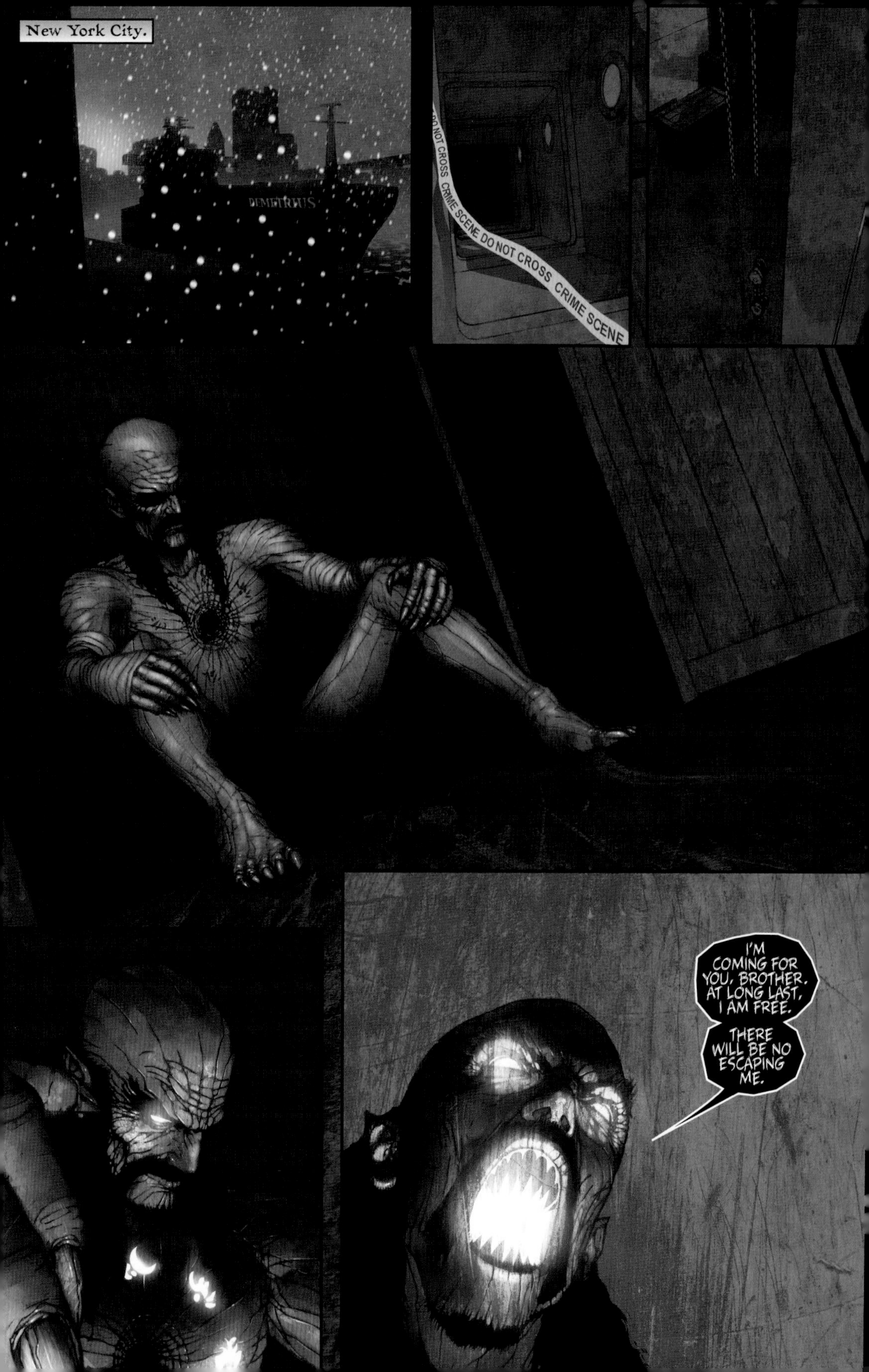
New York City.
DEMETRIUS
DO NOT CROSS CRIME SCENE DO NOT CROSS CRIME SCENE
I'M COMING FOR YOU, BROTHER. AT LONG LAST, I AM FREE.
THERE WILL BE NO ESCAPING ME.

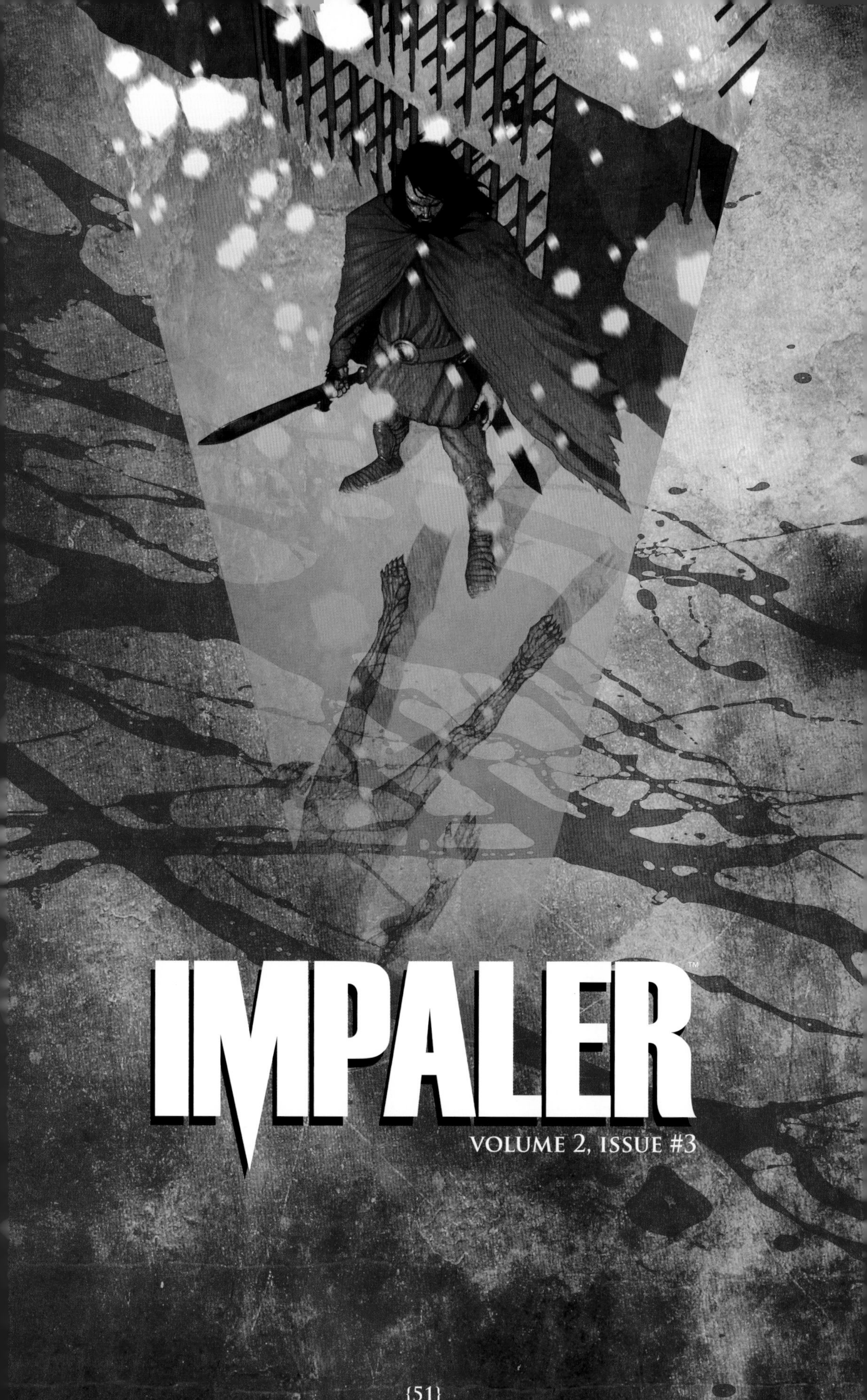
IMPALER™
VOLUME 2, ISSUE #3

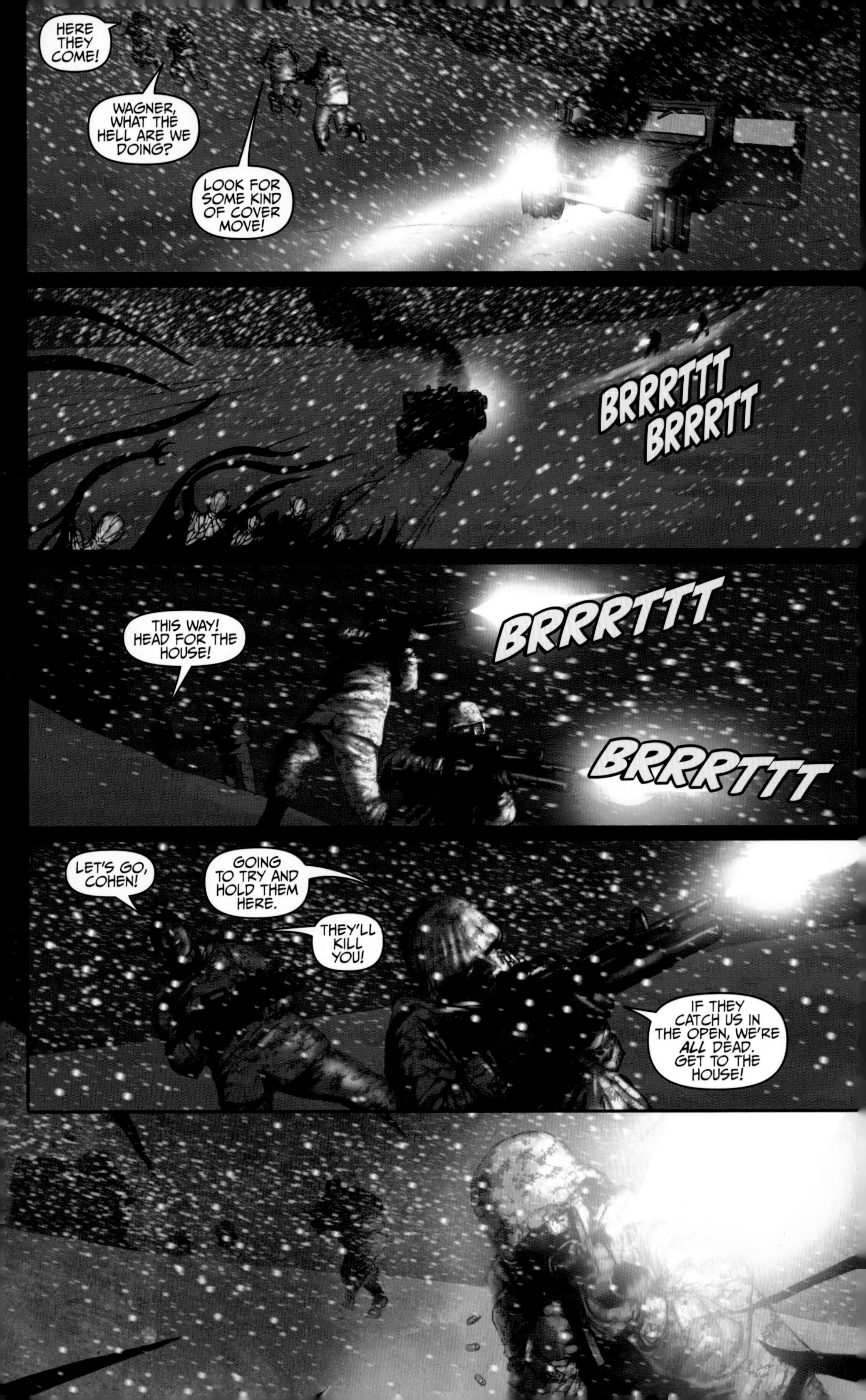
HERE THEY COME!
WAGNER, WHAT THE HELL ARE WE DOING?
LOOK FOR SOME KIND OF COVER MOVE!
BRRRTTT BRRRTT
THIS WAY! HEAD FOR THE HOUSE!
BRRRTTT
BRRRRTTT
LET'S GO, COHEN!
GOING TO TRY AND HOLD THEM HERE.
THEY'LL KILL YOU!
IF THEY CATCH US IN THE OPEN, WE'RE *ALL* DEAD. GET TO THE HOUSE!

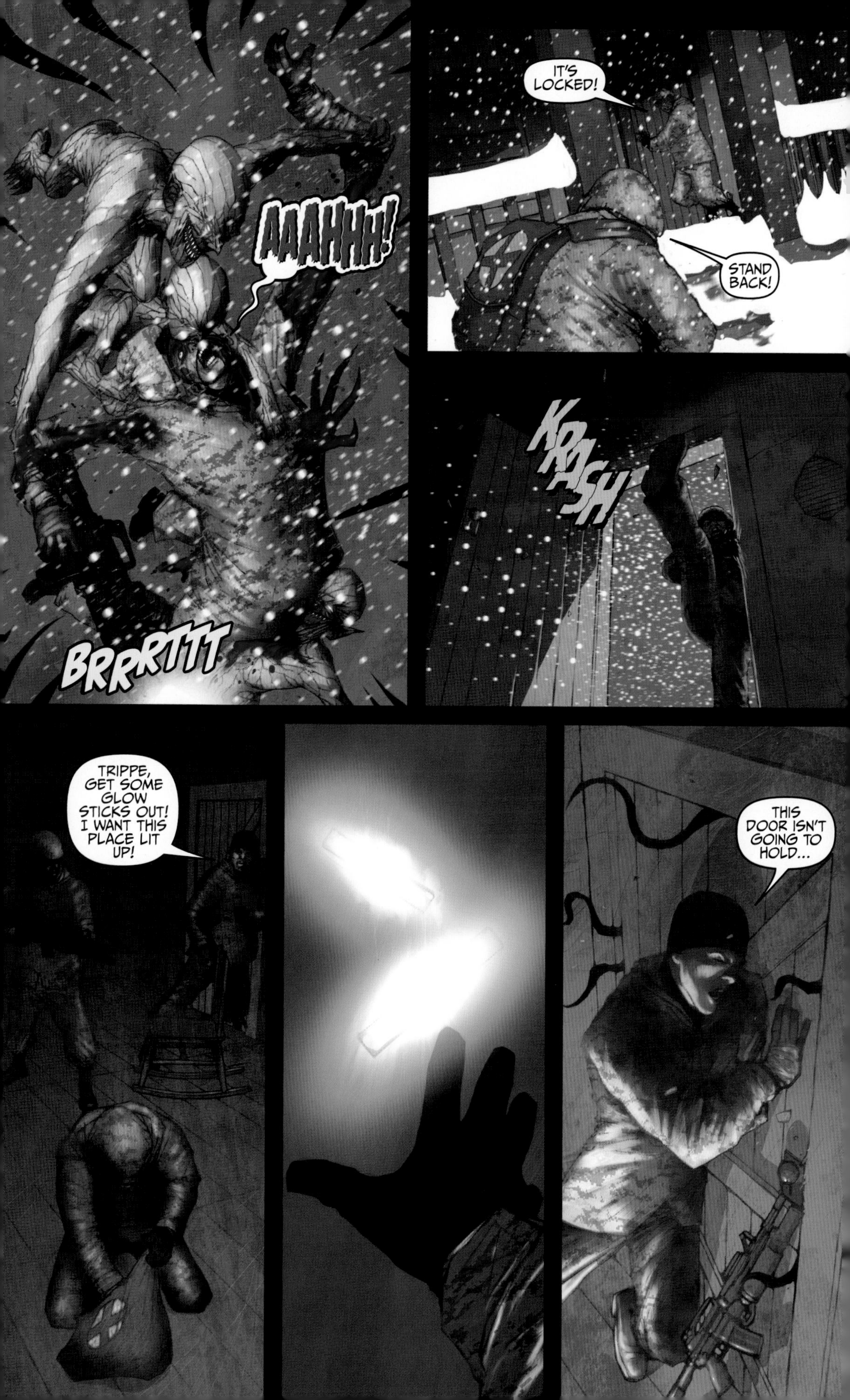
AAAHHH!
BRRRTTT
IT'S LOCKED!
STAND BACK!
KRASH
TRIPPE, GET SOME GLOW STICKS OUT! I WANT THIS PLACE LIT UP!
THIS DOOR ISN'T GOING TO HOLD...

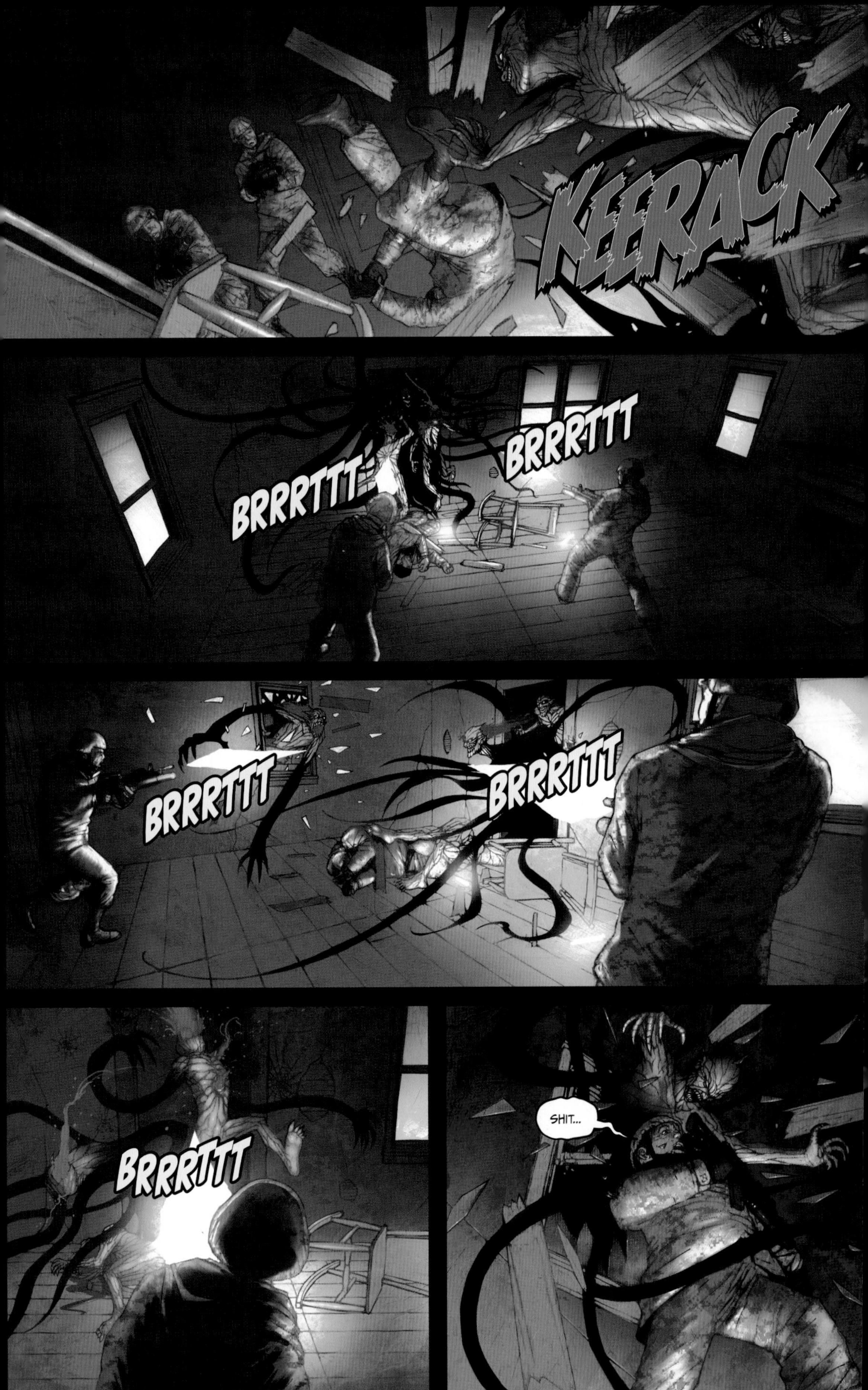
KEERACK
BRRRTTT
BRRRTTT
BRRRTTT
BRRRTTT
BRRRTTT
SHIT...

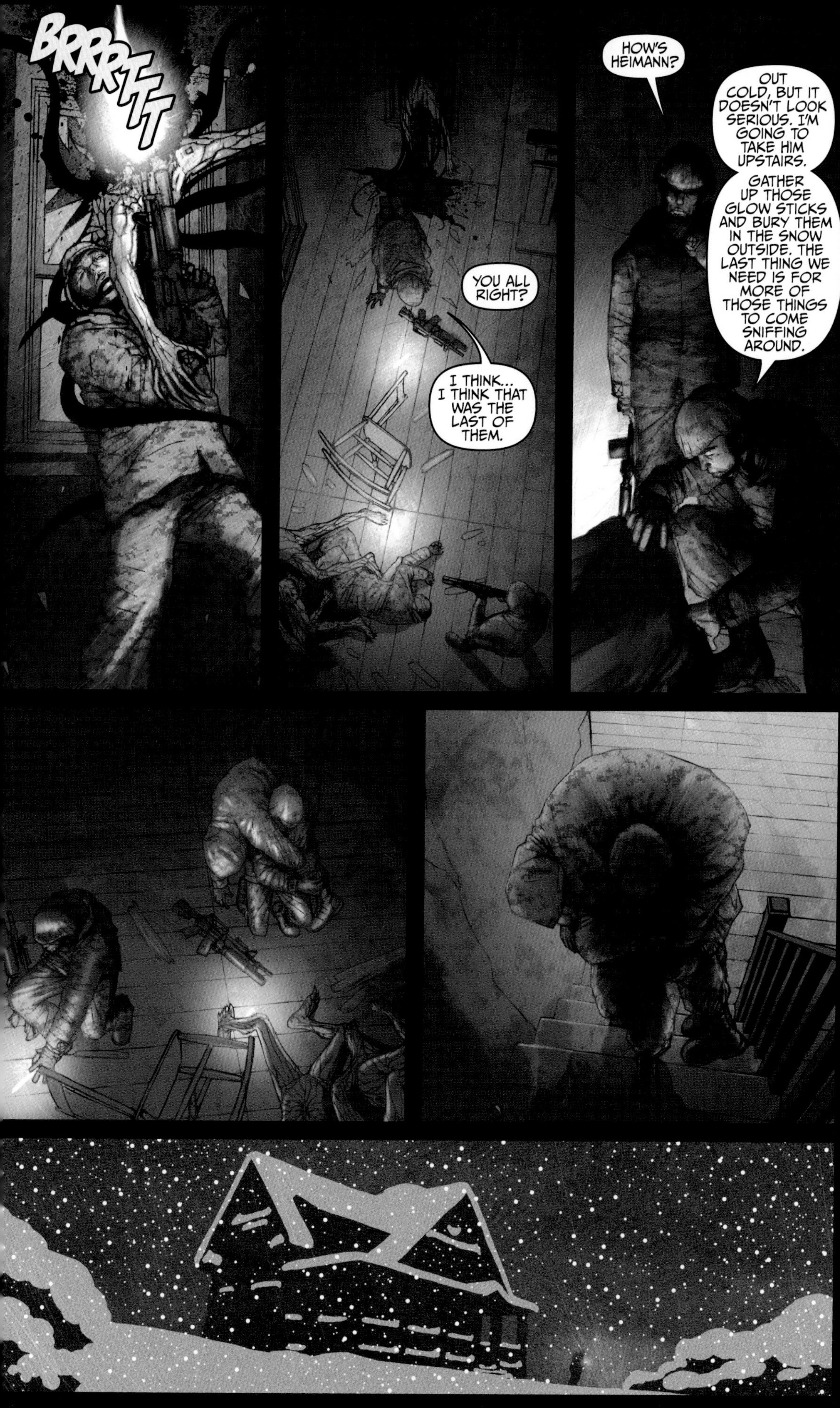
BRRRRTTT
YOU ALL RIGHT?
I THINK... I THINK THAT WAS THE LAST OF THEM.
HOW'S HEIMANN?
OUT COLD, BUT IT DOESN'T LOOK SERIOUS. I'M GOING TO TAKE HIM UPSTAIRS.
GATHER UP THOSE GLOW STICKS AND BURY THEM IN THE SNOW OUTSIDE. THE LAST THING WE NEED IS FOR MORE OF THOSE THINGS TO COME SNIFFING AROUND.

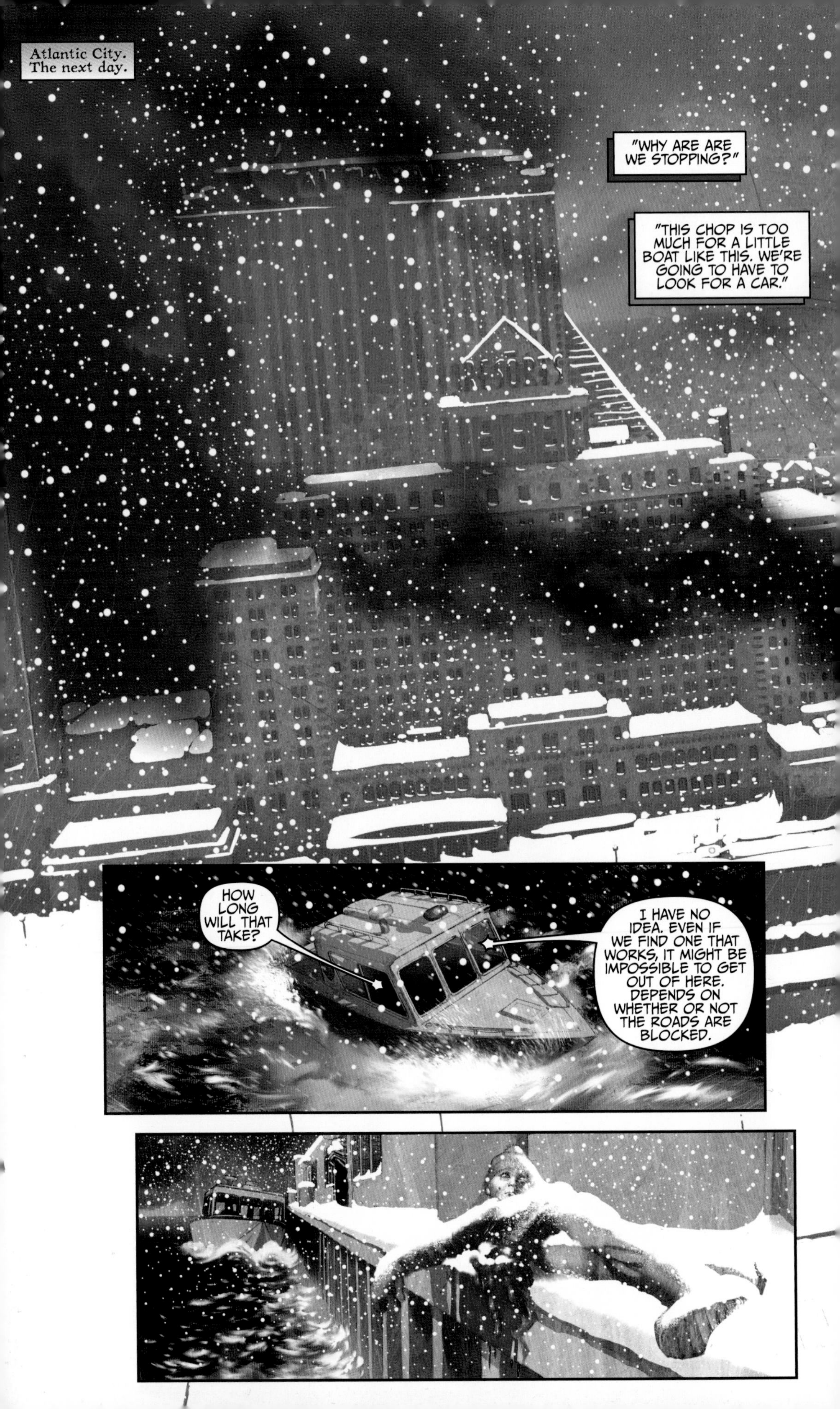
Atlantic City.
The next day.
"WHY ARE ARE WE STOPPING?"
"THIS CHOP IS TOO MUCH FOR A LITTLE BOAT LIKE THIS. WE'RE GOING TO HAVE TO LOOK FOR A CAR."
HOW LONG WILL THAT TAKE?
I HAVE NO IDEA. EVEN IF WE FIND ONE THAT WORKS, IT MIGHT BE IMPOSSIBLE TO GET OUT OF HERE. DEPENDS ON WHETHER OR NOT THE ROADS ARE BLOCKED.

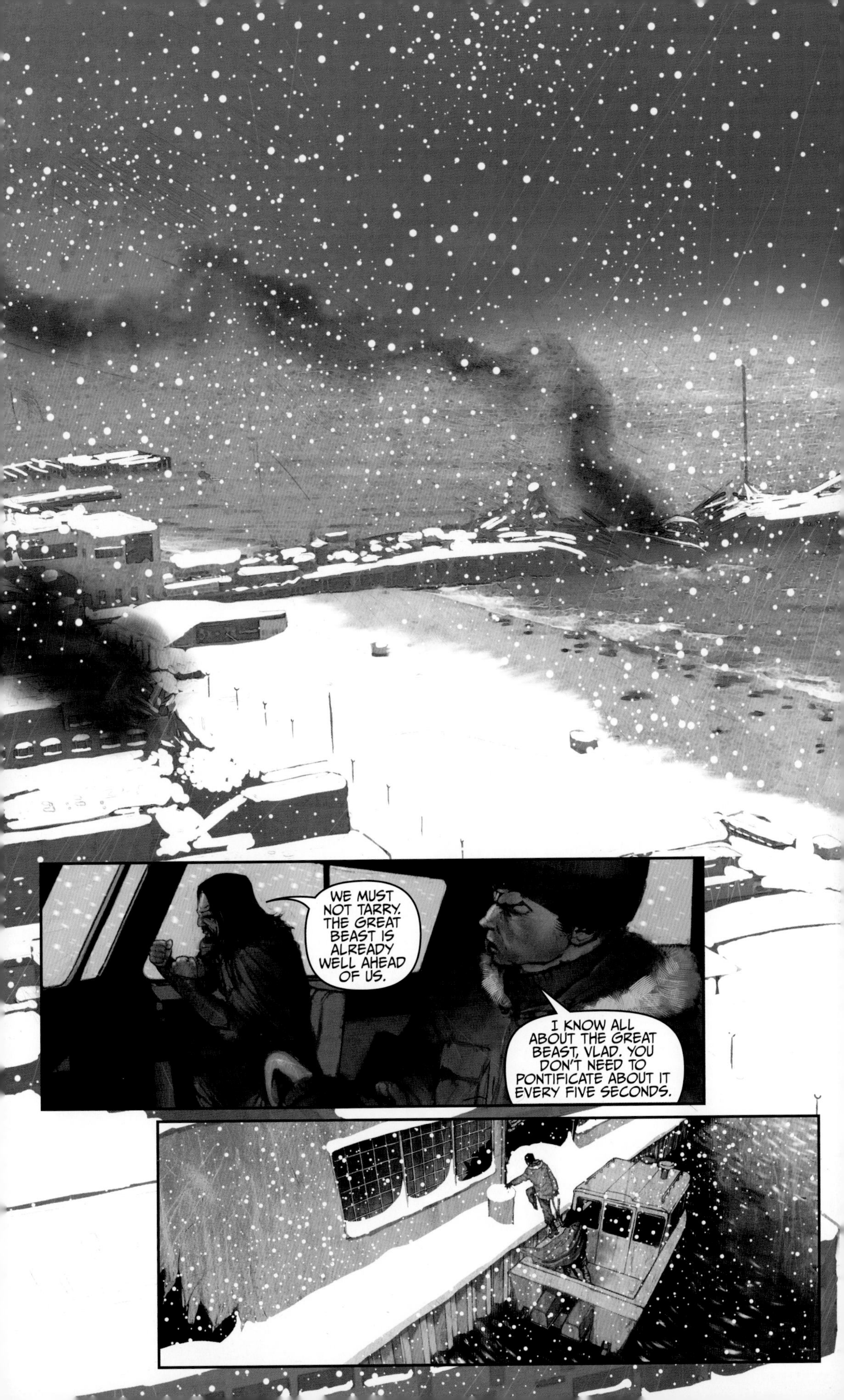
WE MUST NOT TARRY. THE GREAT BEAST IS ALREADY WELL AHEAD OF US.
I KNOW ALL ABOUT THE GREAT BEAST, VLAD. YOU DON'T NEED TO PONTIFICATE ABOUT IT EVERY FIVE SECONDS.

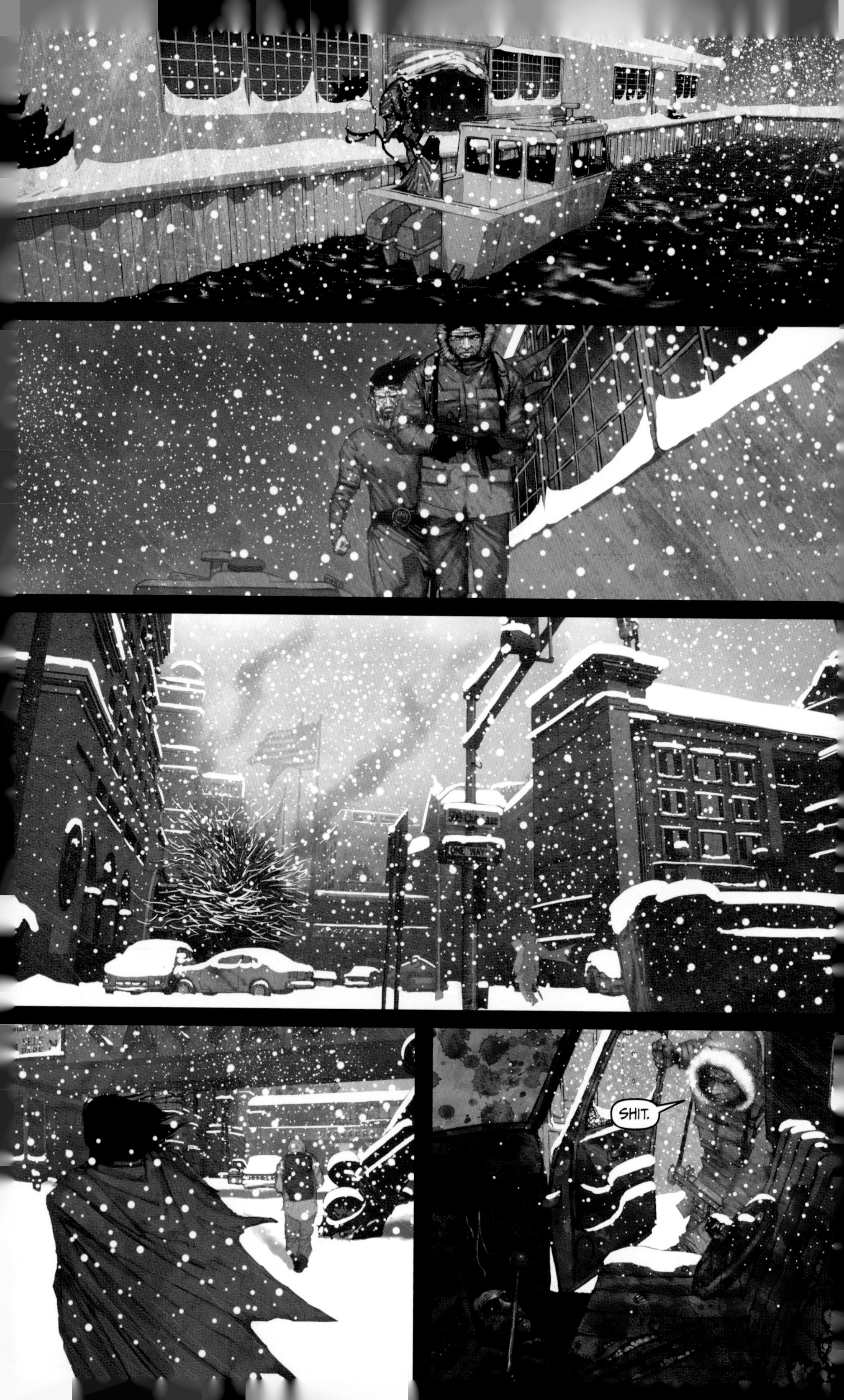
ONE WAY
SHIT.

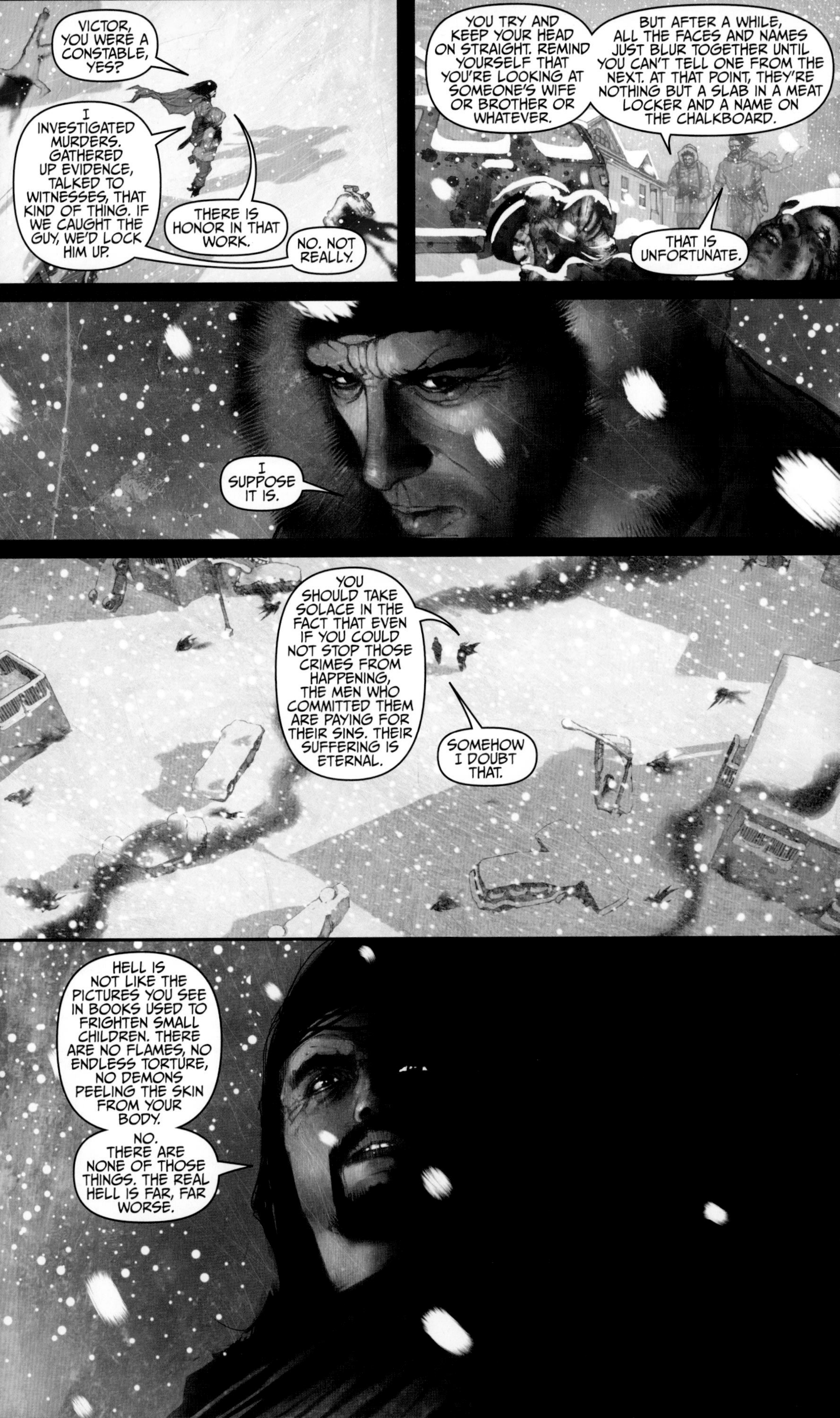
VICTOR, YOU WERE A CONSTABLE, YES?
I INVESTIGATED MURDERS. GATHERED UP EVIDENCE, TALKED TO WITNESSES, THAT KIND OF THING. IF WE CAUGHT THE GUY, WE'D LOCK HIM UP.
THERE IS HONOR IN THAT WORK.
NO. NOT REALLY.
YOU TRY AND KEEP YOUR HEAD ON STRAIGHT. REMIND YOURSELF THAT YOU'RE LOOKING AT SOMEONE'S WIFE OR BROTHER OR WHATEVER.
BUT AFTER A WHILE, ALL THE FACES AND NAMES JUST BLUR TOGETHER UNTIL YOU CAN'T TELL ONE FROM THE NEXT. AT THAT POINT, THEY'RE NOTHING BUT A SLAB IN A MEAT LOCKER AND A NAME ON THE CHALKBOARD.
THAT IS UNFORTUNATE.
I SUPPOSE IT IS.
YOU SHOULD TAKE SOLACE IN THE FACT THAT EVEN IF YOU COULD NOT STOP THOSE CRIMES FROM HAPPENING, THE MEN WHO COMMITTED THEM ARE PAYING FOR THEIR SINS. THEIR SUFFERING IS ETERNAL.
SOMEHOW I DOUBT THAT.
HELL IS NOT LIKE THE PICTURES YOU SEE IN BOOKS USED TO FRIGHTEN SMALL CHILDREN. THERE ARE NO FLAMES, NO ENDLESS TORTURE, NO DEMONS PEELING THE SKIN FROM YOUR BODY.
NO. THERE ARE NONE OF THOSE THINGS. THE REAL HELL IS FAR, FAR WORSE.

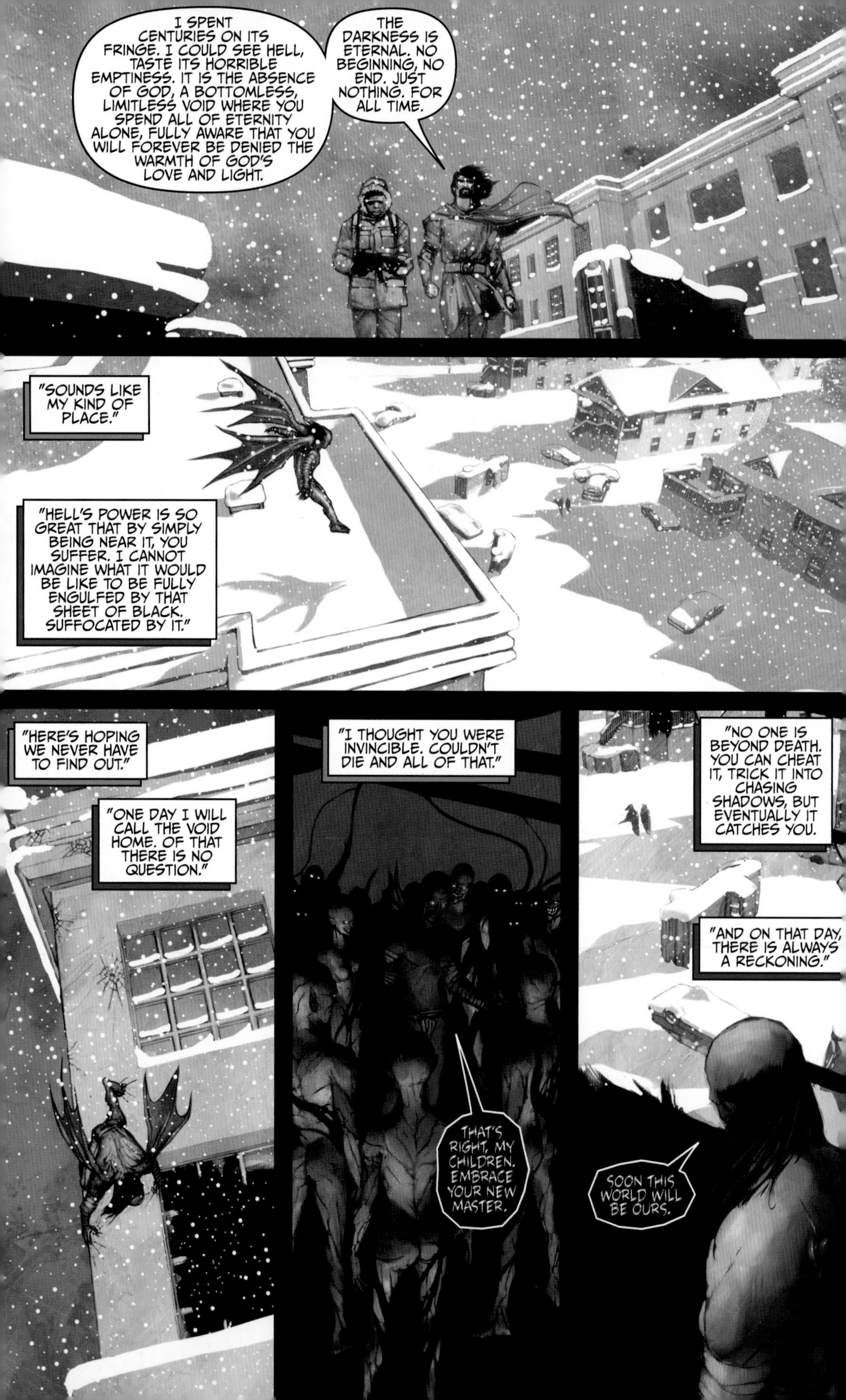
I SPENT CENTURIES ON ITS FRINGE. I COULD SEE HELL, TASTE ITS HORRIBLE EMPTINESS. IT IS THE ABSENCE OF GOD, A BOTTOMLESS, LIMITLESS VOID WHERE YOU SPEND ALL OF ETERNITY ALONE, FULLY AWARE THAT YOU WILL FOREVER BE DENIED THE WARMTH OF GOD'S LOVE AND LIGHT.
THE DARKNESS IS ETERNAL. NO BEGINNING, NO END. JUST NOTHING. FOR ALL TIME.
"SOUNDS LIKE MY KIND OF PLACE."
"HELL'S POWER IS SO GREAT THAT BY SIMPLY BEING NEAR IT, YOU SUFFER. I CANNOT IMAGINE WHAT IT WOULD BE LIKE TO BE FULLY ENGULFED BY THAT SHEET OF BLACK. SUFFOCATED BY IT."
"HERE'S HOPING WE NEVER HAVE TO FIND OUT."
"ONE DAY I WILL CALL THE VOID HOME. OF THAT THERE IS NO QUESTION."
"I THOUGHT YOU WERE INVINCIBLE. COULDN'T DIE AND ALL OF THAT."
THAT'S RIGHT, MY CHILDREN. EMBRACE YOUR NEW MASTER.
"NO ONE IS BEYOND DEATH. YOU CAN CHEAT IT, TRICK IT INTO CHASING SHADOWS, BUT EVENTUALLY IT CATCHES YOU.
"AND ON THAT DAY, THERE IS ALWAYS A RECKONING."
SOON THIS WORLD WILL BE OURS.

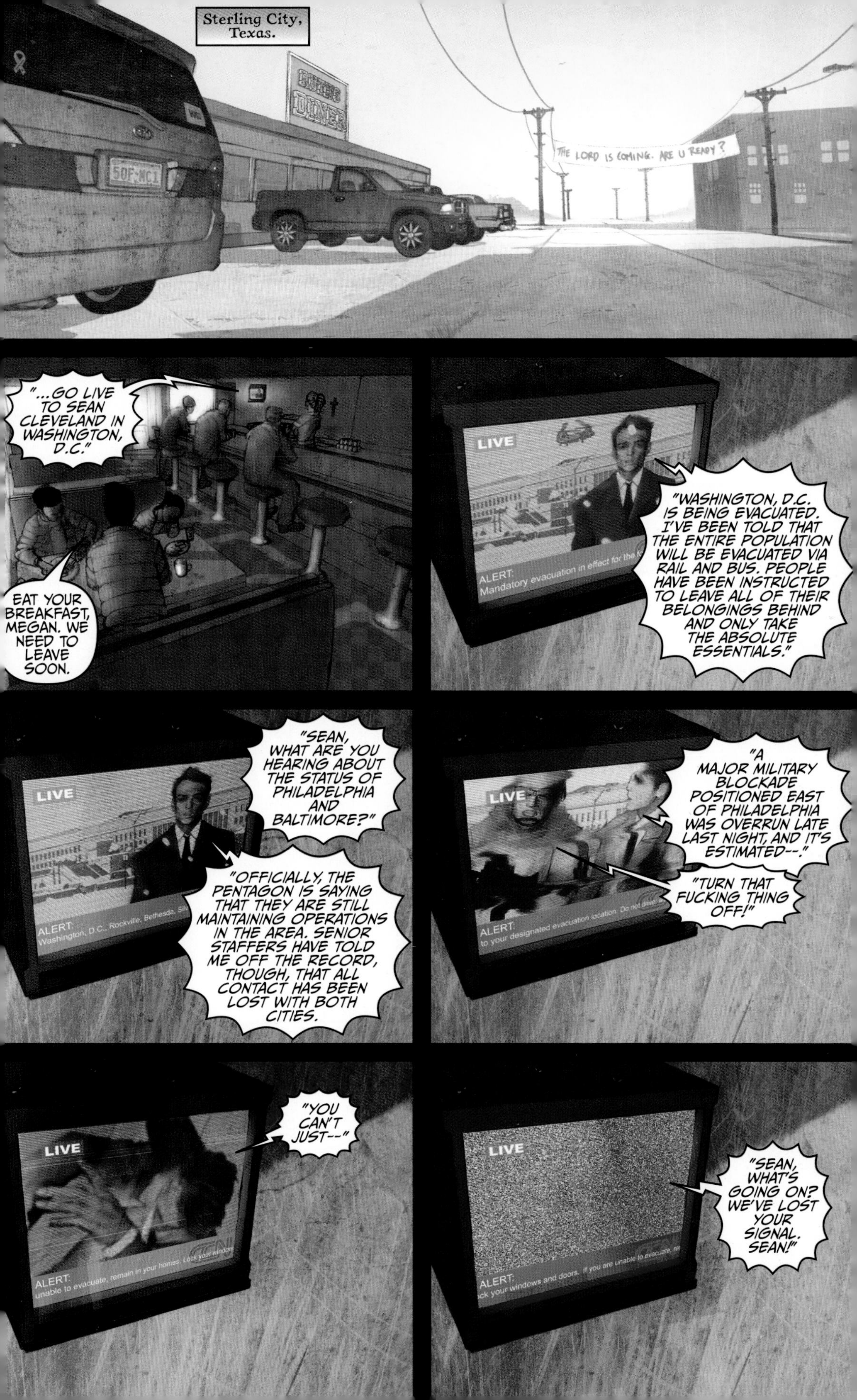

Sterling City, Texas.
THE LORD IS COMING. ARE U READY?
"...GO LIVE TO SEAN CLEVELAND IN WASHINGTON, D.C."
EAT YOUR BREAKFAST, MEGAN. WE NEED TO LEAVE SOON.
LIVE
ALERT: Mandatory evacuation in effect for the
"WASHINGTON, D.C. IS BEING EVACUATED. I'VE BEEN TOLD THAT THE ENTIRE POPULATION WILL BE EVACUATED VIA RAIL AND BUS. PEOPLE HAVE BEEN INSTRUCTED TO LEAVE ALL OF THEIR BELONGINGS BEHIND AND ONLY TAKE THE ABSOLUTE ESSENTIALS."
"SEAN, WHAT ARE YOU HEARING ABOUT THE STATUS OF PHILADELPHIA AND BALTIMORE?"
LIVE
ALERT: Washington, D.C., Rockville, Bethesda,
"OFFICIALLY, THE PENTAGON IS SAYING THAT THEY ARE STILL MAINTAINING OPERATIONS IN THE AREA. SENIOR STAFFERS HAVE TOLD ME OFF THE RECORD, THOUGH, THAT ALL CONTACT HAS BEEN LOST WITH BOTH CITIES.
"A MAJOR MILITARY BLOCKADE POSITIONED EAST OF PHILADELPHIA WAS OVERRUN LATE LAST NIGHT, AND IT'S ESTIMATED--."
"TURN THAT FUCKING THING OFF!"
LIVE
ALERT: to your designated evacuation location. Do not drive
LIVE
"YOU CAN'T JUST--"
ALERT: unable to evacuate, remain in your homes. Lock your windo
LIVE
"SEAN, WHAT'S GOING ON? WE'VE LOST YOUR SIGNAL. SEAN!"
ALERT: ck your windows and doors. If you are unable to evacuate,

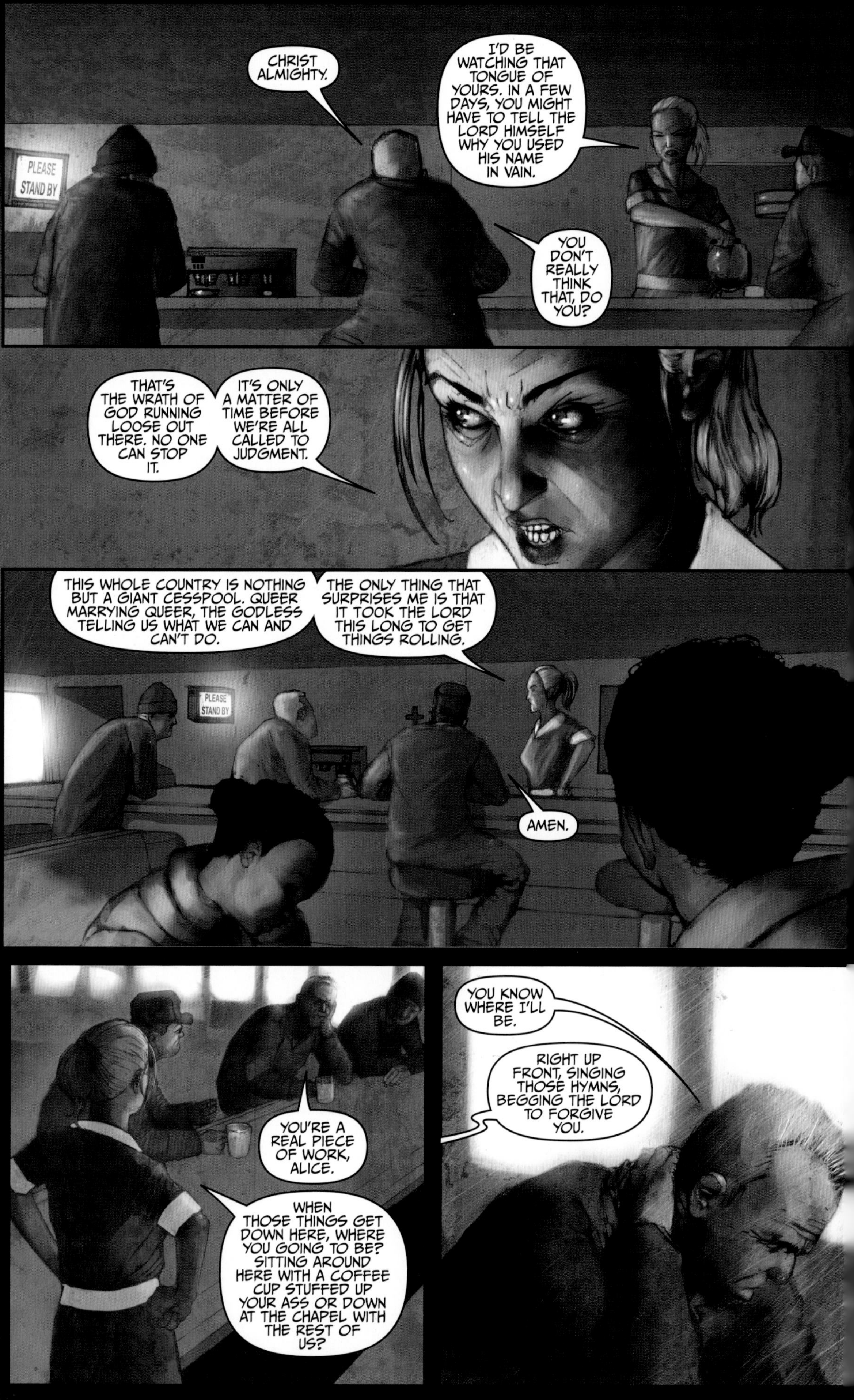
CHRIST ALMIGHTY.
I'D BE WATCHING THAT TONGUE OF YOURS. IN A FEW DAYS, YOU MIGHT HAVE TO TELL THE LORD HIMSELF WHY YOU USED HIS NAME IN VAIN.
PLEASE STAND BY
YOU DON'T REALLY THINK THAT, DO YOU?
THAT'S THE WRATH OF GOD RUNNING LOOSE OUT THERE. NO ONE CAN STOP IT.
IT'S ONLY A MATTER OF TIME BEFORE WE'RE ALL CALLED TO JUDGMENT.
THIS WHOLE COUNTRY IS NOTHING BUT A GIANT CESSPOOL. QUEER MARRYING QUEER, THE GODLESS TELLING US WHAT WE CAN AND CAN'T DO.
THE ONLY THING THAT SURPRISES ME IS THAT IT TOOK THE LORD THIS LONG TO GET THINGS ROLLING.
PLEASE STAND BY
AMEN.
YOU'RE A REAL PIECE OF WORK, ALICE.
WHEN THOSE THINGS GET DOWN HERE, WHERE YOU GOING TO BE? SITTING AROUND HERE WITH A COFFEE CUP STUFFED UP YOUR ASS OR DOWN AT THE CHAPEL WITH THE REST OF US?
YOU KNOW WHERE I'LL BE.
RIGHT UP FRONT, SINGING THOSE HYMNS, BEGGING THE LORD TO FORGIVE YOU.

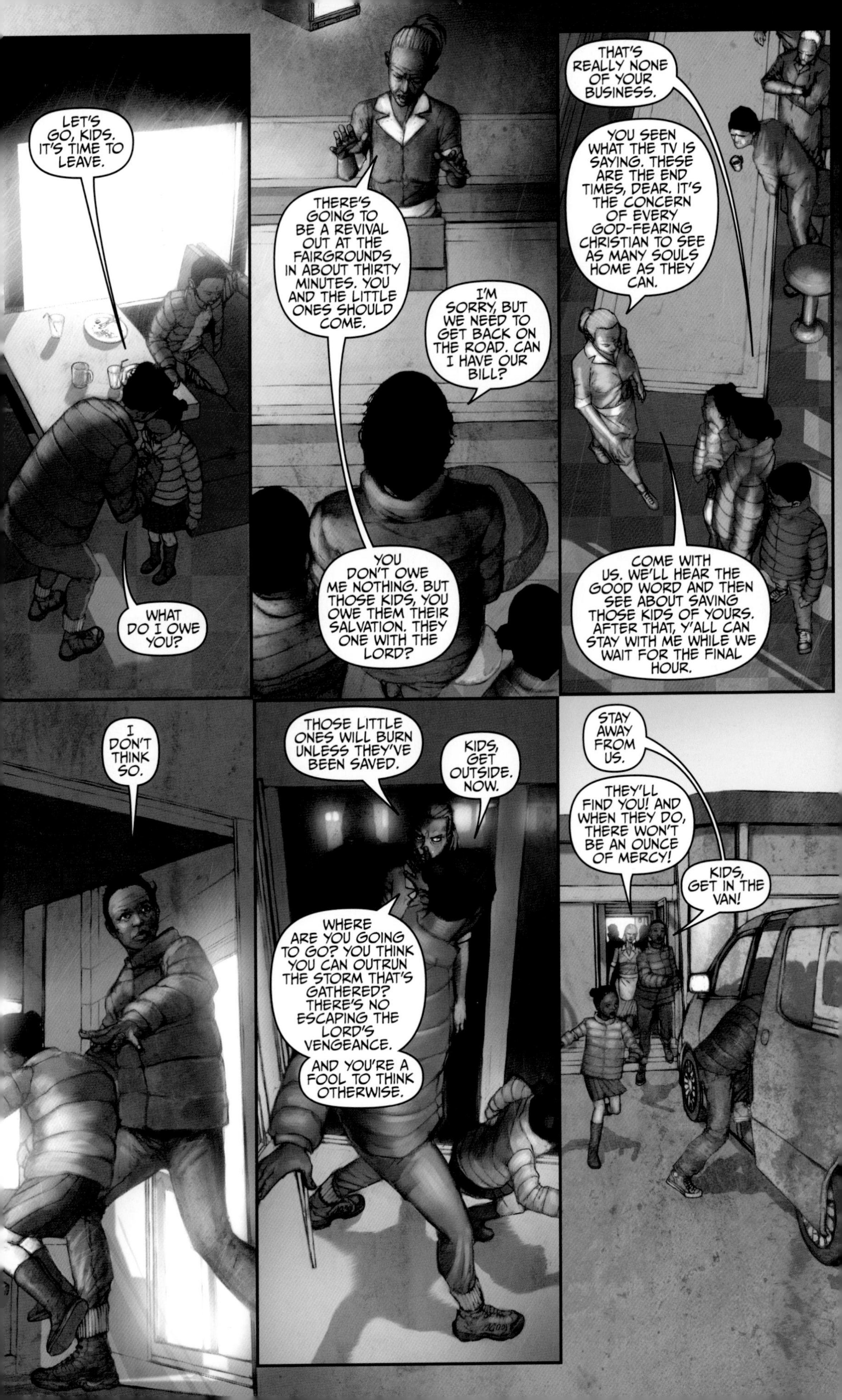

LET'S GO, KIDS. IT'S TIME TO LEAVE.
WHAT DO I OWE YOU?
THERE'S GOING TO BE A REVIVAL OUT AT THE FAIRGROUNDS IN ABOUT THIRTY MINUTES. YOU AND THE LITTLE ONES SHOULD COME.
I'M SORRY, BUT WE NEED TO GET BACK ON THE ROAD. CAN I HAVE OUR BILL?
YOU DON'T OWE ME NOTHING. BUT THOSE KIDS, YOU OWE THEM THEIR SALVATION. THEY ONE WITH THE LORD?
THAT'S REALLY NONE OF YOUR BUSINESS.
YOU SEEN WHAT THE TV IS SAYING. THESE ARE THE END TIMES, DEAR. IT'S THE CONCERN OF EVERY GOD-FEARING CHRISTIAN TO SEE AS MANY SOULS HOME AS THEY CAN.
COME WITH US. WE'LL HEAR THE GOOD WORD AND THEN SEE ABOUT SAVING THOSE KIDS OF YOURS. AFTER THAT, Y'ALL CAN STAY WITH ME WHILE WE WAIT FOR THE FINAL HOUR.
I DON'T THINK SO.
THOSE LITTLE ONES WILL BURN UNLESS THEY'VE BEEN SAVED.
KIDS, GET OUTSIDE. NOW.
WHERE ARE YOU GOING TO GO? YOU THINK YOU CAN OUTRUN THE STORM THAT'S GATHERED? THERE'S NO ESCAPING THE LORD'S VENGEANCE.
AND YOU'RE A FOOL TO THINK OTHERWISE.
STAY AWAY FROM US.
THEY'LL FIND YOU! AND WHEN THEY DO, THERE WON'T BE AN OUNCE OF MERCY!
KIDS, GET IN THE VAN!

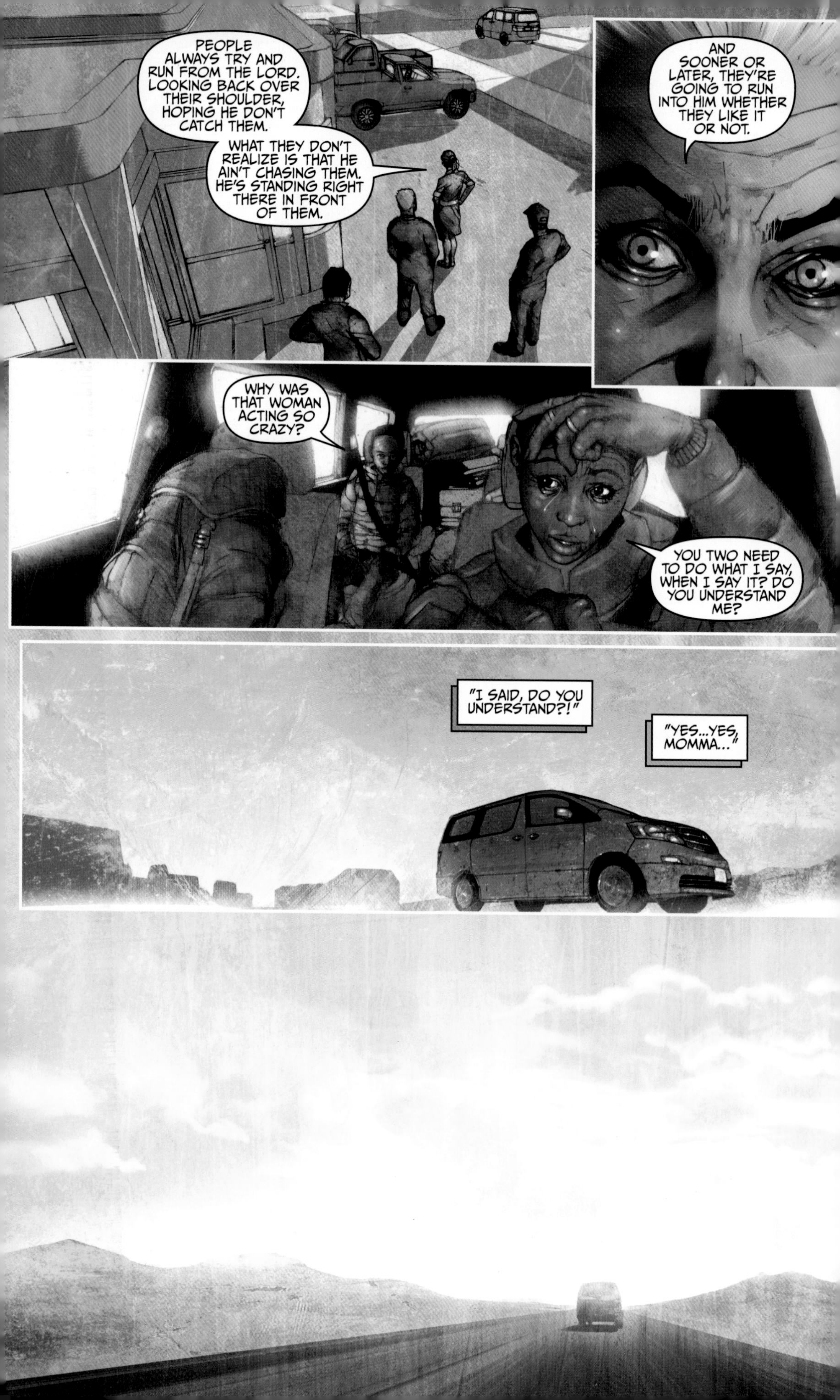
PEOPLE ALWAYS TRY AND RUN FROM THE LORD. LOOKING BACK OVER THEIR SHOULDER, HOPING HE DON'T CATCH THEM.
WHAT THEY DON'T REALIZE IS THAT HE AIN'T CHASING THEM. HE'S STANDING RIGHT THERE IN FRONT OF THEM.
AND SOONER OR LATER, THEY'RE GOING TO RUN INTO HIM WHETHER THEY LIKE IT OR NOT.
WHY WAS THAT WOMAN ACTING SO CRAZY?
YOU TWO NEED TO DO WHAT I SAY, WHEN I SAY IT? DO YOU UNDERSTAND ME?
"I SAID, DO YOU UNDERSTAND?!"
"YES...YES, MOMMA..."

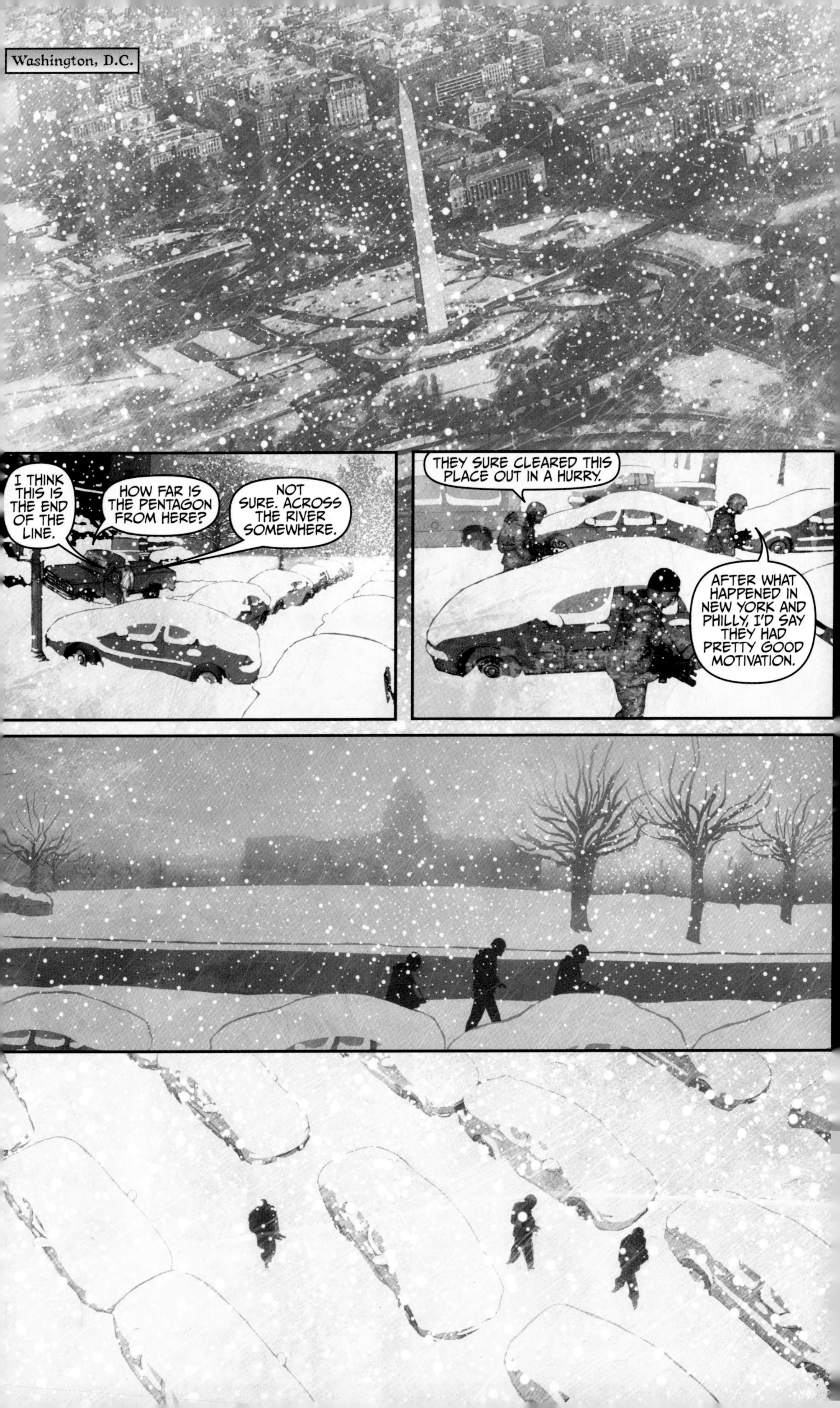
Washington, D.C.
I THINK THIS IS THE END OF THE LINE.
HOW FAR IS THE PENTAGON FROM HERE?
NOT SURE. ACROSS THE RIVER SOMEWHERE.
THEY SURE CLEARED THIS PLACE OUT IN A HURRY.
AFTER WHAT HAPPENED IN NEW YORK AND PHILLY, I'D SAY THEY HAD PRETTY GOOD MOTIVATION.

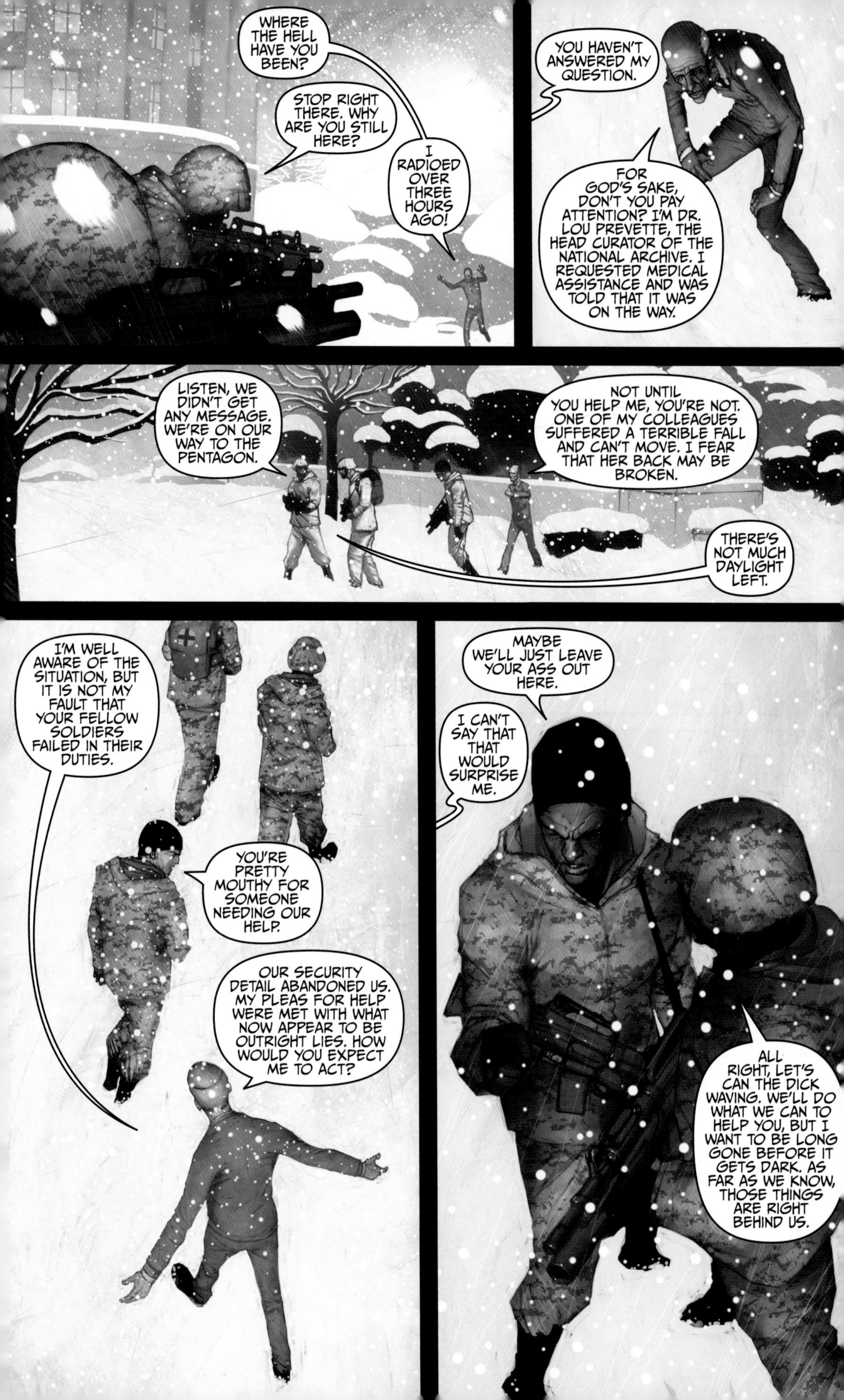
WHERE THE HELL HAVE YOU BEEN?
STOP RIGHT THERE. WHY ARE YOU STILL HERE?
I RADIOED OVER THREE HOURS AGO!
YOU HAVEN'T ANSWERED MY QUESTION.
FOR GOD'S SAKE, DON'T YOU PAY ATTENTION? I'M DR. LOU PREVETTE, THE HEAD CURATOR OF THE NATIONAL ARCHIVE. I REQUESTED MEDICAL ASSISTANCE AND WAS TOLD THAT IT WAS ON THE WAY.
LISTEN, WE DIDN'T GET ANY MESSAGE. WE'RE ON OUR WAY TO THE PENTAGON.
NOT UNTIL YOU HELP ME, YOU'RE NOT. ONE OF MY COLLEAGUES SUFFERED A TERRIBLE FALL AND CAN'T MOVE. I FEAR THAT HER BACK MAY BE BROKEN.
THERE'S NOT MUCH DAYLIGHT LEFT.
I'M WELL AWARE OF THE SITUATION, BUT IT IS NOT MY FAULT THAT YOUR FELLOW SOLDIERS FAILED IN THEIR DUTIES.
YOU'RE PRETTY MOUTHY FOR SOMEONE NEEDING OUR HELP.
OUR SECURITY DETAIL ABANDONED US. MY PLEAS FOR HELP WERE MET WITH WHAT NOW APPEAR TO BE OUTRIGHT LIES. HOW WOULD YOU EXPECT ME TO ACT?
MAYBE WE'LL JUST LEAVE YOUR ASS OUT HERE.
I CAN'T SAY THAT THAT WOULD SURPRISE ME.
ALL RIGHT, LET'S CAN THE DICK WAVING. WE'LL DO WHAT WE CAN TO HELP YOU, BUT I WANT TO BE LONG GONE BEFORE IT GETS DARK. AS FAR AS WE KNOW, THOSE THINGS ARE RIGHT BEHIND US.

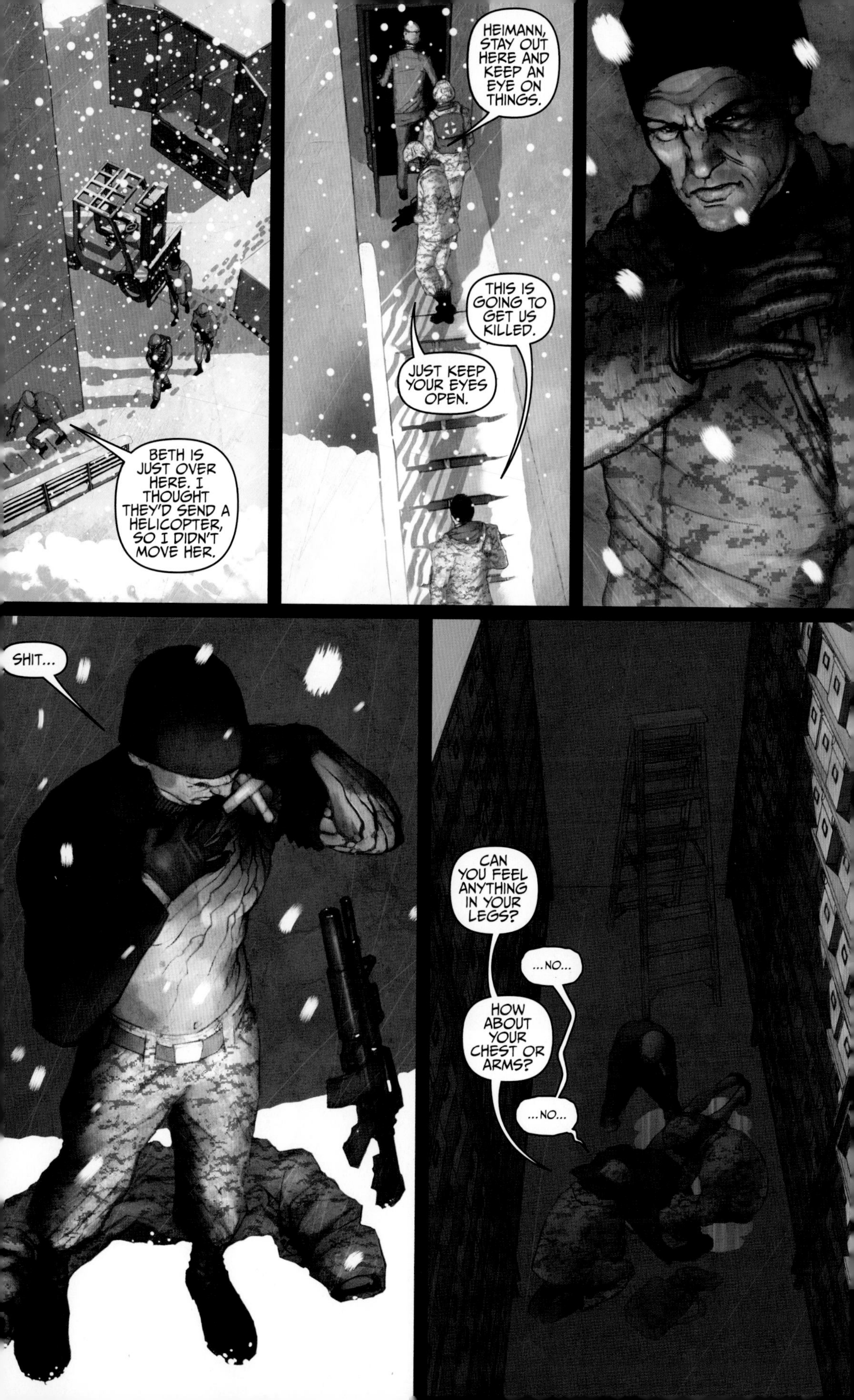
BETH IS JUST OVER HERE. I THOUGHT THEY'D SEND A HELICOPTER, SO I DIDN'T MOVE HER.
HEIMANN, STAY OUT HERE AND KEEP AN EYE ON THINGS.
THIS IS GOING TO GET US KILLED.
JUST KEEP YOUR EYES OPEN.
SHIT...
CAN YOU FEEL ANYTHING IN YOUR LEGS?
...NO...
HOW ABOUT YOUR CHEST OR ARMS?
...NO...

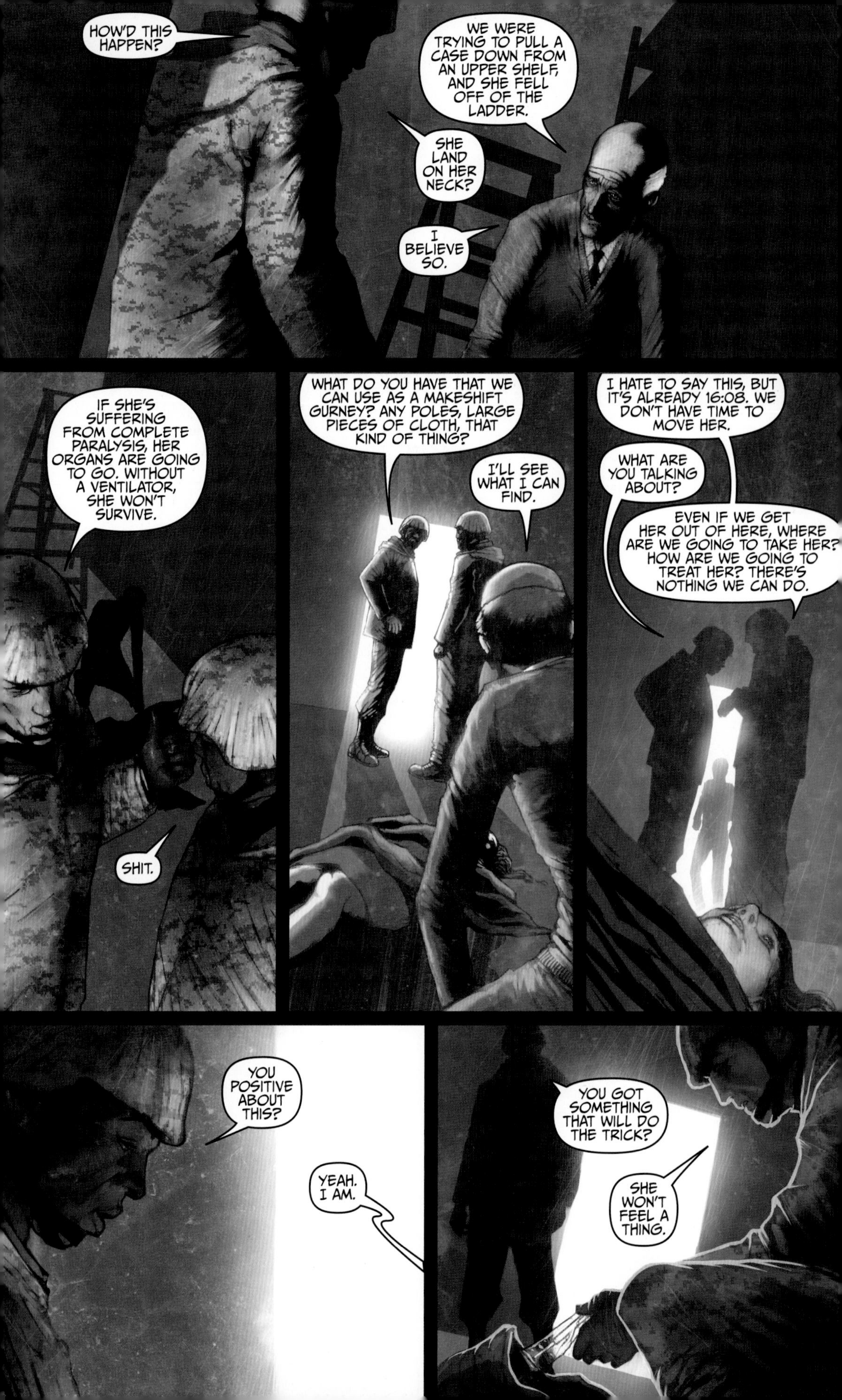
HOW'D THIS HAPPEN?
WE WERE TRYING TO PULL A CASE DOWN FROM AN UPPER SHELF, AND SHE FELL OFF OF THE LADDER.
SHE LAND ON HER NECK?
I BELIEVE SO.
IF SHE'S SUFFERING FROM COMPLETE PARALYSIS, HER ORGANS ARE GOING TO GO. WITHOUT A VENTILATOR, SHE WON'T SURVIVE.
SHIT.
WHAT DO YOU HAVE THAT WE CAN USE AS A MAKESHIFT GURNEY? ANY POLES, LARGE PIECES OF CLOTH, THAT KIND OF THING?
I'LL SEE WHAT I CAN FIND.
I HATE TO SAY THIS, BUT IT'S ALREADY 16:08. WE DON'T HAVE TIME TO MOVE HER.
WHAT ARE YOU TALKING ABOUT?
EVEN IF WE GET HER OUT OF HERE, WHERE ARE WE GOING TO TAKE HER? HOW ARE WE GOING TO TREAT HER? THERE'S NOTHING WE CAN DO.
YOU POSITIVE ABOUT THIS?
YEAH. I AM.
YOU GOT SOMETHING THAT WILL DO THE TRICK?
SHE WON'T FEEL A THING.

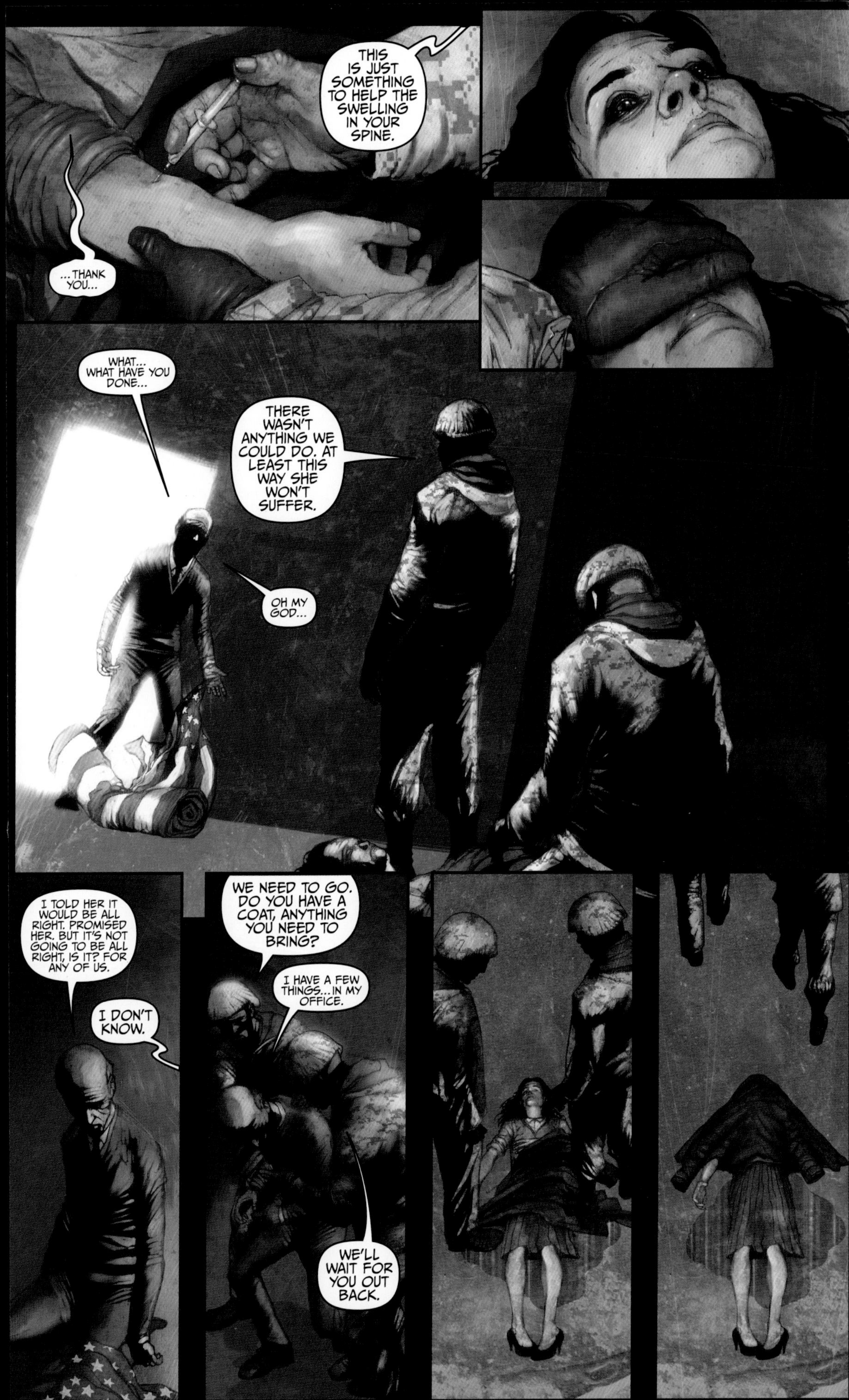
THIS IS JUST SOMETHING TO HELP THE SWELLING IN YOUR SPINE.
...THANK YOU...
WHAT... WHAT HAVE YOU DONE...
THERE WASN'T ANYTHING WE COULD DO. AT LEAST THIS WAY SHE WON'T SUFFER.
OH MY GOD...
I TOLD HER IT WOULD BE ALL RIGHT. PROMISED HER. BUT IT'S NOT GOING TO BE ALL RIGHT, IS IT? FOR ANY OF US.
I DON'T KNOW.
WE NEED TO GO. DO YOU HAVE A COAT, ANYTHING YOU NEED TO BRING?
I HAVE A FEW THINGS...IN MY OFFICE.
WE'LL WAIT FOR YOU OUT BACK.

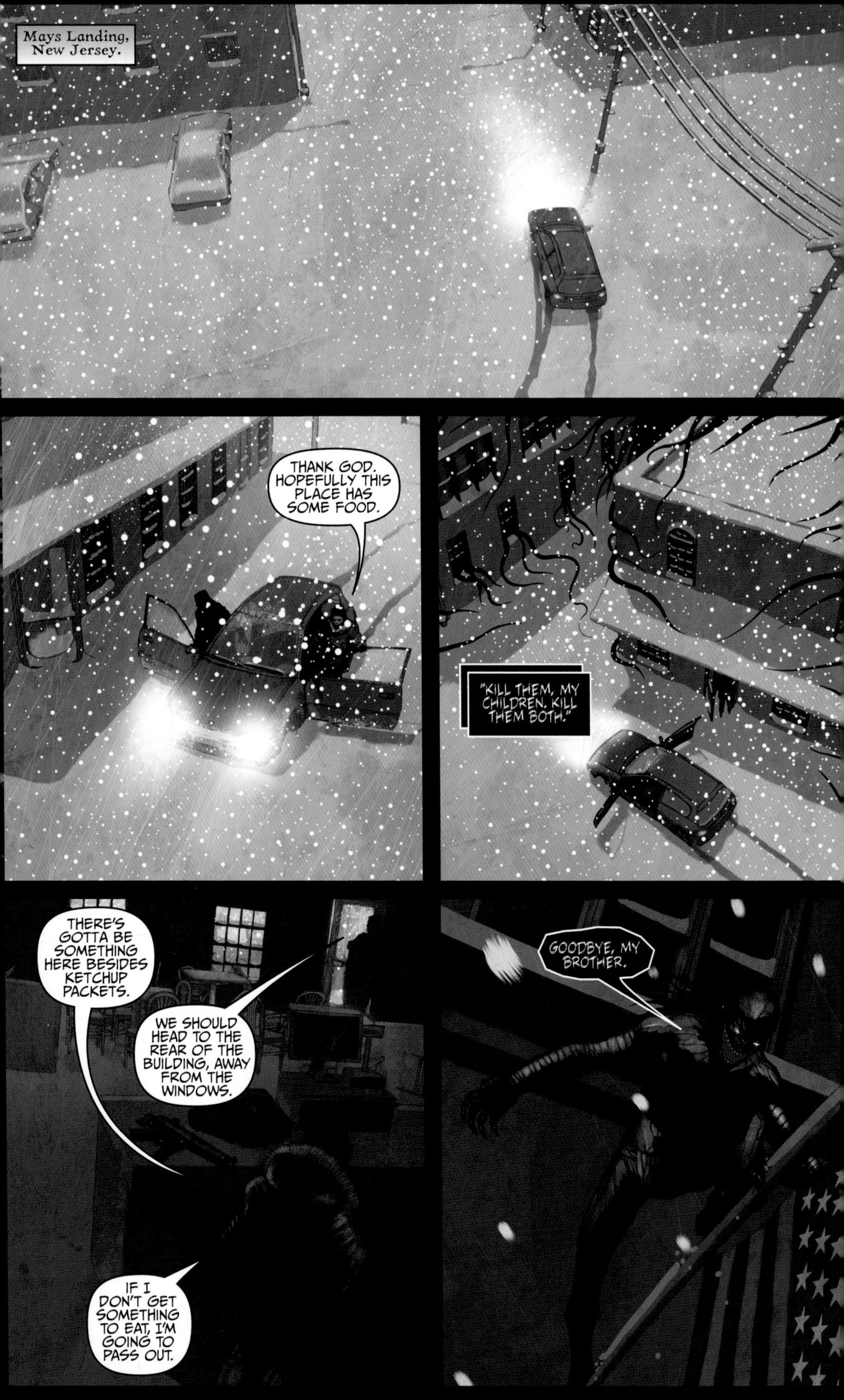
Mays Landing, New Jersey.
THANK GOD. HOPEFULLY THIS PLACE HAS SOME FOOD.
"KILL THEM, MY CHILDREN. KILL THEM BOTH."
THERE'S GOTTA BE SOMETHING HERE BESIDES KETCHUP PACKETS.
WE SHOULD HEAD TO THE REAR OF THE BUILDING, AWAY FROM THE WINDOWS.
IF I DON'T GET SOMETHING TO EAT, I'M GOING TO PASS OUT.
GOODBYE, MY BROTHER.

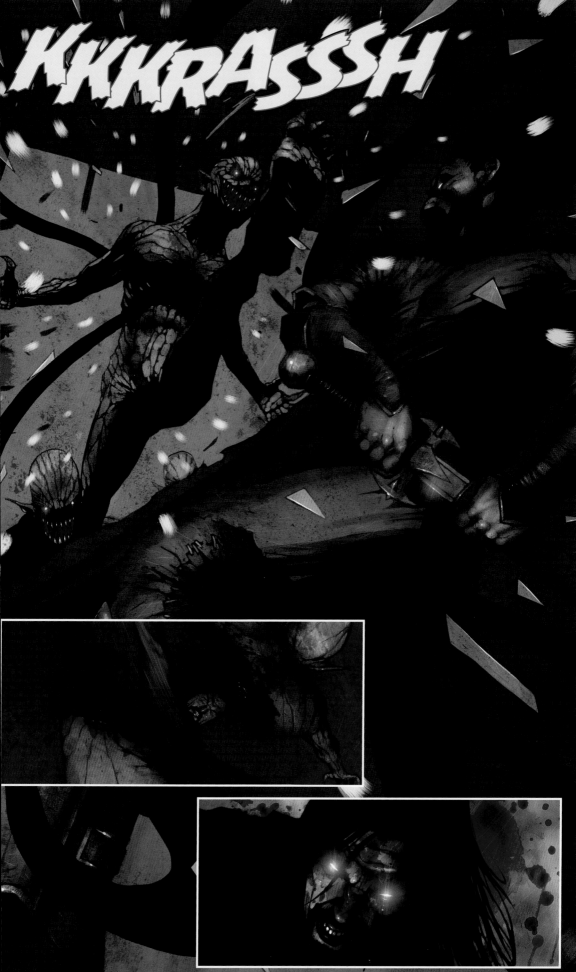

KKKRASSSH

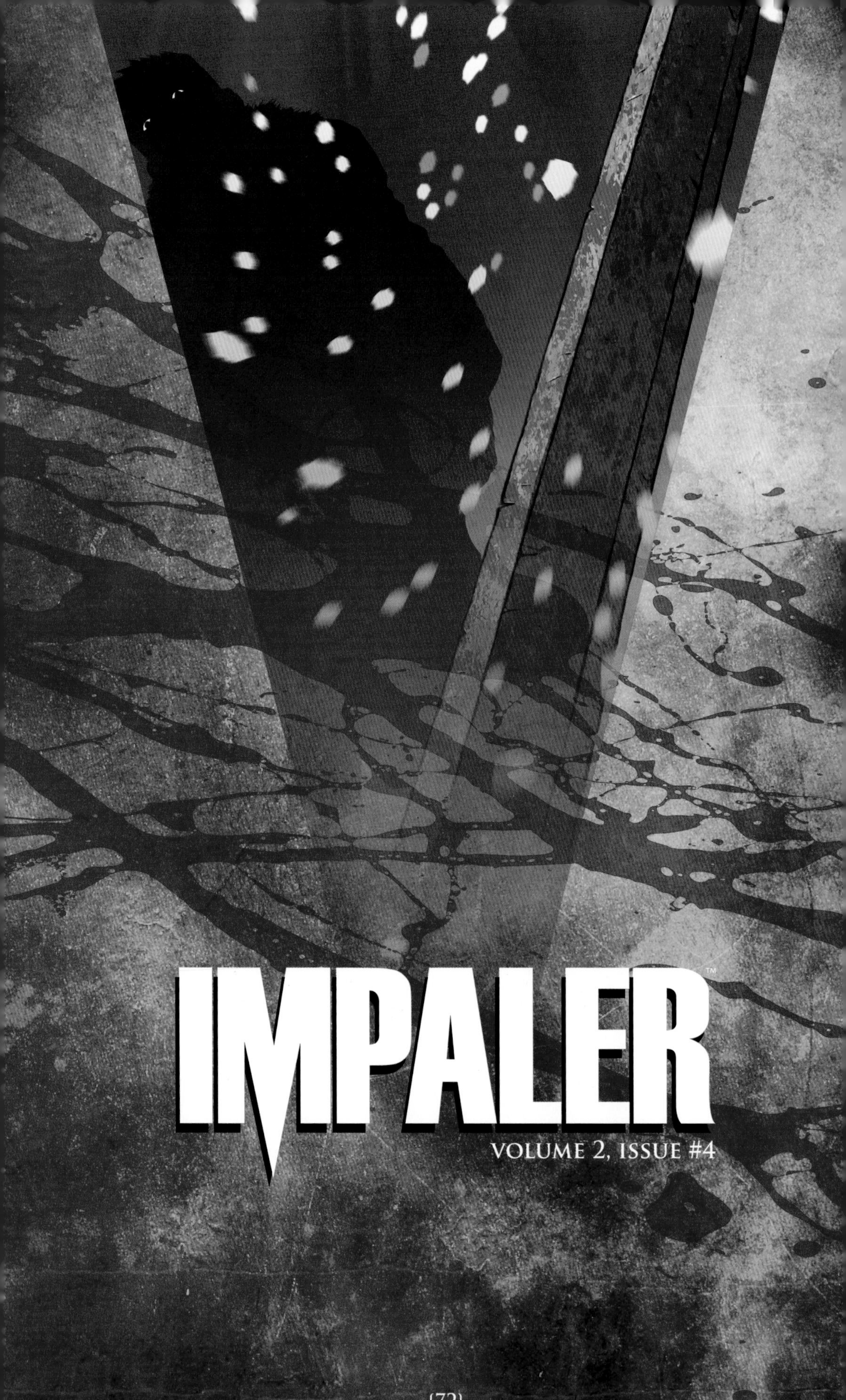
IMPALER™
VOLUME 2, ISSUE #4

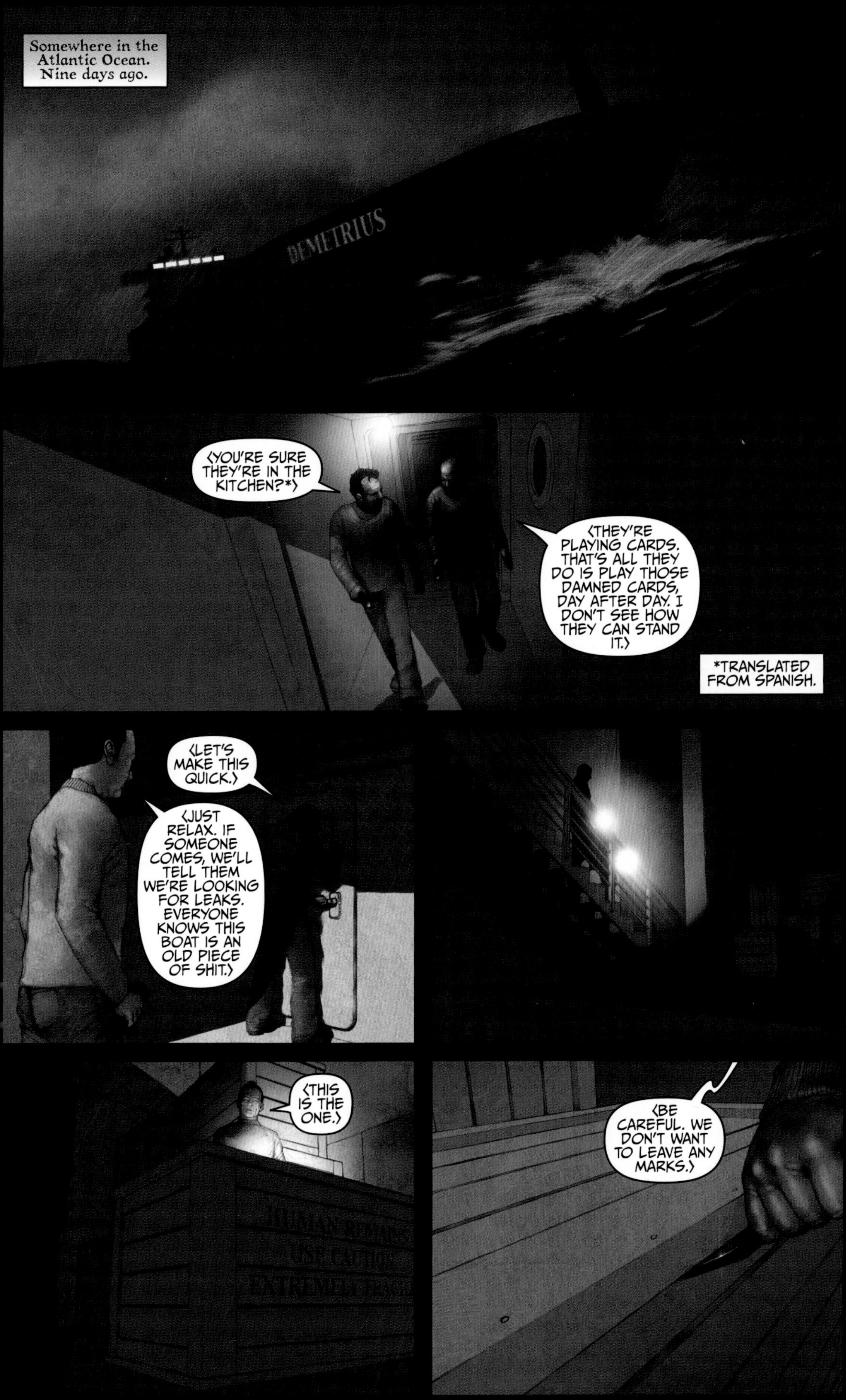

Somewhere in the Atlantic Ocean. Nine days ago.
DEMETRIUS
‹YOU'RE SURE THEY'RE IN THE KITCHEN?*›
‹THEY'RE PLAYING CARDS. THAT'S ALL THEY DO IS PLAY THOSE DAMNED CARDS, DAY AFTER DAY. I DON'T SEE HOW THEY CAN STAND IT.›
*TRANSLATED FROM SPANISH.
‹LET'S MAKE THIS QUICK.›
‹JUST RELAX. IF SOMEONE COMES, WE'LL TELL THEM WE'RE LOOKING FOR LEAKS. EVERYONE KNOWS THIS BOAT IS AN OLD PIECE OF SHIT.›
‹THIS IS THE ONE.›
‹BE CAREFUL. WE DON'T WANT TO LEAVE ANY MARKS.›

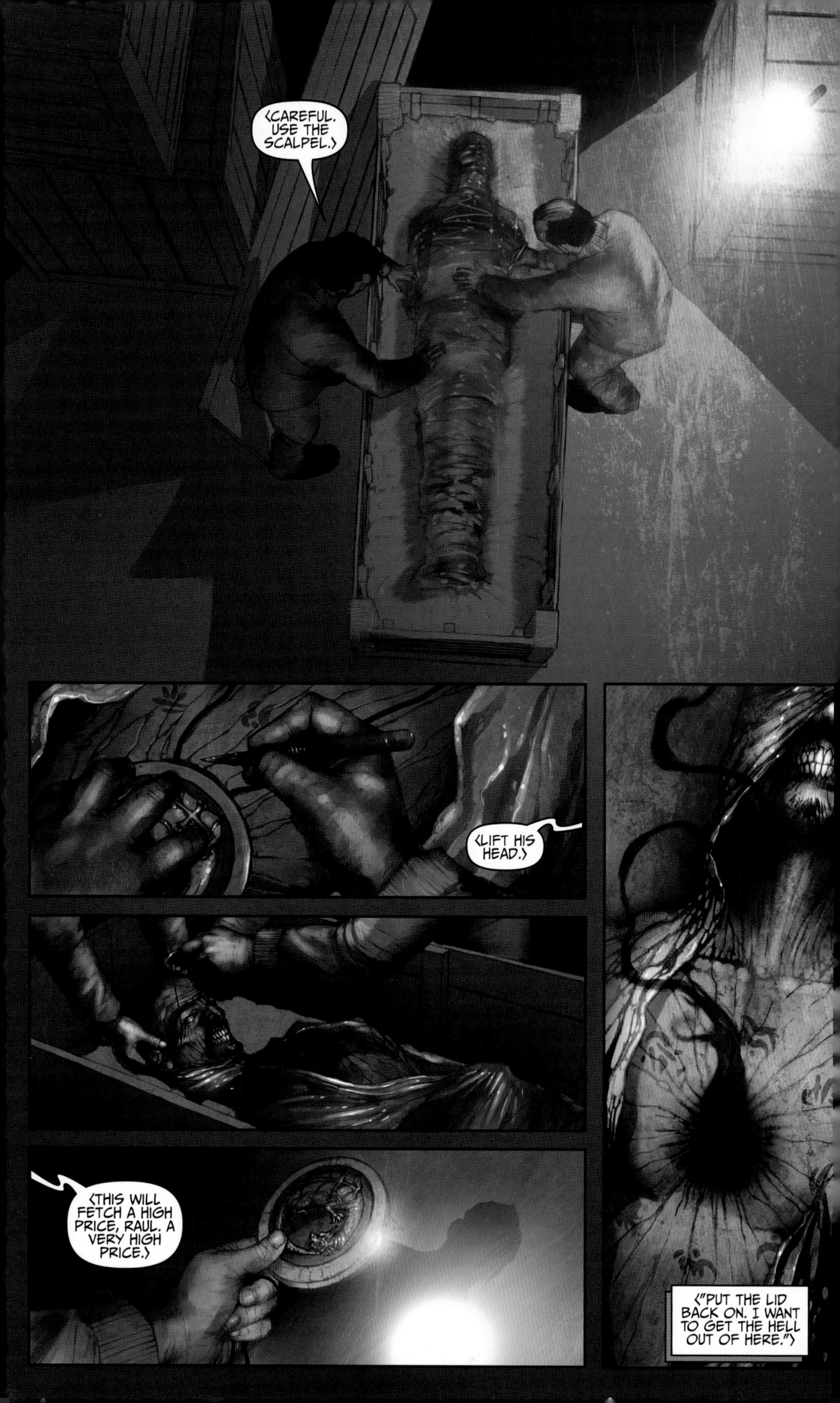

‹CAREFUL. USE THE SCALPEL.›
‹LIFT HIS HEAD.›
‹THIS WILL FETCH A HIGH PRICE, RAUL. A VERY HIGH PRICE.›
‹"PUT THE LID BACK ON. I WANT TO GET THE HELL OUT OF HERE."›

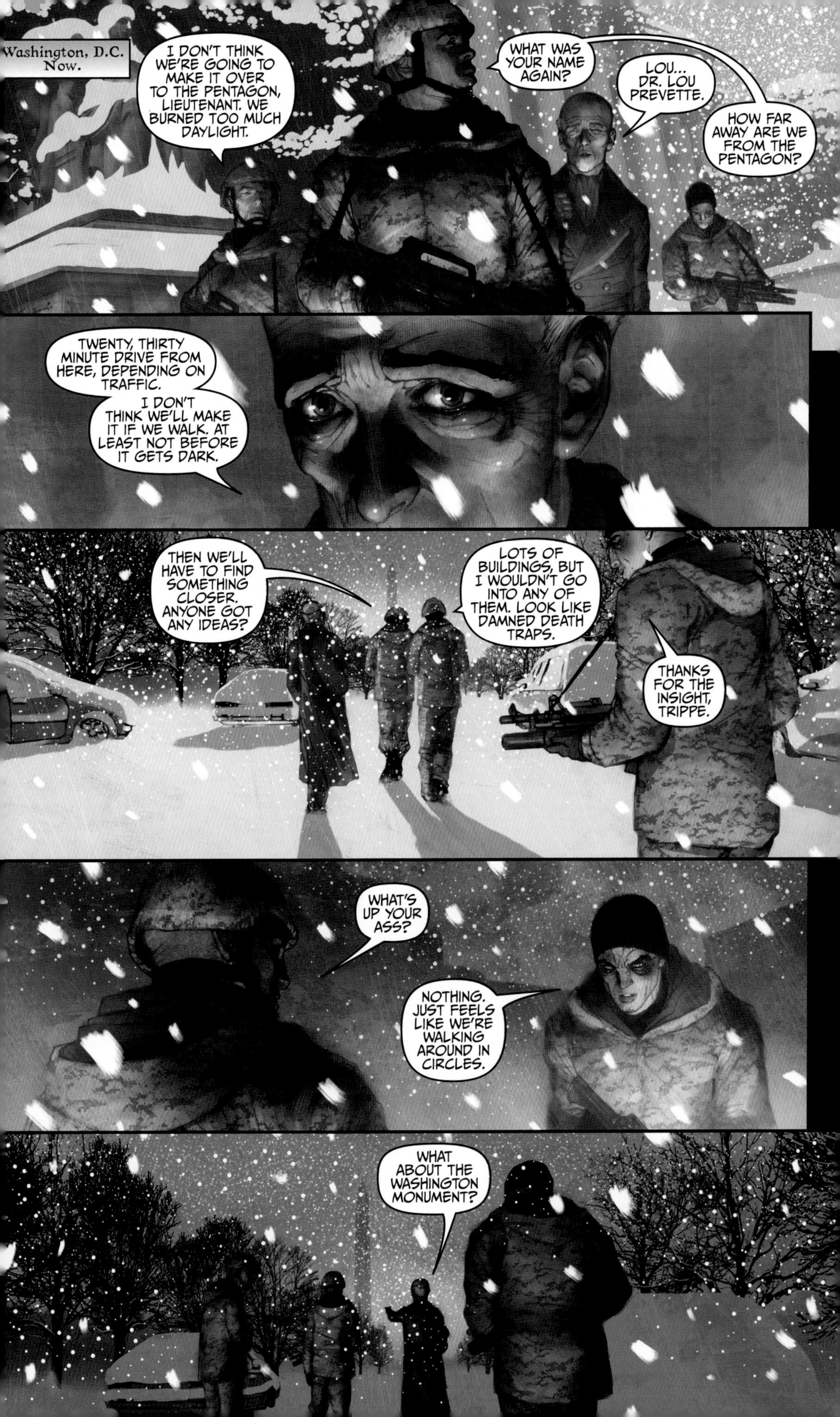
Washington, D.C.
Now.
I DON'T THINK WE'RE GOING TO MAKE IT OVER TO THE PENTAGON, LIEUTENANT. WE BURNED TOO MUCH DAYLIGHT.
WHAT WAS YOUR NAME AGAIN?
LOU... DR. LOU PREVETTE.
HOW FAR AWAY ARE WE FROM THE PENTAGON?
TWENTY, THIRTY MINUTE DRIVE FROM HERE, DEPENDING ON TRAFFIC.
I DON'T THINK WE'LL MAKE IT IF WE WALK. AT LEAST NOT BEFORE IT GETS DARK.
THEN WE'LL HAVE TO FIND SOMETHING CLOSER. ANYONE GOT ANY IDEAS?
LOTS OF BUILDINGS, BUT I WOULDN'T GO INTO ANY OF THEM. LOOK LIKE DAMNED DEATH TRAPS.
THANKS FOR THE INSIGHT, TRIPPE.
WHAT'S UP YOUR ASS?
NOTHING. JUST FEELS LIKE WE'RE WALKING AROUND IN CIRCLES.
WHAT ABOUT THE WASHINGTON MONUMENT?

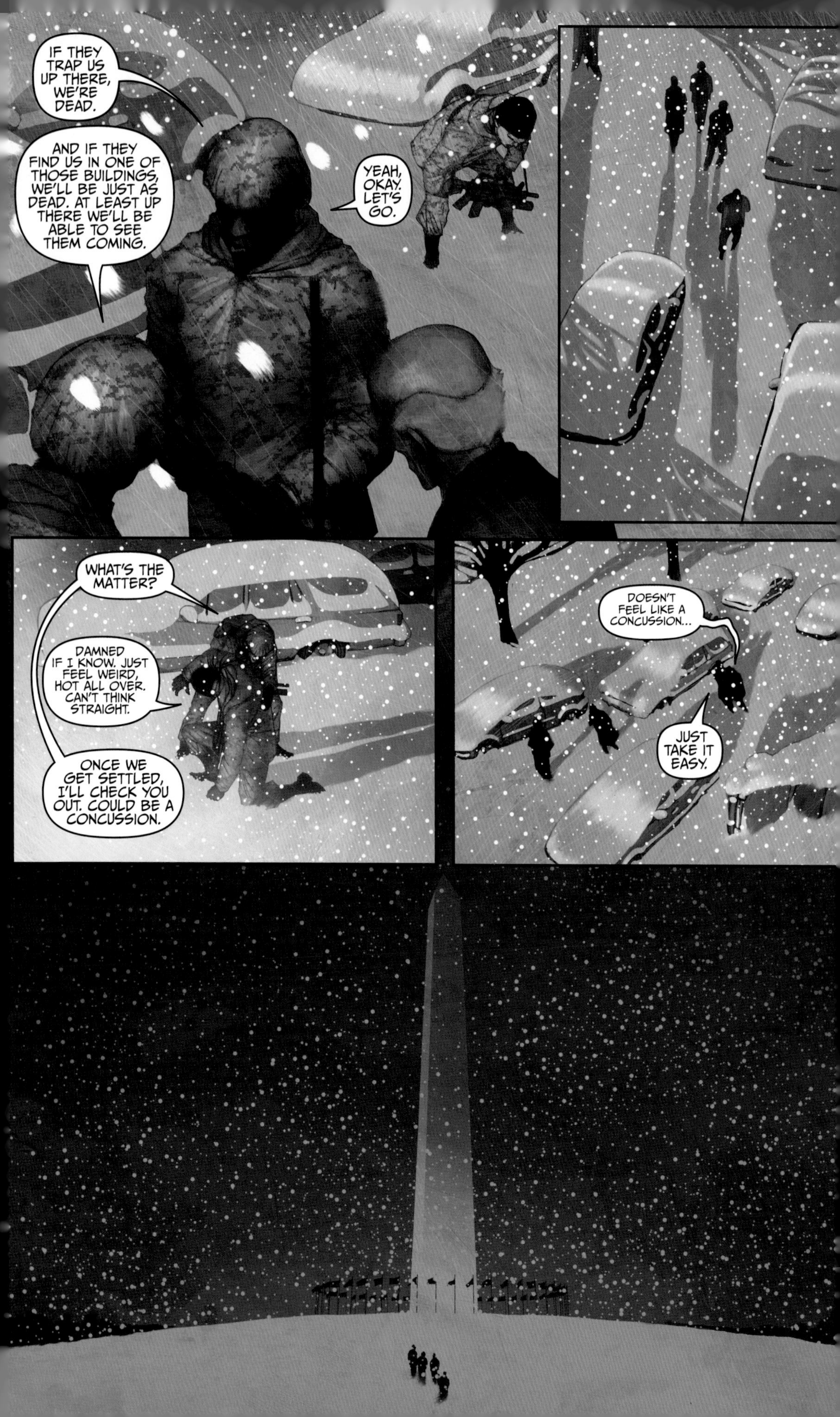
IF THEY TRAP US UP THERE, WE'RE DEAD.
AND IF THEY FIND US IN ONE OF THOSE BUILDINGS, WE'LL BE JUST AS DEAD. AT LEAST UP THERE WE'LL BE ABLE TO SEE THEM COMING.
YEAH, OKAY. LET'S GO.
WHAT'S THE MATTER?
DAMNED IF I KNOW. JUST FEEL WEIRD, HOT ALL OVER. CAN'T THINK STRAIGHT.
ONCE WE GET SETTLED, I'LL CHECK YOU OUT. COULD BE A CONCUSSION.
DOESN'T FEEL LIKE A CONCUSSION...
JUST TAKE IT EASY.

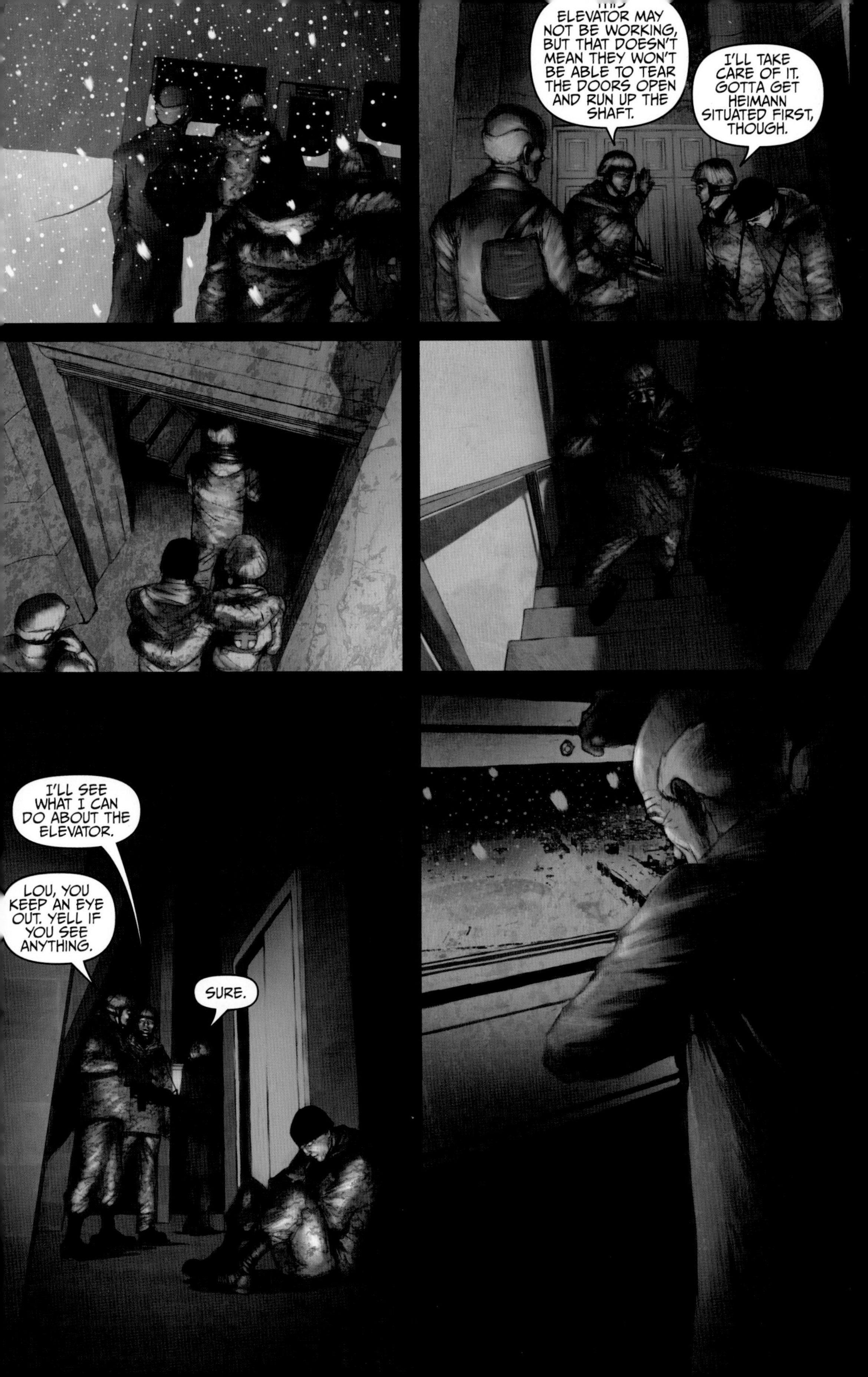
THIS ELEVATOR MAY NOT BE WORKING, BUT THAT DOESN'T MEAN THEY WON'T BE ABLE TO TEAR THE DOORS OPEN AND RUN UP THE SHAFT.
I'LL TAKE CARE OF IT. GOTTA GET HEIMANN SITUATED FIRST, THOUGH.
I'LL SEE WHAT I CAN DO ABOUT THE ELEVATOR.
LOU, YOU KEEP AN EYE OUT. YELL IF YOU SEE ANYTHING.
SURE.

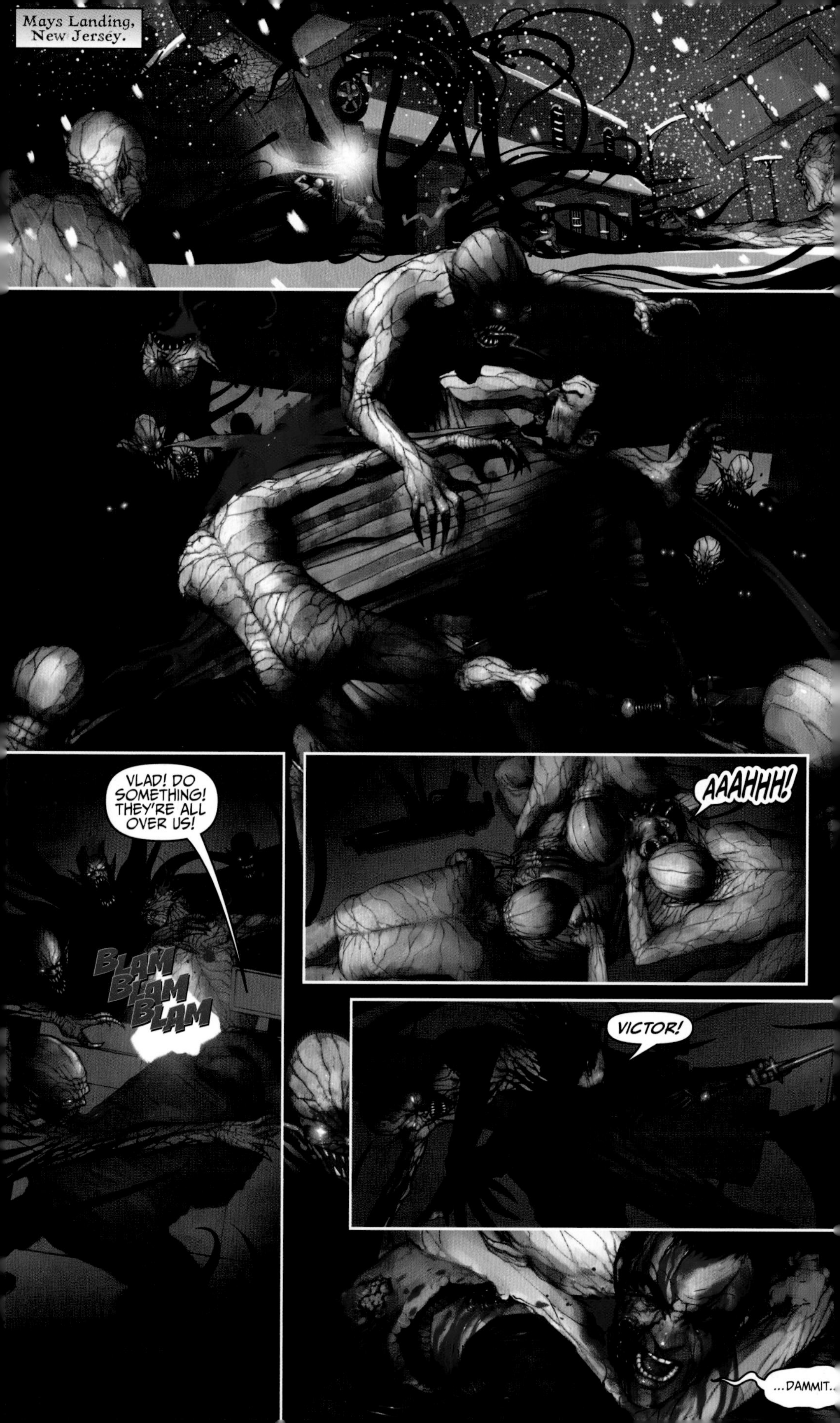
Mays Landing, New Jersey.
VLAD! DO SOMETHING! THEY'RE ALL OVER US!
BLAM BLAM BLAM
AAAHHH!
VICTOR!
...DAMMIT...

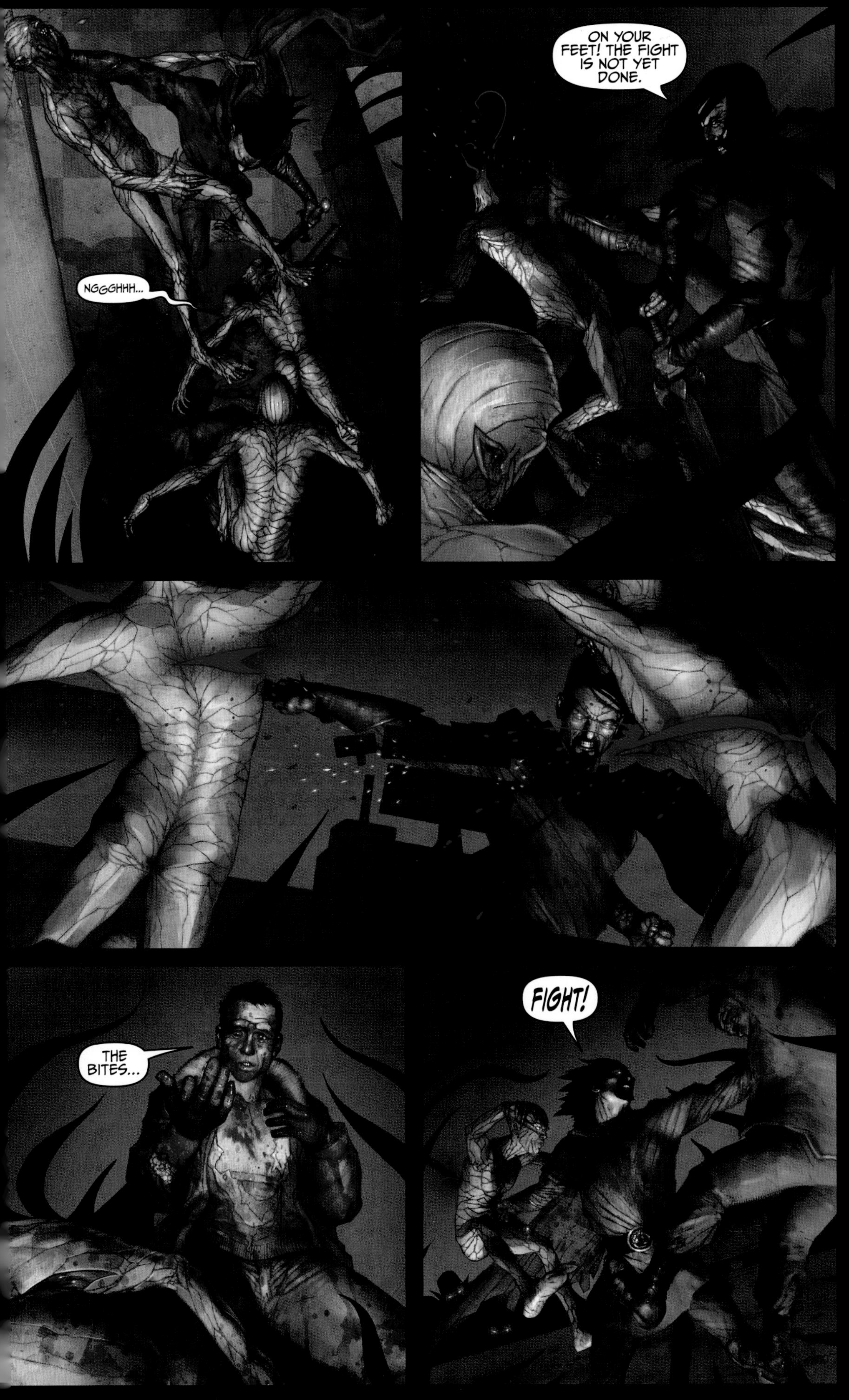
NGGGHHH...
ON YOUR FEET! THE FIGHT IS NOT YET DONE.
THE BITES...
FIGHT!

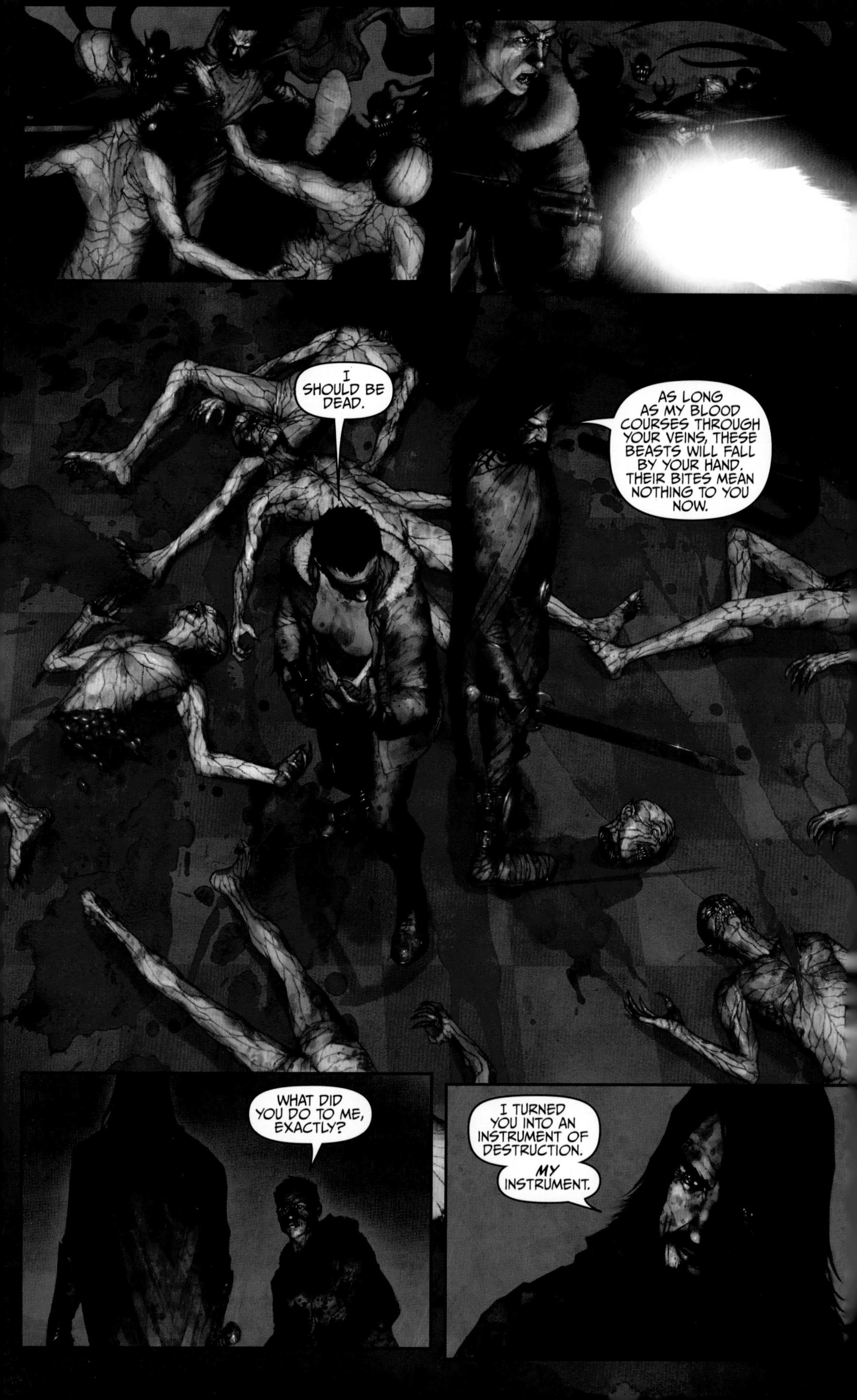
I SHOULD BE DEAD.
AS LONG AS MY BLOOD COURSES THROUGH YOUR VEINS, THESE BEASTS WILL FALL BY YOUR HAND. THEIR BITES MEAN NOTHING TO YOU NOW.
WHAT DID YOU DO TO ME, EXACTLY?
I TURNED YOU INTO AN INSTRUMENT OF DESTRUCTION.
MY INSTRUMENT.

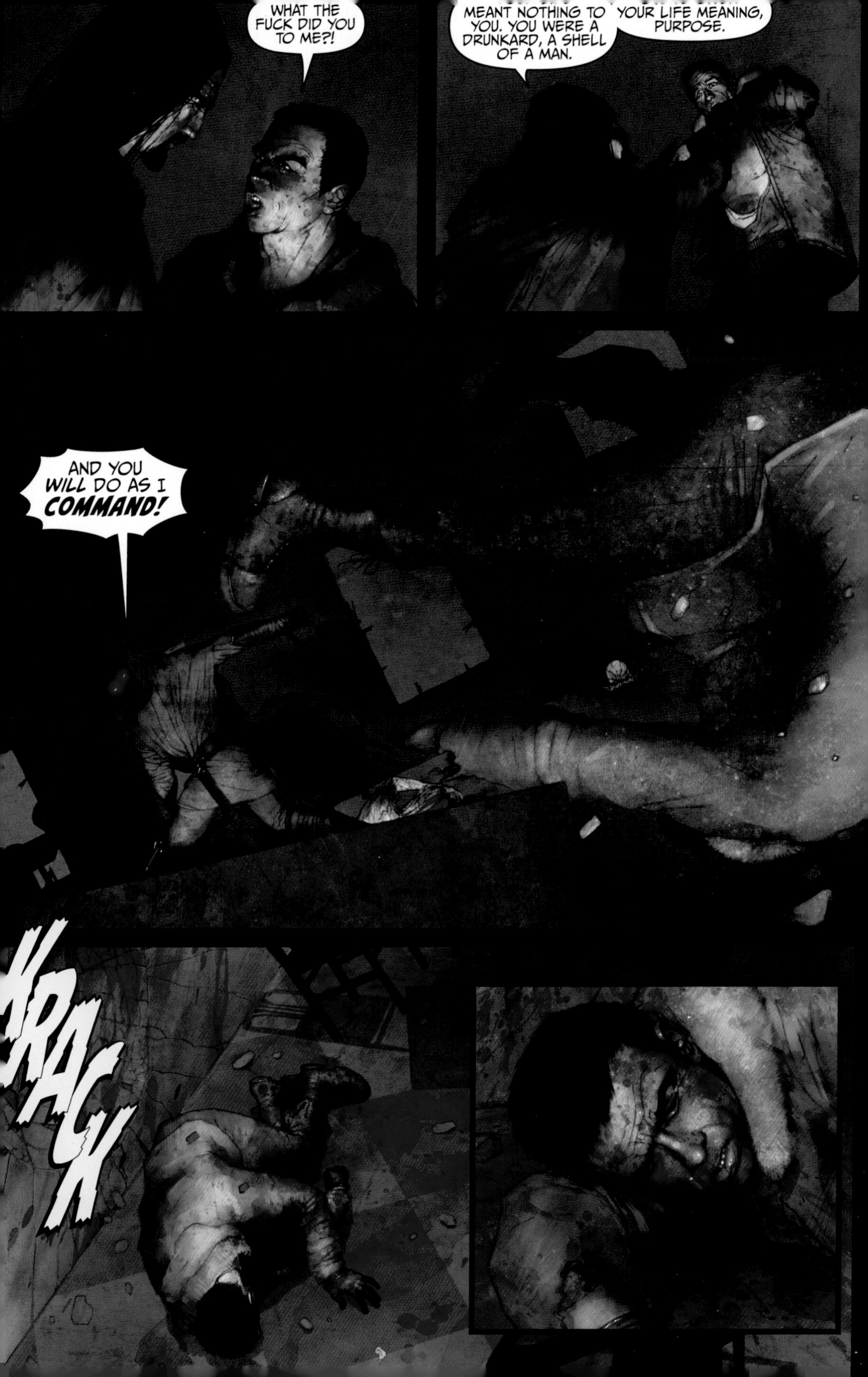
WHAT THE FUCK DID YOU TO ME?!
MEANT NOTHING TO YOU. YOU WERE A DRUNKARD, A SHELL OF A MAN.
YOUR LIFE MEANING, PURPOSE.
AND YOU WILL DO AS I COMMAND!
KRACK

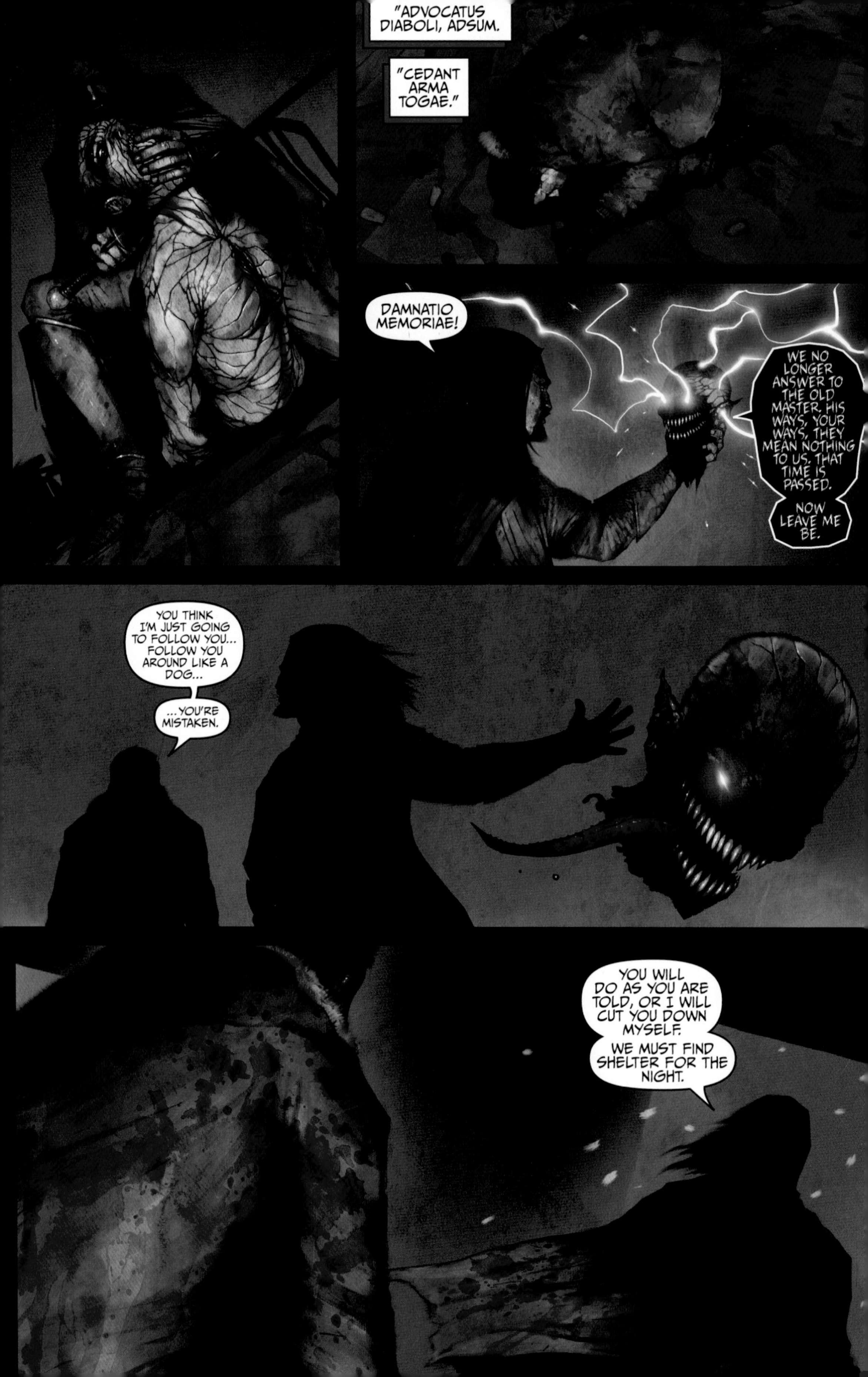
"ADVOCATUS DIABOLI, ADSUM.
"CEDANT ARMA TOGAE."
DAMNATIO MEMORIAE!
WE NO LONGER ANSWER TO THE OLD MASTER. HIS WAYS, YOUR WAYS, THEY MEAN NOTHING TO US. THAT TIME IS PASSED.
NOW LEAVE ME BE.
YOU THINK I'M JUST GOING TO FOLLOW YOU... FOLLOW YOU AROUND LIKE A DOG...
...YOU'RE MISTAKEN.
YOU WILL DO AS YOU ARE TOLD, OR I WILL CUT YOU DOWN MYSELF.
WE MUST FIND SHELTER FOR THE NIGHT.

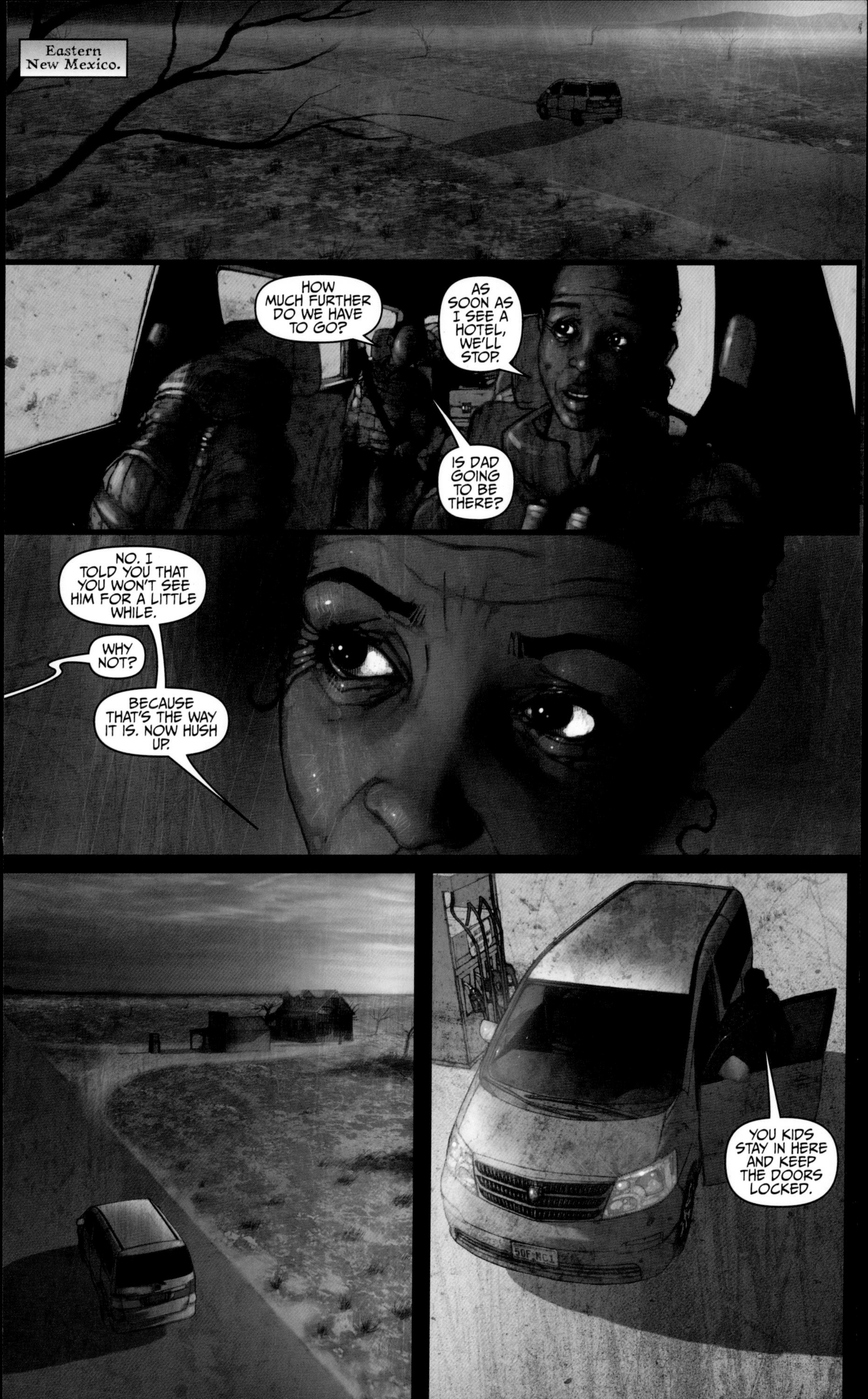
Eastern New Mexico.
HOW MUCH FURTHER DO WE HAVE TO GO?
AS SOON AS I SEE A HOTEL, WE'LL STOP.
IS DAD GOING TO BE THERE?
NO. I TOLD YOU THAT YOU WON'T SEE HIM FOR A LITTLE WHILE.
WHY NOT?
BECAUSE THAT'S THE WAY IT IS. NOW HUSH UP.
YOU KIDS STAY IN HERE AND KEEP THE DOORS LOCKED.

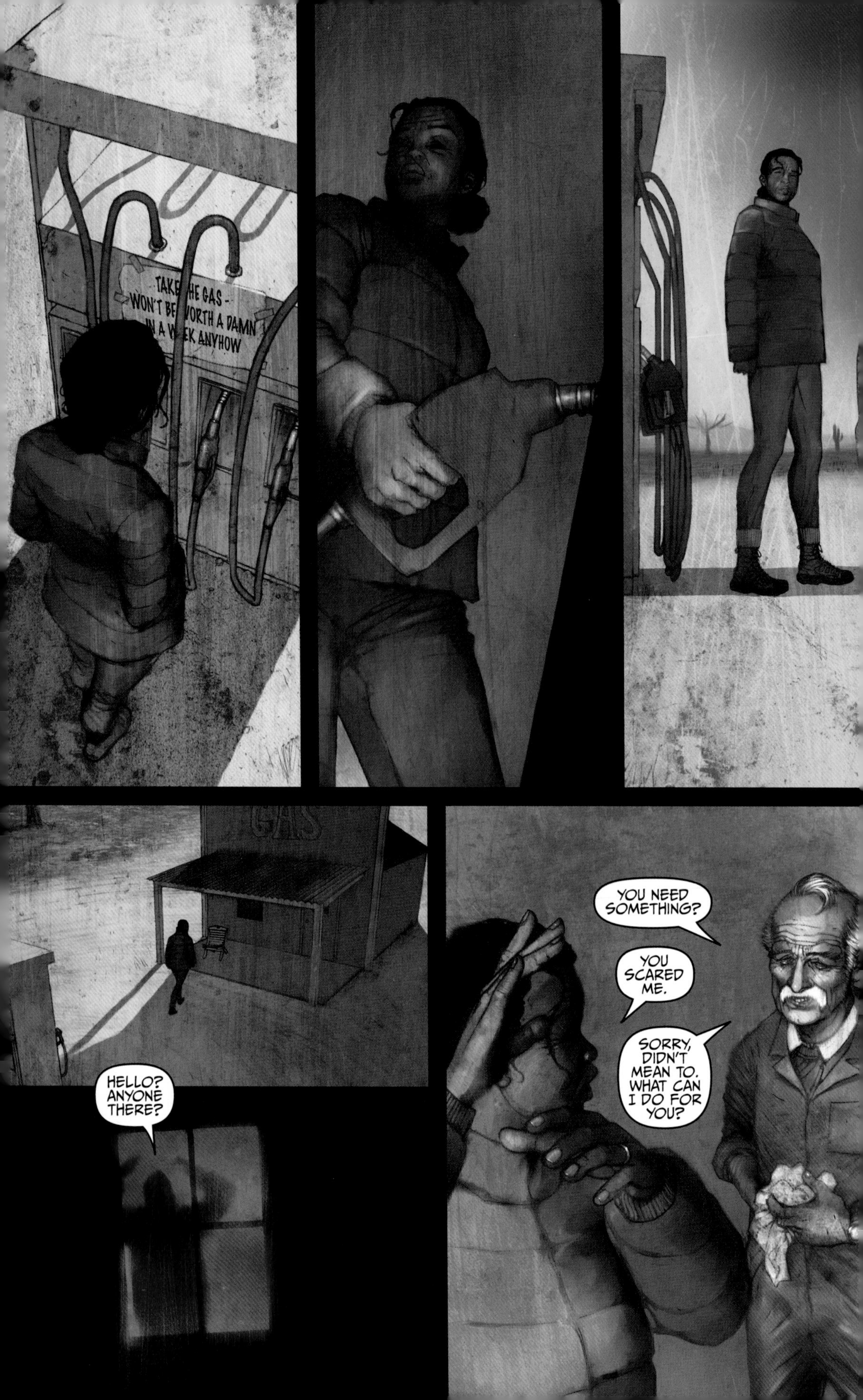

TAKE HE GAS -
WON'T BE WORTH A DAMN
IN A W EK ANYHOW
GAS
HELLO? ANYONE THERE?
YOU NEED SOMETHING?
YOU SCARED ME.
SORRY, DIDN'T MEAN TO. WHAT CAN I DO FOR YOU?

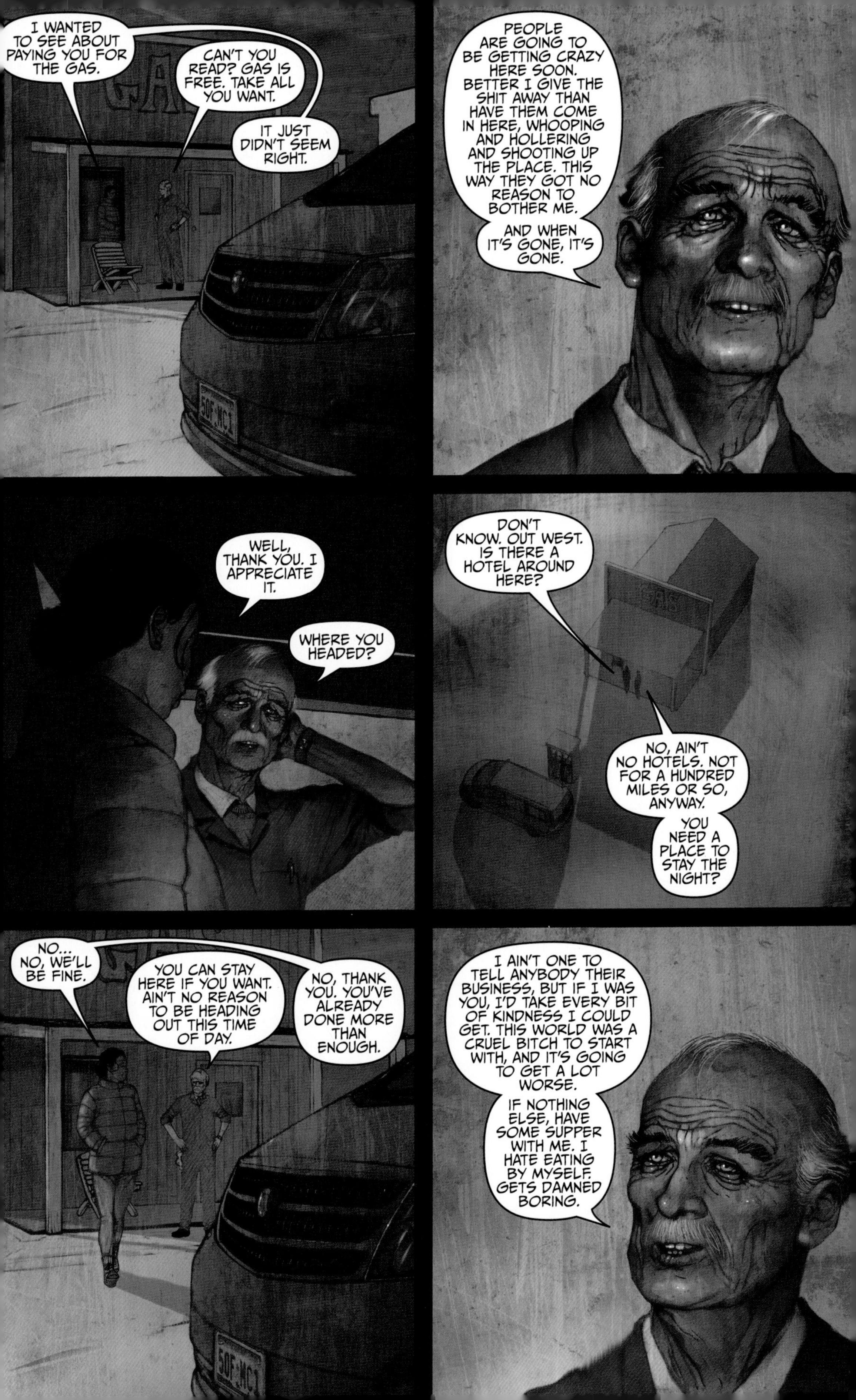
I WANTED TO SEE ABOUT PAYING YOU FOR THE GAS.
CAN'T YOU READ? GAS IS FREE. TAKE ALL YOU WANT.
IT JUST DIDN'T SEEM RIGHT.
PEOPLE ARE GOING TO BE GETTING CRAZY HERE SOON. BETTER I GIVE THE SHIT AWAY THAN HAVE THEM COME IN HERE, WHOOPING AND HOLLERING AND SHOOTING UP THE PLACE. THIS WAY THEY GOT NO REASON TO BOTHER ME.
AND WHEN IT'S GONE, IT'S GONE.
WELL, THANK YOU. I APPRECIATE IT.
WHERE YOU HEADED?
DON'T KNOW. OUT WEST. IS THERE A HOTEL AROUND HERE?
NO, AIN'T NO HOTELS. NOT FOR A HUNDRED MILES OR SO, ANYWAY.
YOU NEED A PLACE TO STAY THE NIGHT?
NO... NO, WE'LL BE FINE.
YOU CAN STAY HERE IF YOU WANT. AIN'T NO REASON TO BE HEADING OUT THIS TIME OF DAY.
NO, THANK YOU. YOU'VE ALREADY DONE MORE THAN ENOUGH.
I AIN'T ONE TO TELL ANYBODY THEIR BUSINESS, BUT IF I WAS YOU, I'D TAKE EVERY BIT OF KINDNESS I COULD GET. THIS WORLD WAS A CRUEL BITCH TO START WITH, AND IT'S GOING TO GET A LOT WORSE.
IF NOTHING ELSE, HAVE SOME SUPPER WITH ME. I HATE EATING BY MYSELF. GETS DAMNED BORING.

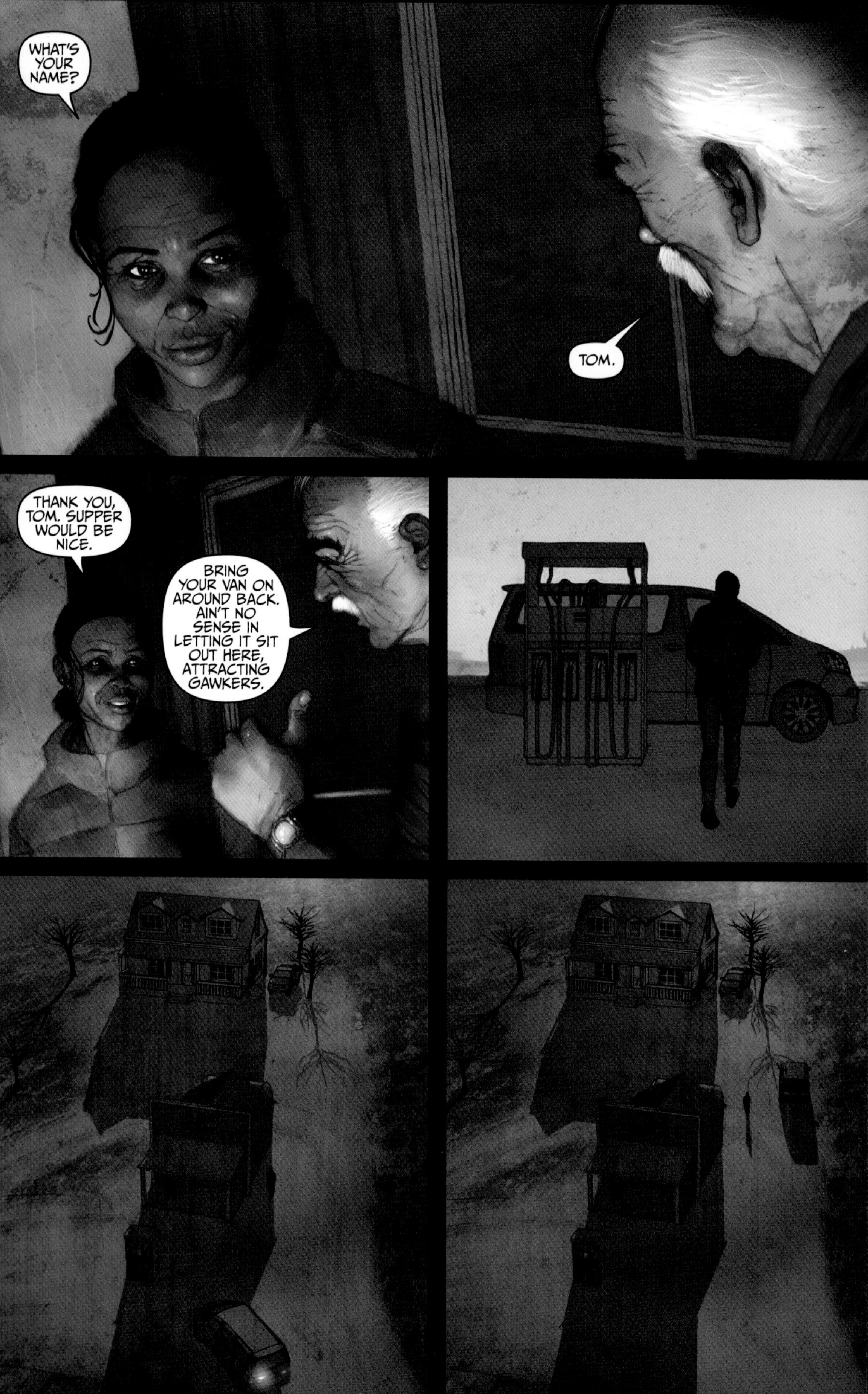
WHAT'S YOUR NAME?
TOM.
THANK YOU, TOM. SUPPER WOULD BE NICE.
BRING YOUR VAN ON AROUND BACK. AIN'T NO SENSE IN LETTING IT SIT OUT HERE, ATTRACTING GAWKERS.

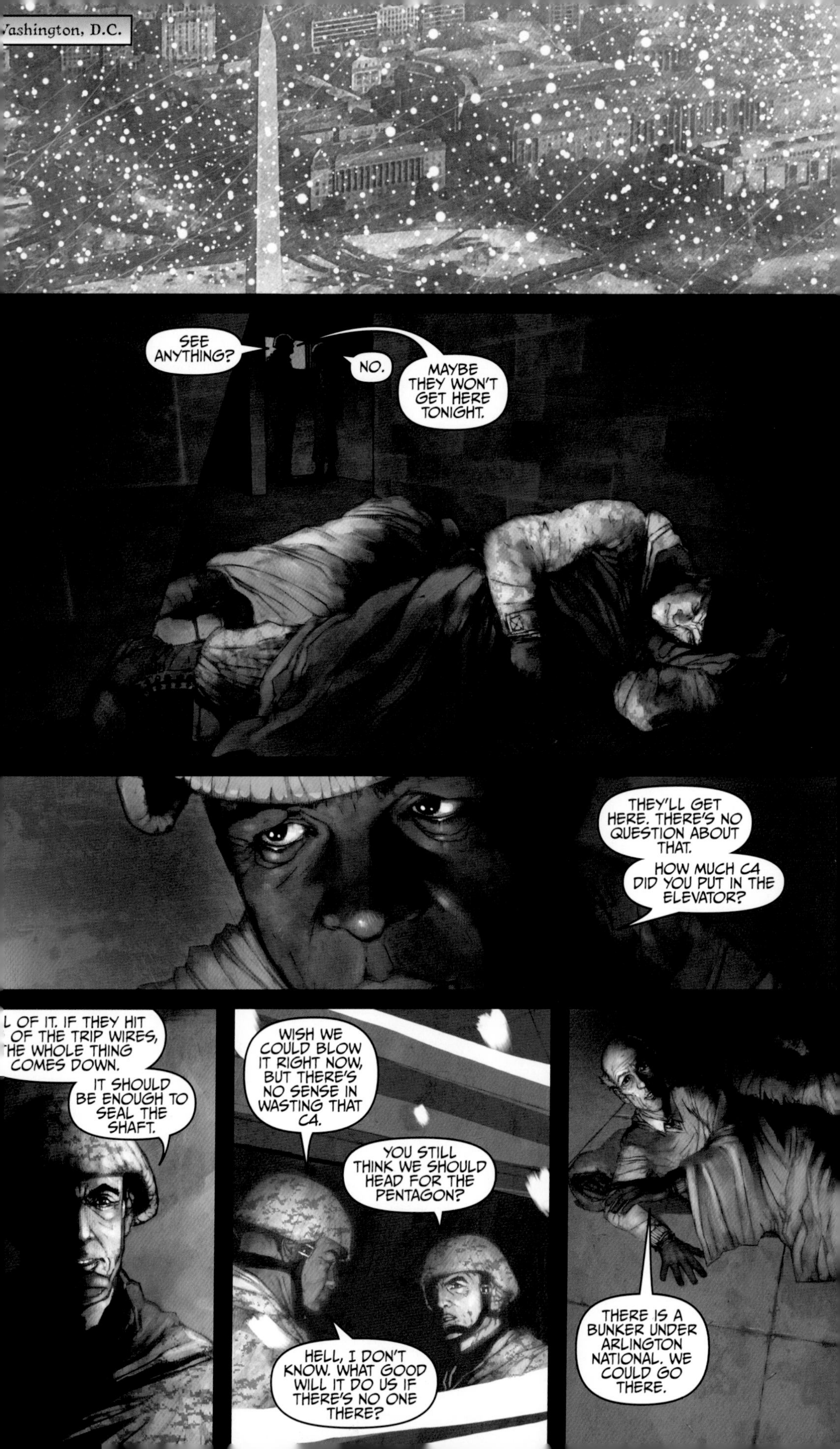
Washington, D.C.
SEE ANYTHING?
NO.
MAYBE THEY WON'T GET HERE TONIGHT.
THEY'LL GET HERE. THERE'S NO QUESTION ABOUT THAT.
HOW MUCH C4 DID YOU PUT IN THE ELEVATOR?
L OF IT. IF THEY HIT OF THE TRIP WIRES, HE WHOLE THING COMES DOWN.
IT SHOULD BE ENOUGH TO SEAL THE SHAFT.
WISH WE COULD BLOW IT RIGHT NOW, BUT THERE'S NO SENSE IN WASTING THAT C4.
YOU STILL THINK WE SHOULD HEAD FOR THE PENTAGON?
HELL, I DON'T KNOW. WHAT GOOD WILL IT DO US IF THERE'S NO ONE THERE?
THERE IS A BUNKER UNDER ARLINGTON NATIONAL. WE COULD GO THERE.

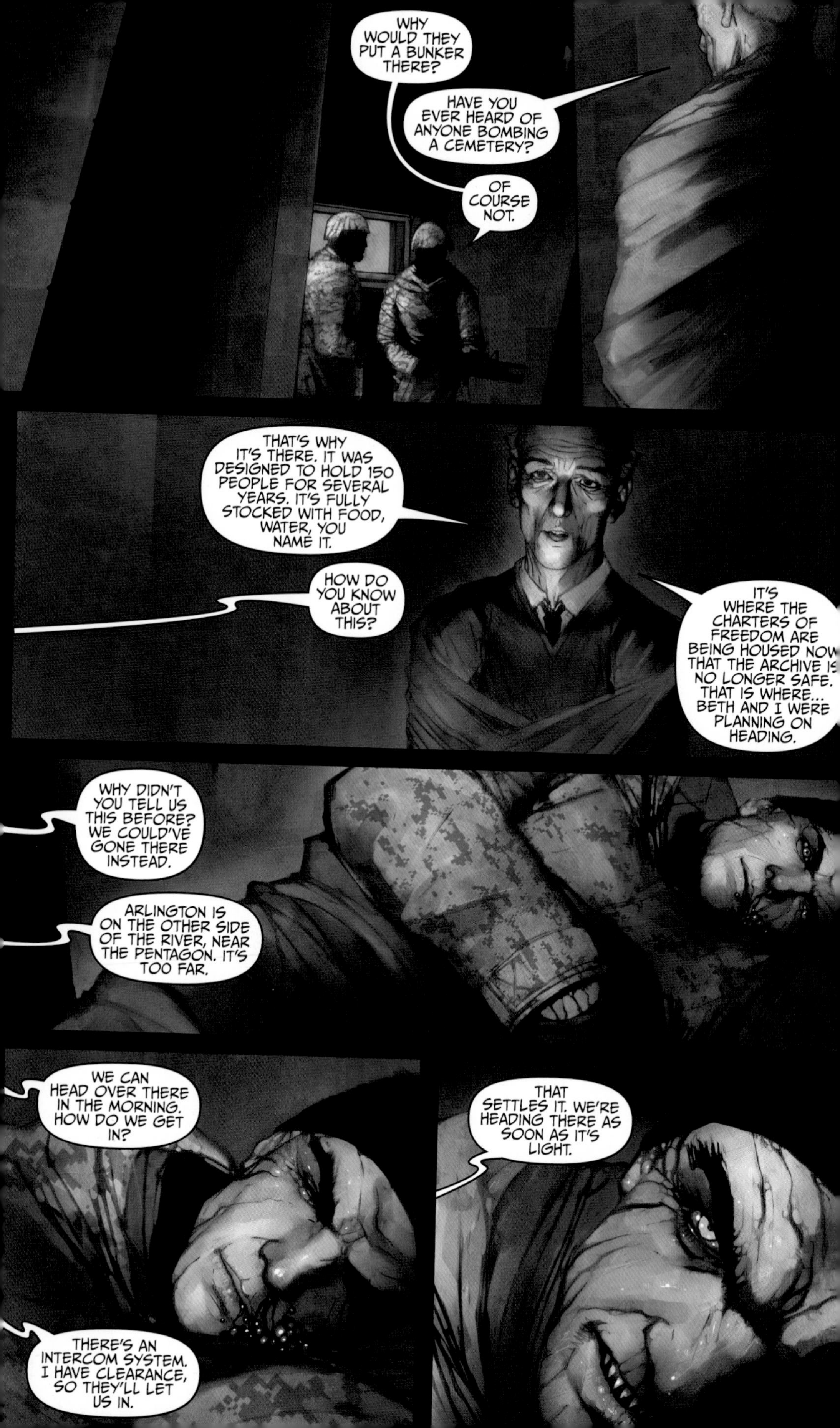
WHY WOULD THEY PUT A BUNKER THERE?
HAVE YOU EVER HEARD OF ANYONE BOMBING A CEMETERY?
OF COURSE NOT.
THAT'S WHY IT'S THERE. IT WAS DESIGNED TO HOLD 150 PEOPLE FOR SEVERAL YEARS. IT'S FULLY STOCKED WITH FOOD, WATER, YOU NAME IT.
HOW DO YOU KNOW ABOUT THIS?
IT'S WHERE THE CHARTERS OF FREEDOM ARE BEING HOUSED NOW THAT THE ARCHIVE IS NO LONGER SAFE. THAT IS WHERE... BETH AND I WERE PLANNING ON HEADING.
WHY DIDN'T YOU TELL US THIS BEFORE? WE COULD'VE GONE THERE INSTEAD.
ARLINGTON IS ON THE OTHER SIDE OF THE RIVER, NEAR THE PENTAGON. IT'S TOO FAR.
WE CAN HEAD OVER THERE IN THE MORNING. HOW DO WE GET IN?
THERE'S AN INTERCOM SYSTEM. I HAVE CLEARANCE, SO THEY'LL LET US IN.
THAT SETTLES IT. WE'RE HEADING THERE AS SOON AS IT'S LIGHT.

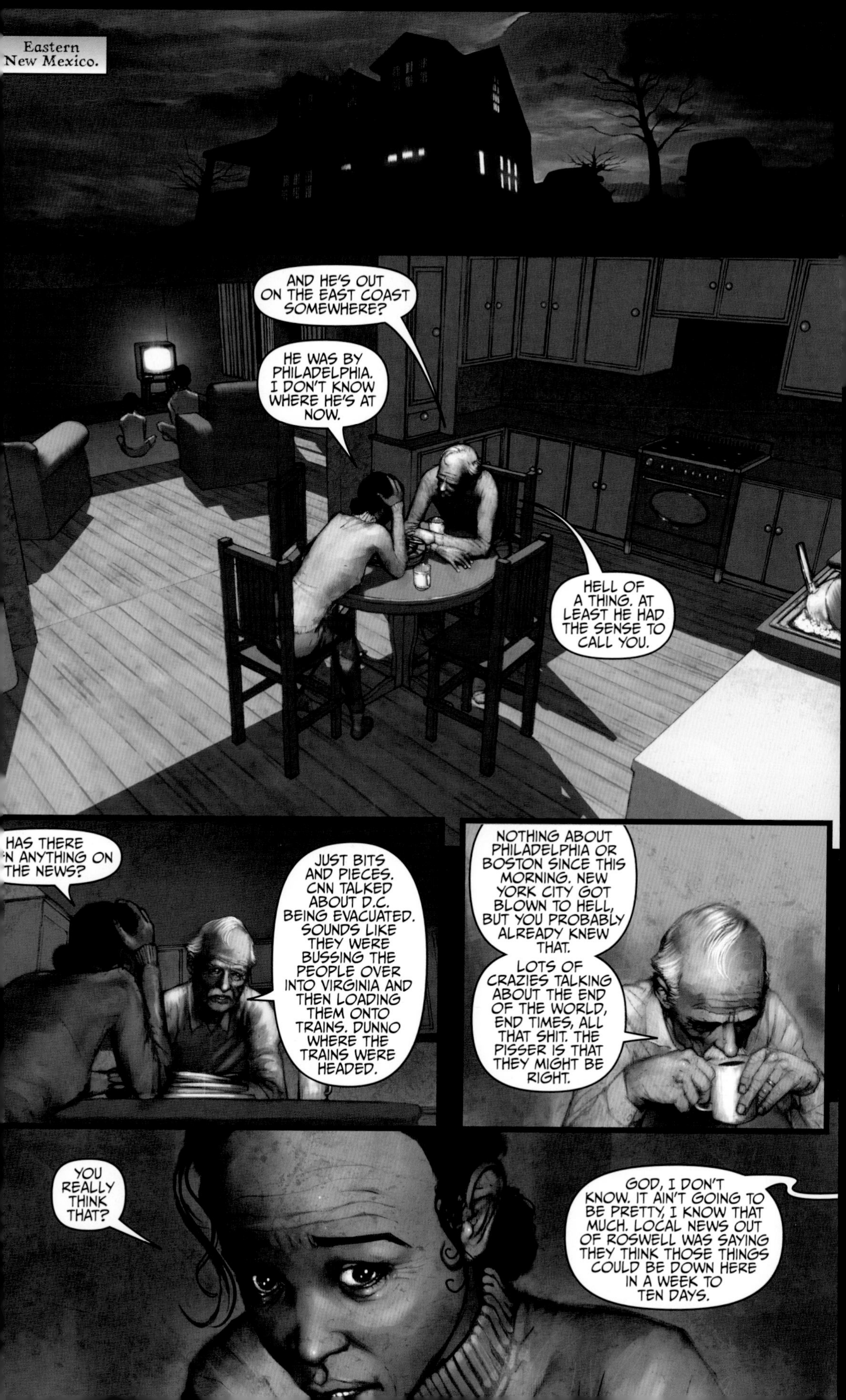
Eastern New Mexico.
AND HE'S OUT ON THE EAST COAST SOMEWHERE?
HE WAS BY PHILADELPHIA. I DON'T KNOW WHERE HE'S AT NOW.
HELL OF A THING. AT LEAST HE HAD THE SENSE TO CALL YOU.
HAS THERE N ANYTHING ON THE NEWS?
JUST BITS AND PIECES. CNN TALKED ABOUT D.C. BEING EVACUATED. SOUNDS LIKE THEY WERE BUSSING THE PEOPLE OVER INTO VIRGINIA AND THEN LOADING THEM ONTO TRAINS. DUNNO WHERE THE TRAINS WERE HEADED.
NOTHING ABOUT PHILADELPHIA OR BOSTON SINCE THIS MORNING. NEW YORK CITY GOT BLOWN TO HELL, BUT YOU PROBABLY ALREADY KNEW THAT.
LOTS OF CRAZIES TALKING ABOUT THE END OF THE WORLD, END TIMES, ALL THAT SHIT. THE PISSER IS THAT THEY MIGHT BE RIGHT.
YOU REALLY THINK THAT?
GOD, I DON'T KNOW. IT AIN'T GOING TO BE PRETTY, I KNOW THAT MUCH. LOCAL NEWS OUT OF ROSWELL WAS SAYING THEY THINK THOSE THINGS COULD BE DOWN HERE IN A WEEK TO TEN DAYS.

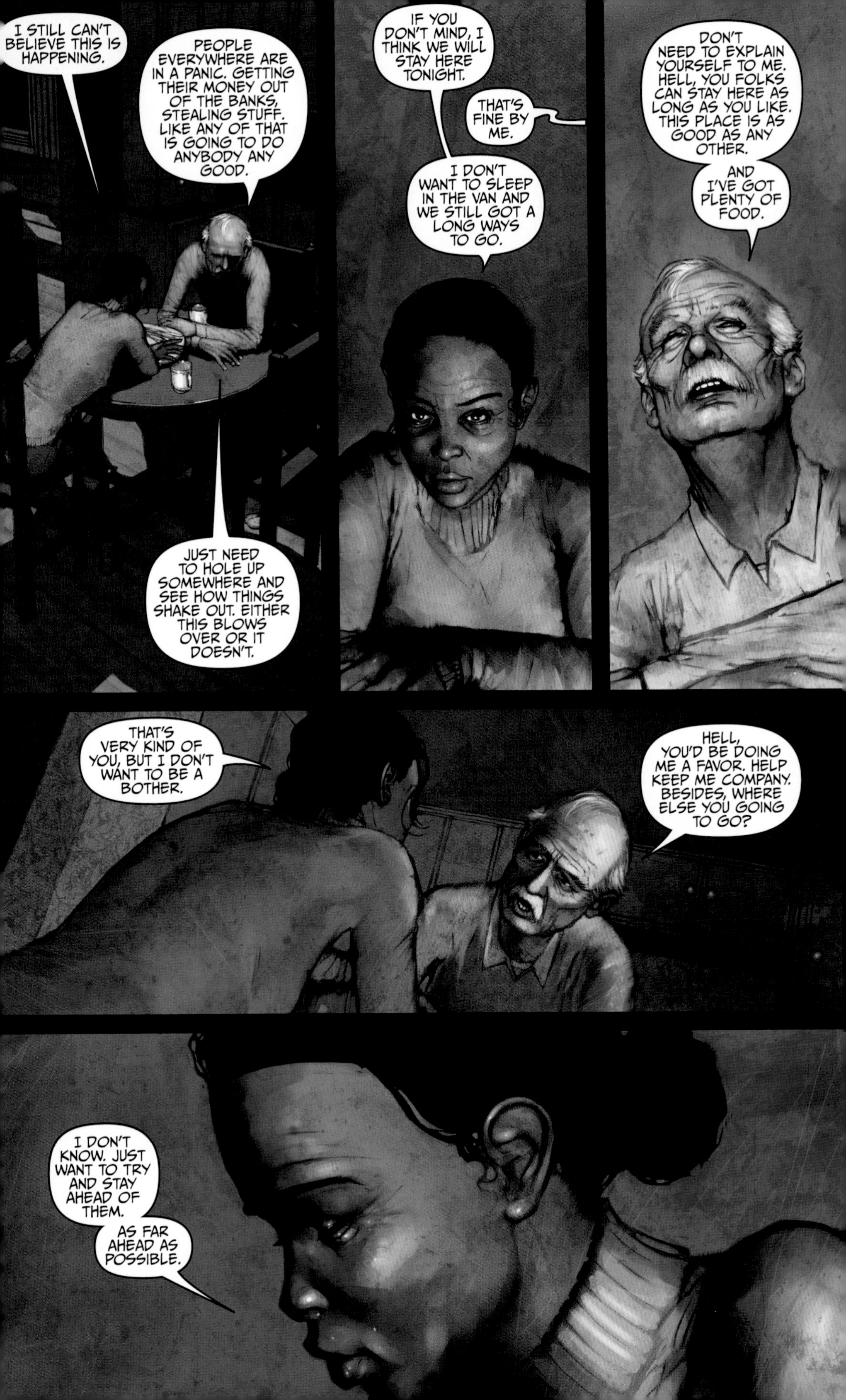
I STILL CAN'T BELIEVE THIS IS HAPPENING.
PEOPLE EVERYWHERE ARE IN A PANIC. GETTING THEIR MONEY OUT OF THE BANKS, STEALING STUFF. LIKE ANY OF THAT IS GOING TO DO ANYBODY ANY GOOD.
JUST NEED TO HOLE UP SOMEWHERE AND SEE HOW THINGS SHAKE OUT. EITHER THIS BLOWS OVER OR IT DOESN'T.
IF YOU DON'T MIND, I THINK WE WILL STAY HERE TONIGHT.
THAT'S FINE BY ME.
I DON'T WANT TO SLEEP IN THE VAN AND WE STILL GOT A LONG WAYS TO GO.
DON'T NEED TO EXPLAIN YOURSELF TO ME. HELL, YOU FOLKS CAN STAY HERE AS LONG AS YOU LIKE. THIS PLACE IS AS GOOD AS ANY OTHER.
AND I'VE GOT PLENTY OF FOOD.
THAT'S VERY KIND OF YOU, BUT I DON'T WANT TO BE A BOTHER.
HELL, YOU'D BE DOING ME A FAVOR. HELP KEEP ME COMPANY. BESIDES, WHERE ELSE YOU GOING TO GO?
I DON'T KNOW. JUST WANT TO TRY AND STAY AHEAD OF THEM.
AS FAR AHEAD AS POSSIBLE.

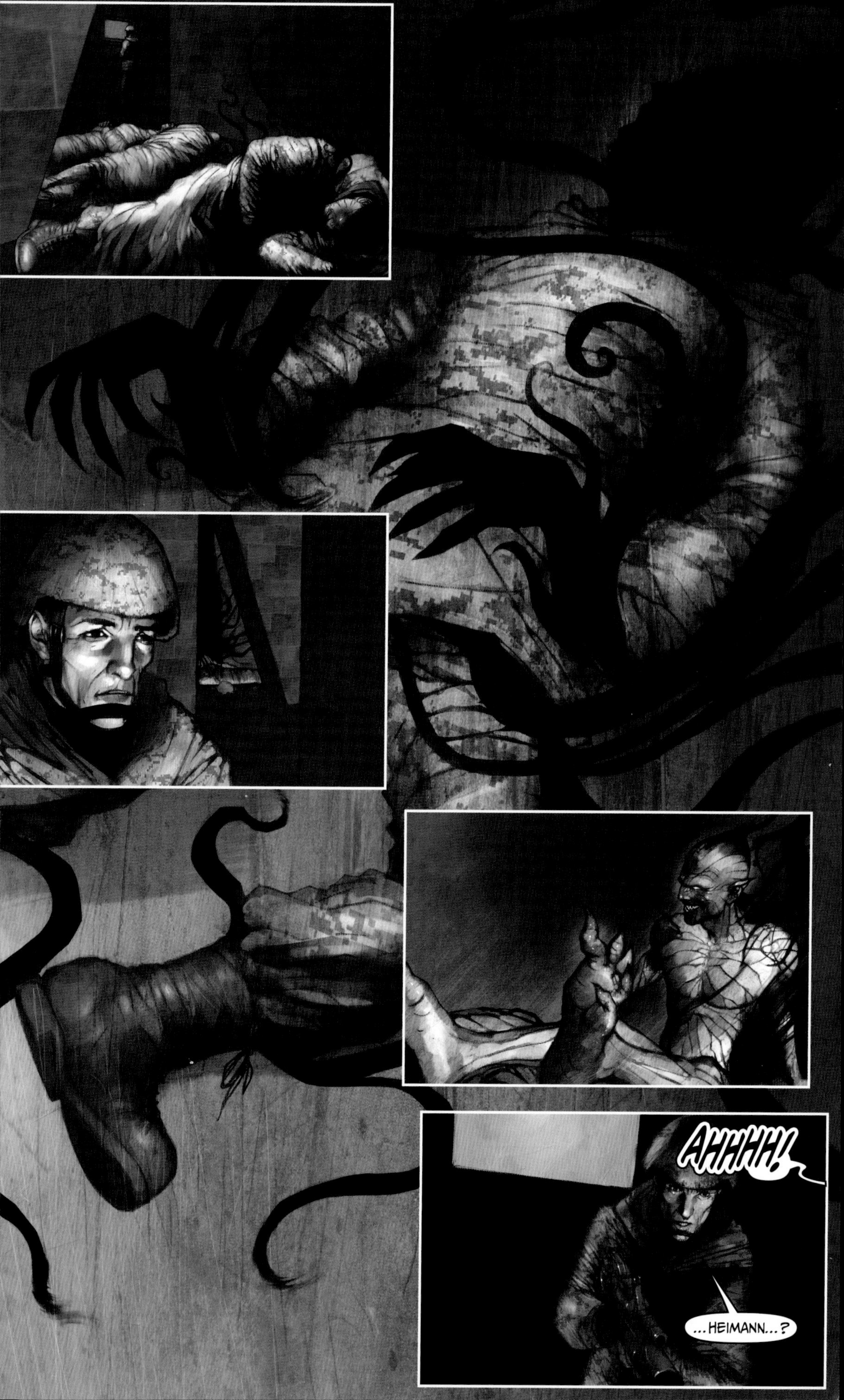
AHHHH!
...HEIMANN...?

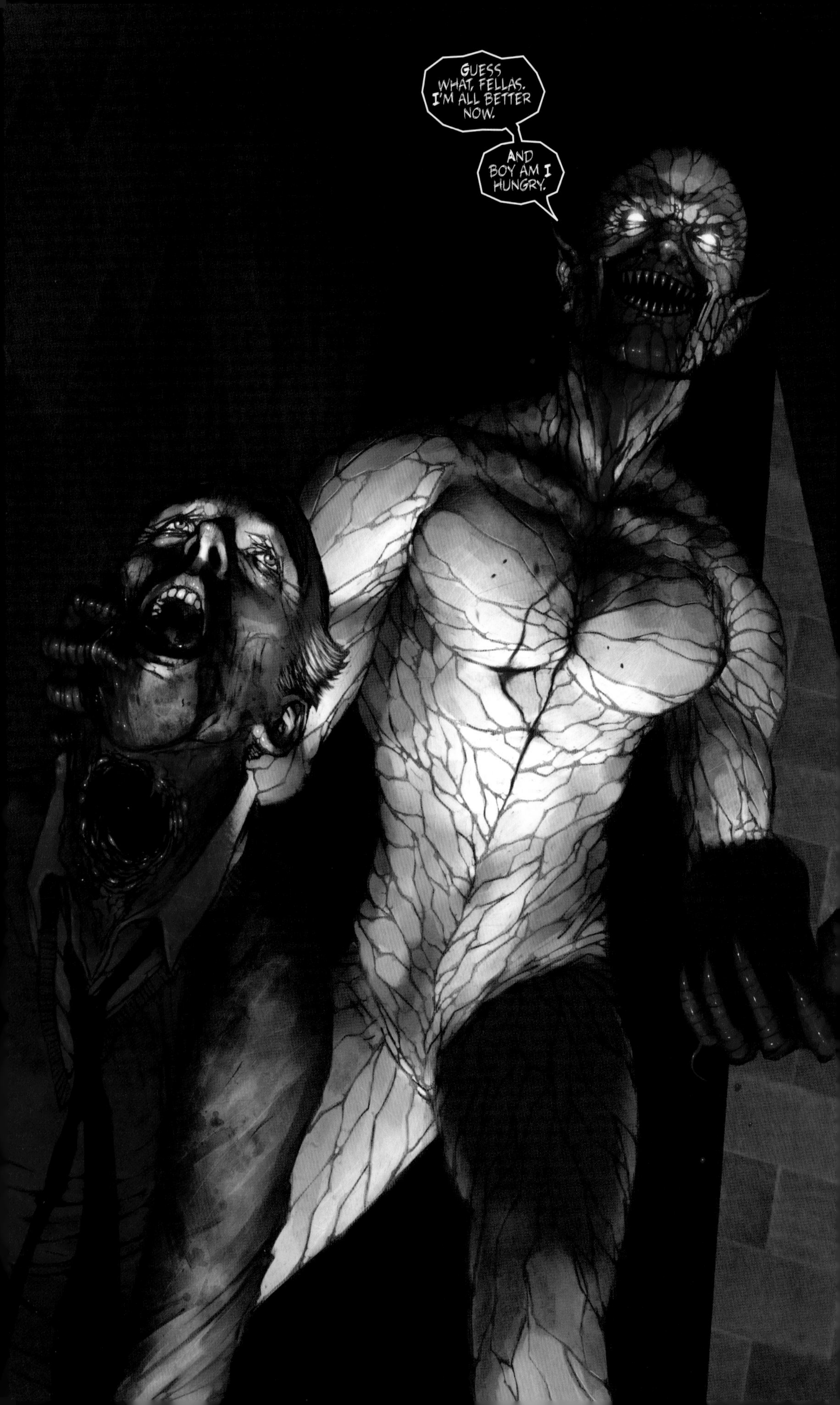
GUESS WHAT, FELLAS. I'M ALL BETTER NOW.
AND BOY AM I HUNGRY.

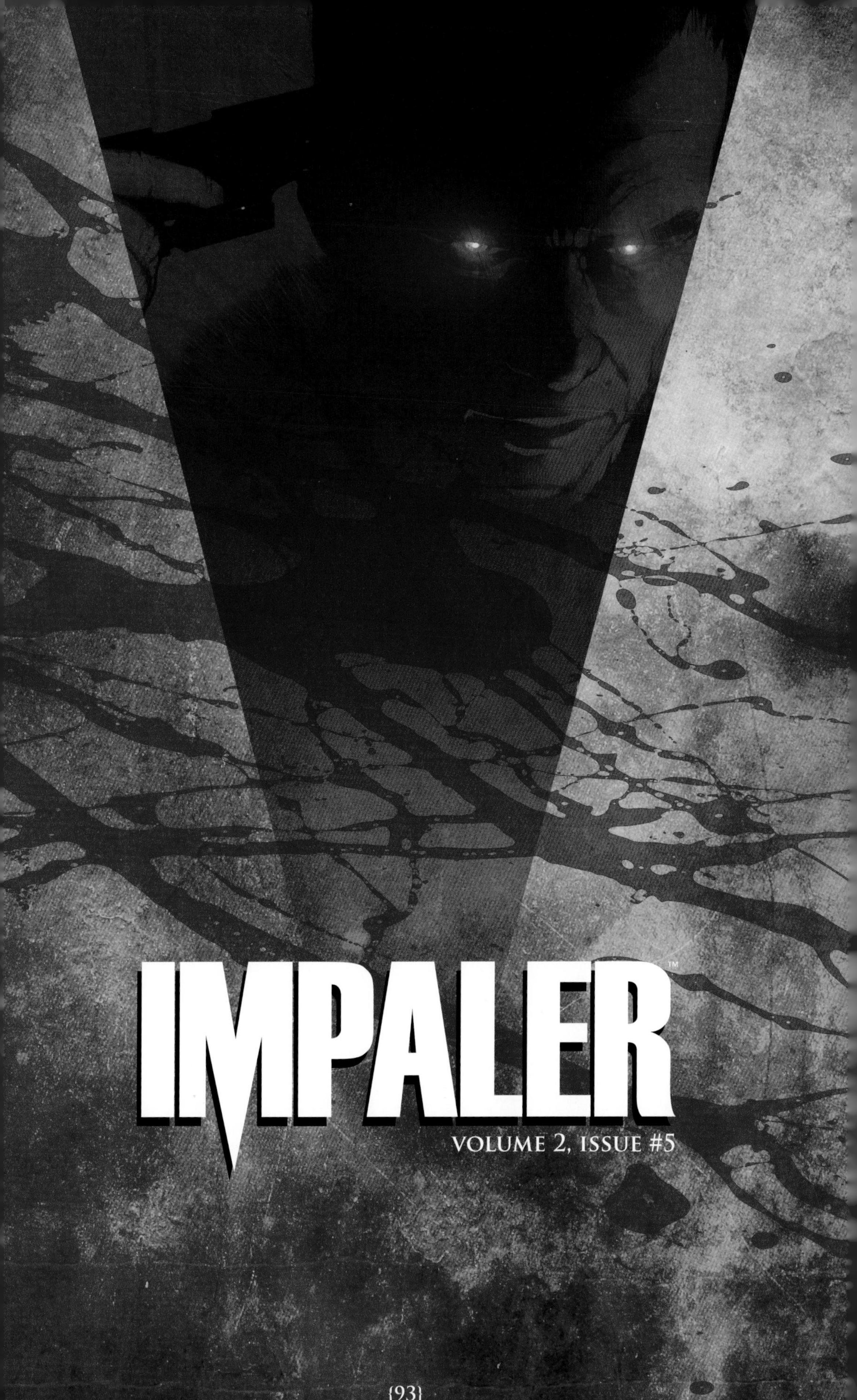
IMPALER™
VOLUME 2, ISSUE #5

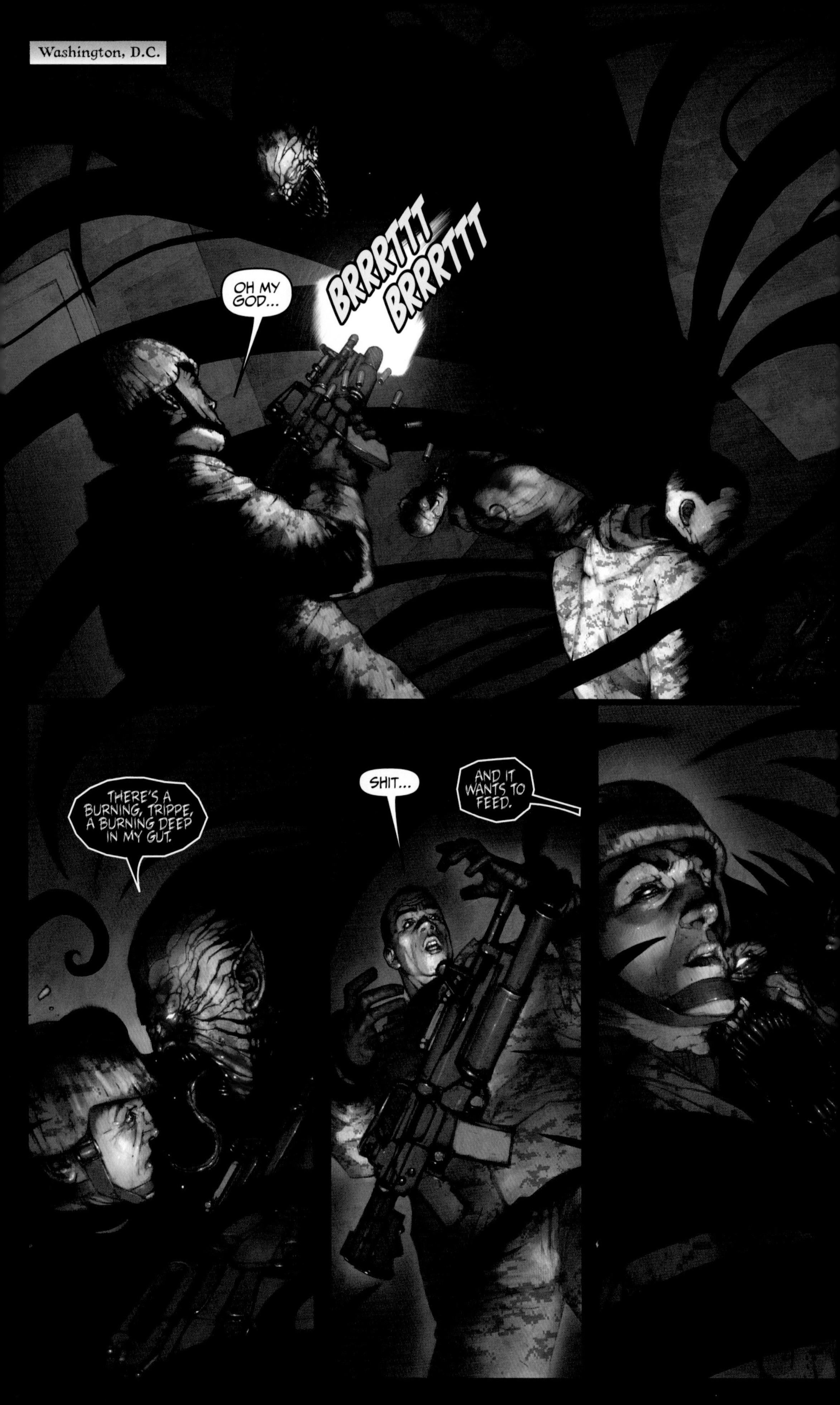
Washington, D.C.
OH MY GOD...
BRRRTTT BRRRTTT
THERE'S A BURNING, TRIPPE, A BURNING DEEP IN MY GUT.
SHIT...
AND IT WANTS TO FEED.

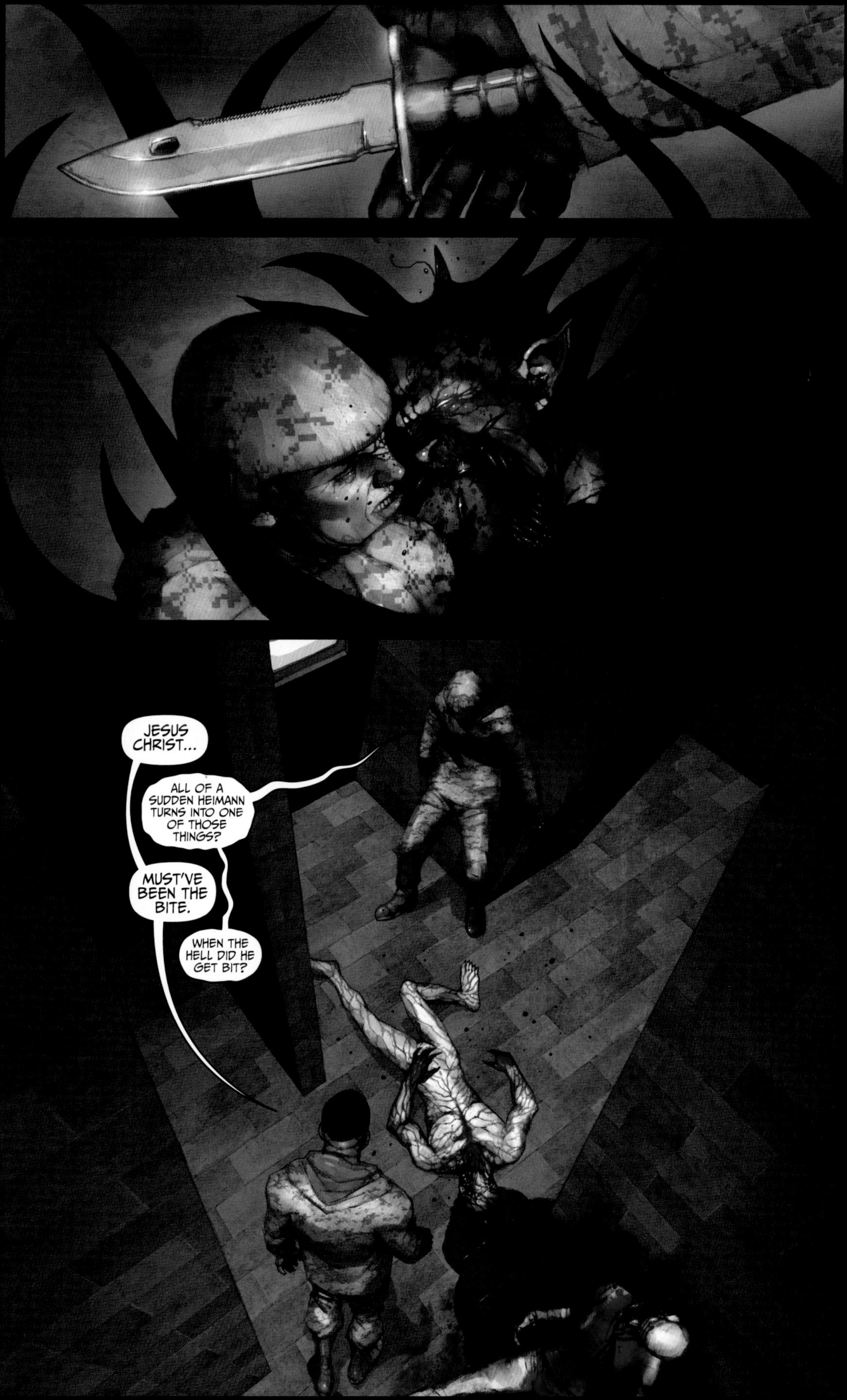

JESUS CHRIST...
ALL OF A SUDDEN HEIMANN TURNS INTO ONE OF THOSE THINGS?
MUST'VE BEEN THE BITE.
WHEN THE HELL DID HE GET BIT?

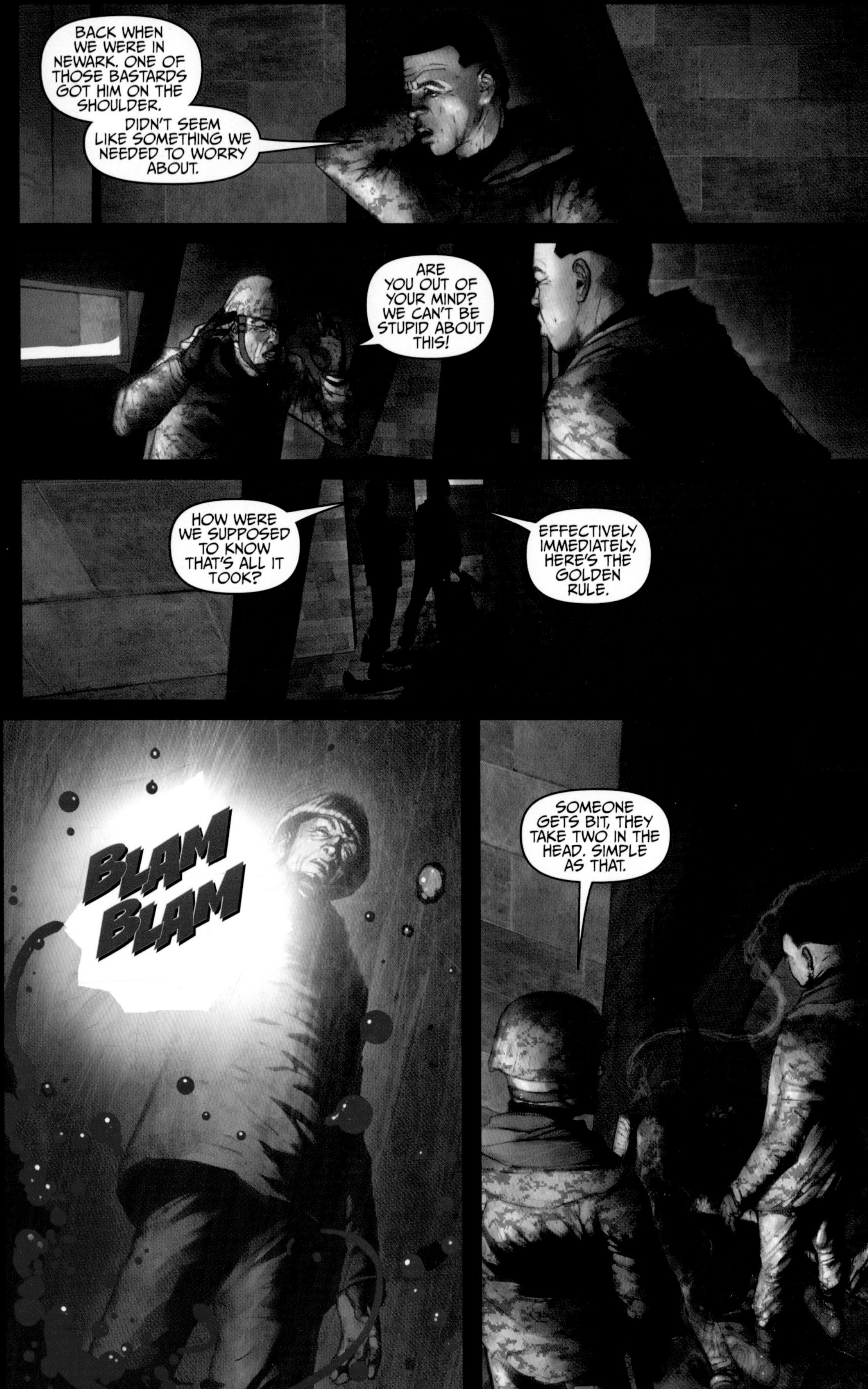
BACK WHEN WE WERE IN NEWARK. ONE OF THOSE BASTARDS GOT HIM ON THE SHOULDER.
DIDN'T SEEM LIKE SOMETHING WE NEEDED TO WORRY ABOUT.
ARE YOU OUT OF YOUR MIND? WE CAN'T BE STUPID ABOUT THIS!
HOW WERE WE SUPPOSED TO KNOW THAT'S ALL IT TOOK?
EFFECTIVELY IMMEDIATELY, HERE'S THE GOLDEN RULE.
BLAM BLAM
SOMEONE GETS BIT, THEY TAKE TWO IN THE HEAD. SIMPLE AS THAT.

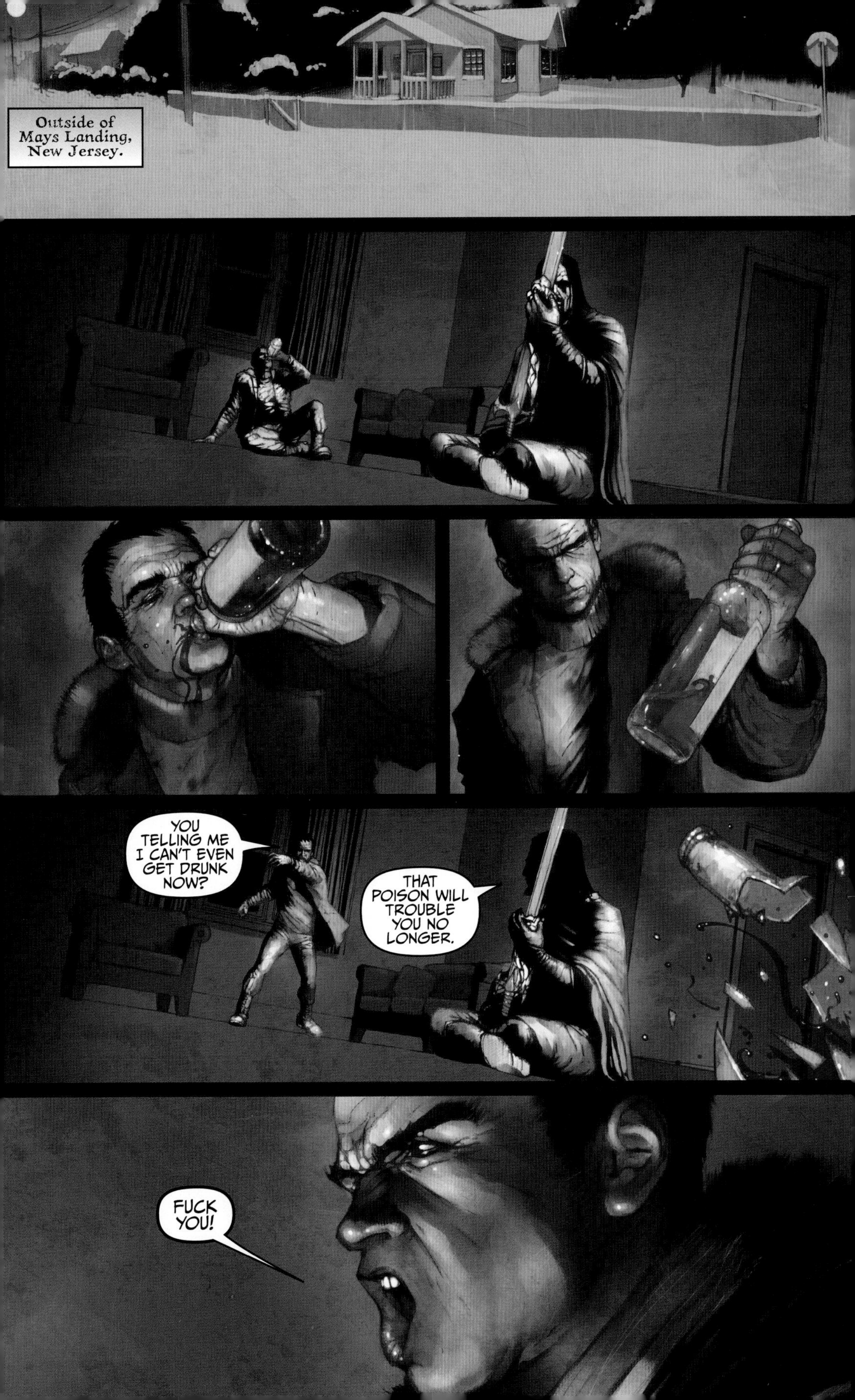
Outside of Mays Landing, New Jersey.
YOU TELLING ME I CAN'T EVEN GET DRUNK NOW?
THAT POISON WILL TROUBLE YOU NO LONGER.
FUCK YOU!

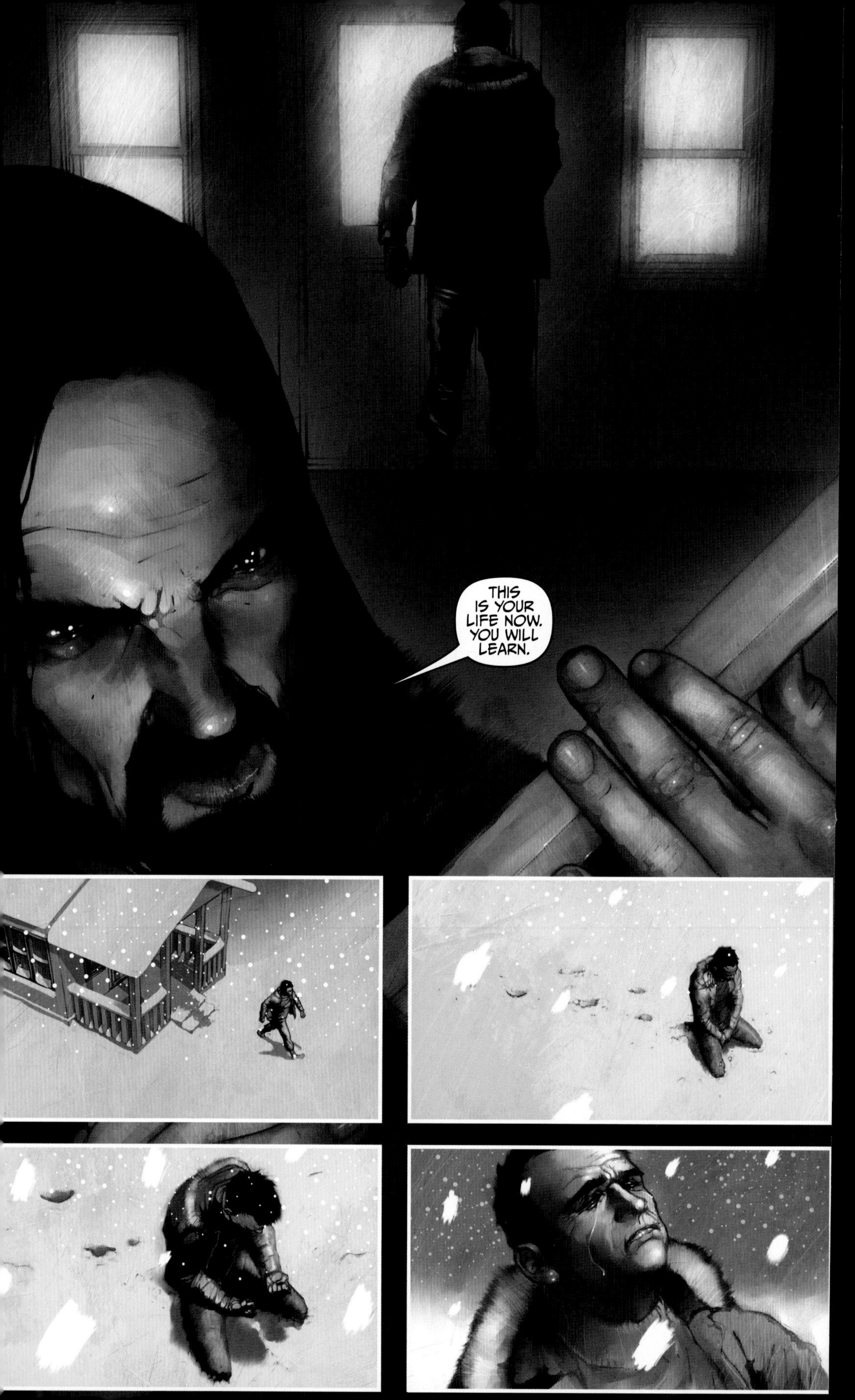
THIS IS YOUR LIFE NOW. YOU WILL LEARN.

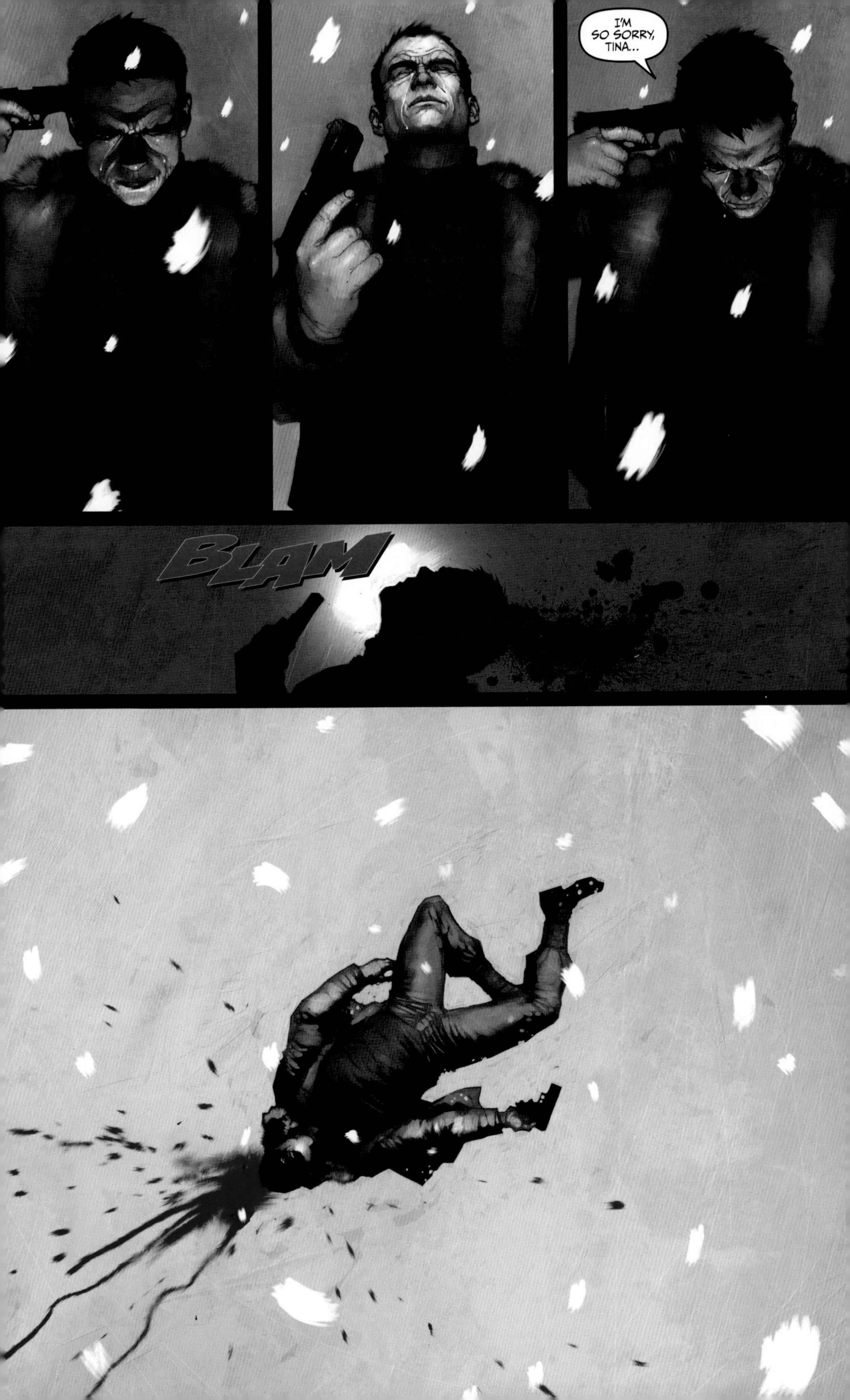
I'M SO SORRY, TINA...
BLAM

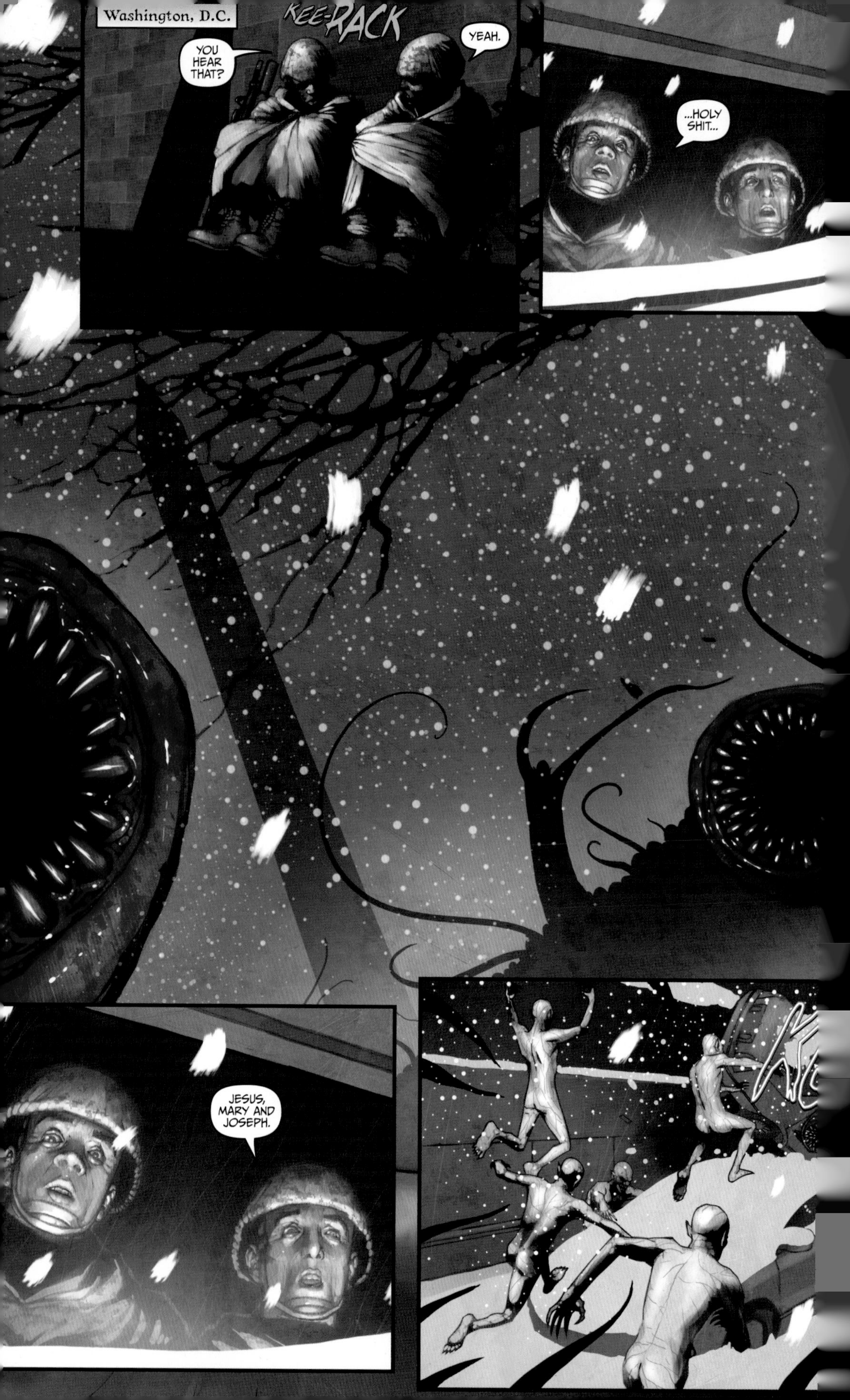
Washington, D.C.
KEE-RACK
YOU HEAR THAT?
YEAH.
...HOLY SHIT...
JESUS, MARY AND JOSEPH.

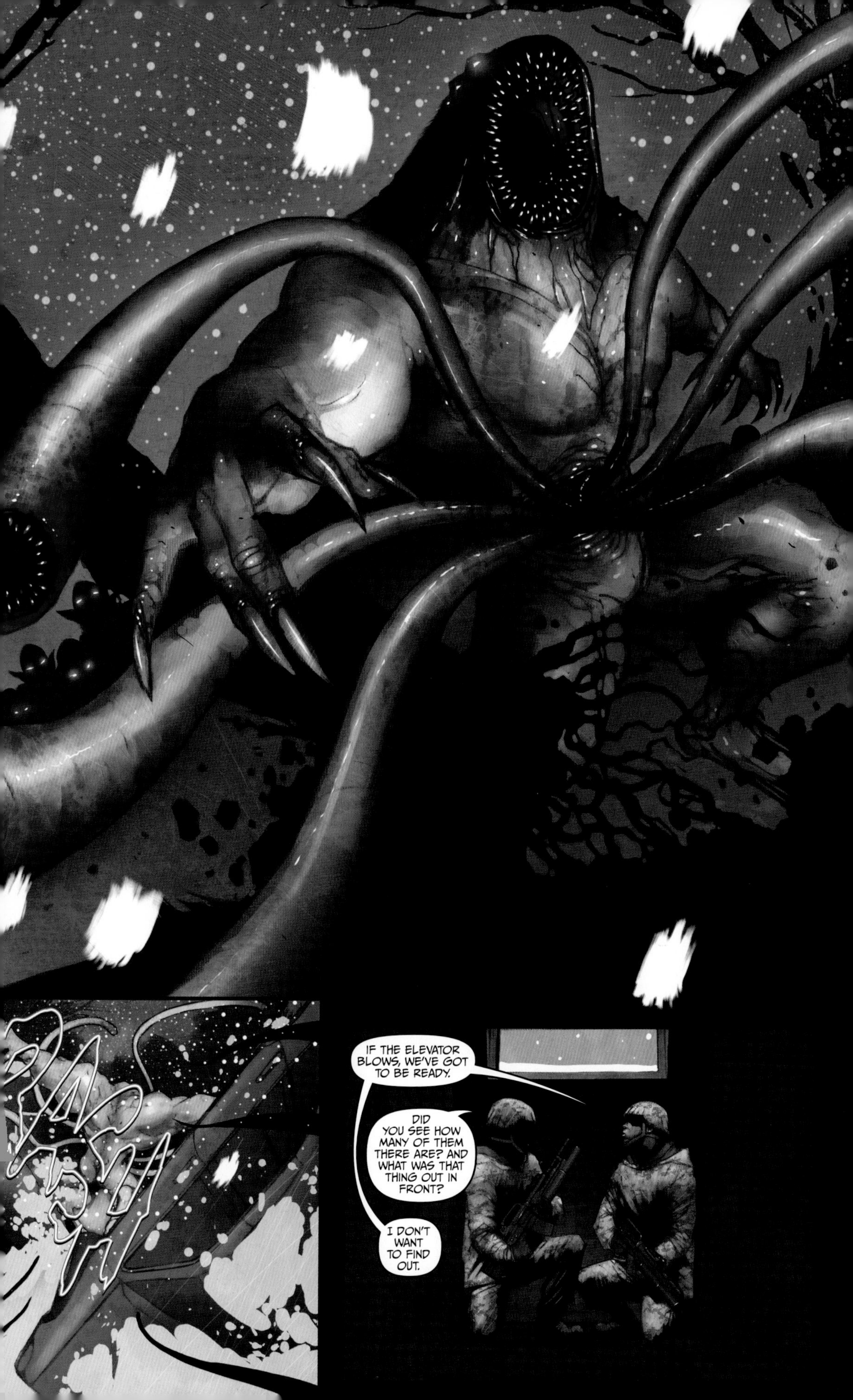
IF THE ELEVATOR BLOWS, WE'VE GOT TO BE READY.
DID YOU SEE HOW MANY OF THEM THERE ARE? AND WHAT WAS THAT THING OUT IN FRONT?
I DON'T WANT TO FIND OUT.

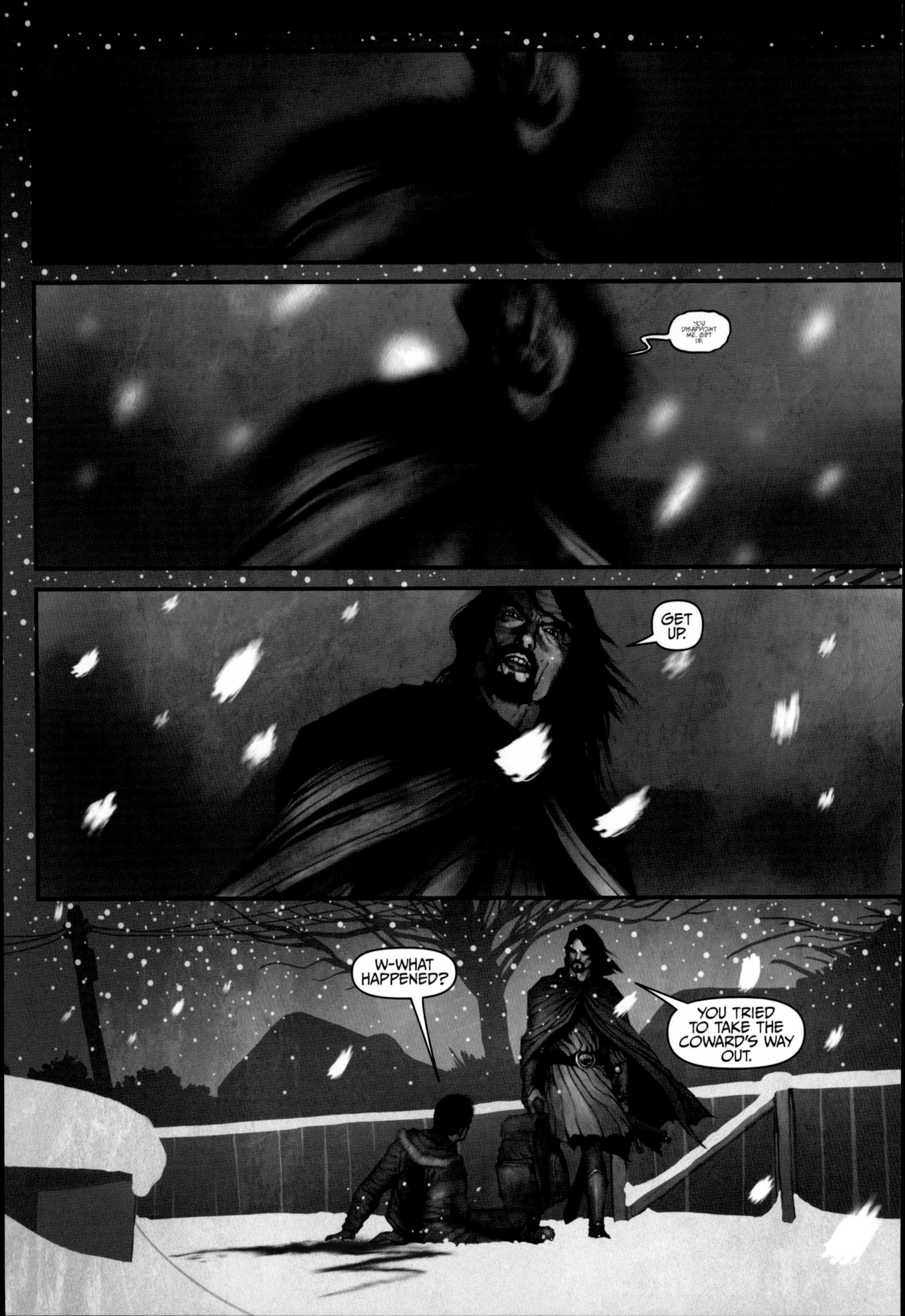
YOU DISAPPOINT ME. GET UP.
GET UP.
W-WHAT HAPPENED?
YOU TRIED TO TAKE THE COWARD'S WAY OUT.

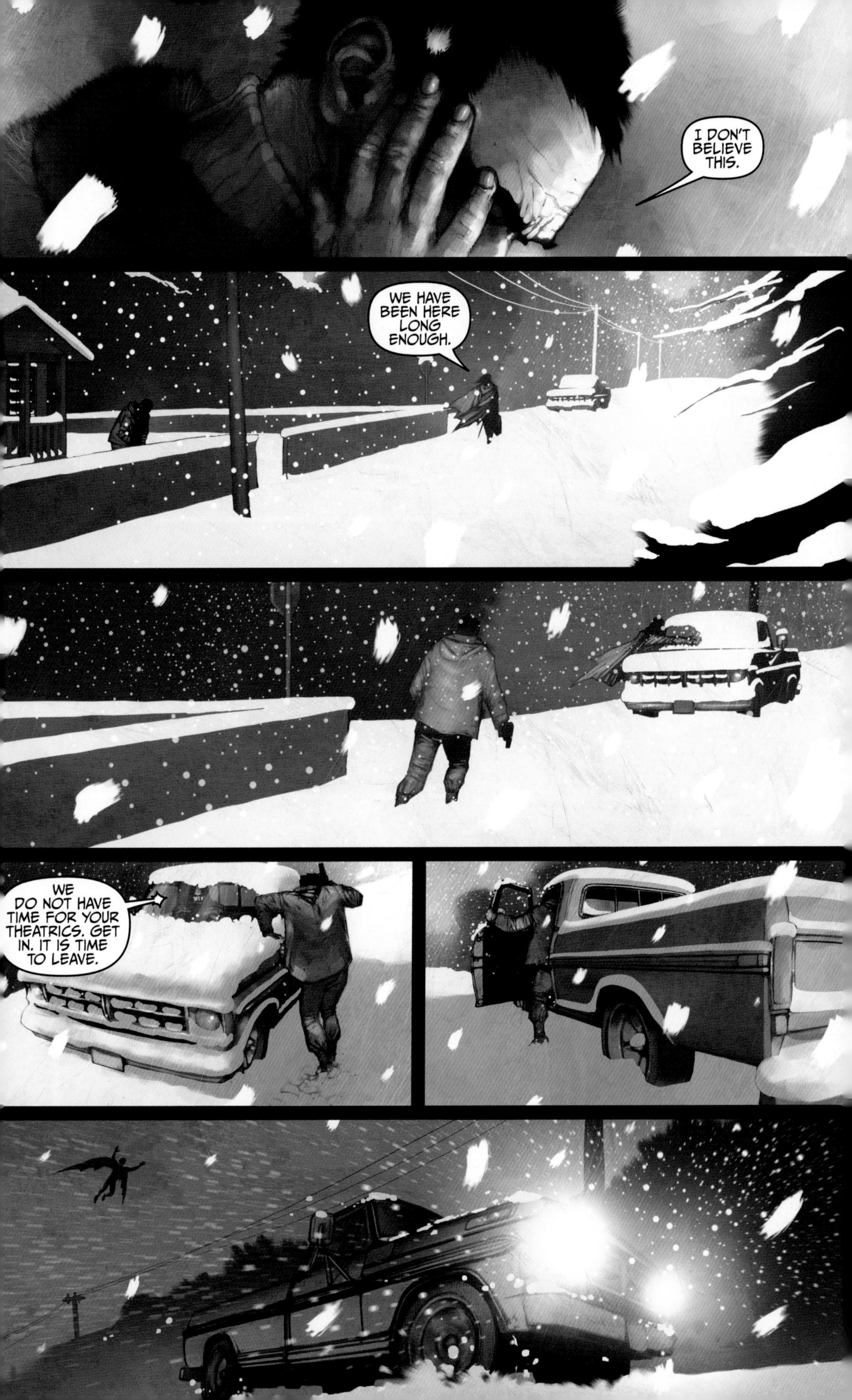
I DON'T BELIEVE THIS.
WE HAVE BEEN HERE LONG ENOUGH.
WE DO NOT HAVE TIME FOR YOUR THEATRICS. GET IN. IT IS TIME TO LEAVE.

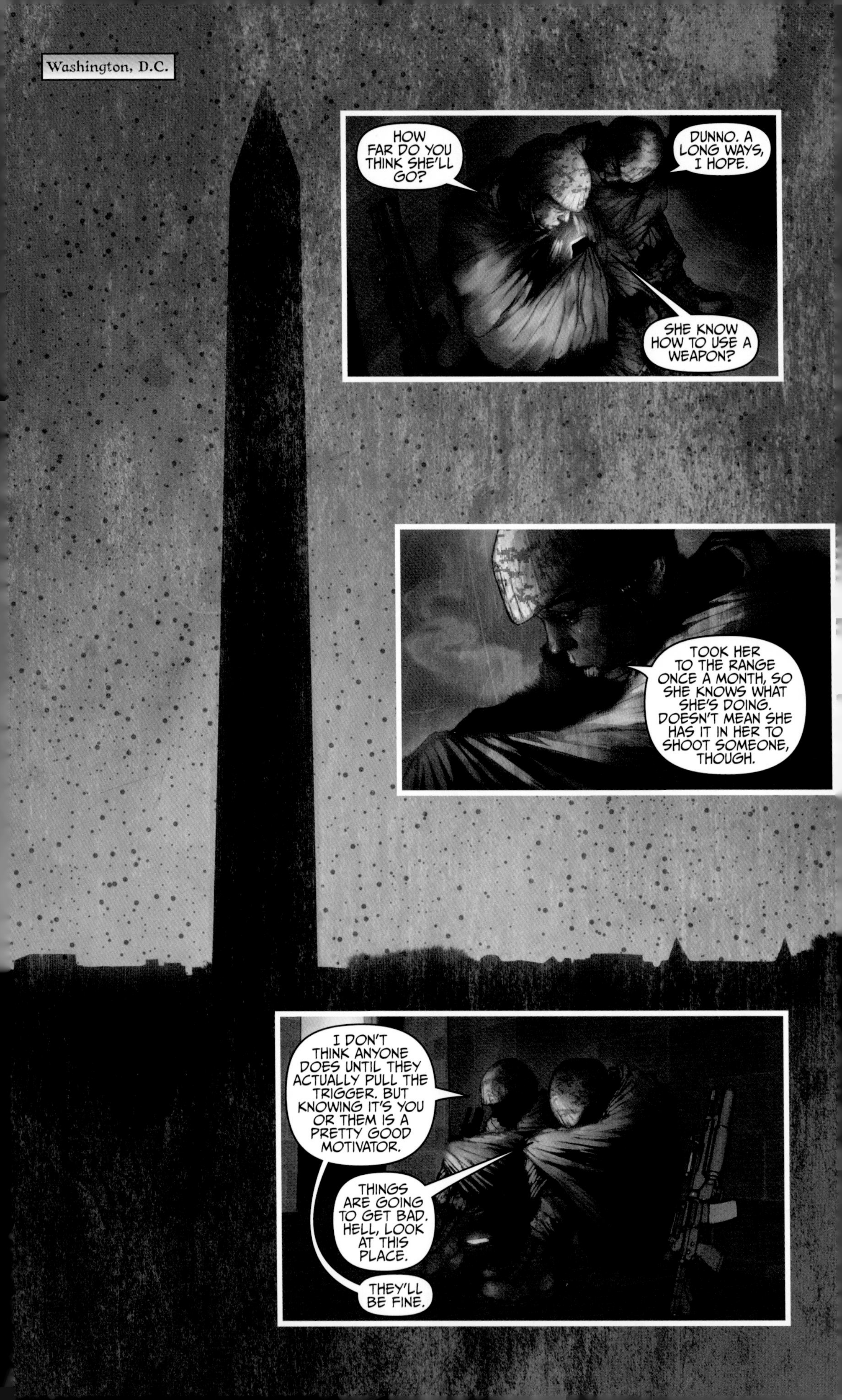

Washington, D.C.
HOW FAR DO YOU THINK SHE'LL GO?
DUNNO. A LONG WAYS, I HOPE.
SHE KNOW HOW TO USE A WEAPON?
TOOK HER TO THE RANGE ONCE A MONTH, SO SHE KNOWS WHAT SHE'S DOING. DOESN'T MEAN SHE HAS IT IN HER TO SHOOT SOMEONE, THOUGH.
I DON'T THINK ANYONE DOES UNTIL THEY ACTUALLY PULL THE TRIGGER. BUT KNOWING IT'S YOU OR THEM IS A PRETTY GOOD MOTIVATOR.
THINGS ARE GOING TO GET BAD. HELL, LOOK AT THIS PLACE.
THEY'LL BE FINE.

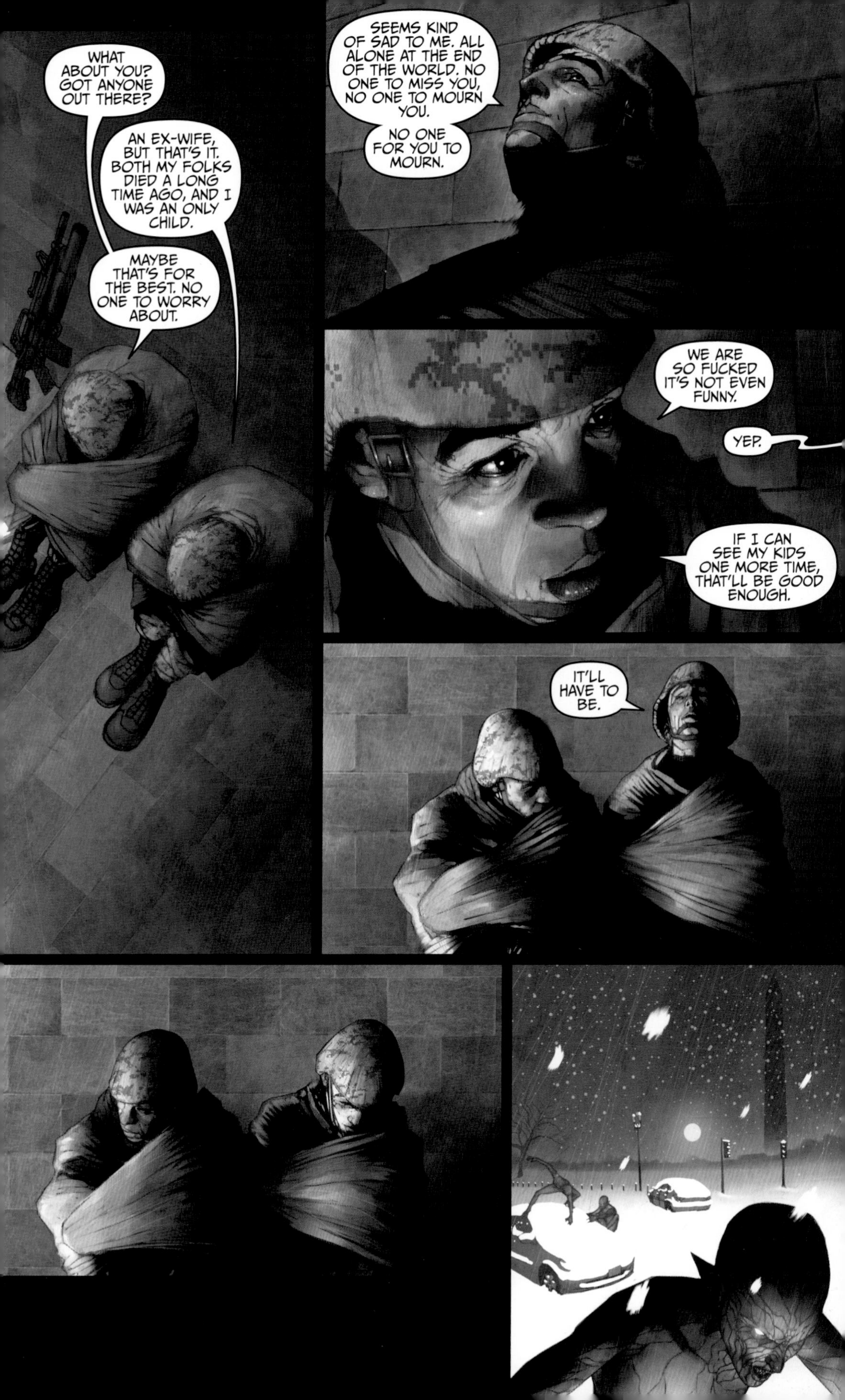
WHAT ABOUT YOU? GOT ANYONE OUT THERE?
AN EX-WIFE, BUT THAT'S IT. BOTH MY FOLKS DIED A LONG TIME AGO, AND I WAS AN ONLY CHILD.
MAYBE THAT'S FOR THE BEST. NO ONE TO WORRY ABOUT.
SEEMS KIND OF SAD TO ME. ALL ALONE AT THE END OF THE WORLD. NO ONE TO MISS YOU, NO ONE TO MOURN YOU.
NO ONE FOR YOU TO MOURN.
WE ARE SO FUCKED IT'S NOT EVEN FUNNY.
YEP.
IF I CAN SEE MY KIDS ONE MORE TIME, THAT'LL BE GOOD ENOUGH.
IT'LL HAVE TO BE.

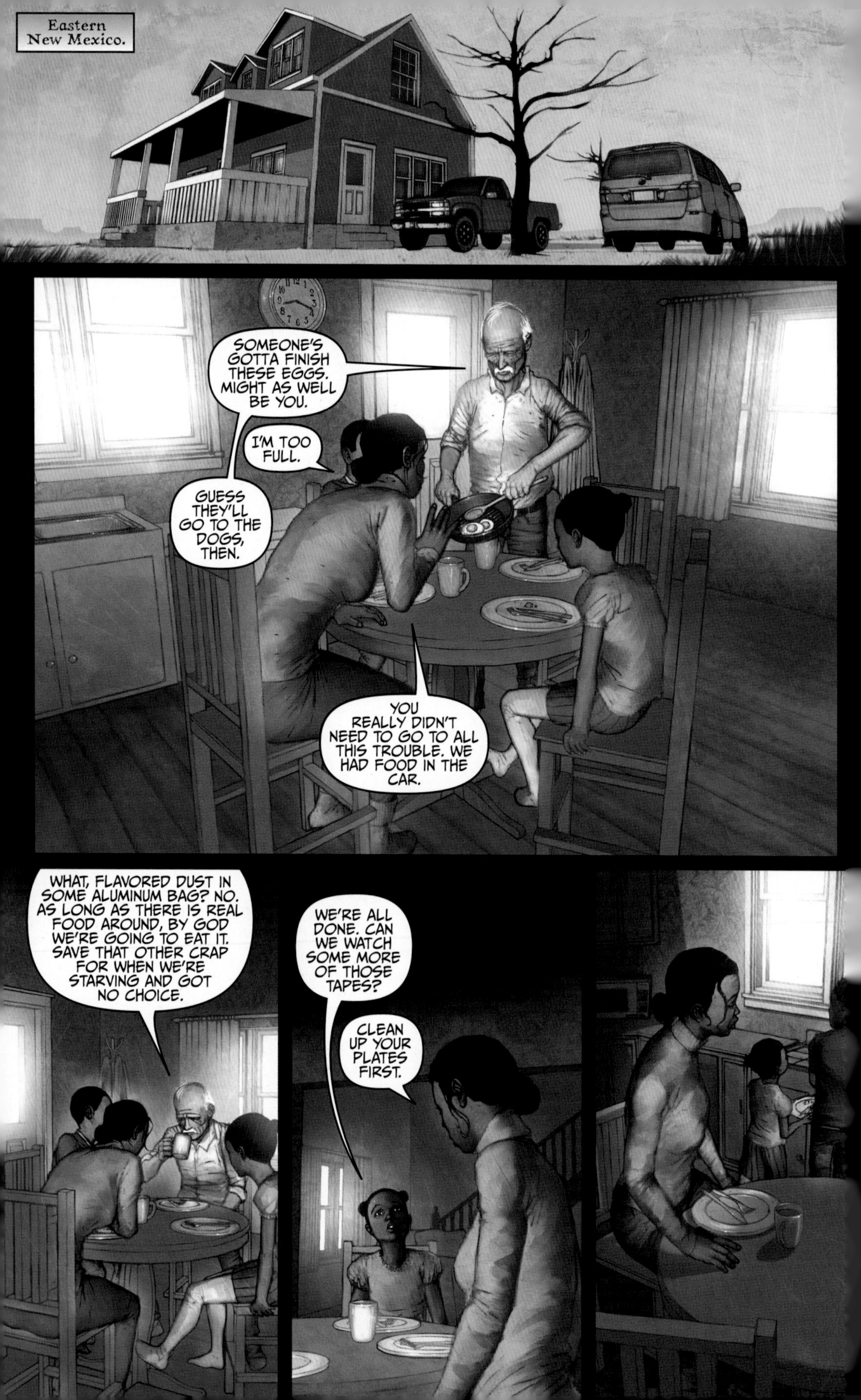
Eastern New Mexico.
SOMEONE'S GOTTA FINISH THESE EGGS. MIGHT AS WELL BE YOU.
I'M TOO FULL.
GUESS THEY'LL GO TO THE DOGS, THEN.
YOU REALLY DIDN'T NEED TO GO TO ALL THIS TROUBLE. WE HAD FOOD IN THE CAR.
WHAT, FLAVORED DUST IN SOME ALUMINUM BAG? NO. AS LONG AS THERE IS REAL FOOD AROUND, BY GOD WE'RE GOING TO EAT IT. SAVE THAT OTHER CRAP FOR WHEN WE'RE STARVING AND GOT NO CHOICE.
WE'RE ALL DONE. CAN WE WATCH SOME MORE OF THOSE TAPES?
CLEAN UP YOUR PLATES FIRST.

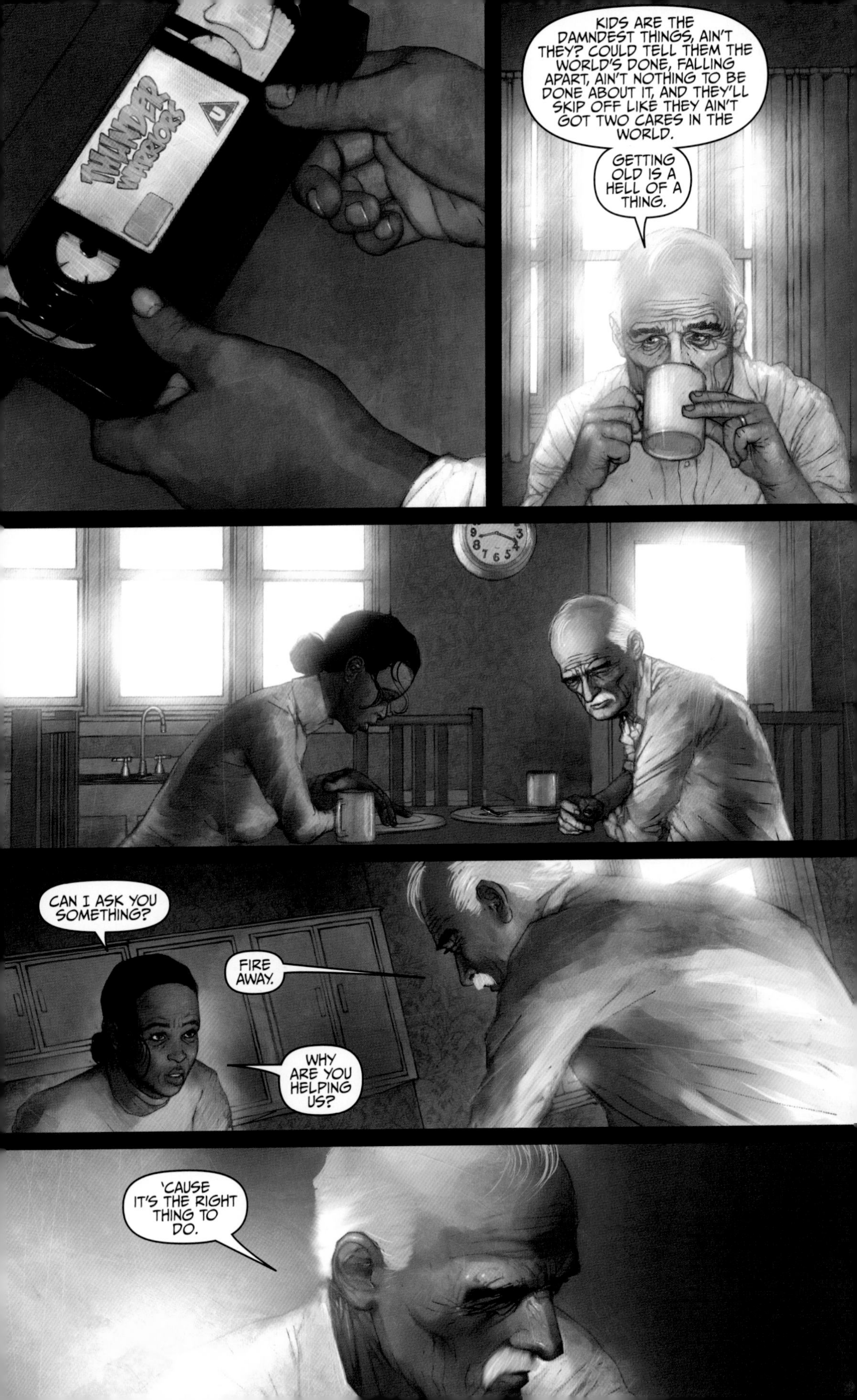
THUNDER WARRIORS
U
KIDS ARE THE DAMNDEST THINGS, AIN'T THEY? COULD TELL THEM THE WORLD'S DONE, FALLING APART, AIN'T NOTHING TO BE DONE ABOUT IT, AND THEY'LL SKIP OFF LIKE THEY AIN'T GOT TWO CARES IN THE WORLD.
GETTING OLD IS A HELL OF A THING.
CAN I ASK YOU SOMETHING?
FIRE AWAY.
WHY ARE YOU HELPING US?
'CAUSE IT'S THE RIGHT THING TO DO.

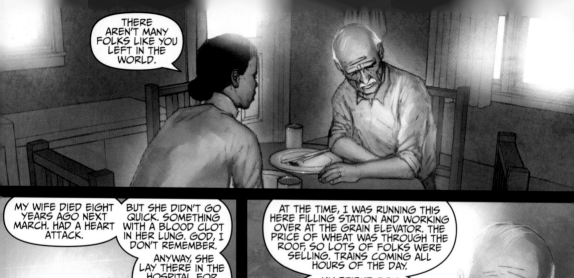

THERE AREN'T MANY FOLKS LIKE YOU LEFT IN THE WORLD.

MY WIFE DIED EIGHT YEARS AGO NEXT MARCH. HAD A HEART ATTACK.

BUT SHE DIDN'T GO QUICK. SOMETHING WITH A BLOOD CLOT IN HER LUNG. GOD, I DON'T REMEMBER.

ANYWAY, SHE LAY THERE IN THE HOSPITAL FOR ABOUT A WEEK BEFORE SHE PASSED ON.

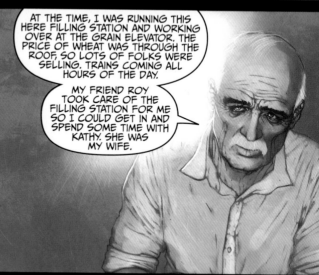

AT THE TIME, I WAS RUNNING THIS HERE FILLING STATION AND WORKING OVER AT THE GRAIN ELEVATOR. THE PRICE OF WHEAT WAS THROUGH THE ROOF, SO LOTS OF FOLKS WERE SELLING. TRAINS COMING ALL HOURS OF THE DAY.

MY FRIEND ROY TOOK CARE OF THE FILLING STATION FOR ME SO I COULD GET IN AND SPEND SOME TIME WITH KATHY. SHE WAS MY WIFE.

ANYWAY, AFTER KATHY'D BEEN IN THE HOSPITAL FOR A COUPLE THREE DAYS, THEY CALL OVER AT THE GRAIN ELEVATOR AND TELL ME SHE'S SLIPPING FAST. IF I WANT TO SEE HER, I'D BETTER GET OVER THERE.

SO I GO TO THE FOREMAN AND SAY, I'VE GOT TO GO SEE MY WIFE. SHE'S IN BAD SHAPE OVER AT THE HOSPITAL. HE LOOKS AT ME AND SAYS, THAT'S NOT MY PROBLEM AND YOU'RE NOT GOING NOWHERE UNTIL WE GET THIS ORDER FILLED.

I TURN AND WALK AWAY, AND HE YELLS AFTER ME, GOING ON ABOUT HOW HE WAS GOING TO FIRE ME IF I WALKED OUT THE DOOR. BUT WALK OUT I DID, AND I SPENT THE LAST FEW HOURS OF MY WIFE'S LIFE BY HER SIDE.

THE NEXT DAY, THAT SON OF A BITCH CALLED ME AND SAID I WAS FIRED. AND HE WAS DOCKING ME A DAY'S PAY BECAUSE THE ORDER WAS LATE.

JUST BECAUSE THAT'S THE WAY THE WORLD WANTS TO BE DOESN'T MEAN THAT'S THE WAY IT HAS TO BE.

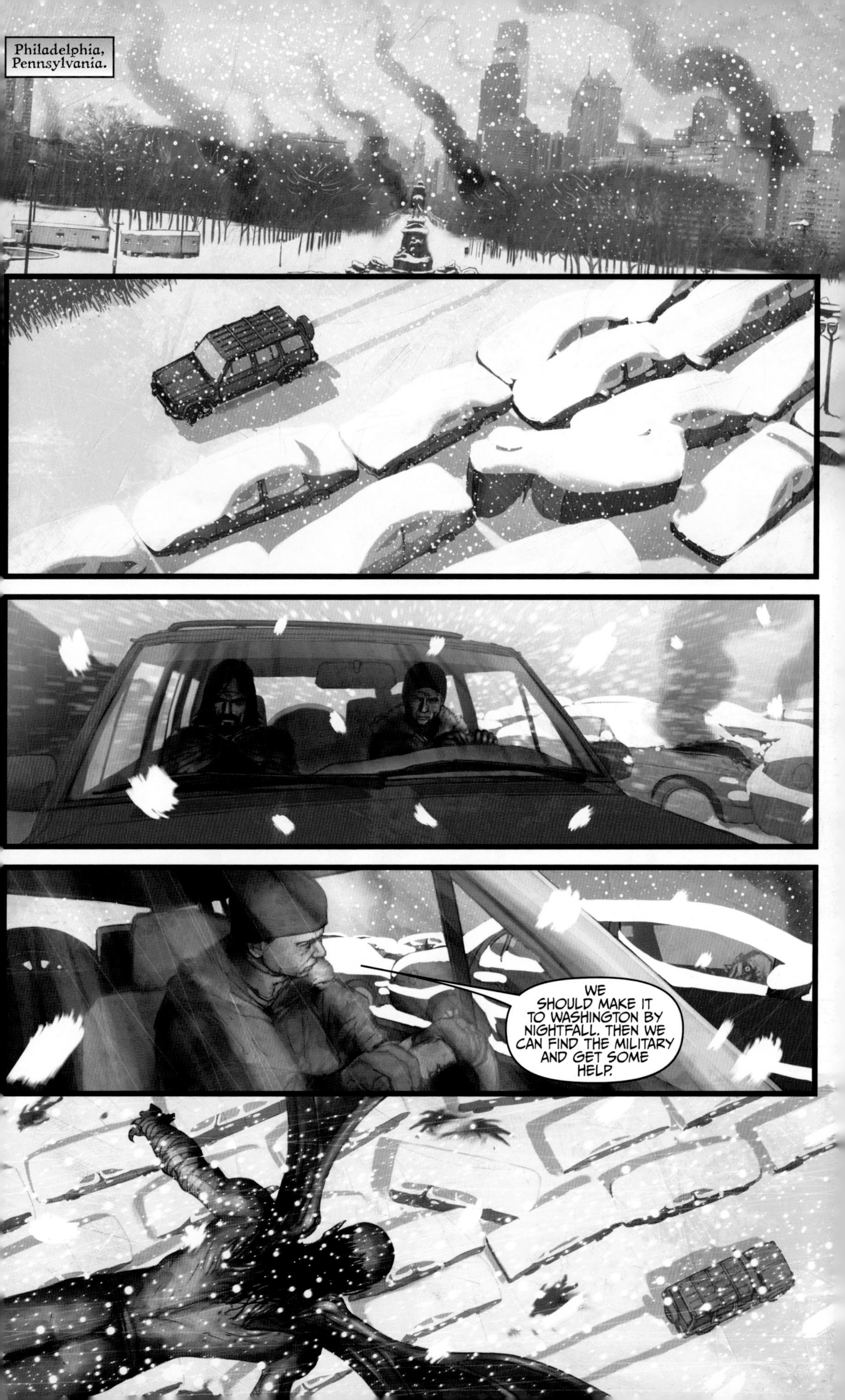
Philadelphia, Pennsylvania.
WE SHOULD MAKE IT TO WASHINGTON BY NIGHTFALL. THEN WE CAN FIND THE MILITARY AND GET SOME HELP.

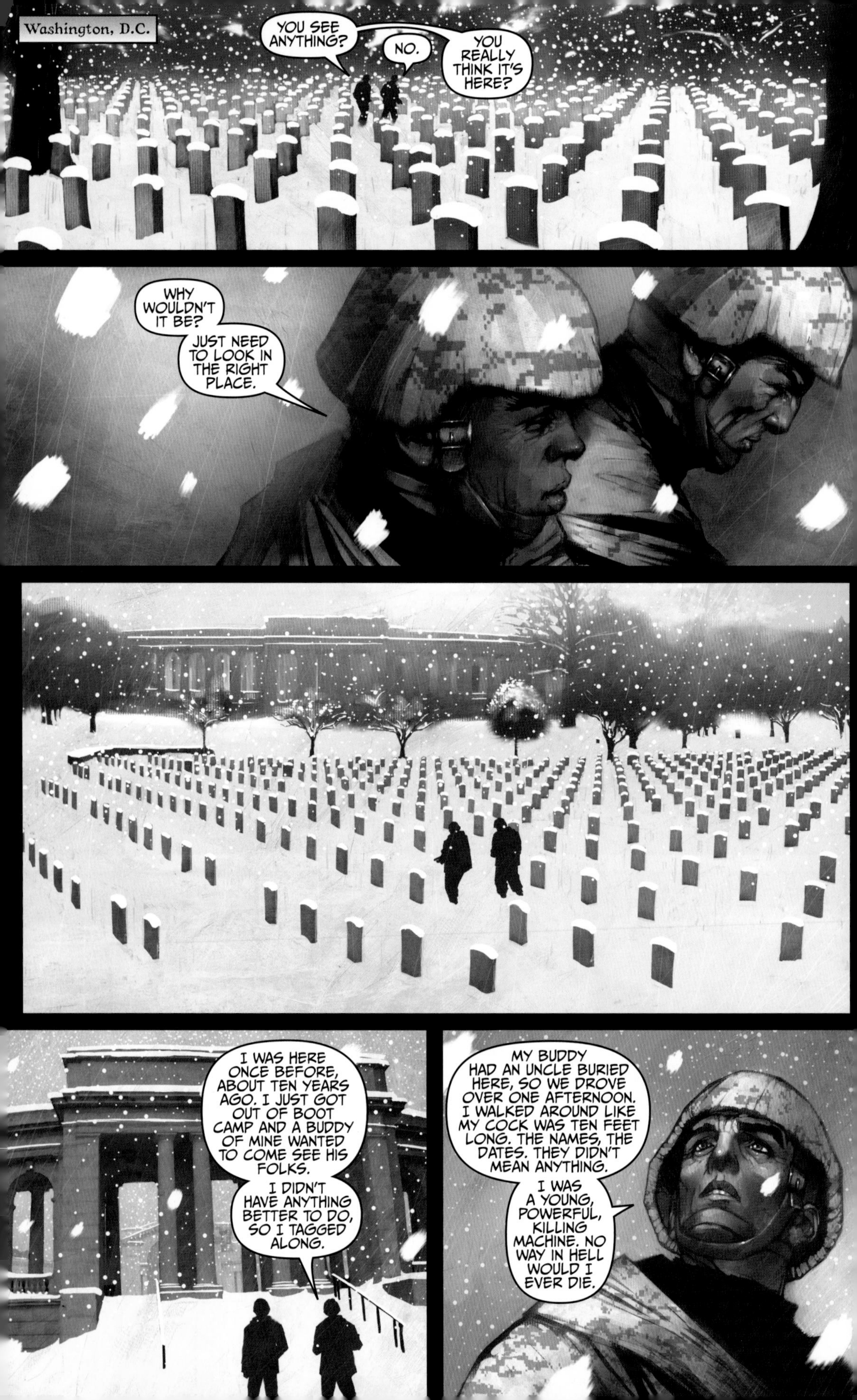
Washington, D.C.
YOU SEE ANYTHING?
NO.
YOU REALLY THINK IT'S HERE?
WHY WOULDN'T IT BE?
JUST NEED TO LOOK IN THE RIGHT PLACE.
I WAS HERE ONCE BEFORE, ABOUT TEN YEARS AGO. I JUST GOT OUT OF BOOT CAMP AND A BUDDY OF MINE WANTED TO COME SEE HIS FOLKS.
I DIDN'T HAVE ANYTHING BETTER TO DO, SO I TAGGED ALONG.
MY BUDDY HAD AN UNCLE BURIED HERE, SO WE DROVE OVER ONE AFTERNOON. I WALKED AROUND LIKE MY COCK WAS TEN FEET LONG. THE NAMES, THE DATES. THEY DIDN'T MEAN ANYTHING.
I WAS A YOUNG, POWERFUL, KILLING MACHINE. NO WAY IN HELL WOULD I EVER DIE.

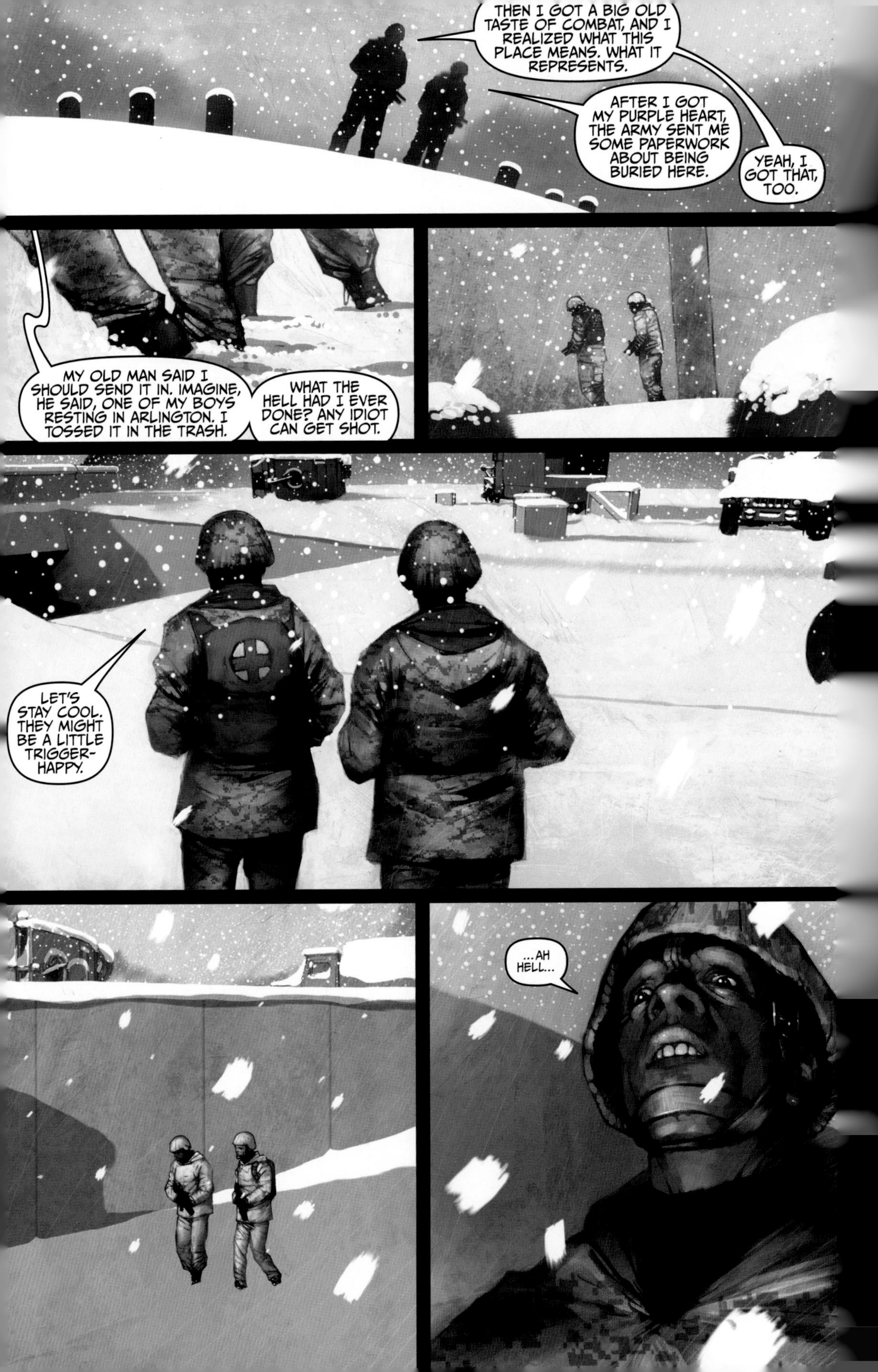
THEN I GOT A BIG OLD TASTE OF COMBAT, AND I REALIZED WHAT THIS PLACE MEANS. WHAT IT REPRESENTS.
AFTER I GOT MY PURPLE HEART, THE ARMY SENT ME SOME PAPERWORK ABOUT BEING BURIED HERE.
YEAH, I GOT THAT, TOO.
MY OLD MAN SAID I SHOULD SEND IT IN. IMAGINE, HE SAID, ONE OF MY BOYS RESTING IN ARLINGTON. I TOSSED IT IN THE TRASH.
WHAT THE HELL HAD I EVER DONE? ANY IDIOT CAN GET SHOT.
LET'S STAY COOL. THEY MIGHT BE A LITTLE TRIGGER-HAPPY.
...AH HELL...

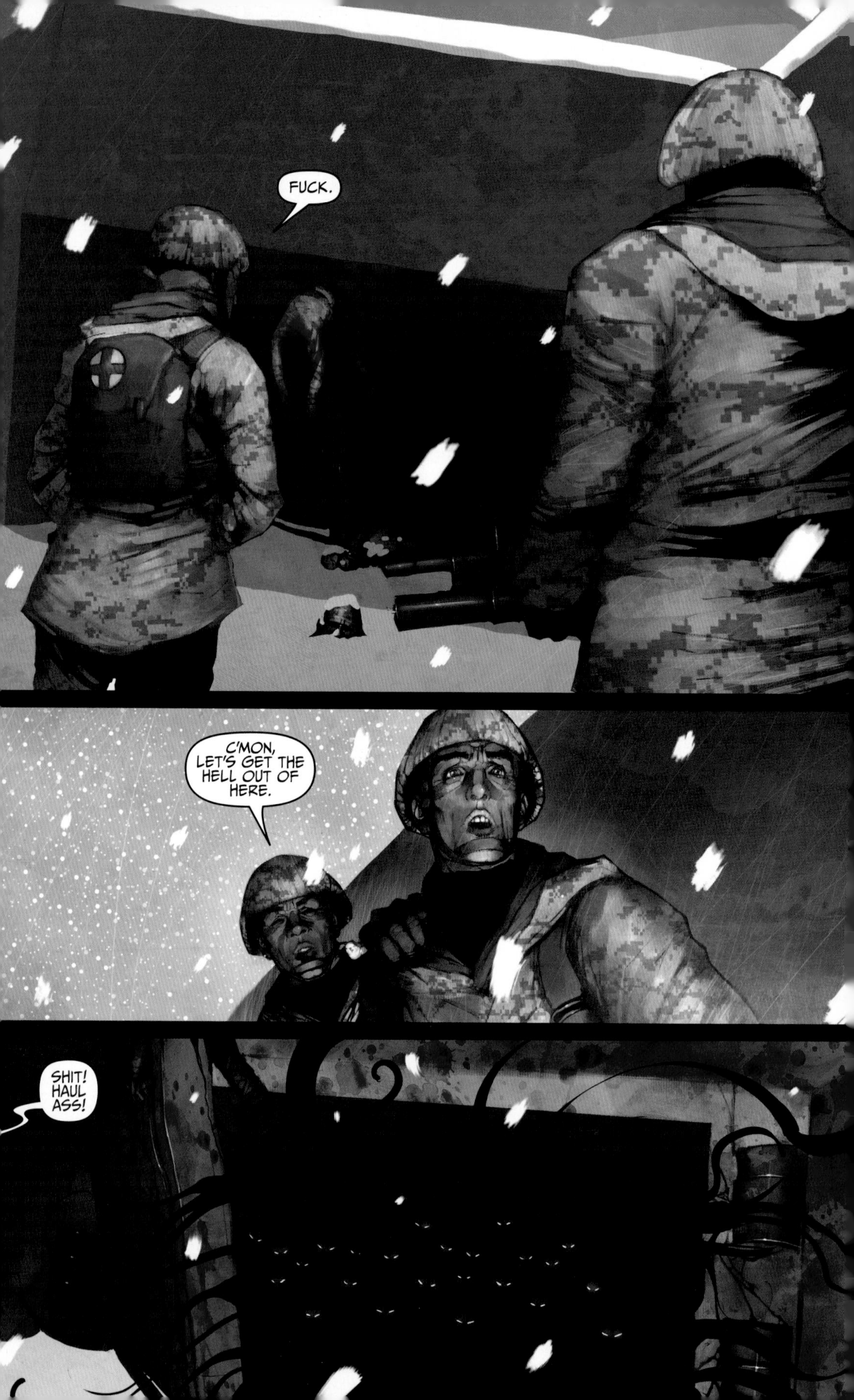
FUCK.
C'MON, LET'S GET THE HELL OUT OF HERE.
SHIT! HAUL ASS!

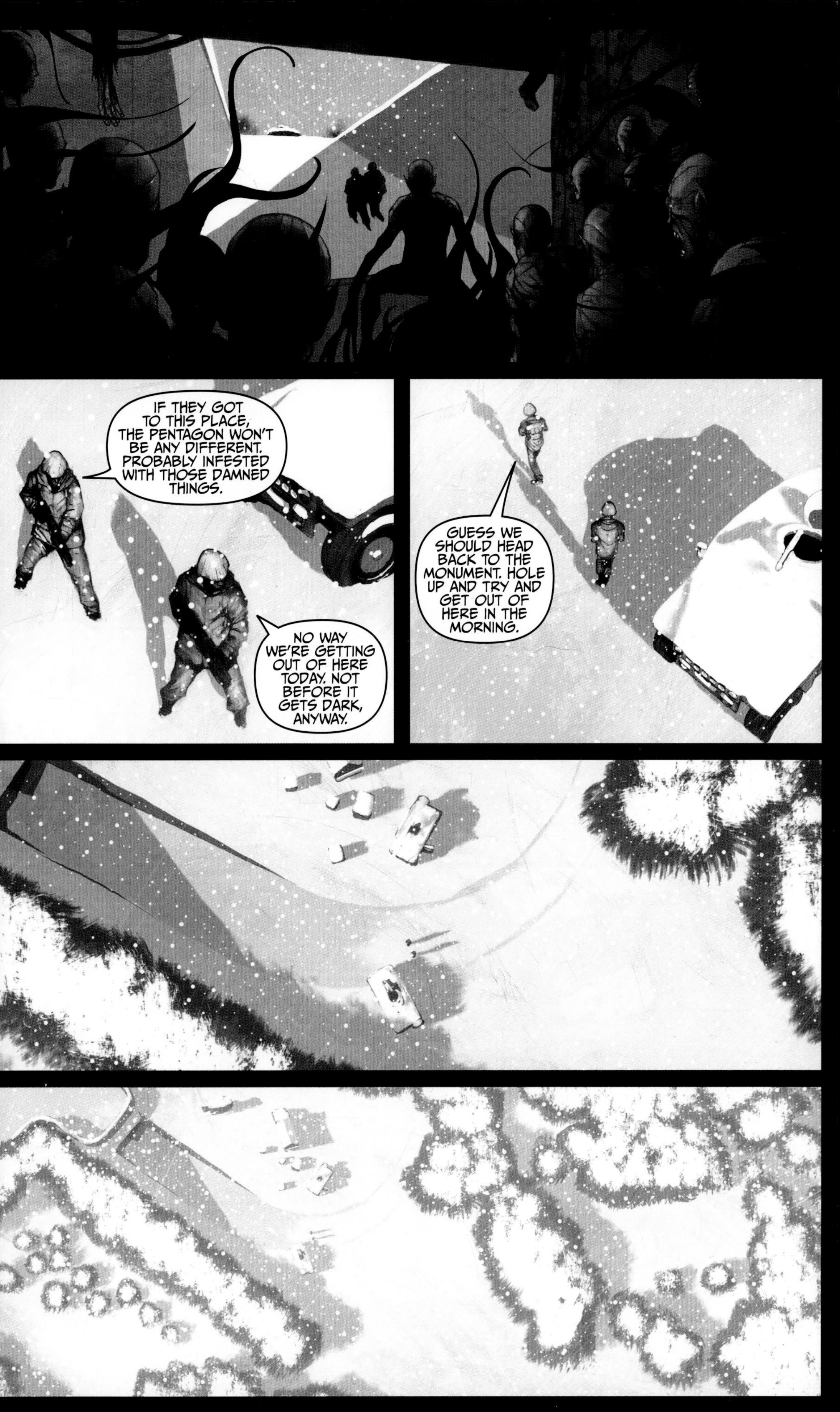
IF THEY GOT TO THIS PLACE, THE PENTAGON WON'T BE ANY DIFFERENT. PROBABLY INFESTED WITH THOSE DAMNED THINGS.
NO WAY WE'RE GETTING OUT OF HERE TODAY. NOT BEFORE IT GETS DARK, ANYWAY.
GUESS WE SHOULD HEAD BACK TO THE MONUMENT. HOLE UP AND TRY AND GET OUT OF HERE IN THE MORNING.

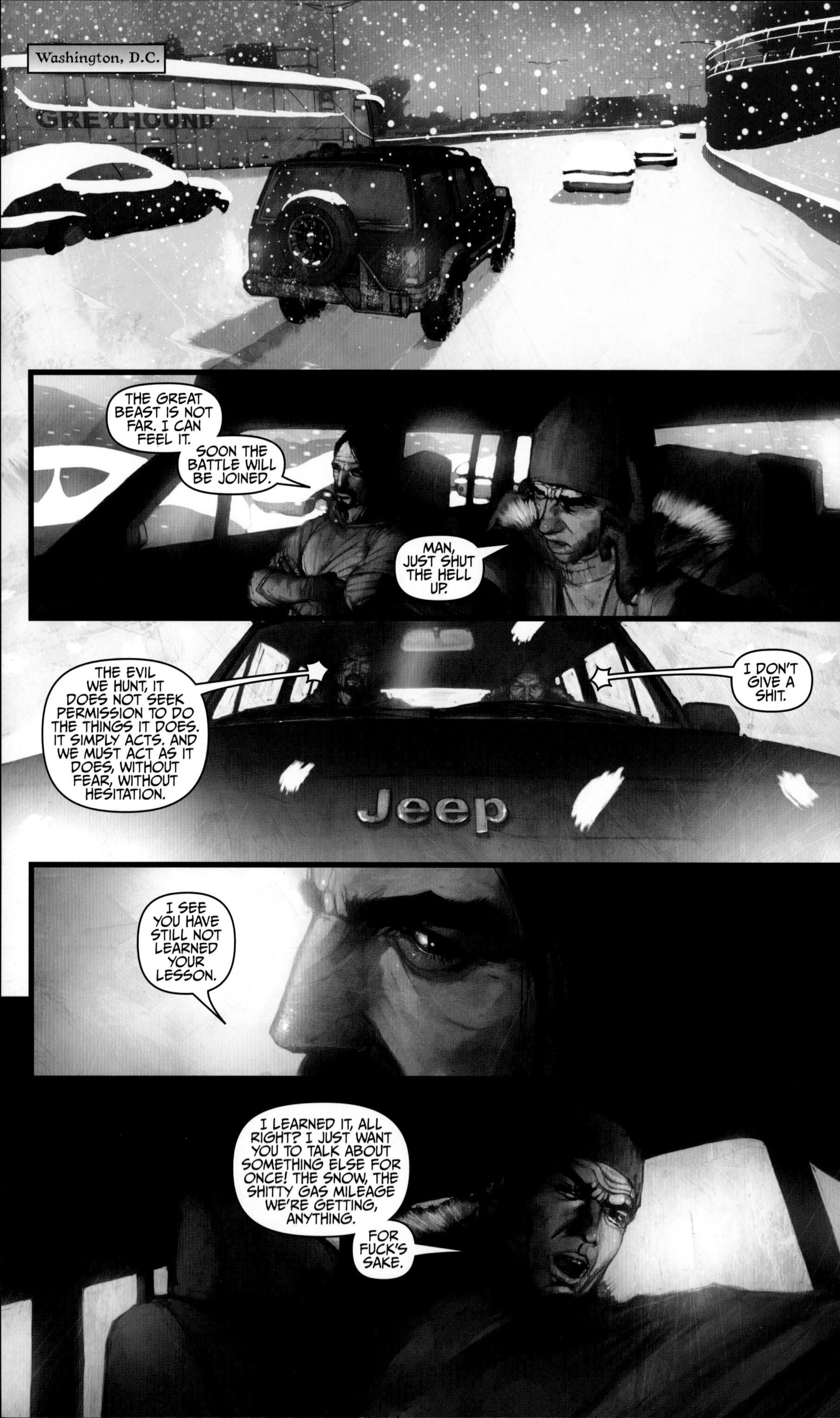
Washington, D.C.
GREYHOUND
THE GREAT BEAST IS NOT FAR. I CAN FEEL IT.
SOON THE BATTLE WILL BE JOINED.
MAN, JUST SHUT THE HELL UP.
THE EVIL WE HUNT, IT DOES NOT SEEK PERMISSION TO DO THE THINGS IT DOES. IT SIMPLY ACTS. AND WE MUST ACT AS IT DOES, WITHOUT FEAR, WITHOUT HESITATION.
I DON'T GIVE A SHIT.
Jeep
I SEE YOU HAVE STILL NOT LEARNED YOUR LESSON.
I LEARNED IT, ALL RIGHT? I JUST WANT YOU TO TALK ABOUT SOMETHING ELSE FOR ONCE! THE SNOW, THE SHITTY GAS MILEAGE WE'RE GETTING, ANYTHING.
FOR FUCK'S SAKE.

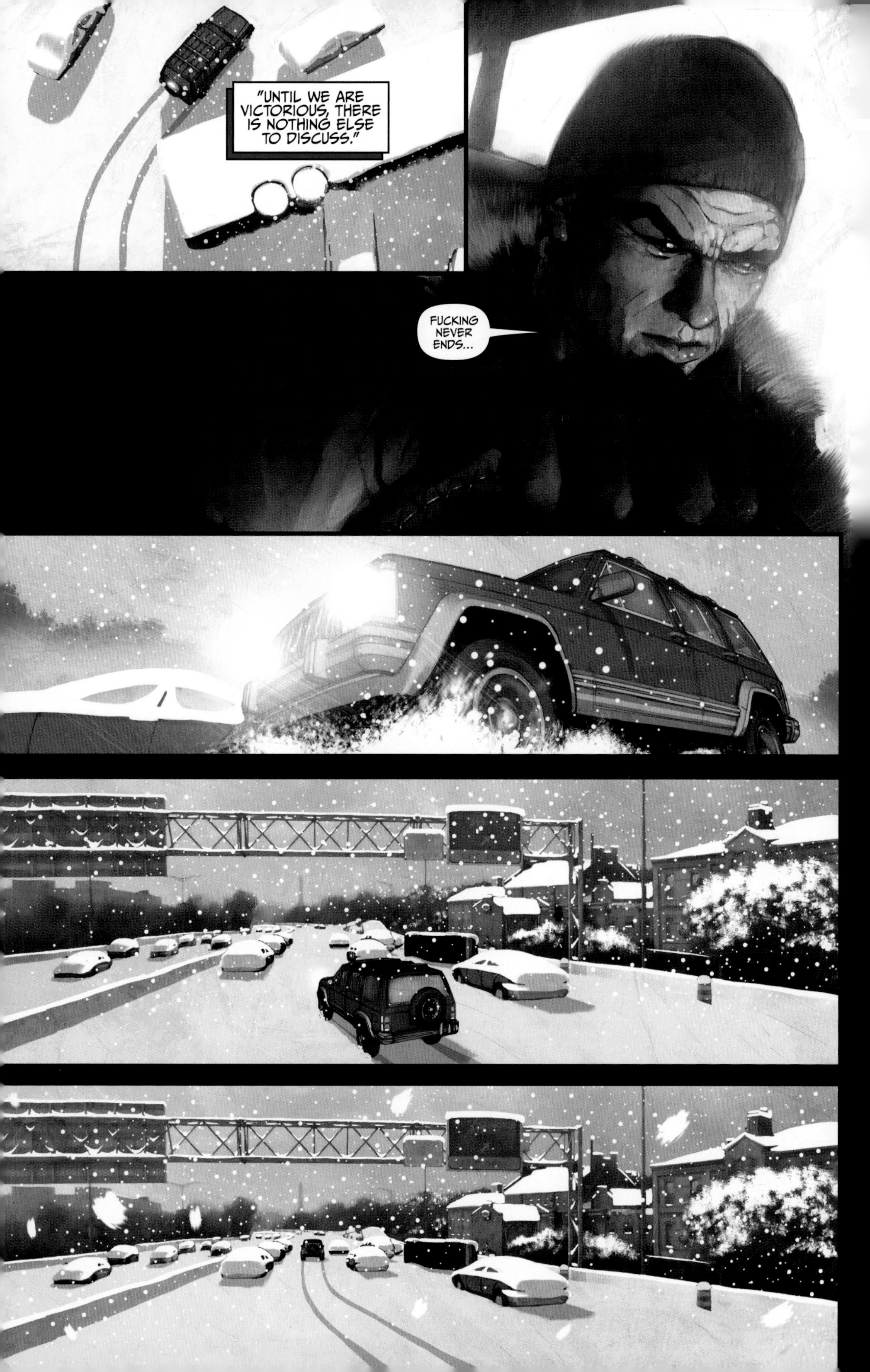
"UNTIL WE ARE VICTORIOUS, THERE IS NOTHING ELSE TO DISCUSS."
FUCKING NEVER ENDS...

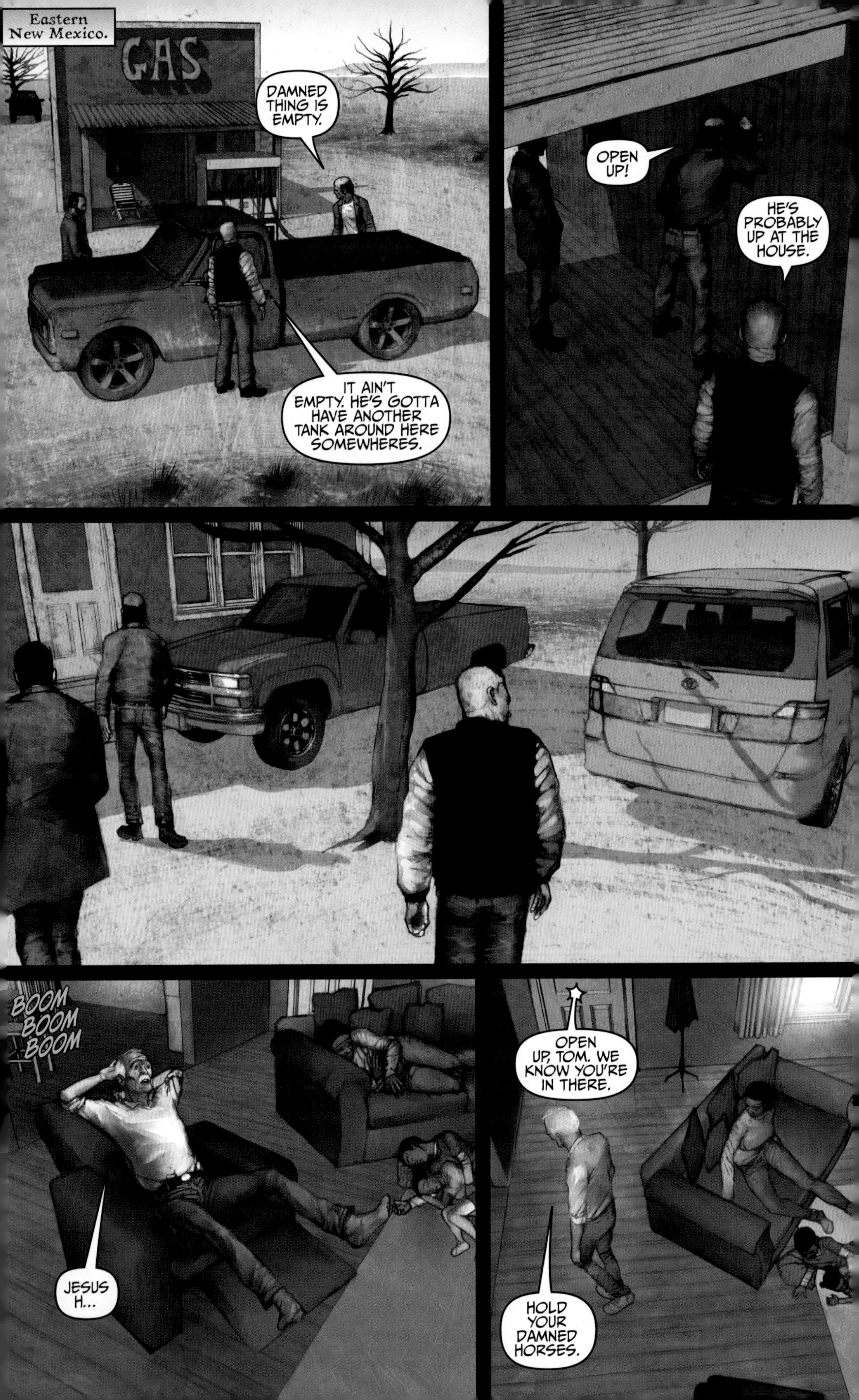
Eastern New Mexico.
GAS
DAMNED THING IS EMPTY.
IT AIN'T EMPTY. HE'S GOTTA HAVE ANOTHER TANK AROUND HERE SOMEWHERES.
OPEN UP!
HE'S PROBABLY UP AT THE HOUSE.
BOOM BOOM BOOM
JESUS H...
OPEN UP, TOM. WE KNOW YOU'RE IN THERE.
HOLD YOUR DAMNED HORSES.

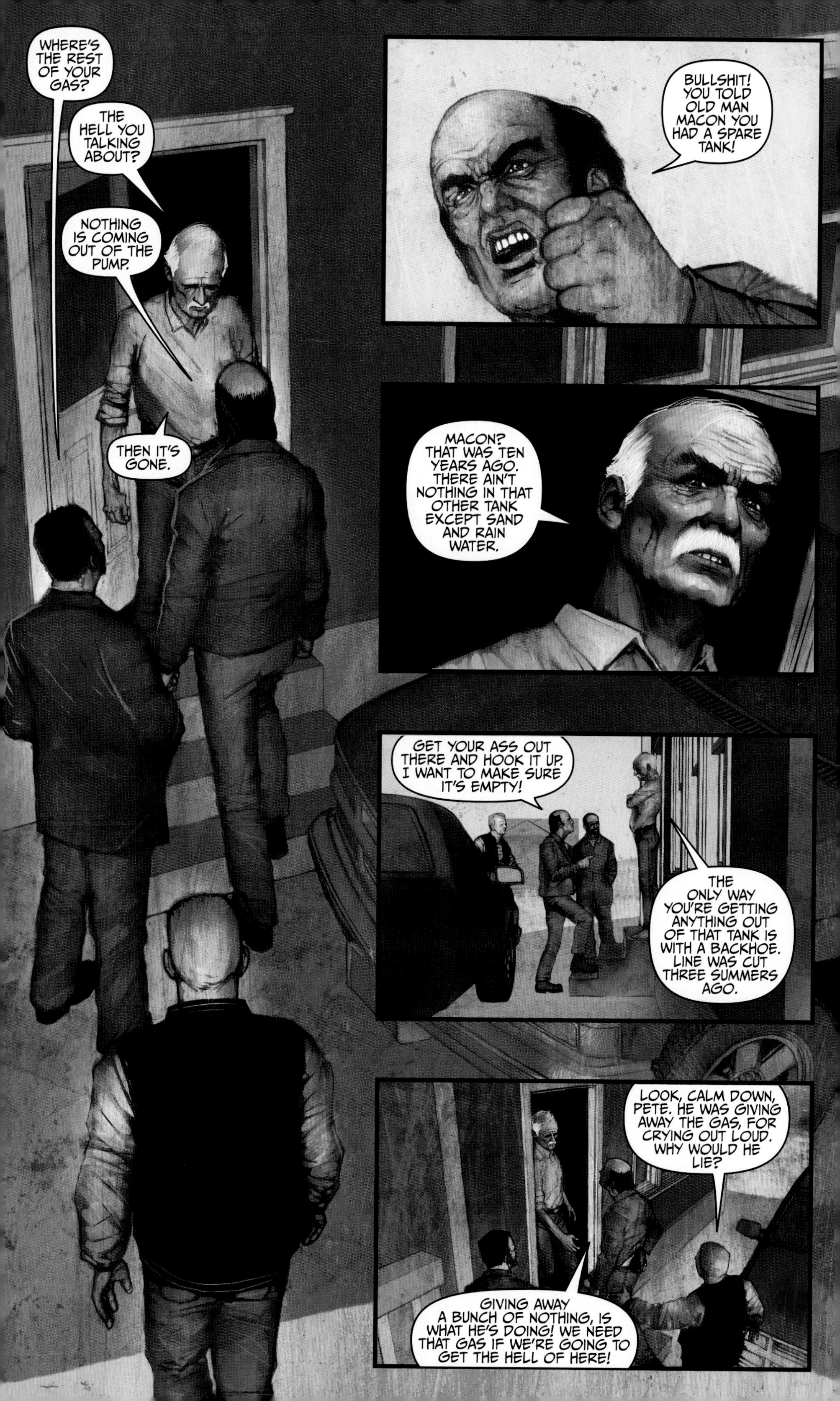
WHERE'S THE REST OF YOUR GAS?
THE HELL YOU TALKING ABOUT?
NOTHING IS COMING OUT OF THE PUMP.
THEN IT'S GONE.
BULLSHIT! YOU TOLD OLD MAN MACON YOU HAD A SPARE TANK!
MACON? THAT WAS TEN YEARS AGO. THERE AIN'T NOTHING IN THAT OTHER TANK EXCEPT SAND AND RAIN WATER.
GET YOUR ASS OUT THERE AND HOOK IT UP. I WANT TO MAKE SURE IT'S EMPTY!
THE ONLY WAY YOU'RE GETTING ANYTHING OUT OF THAT TANK IS WITH A BACKHOE. LINE WAS CUT THREE SUMMERS AGO.
LOOK, CALM DOWN, PETE. HE WAS GIVING AWAY THE GAS, FOR CRYING OUT LOUD. WHY WOULD HE LIE?
GIVING AWAY A BUNCH OF NOTHING, IS WHAT HE'S DOING! WE NEED THAT GAS IF WE'RE GOING TO GET THE HELL OF HERE!

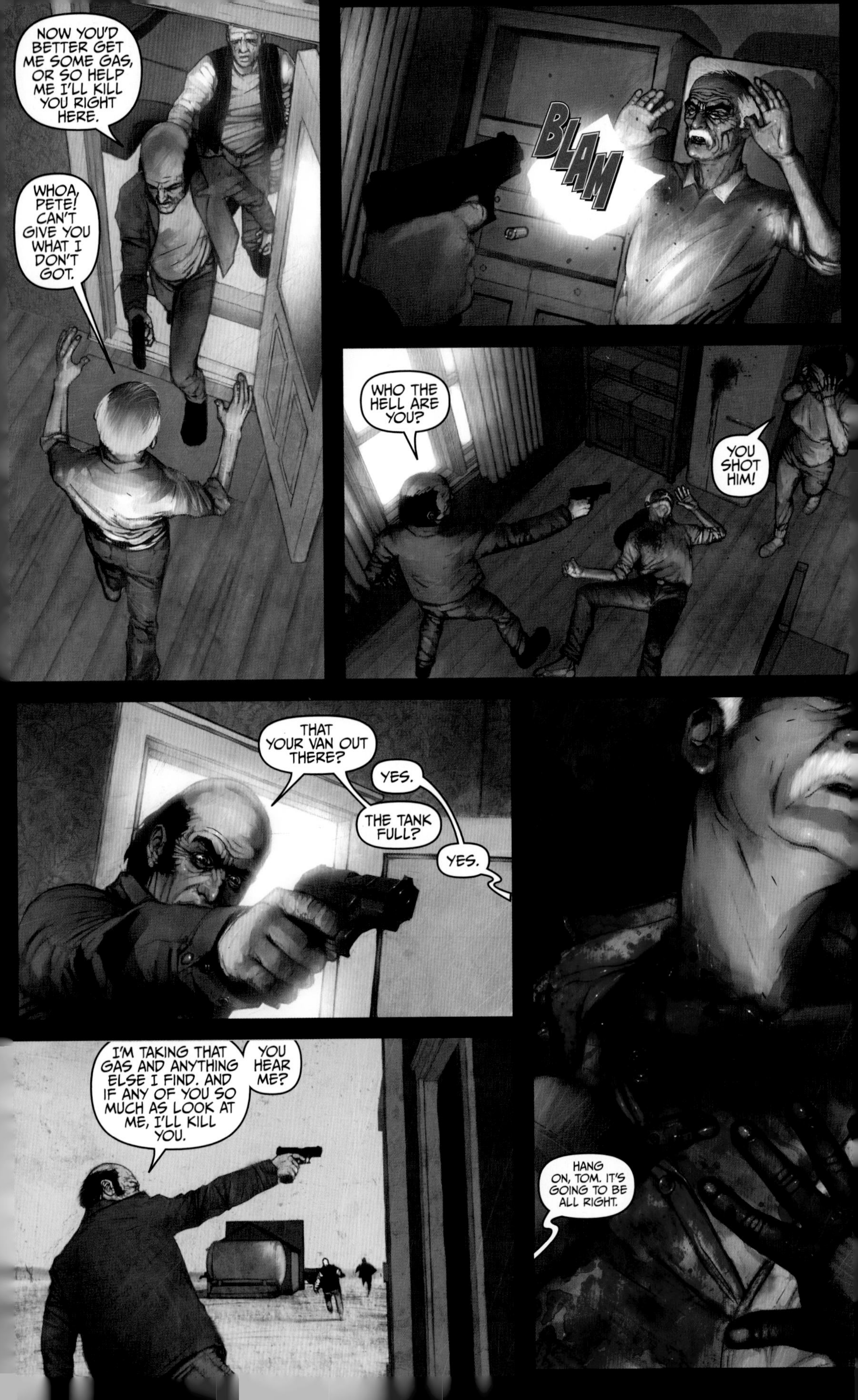
NOW YOU'D BETTER GET ME SOME GAS, OR SO HELP ME I'LL KILL YOU RIGHT HERE.
WHOA, PETE! CAN'T GIVE YOU WHAT I DON'T GOT.
BLAM
WHO THE HELL ARE YOU?
YOU SHOT HIM!
THAT YOUR VAN OUT THERE?
YES.
THE TANK FULL?
YES.
I'M TAKING THAT GAS AND ANYTHING ELSE I FIND. AND IF ANY OF YOU SO MUCH AS LOOK AT ME, I'LL KILL YOU.
YOU HEAR ME?
HANG ON, TOM. IT'S GOING TO BE ALL RIGHT.

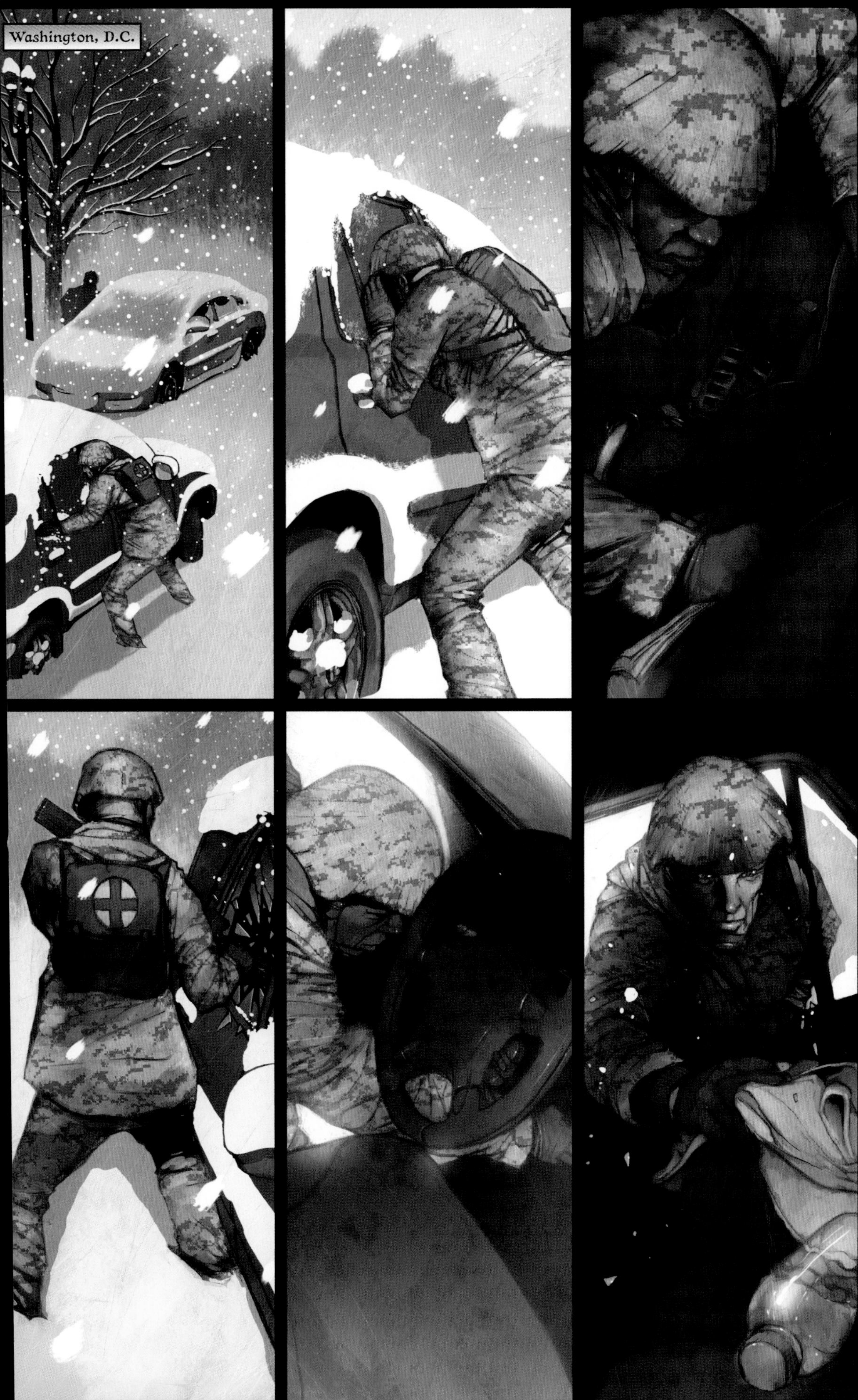
Washington, D.C.

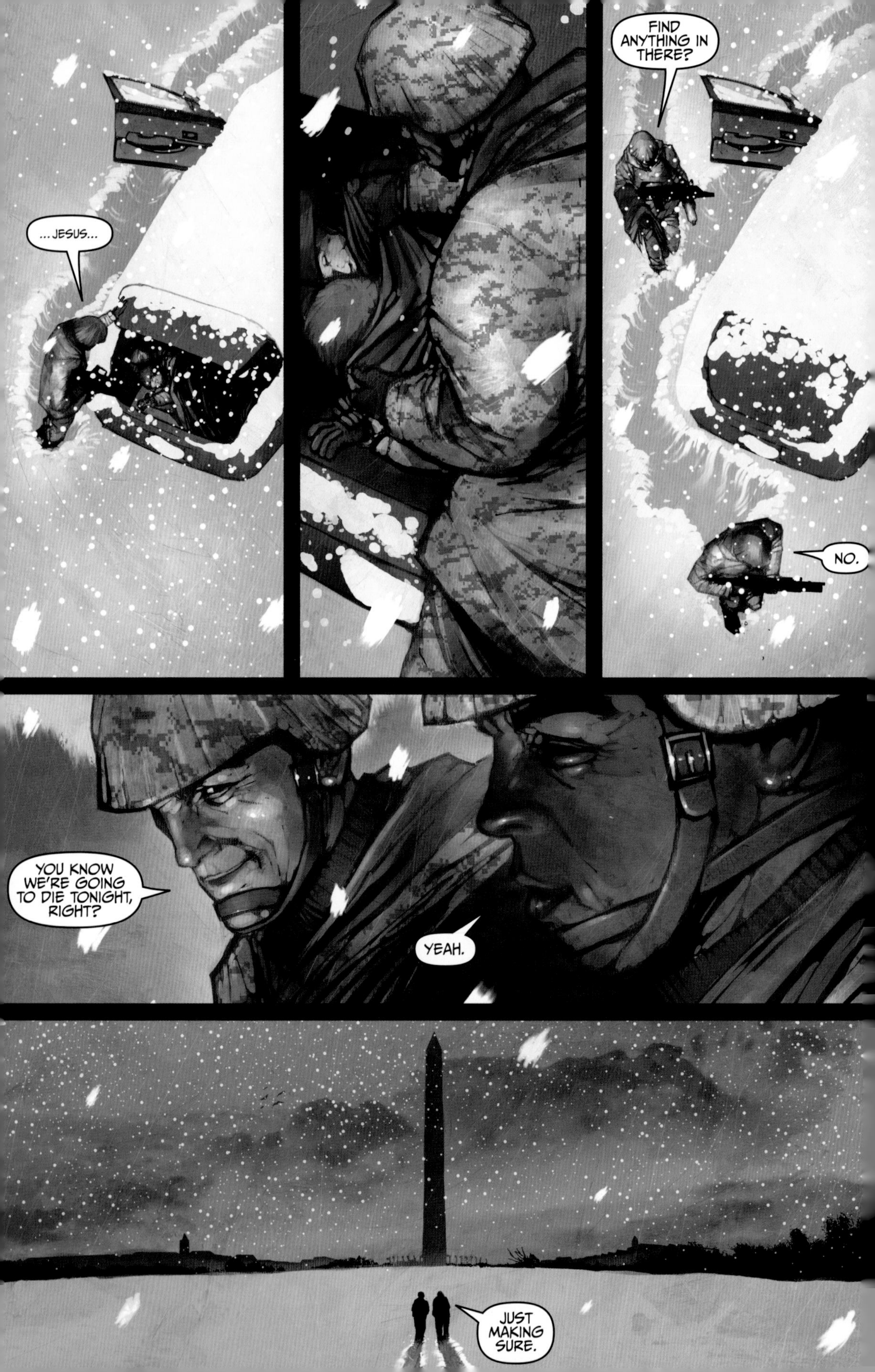
...JESUS...
FIND ANYTHING IN THERE?
NO.
YOU KNOW WE'RE GOING TO DIE TONIGHT, RIGHT?
YEAH.
JUST MAKING SURE.

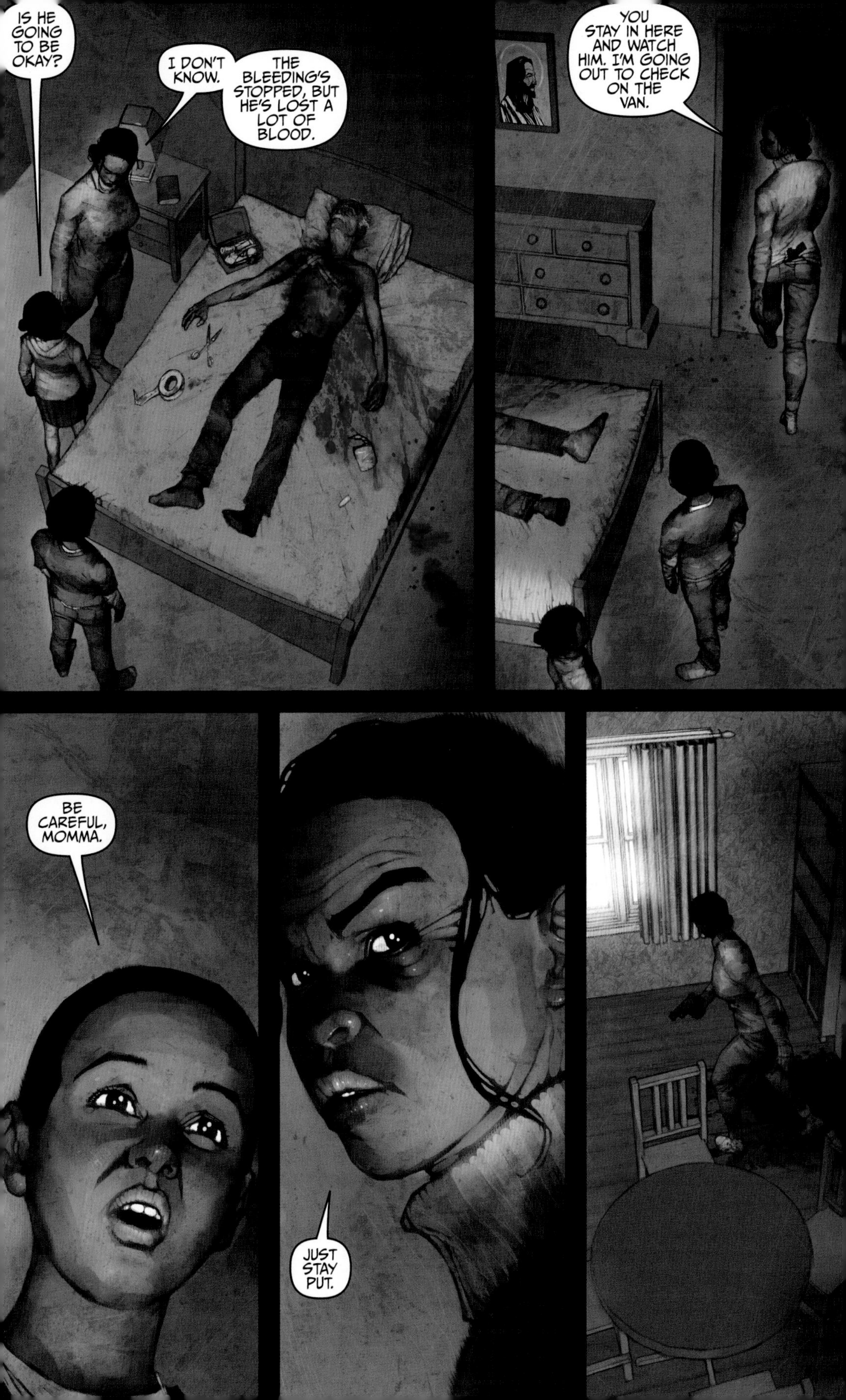
IS HE GOING TO BE OKAY?
I DON'T KNOW.
THE BLEEDING'S STOPPED, BUT HE'S LOST A LOT OF BLOOD.
YOU STAY IN HERE AND WATCH HIM. I'M GOING OUT TO CHECK ON THE VAN.
BE CAREFUL, MOMMA.
JUST STAY PUT.

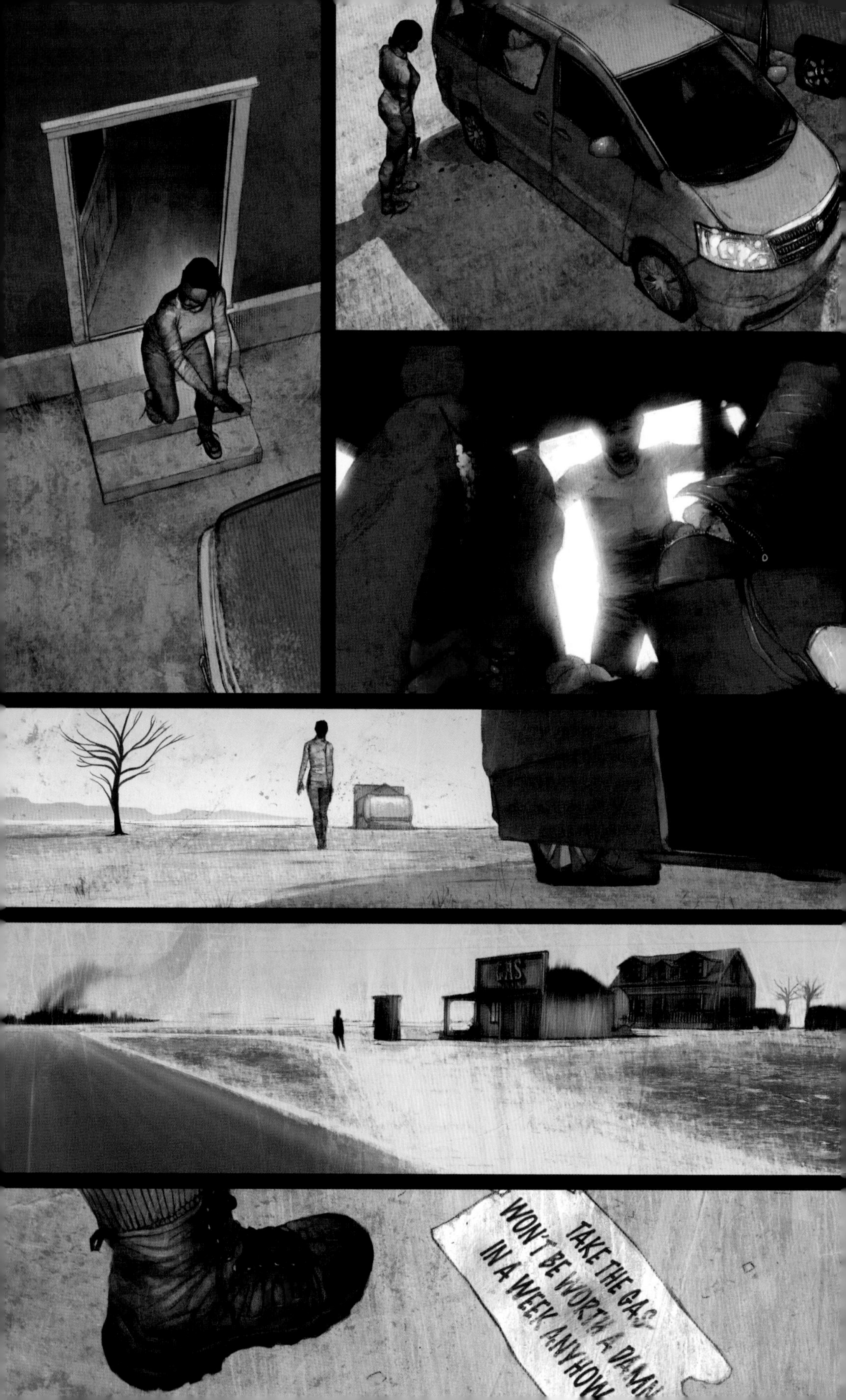
GAS
TAKE THE GAS
WON'T BE WORTH A DAMN
IN A WEEK ANYHOW

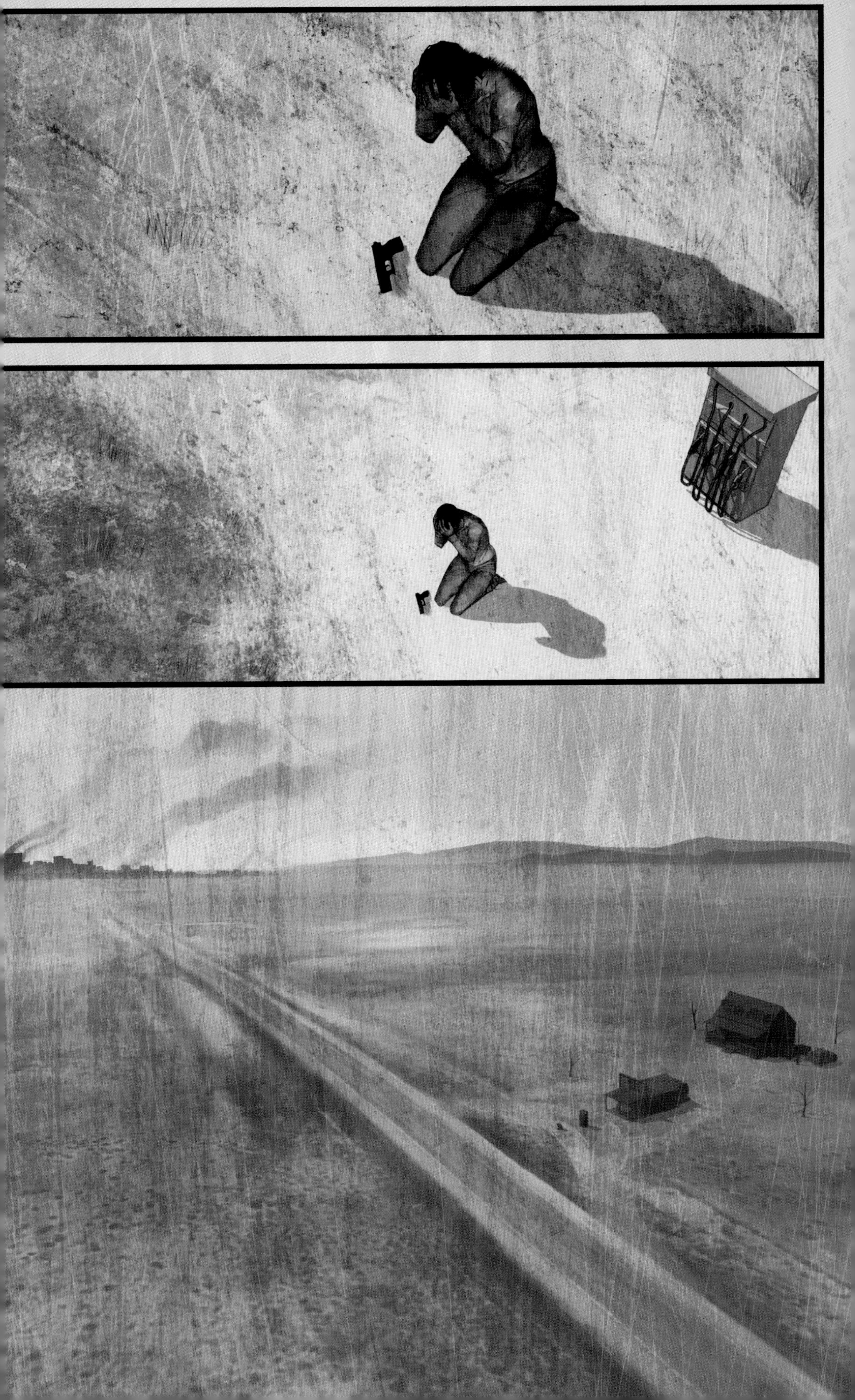

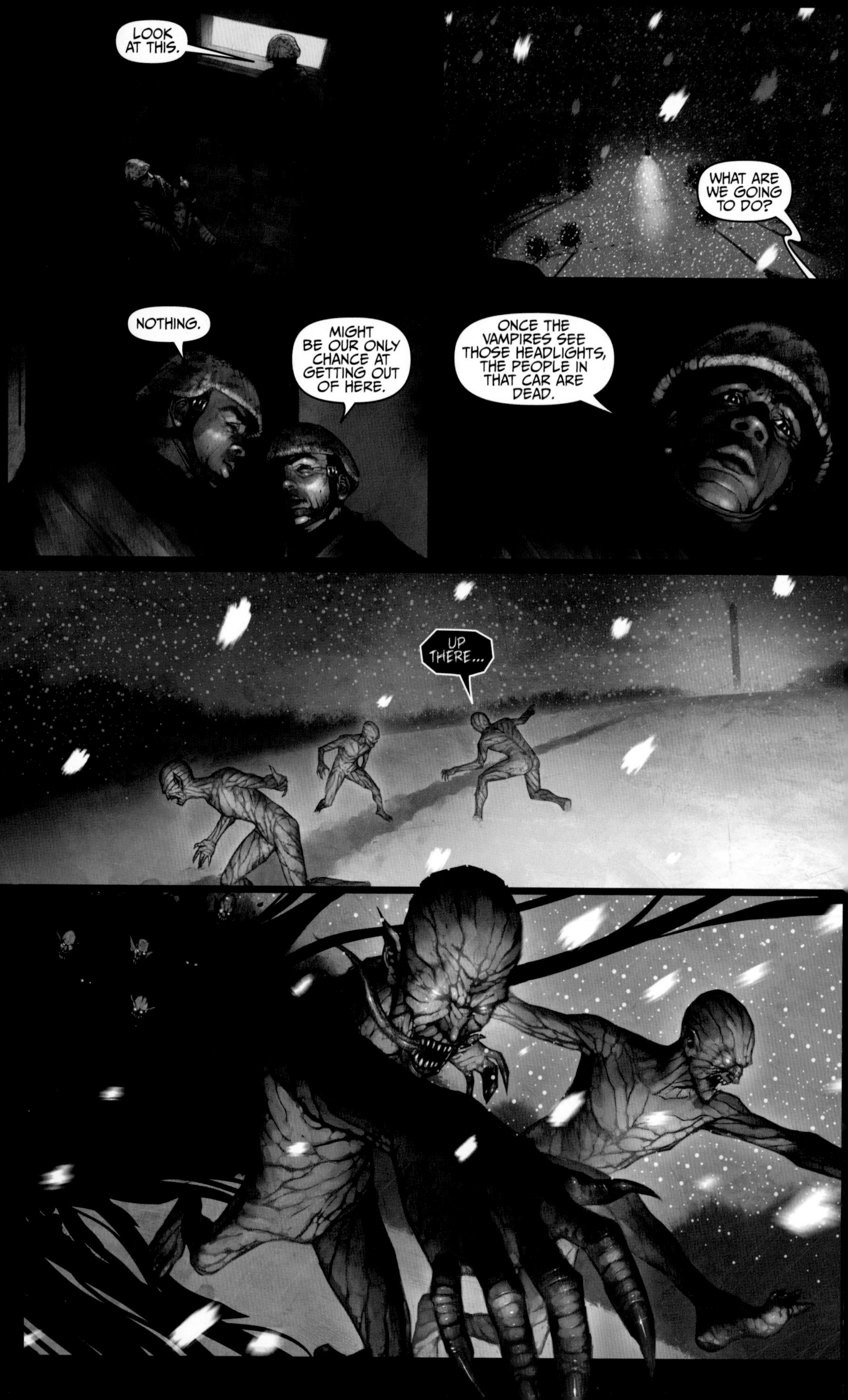
LOOK AT THIS.
WHAT ARE WE GOING TO DO?
NOTHING.
MIGHT BE OUR ONLY CHANCE AT GETTING OUT OF HERE.
ONCE THE VAMPIRES SEE THOSE HEADLIGHTS, THE PEOPLE IN THAT CAR ARE DEAD.
UP THERE...

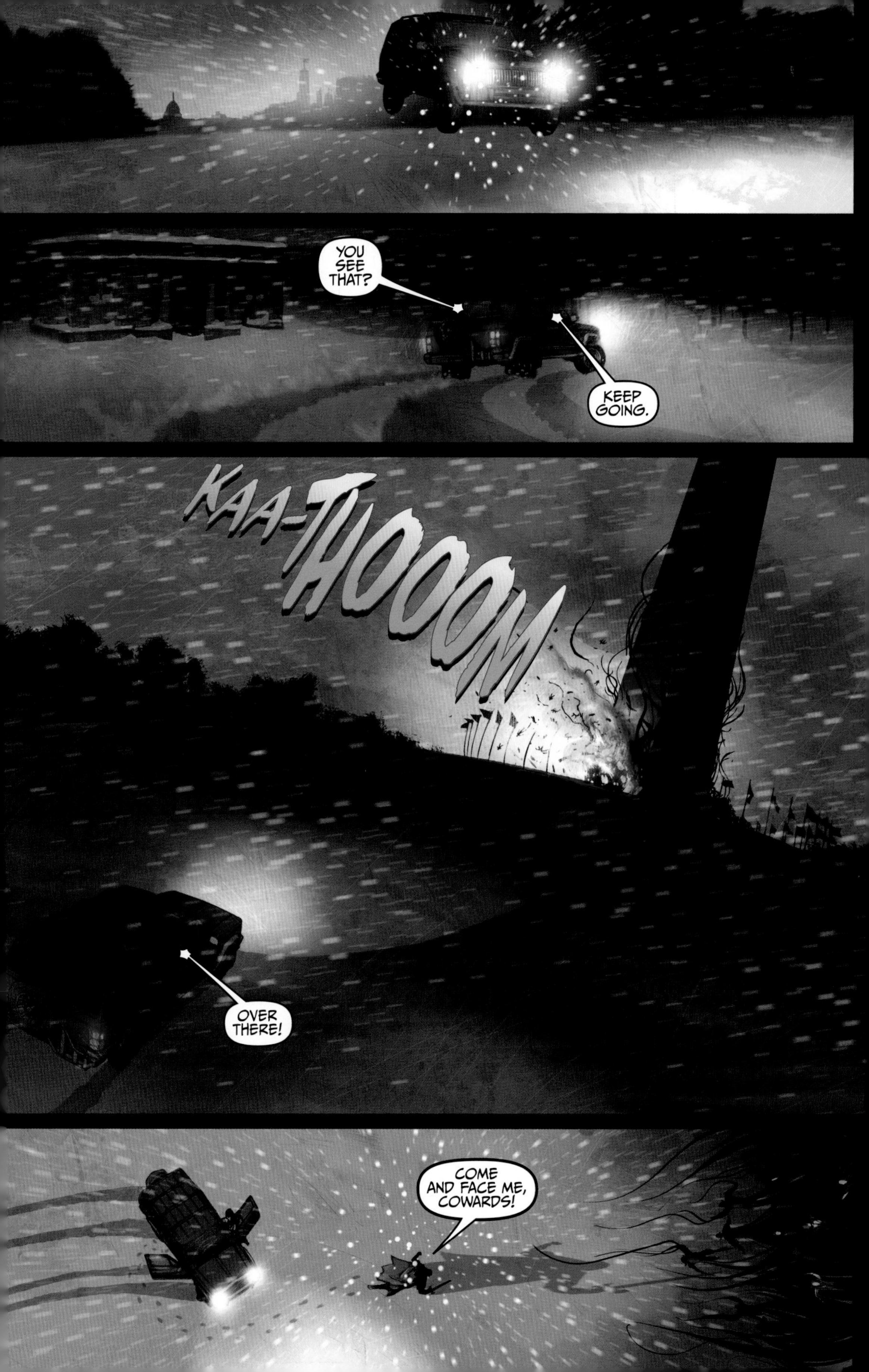
YOU SEE THAT?
KEEP GOING.
KAA-THOOOM
OVER THERE!
COME AND FACE ME, COWARDS!

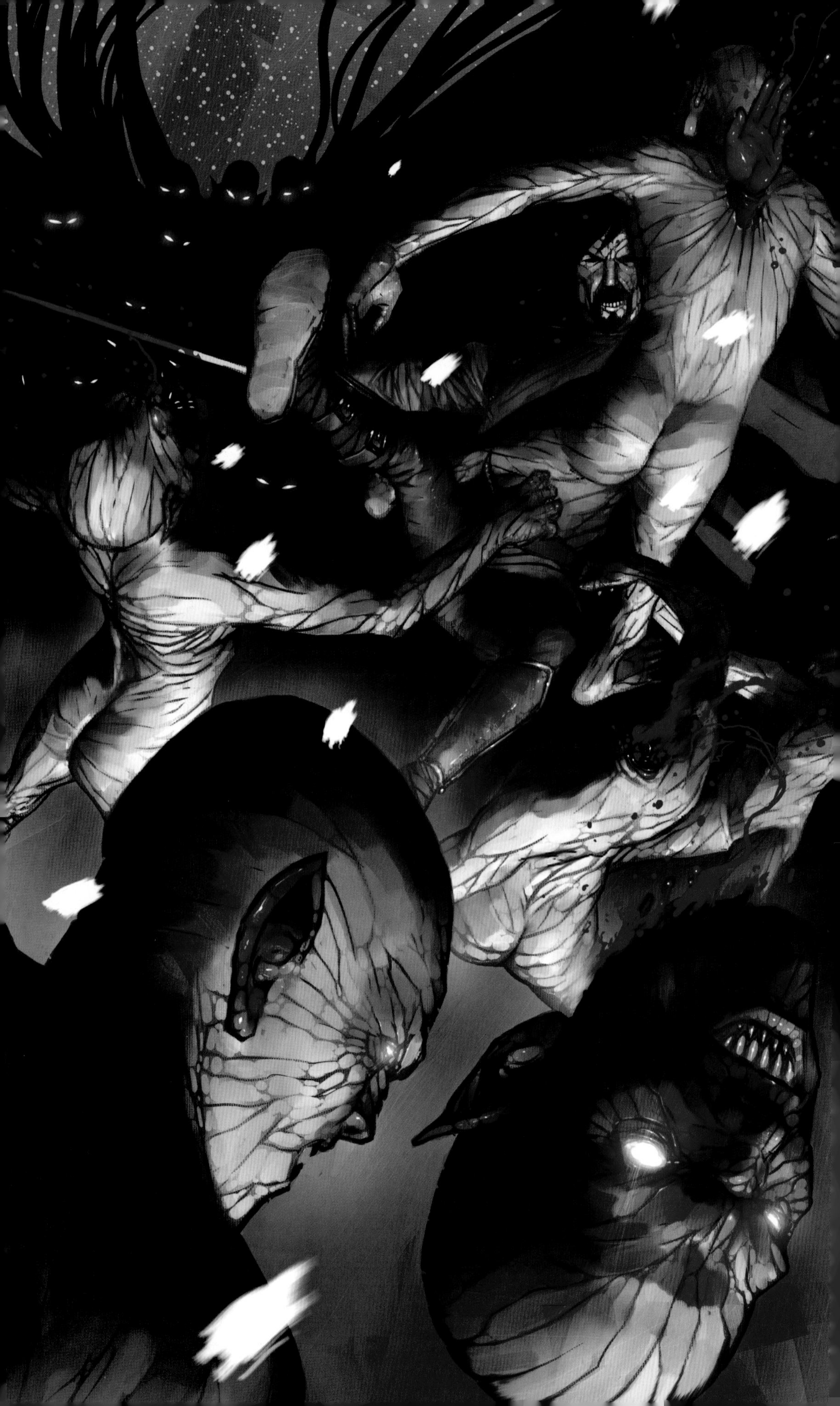

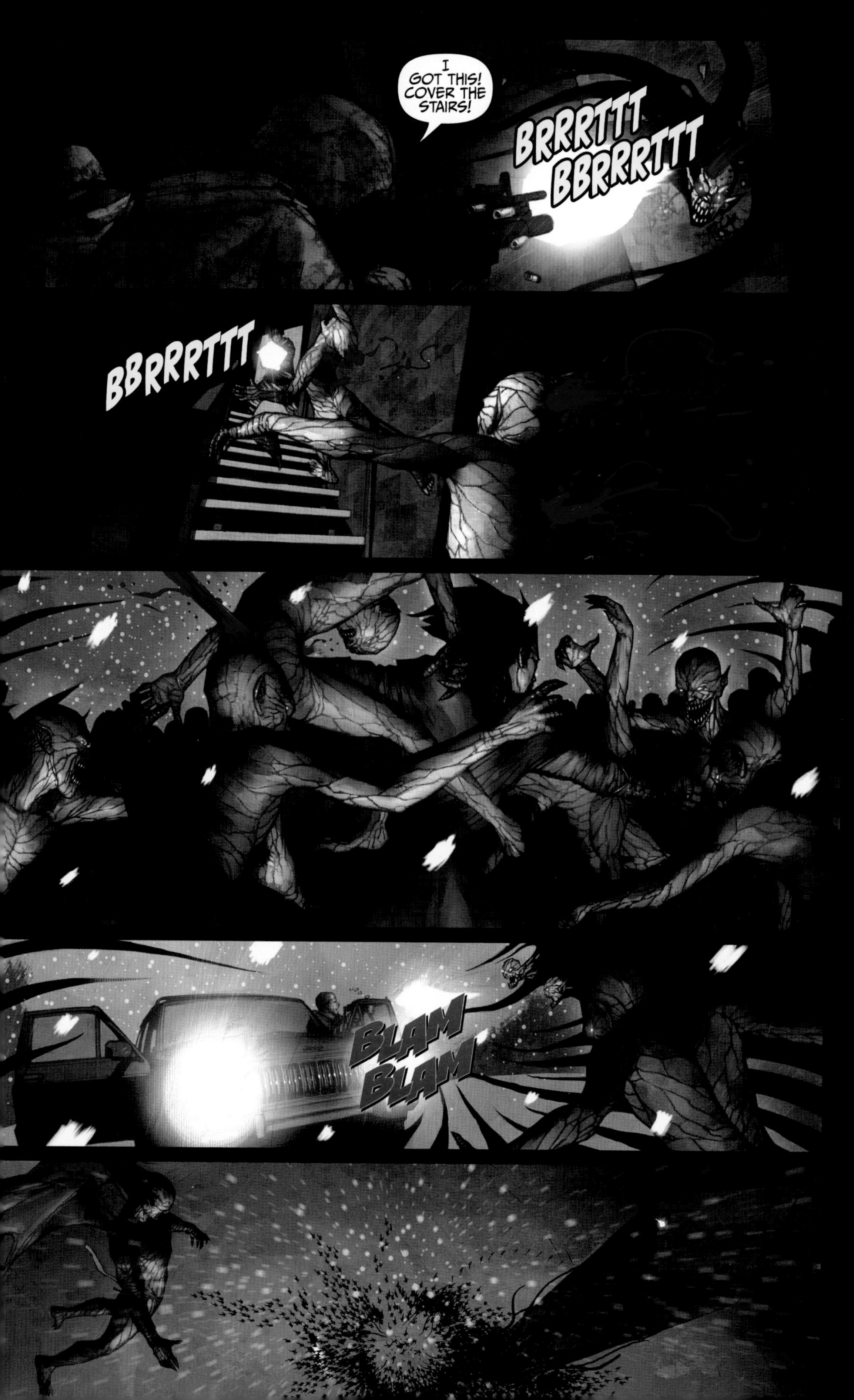

I GOT THIS! COVER THE STAIRS!
BRRRTTT
BBRRRTTT
BBRRRTTT
BLAM
BLAM

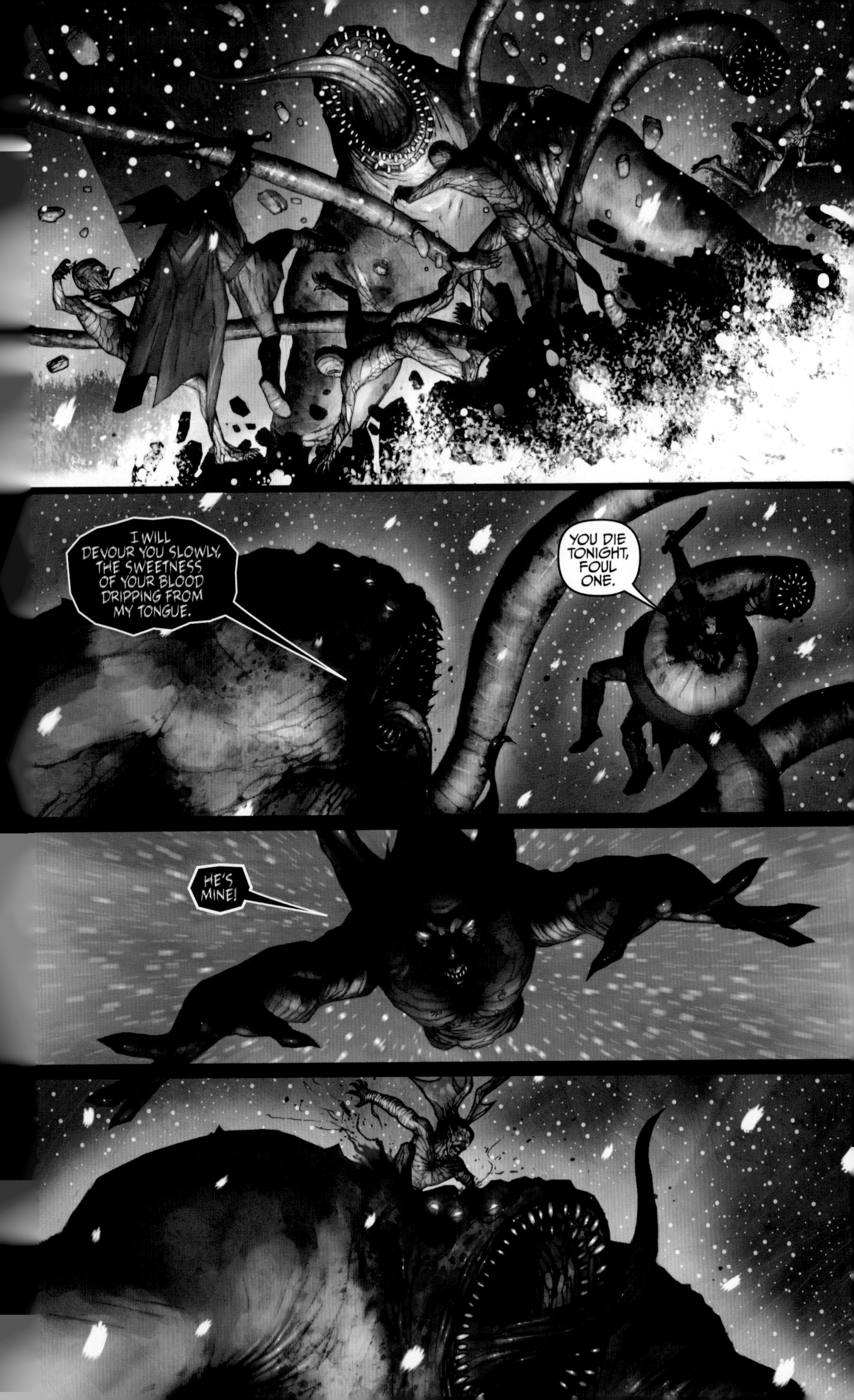
I WILL DEVOUR YOU SLOWLY, THE SWEETNESS OF YOUR BLOOD DRIPPING FROM MY TONGUE.
YOU DIE TONIGHT, FOUL ONE.
HE'S MINE!

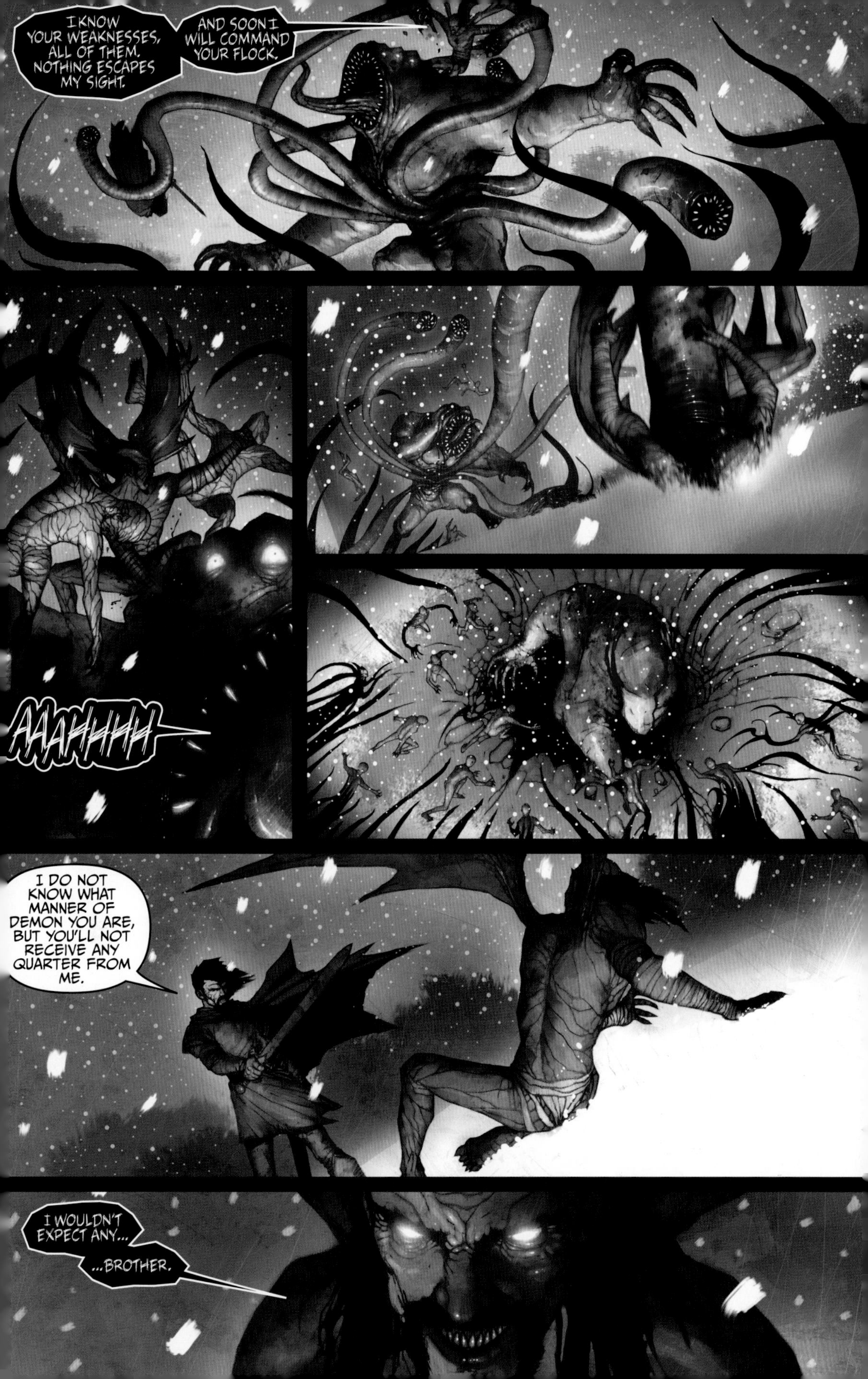
I KNOW YOUR WEAKNESSES, ALL OF THEM. NOTHING ESCAPES MY SIGHT.
AND SOON I WILL COMMAND YOUR FLOCK.
AAAHHHH
I DO NOT KNOW WHAT MANNER OF DEMON YOU ARE, BUT YOU'LL NOT RECEIVE ANY QUARTER FROM ME.
I WOULDN'T EXPECT ANY...
...BROTHER.

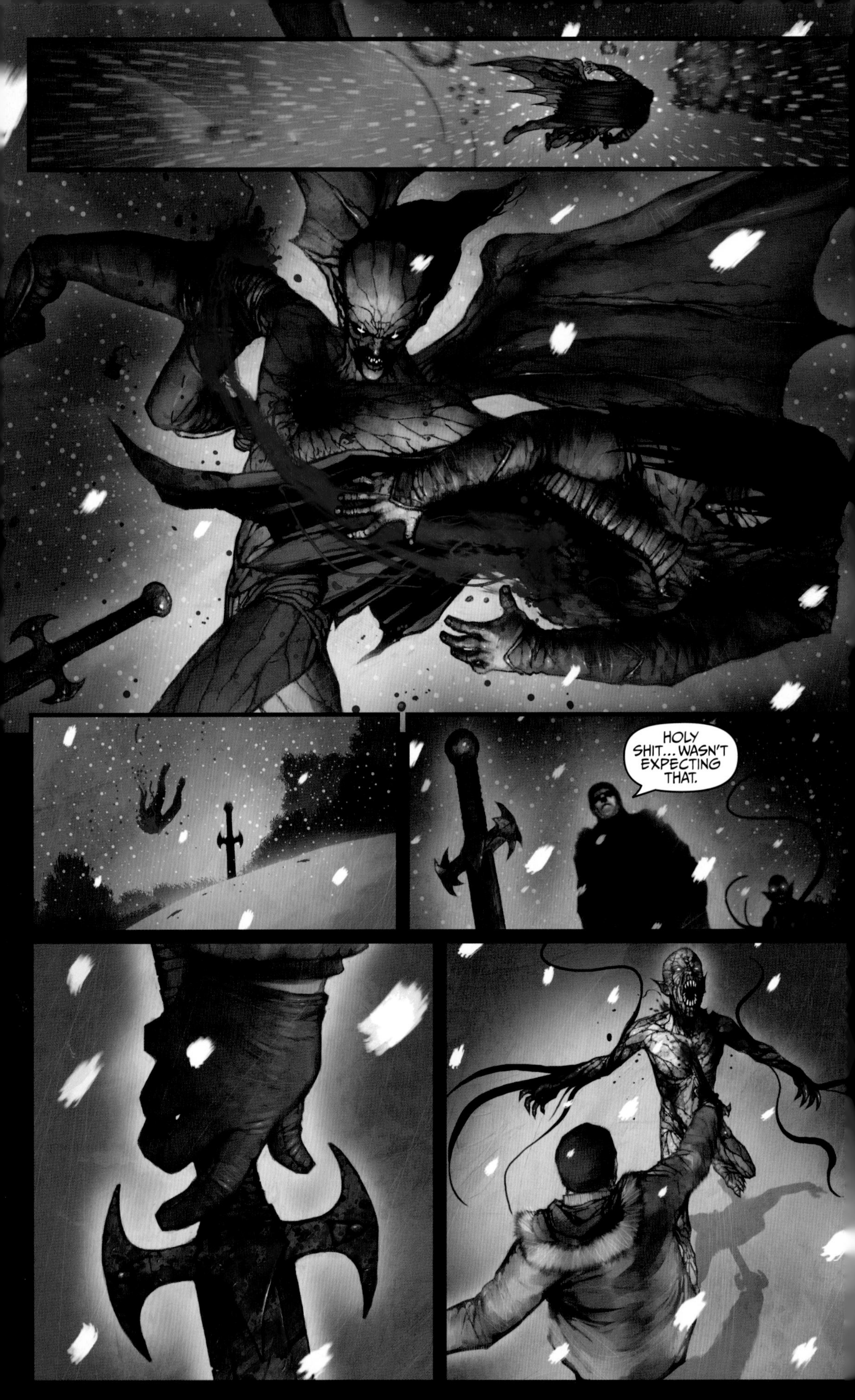
HOLY SHIT...WASN'T EXPECTING THAT.

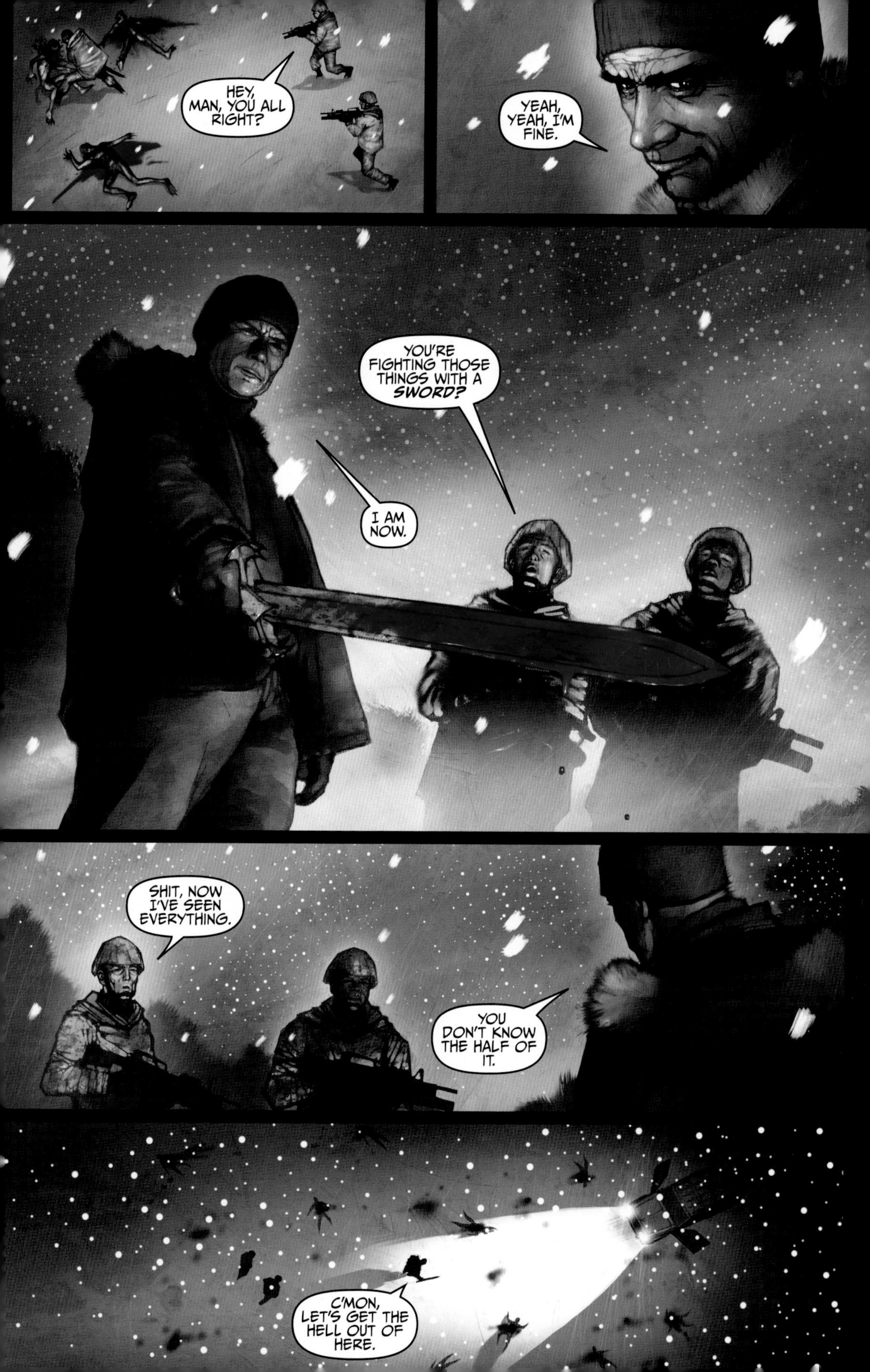
HEY, MAN, YOU ALL RIGHT?
YEAH, YEAH, I'M FINE.
YOU'RE FIGHTING THOSE THINGS WITH A SWORD?
I AM NOW.
SHIT, NOW I'VE SEEN EVERYTHING.
YOU DON'T KNOW THE HALF OF IT.
C'MON, LET'S GET THE HELL OUT OF HERE.

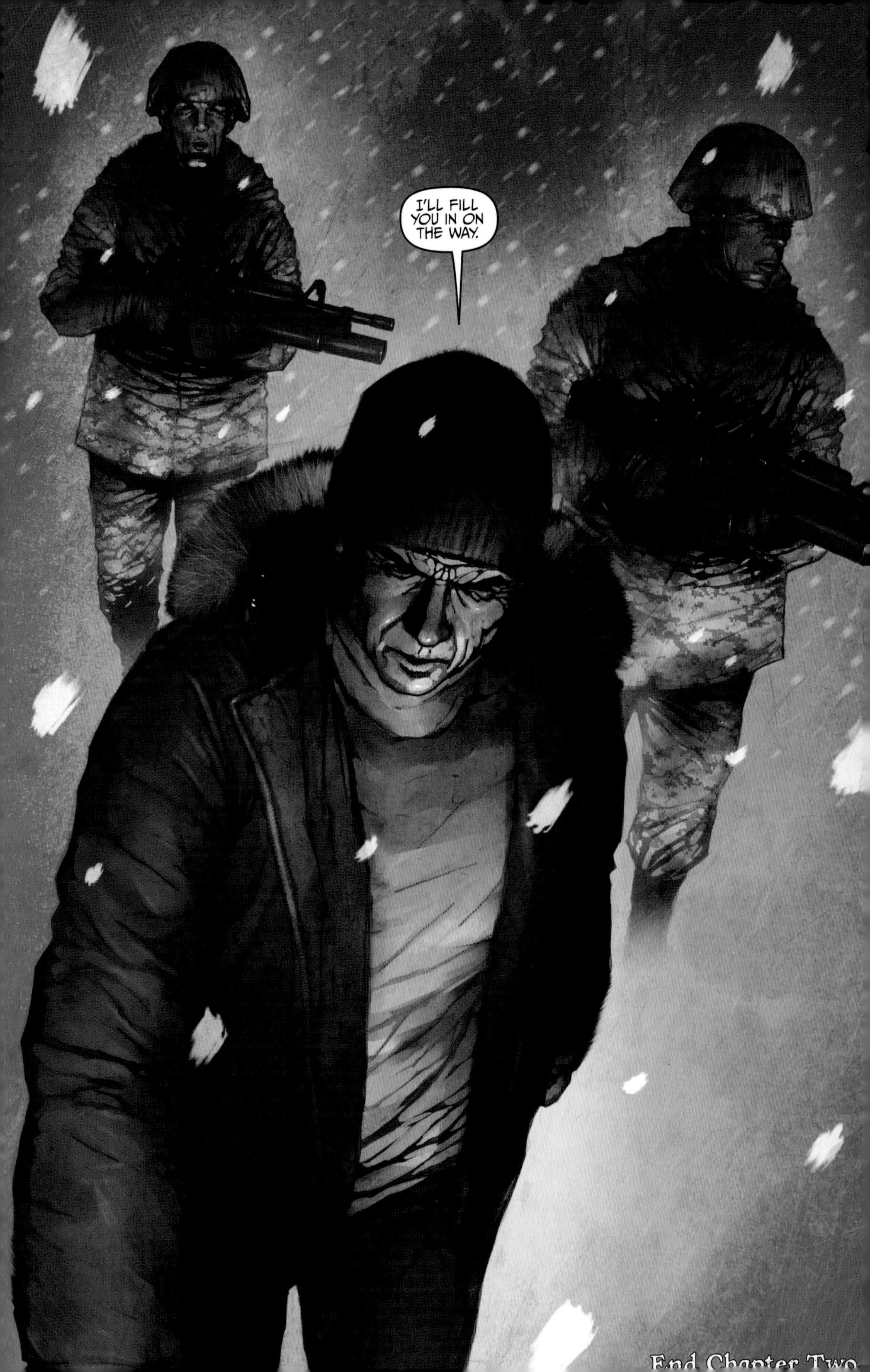
I'LL FILL YOU IN ON THE WAY.
End Chapter Two.

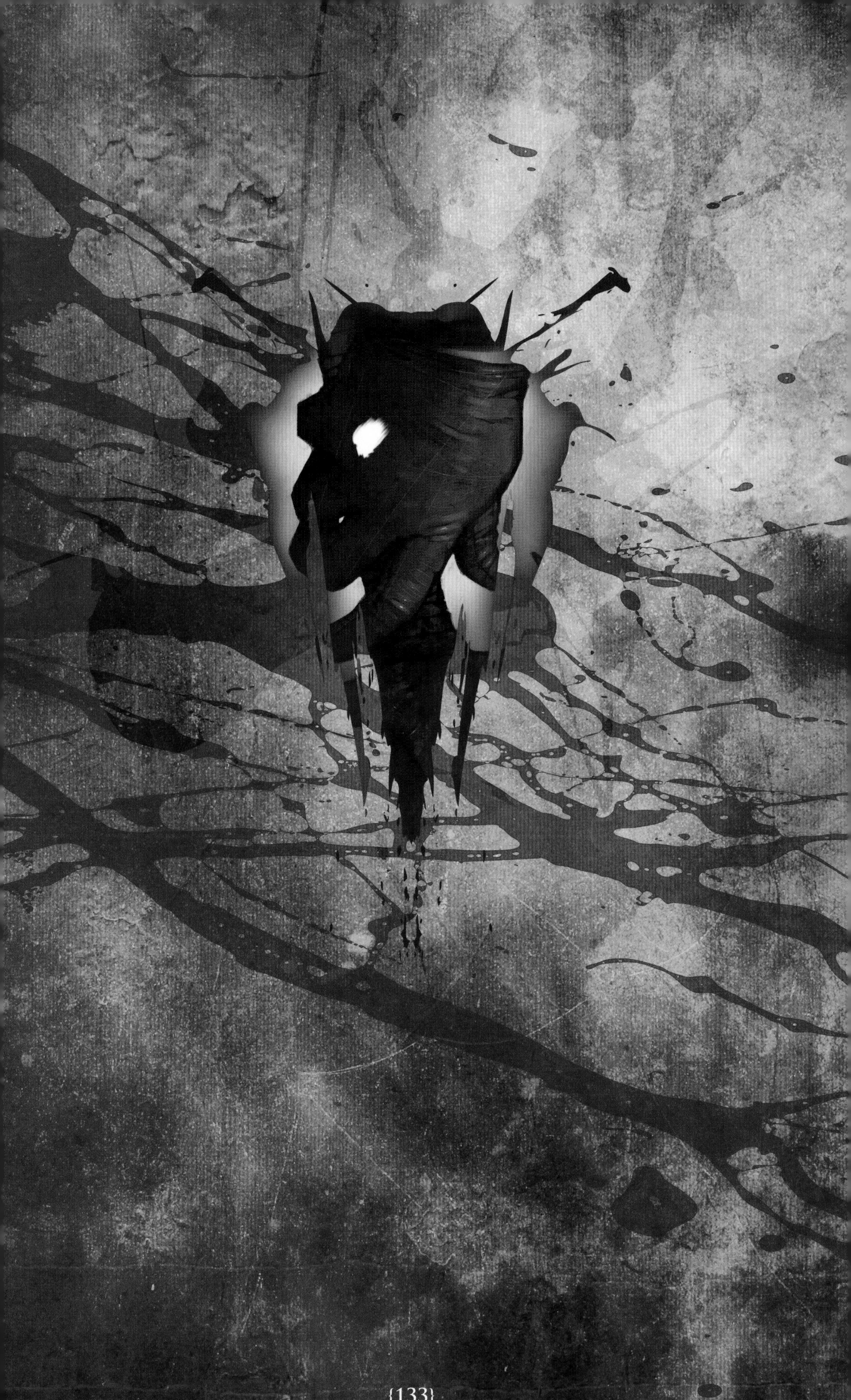

IMPALER

VOLUME 2

{COVER GALLERY}

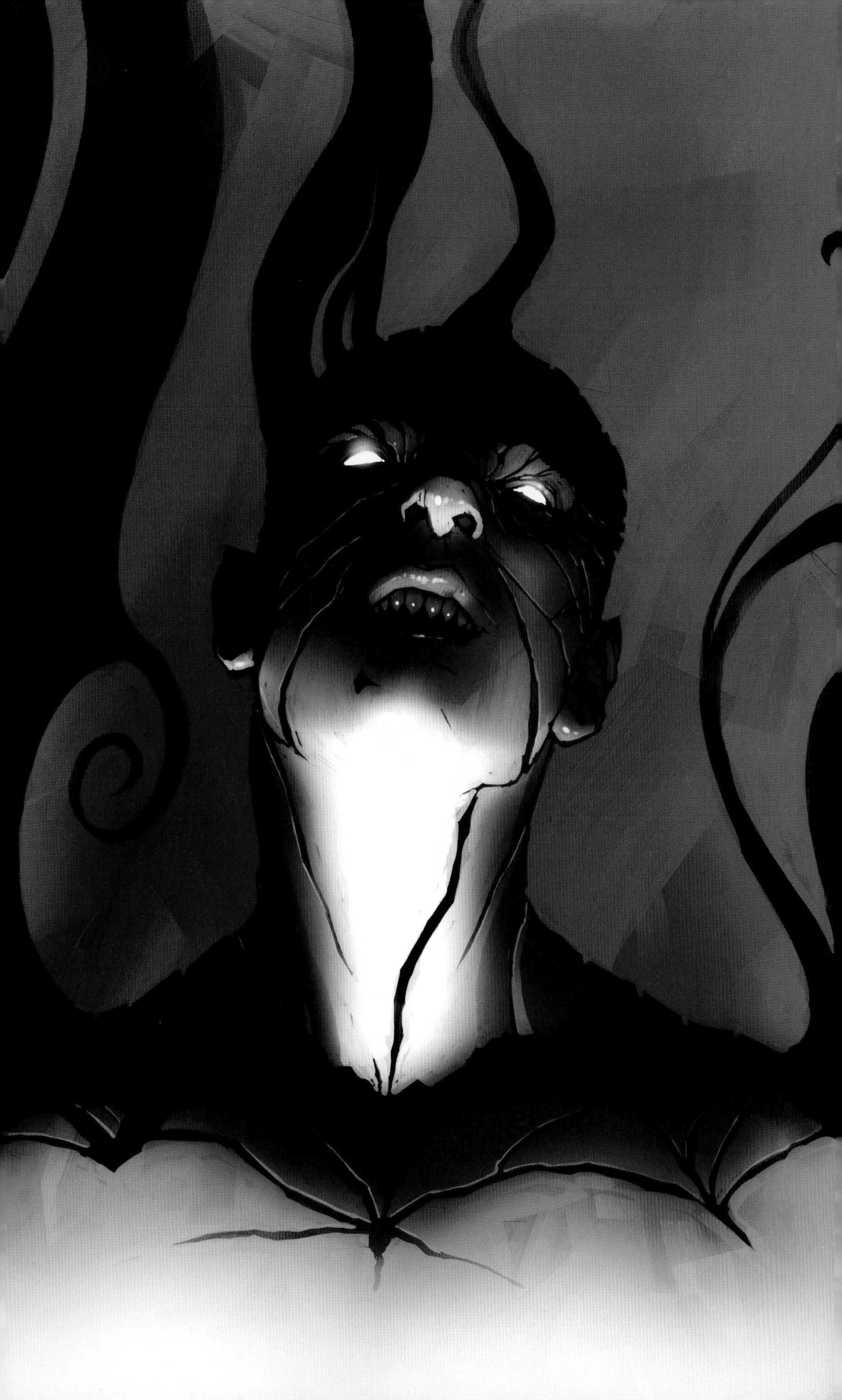

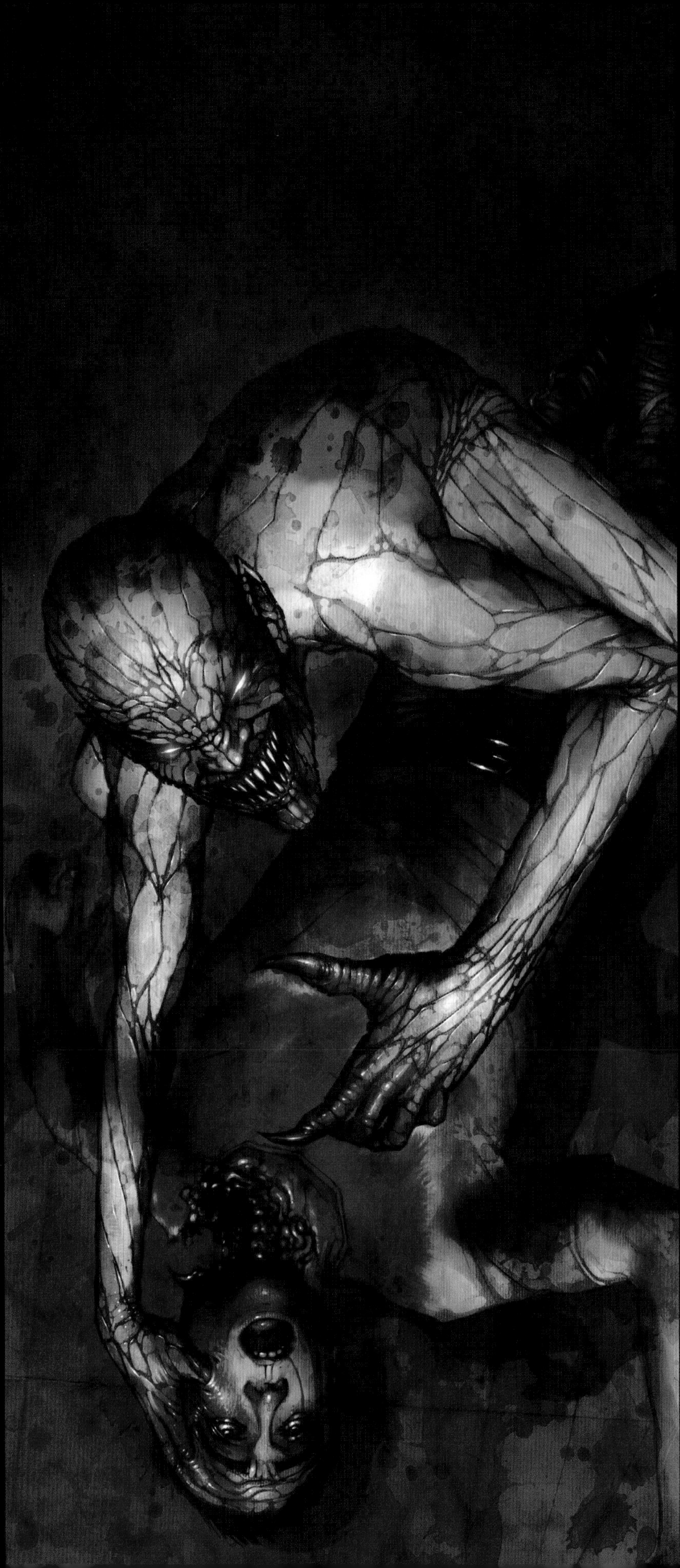

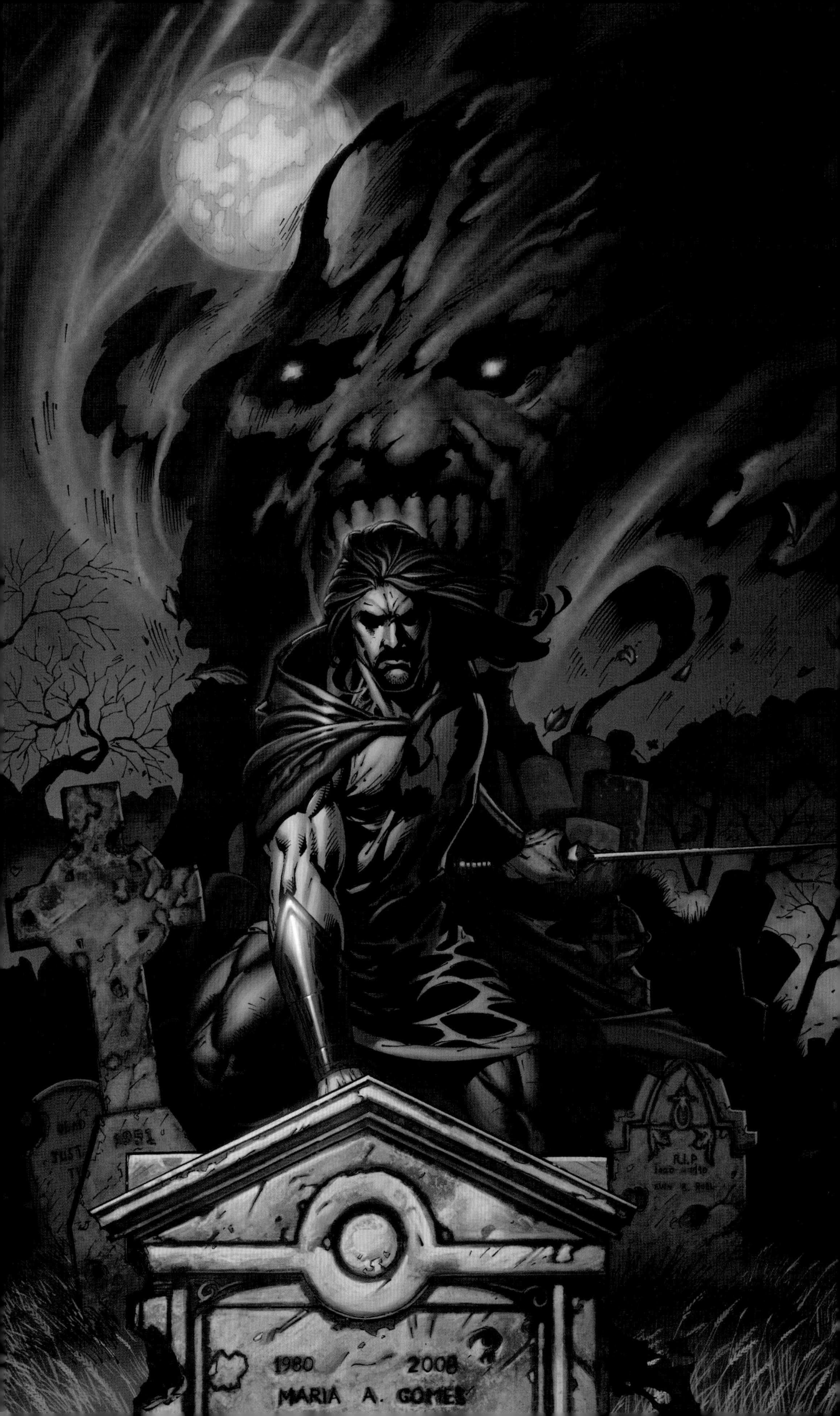
1951
R.I.P.
1980 2008
MARIA A. GOMES

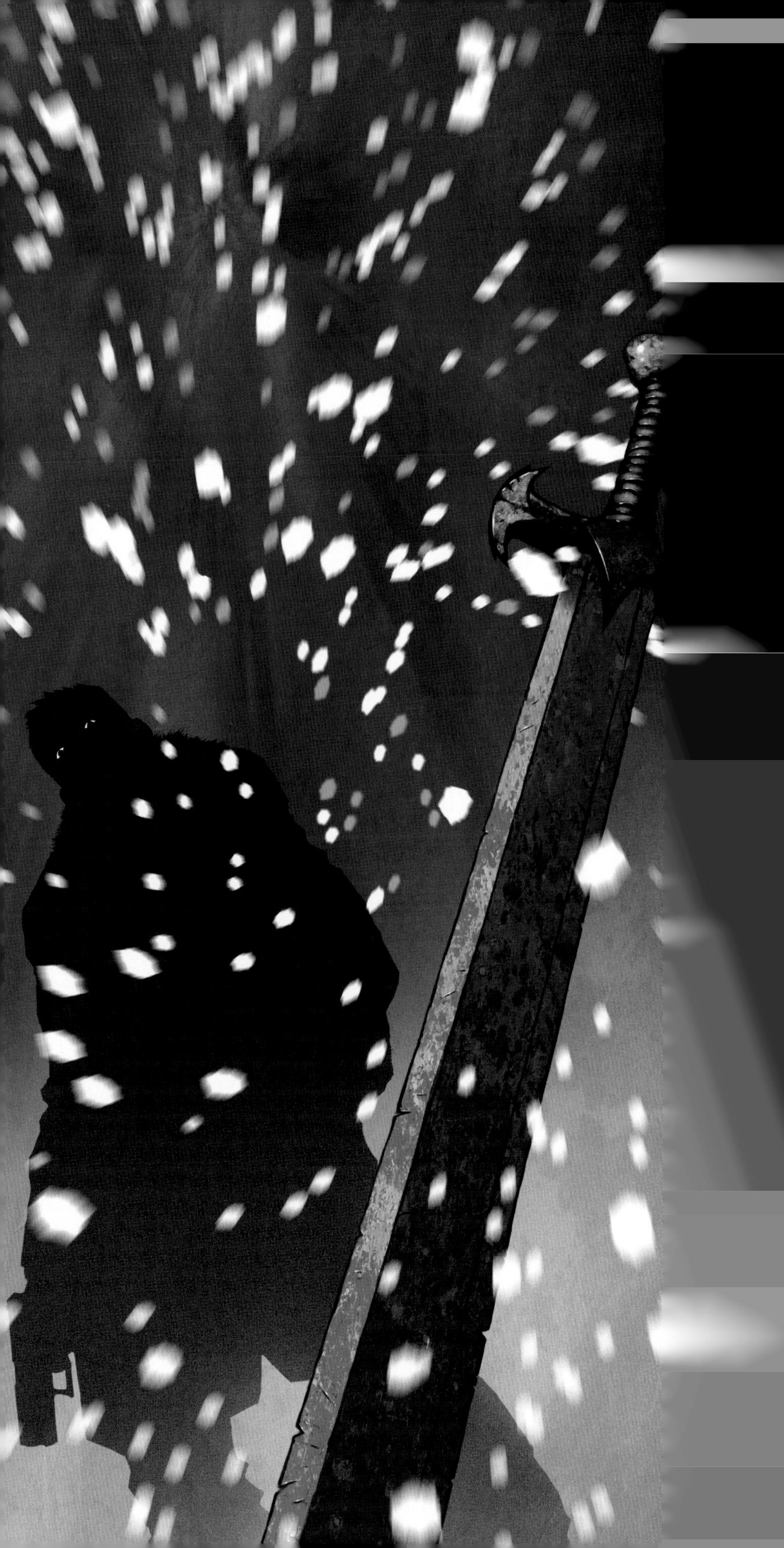

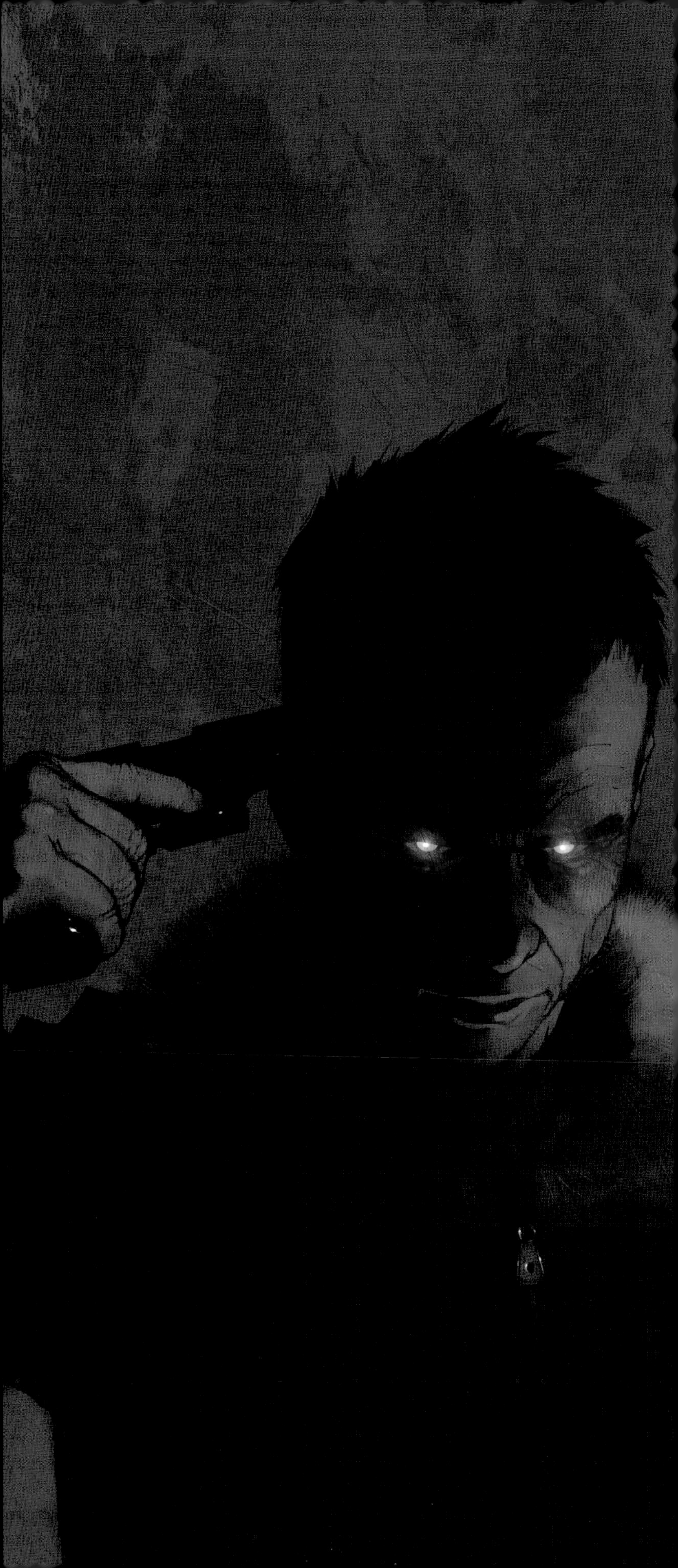

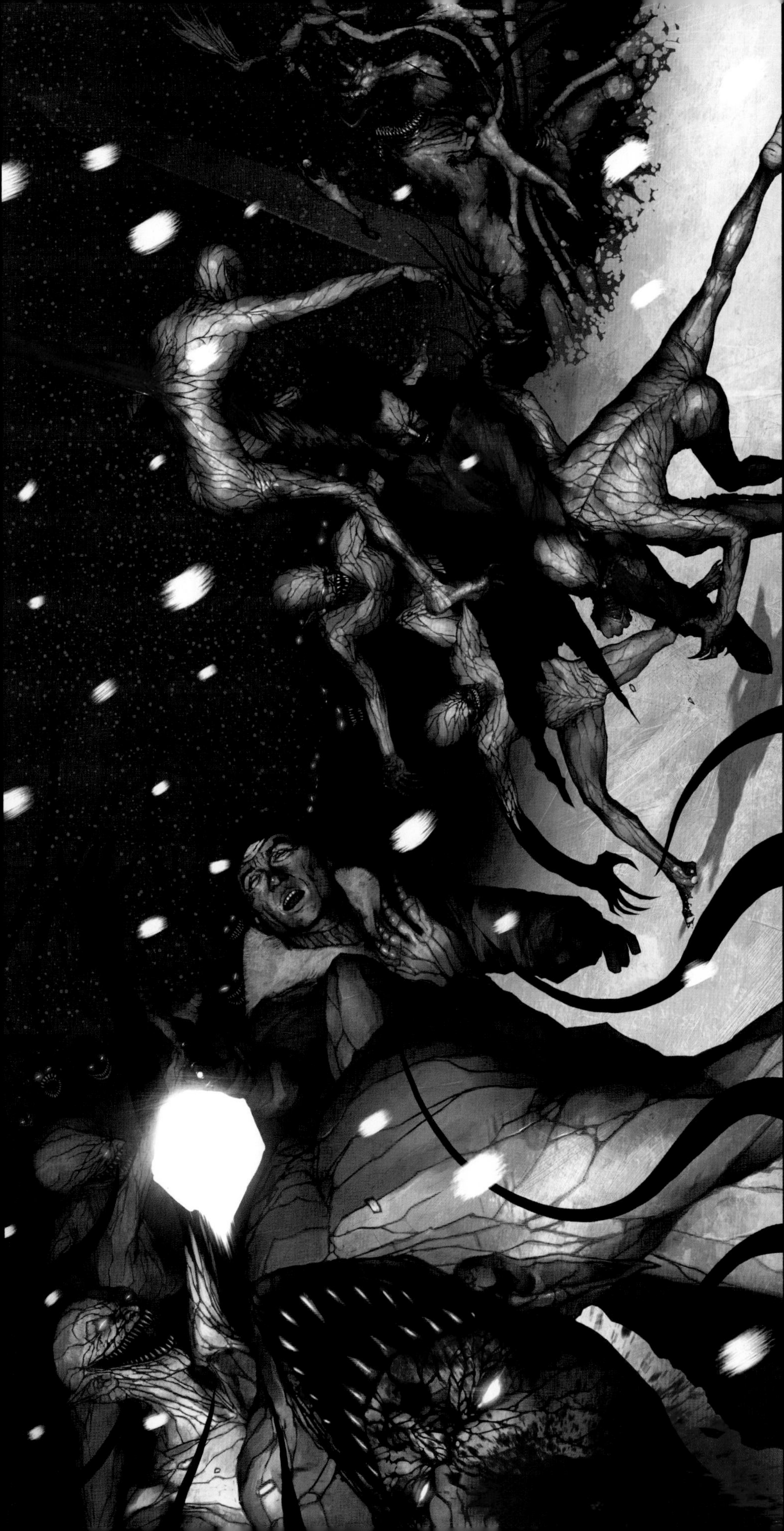

IMPALER
VOLUME 2

{BONUS MATERIALS}

Deleted Scene: Final Fate of the Demetrius

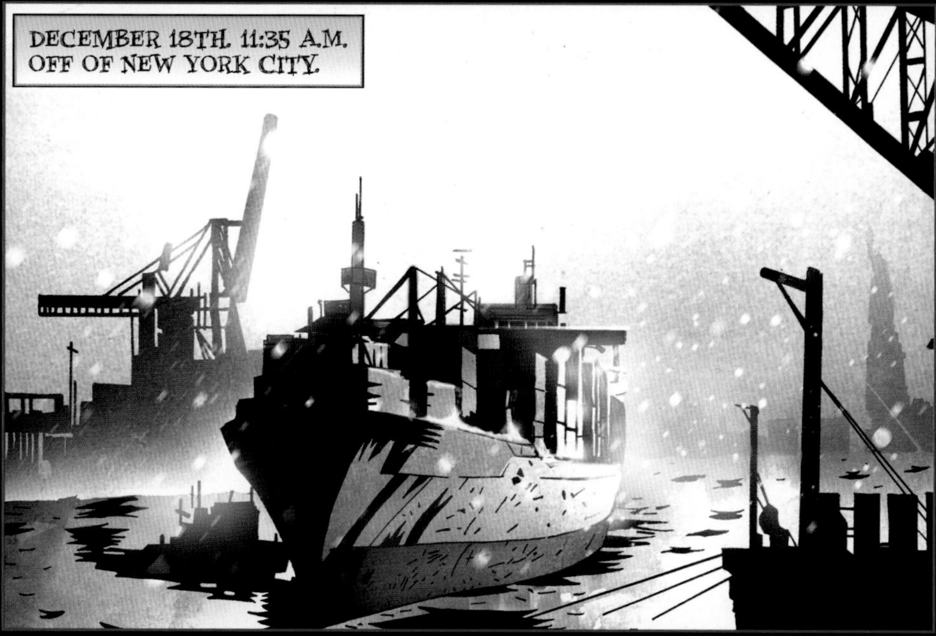
DECEMBER 18TH. 11:35 A.M.
OFF OF NEW YORK CITY.

Impaler volume 1, issue #1 page 7

Long-time readers will remember the Demetrius as the cargo ship that was found adrift off the coast of New York way back in Impaler # 1 (volume one). It's from the Demetrius that the vampire menace was birthed, and a lot of readers have written wanting to know more about the ship and its last journey.

Originally the second volume of Impaler was going to be six issues, but when we decided to combine issues five and six into a single double-sized book, we had to cut some pages. The scene that follows was going to open issue six.

The character "Gladstone" is named after my good friend Darren Gladstone. (I was even going to ask Matt to draw him into the book.) Before the pages got cut, I had Darren take some reference photos -- I've included one with these script pages -- so that Matt would know what Darren looked like.

-William

Impaler volume 1, issue #1 page 9

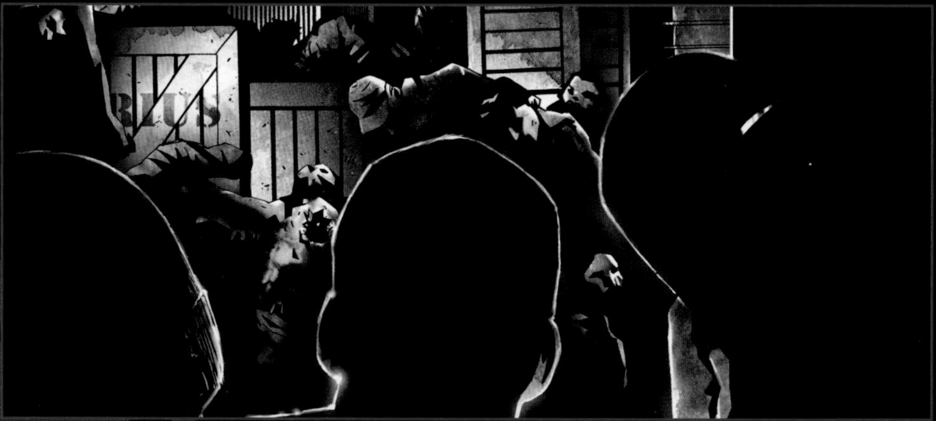

PAGE 2

PANEL 1: Establishing shot of the DEMETRIUS at sea. It's night and the ship plows through choppy seas, thin, cold snowflakes hanging in the air.

CAPTION: Somewhere in the Atlantic Ocean. Seven days ago.

PANEL 2: Inside of the ship's bridge. A crusty old SEA CAPTAIN and GLAD-STONE are on the bridge. The door to the bridge is barricaded with a desk and chair. The windows to the bridge open outward and are large enough for some-one to get through them. There is a small external ledge on the outside of the bridge, just below the windows.

Gladstone and the Captain are both armed -- the Captain has a pistol and Glad-stone has a flare gun. Both men look tired and battered, their clothing torn and spotted with blood. They're pulling on life preservers.

GLADSTONE: How many of them did you see?

CAPTAIN: Four or five at least.

GLADSTONE: Shit.

PANEL 3: The Captain looks out of the windows on the bridge, his eyes looking for movement. His life preserver is now on.

GLADSTONE (OP): You sure this is a good idea?

CAPTAIN: Got no other choice. They destroyed the life rafts, and we sure as shit can't stay here.

PANEL 4: Shot looking toward the door. It buckles from impact, the metal bend-ing inward. Black tentacles start to creep in through the cracks. Gladstone (life preserver on) looks at the door in terror.

SFX: THRACK

GLADSTONE: God help us.

PANEL 5: The Captain has opened a window and Gladstone is moving toward him. We're looking in through the open window, and the door is visible in the background, the Captain looking toward the door, motioning for Gladstone to get a move on.

SFX: THRACK

CAPTAIN: When you hit the water, make damn sure you keep your mouth closed. And hold your breath until you surface, got it?

GLADSTONE: Yeah…

PAGE 3

PANEL 1: External shot. Gladstone squeezes through the window, climbing out onto the ledge.

PANEL 2: Inside the bridge. The door buckles inward, shadows and tentacles rocketing in through the opening. The Captain ducks down, trying to shield himself. He yells out the window, toward Gladstone.

CAPTAIN: Jump! Jump now!

PANEL 3: Gladstone jumps off of the ledge, toward the black water, his body hanging in the air.

PANEL 4: Vampires rush into the bridge, the Captain firing his gun at them.

SFX: BLAM BLAM

PANEL 5: Tight shot, on Gladstone as he plummets toward the water. He's now about four feet from the water, his face etched in terror as a black tentacle wraps around his mid-section. He has one hand outstretched toward the water, as if he's trying to grab it and hold on.

GLADSTONE (weak): …no…

PANEL 6: Pulled back shot. Gladstone is being yanked back toward the ship, the tentacle cracking like a whip. Gladstone is beyond terrified, his hands helplessly looking for something to grab onto. The water below is black.

PANEL 7: Exterior shot of the ship. It trundles along through the black water, snow swirling around.

SFX: AAAHHHHH

This is Darren. Who wouldn't want to see him get ripped apart by vampires?
-William

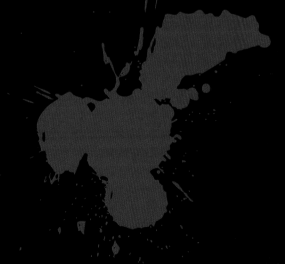

Pin-Up: Vlad at 40

One of the great things about being a comic book writer is that you get to run around with comic book artists, and occasionally they draw things for you.

This pin-up was drawn by my good friend Rob Osborne (*1000 Steps to World Domination*) for my 40th birthday. The original now hangs in my office.

-William

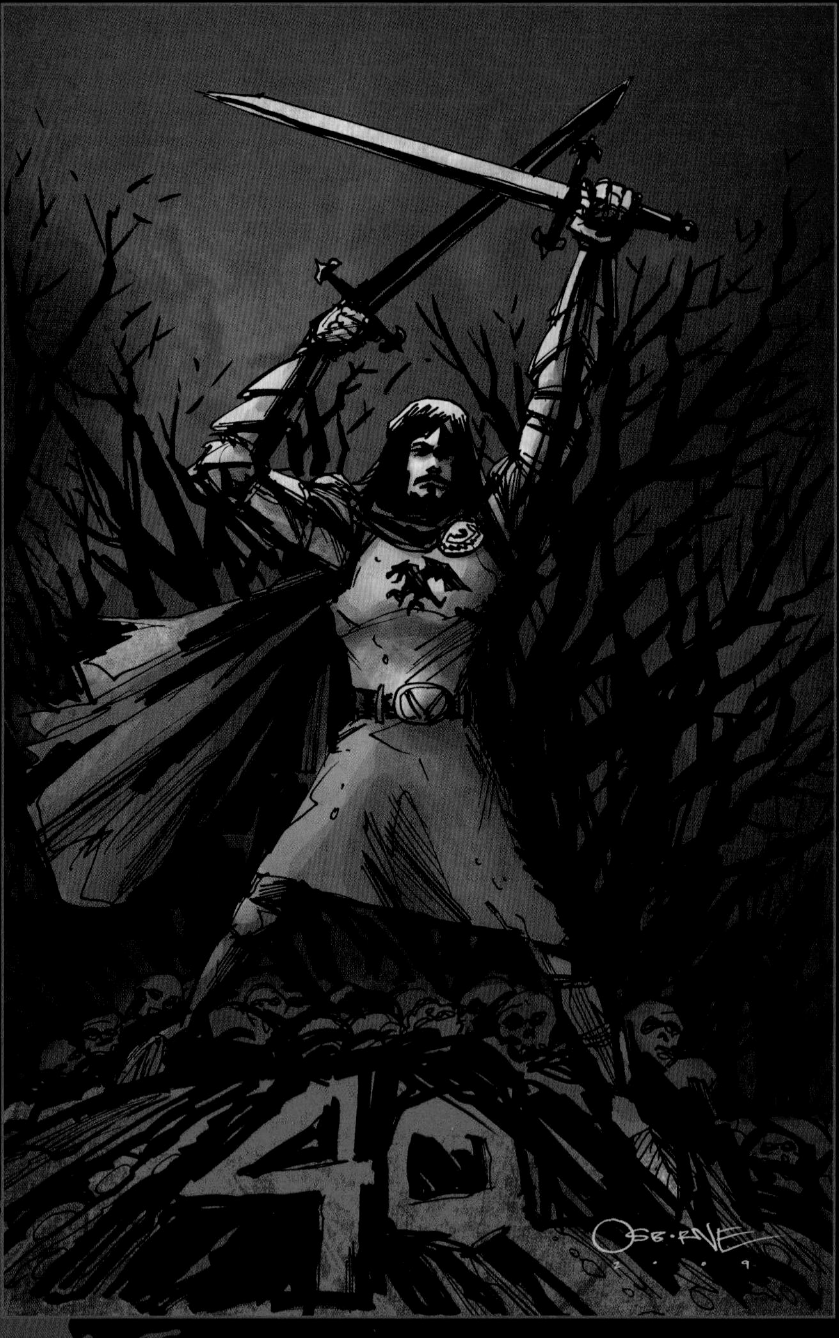

Impaler vol.2, issue #1
Cover Process, by: Matt Timson
Originally featured on: www.comicmonsters.com

My name is Matt Timson (and not Tim Matthews- which is a common misconception) and I'm currently lucky enough to be the artist for Impaler, written by William (Bill) Harms and published by Top Cow.

Having previously worked on zombie stuff, I was quite keen to make the switch to vampires, as there's something inherently nasty and evil about a vampire that makes it even more frightening than a zombie to me. A zombie doesn't really know what it's doing- it's all about staggering from place to place, looking for the ever more elusive brains it seems to hanker after. You can outrun a zombie. You can outwit a zombie (and if you can't, frankly, you deserve to get eaten). You can even stand your ground against one or two, if you keep your wits about you and don't mind bashing their brains in. Vampires, on the other hand, are genuinely evil in my book. They're fast, deadly, intelligent and extremely difficult to kill if you're just some poor slob in the wrong place at the wrong time. The best you can hope for is that the Sun will rise before they find your hiding place, or that they'll kill you quick if not. They delight in what they do and I get the impression that feeding is secondary to the enjoyment of simply tearing people apart for fun. That's something I really wanted to get across- that these guys are having the time of their (un)lives as they peel your face off, crush your skull and lap up the resulting rivers of blood that gush out- which is why most of my vampires are grinning or laughing. They can get a bit angry too, of course, but the main thing I'm going for is a sense of enjoyment.

My first stumbling block was following the amazingly talented two Nicks (that's Marinkovich and Postic). I mean, seriously, how do you follow that? Long story short, I decided not to even bother trying and went for a slightly different look instead. As all of my work is digital, I tend to end up working over my roughs as I go, so there's actually surprisingly little of the earlier stages of what I do knocking about. Fortunately, as luck would have it, I've still got most of the original layers for the cover of issue #1, so that's what I'm going to talk you through today.

As you can see, I've decided to stick to the theme of the original covers (just using the band in the middle for the art) because I like the way it looks and I don't mind admitting that I couldn't think of anything more aesthetically pleasing.

I start with what really ought to be a doodle, but, as often happens, I tend to get a bit carried away with colours, textures and other totally unnecessary details that will just mean extra work for me if the cover gets rejected. In this case, I get lucky and both Bill and Rob (Rob Levin, my editor) like the concept and tell me to get on with it (Rob is like a cross between my nemesis and my conscience. I feel like punching him in the throat when he dares to suggest a change to my work, but after I've reluctantly made the change, he is invariably proved correct and I am extremely grateful for his input- at which point, I'm glad he doesn't live closer, as I would have punched him in the throat for nothing).

Before I go any further, I've got to tell you that I work in a totally arse backwards kind of way and I expect to have all manner of scorn poured all over me- but the way I work is the way I work, so…

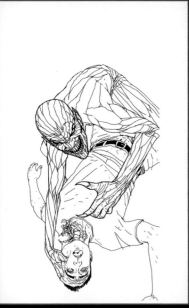

I make a lovely neat line drawing of the scene in Photoshop. I say scene, but it's really just the vamp and his unfortunate victim.

I then take these lovely clean lines and open them up in Painter, where I proceed to smudge all over them with the grainy water tool, having first selected a paper texture (usually ribbed pastel) that will show up after the smudging.

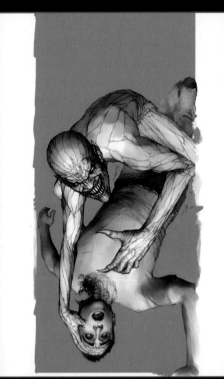

Back to Photoshop and I paint all the white areas back in again on a separate layer, to redefine the lines. Yes, you read that correctly. I draw lines, then I obliterate them and then I draw them all back in again. The hard way. Hopefully, you can see the effect that I'm going for here. The lines are less harsh and distinct, but at the same time, they're still clearly visible. There are probably a lot of ways to do this far more effectively and with a lot less work but, for the time being, this is how I like to do it.

Next up is some block greys and shading. The greys are on a separate, multiply layer, created in Photoshop, which I then take into Painter and smudge with the grainy water tool, again with the same paper selected as before.

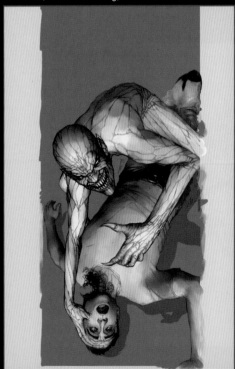

Back to Photoshop and another multiply layer, set at about 50% opacity. This is for the basic colours. There's also a shadow layer added at this point- black, probably about 30%

Another multiply layer, this time for basic blood. There's also a layer with some minute airbrush shading (black and red), as well as a highlight layer- which can be seen on the victim' shoes, belt buckle and face and on the vamp's teeth and hands.

Next up is a colour burn layer of a texture/paint thingy that I already had lying around- probably around 10% opacity. This adds some texture to the pic and throws in some random colour, making me look far more artistic and clever with colour than I actually am.

Here, I've added two more colour burn layers for the blood. These are actually made from tea that I've splattered on paper, left to dry and scanned in. Lovely, aren't they?

Finally, I add in the black bands at the sides and some shadow at the top of the picture, again, on separate layers. I also add a little glow to the vamp's eyes with the airbrush tool.

Basically, the interior pages are handled pretty much the same way. I lay them out, like in the initial sketch, but without colour (although I usually end up adding grey tones to them). After I've laid the page out, I tend to work on one panel at a time (unless they're really simple panels) because it's not unusual for me to have 20+ layers on the go at once, per panel. 6 panels of that on one page would probably make my brain bleed.

And that's about it- apart from to say that, originally, I had the victim's feet hidden from view. Basically, his legs were apart, rather than together, which was fine for the right foot, which disappeared off the page, but it made the left foot look like it was growing out of the vamp's ass. No problem, I thought- and just decided that the left leg would be bent at the knee, so that we'd end up seeing neither of his feet.

The nemesis picked up on this only after the final was submitted for approval and asked me to add the feet in. I briefly considered getting on a plane so that I could punch him in the throat, but eventually reasoned that it'd probably be quicker and easier for all concerned to just add the feet, moving the legs closer together to avoid the whole foot-and-ass thing. This is why the feet don't appear on the initial sketch and line drawings.

Needless to say, Rob was correct (as usual). In retrospect, it looked stupid without the feet and I don't know what I was thinking about! Rob's quite good at his job really- I ought to listen to him more.

Anyway- that really is it. I'd like to thank Rob Caprilozzi for inviting me to contribute and, also, you guys for reading- I hope that you enjoyed it.

Cheers-
Matt

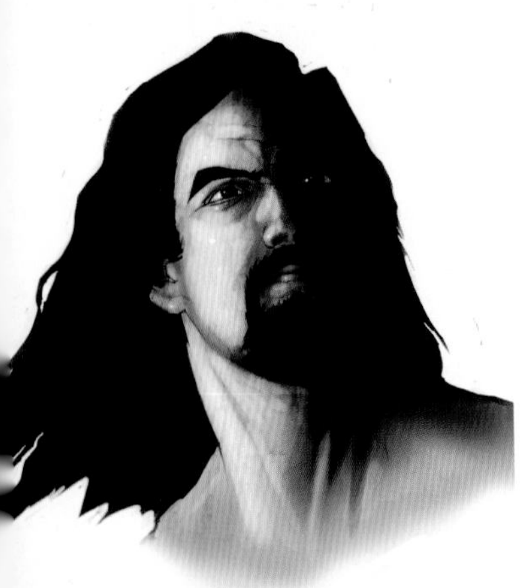

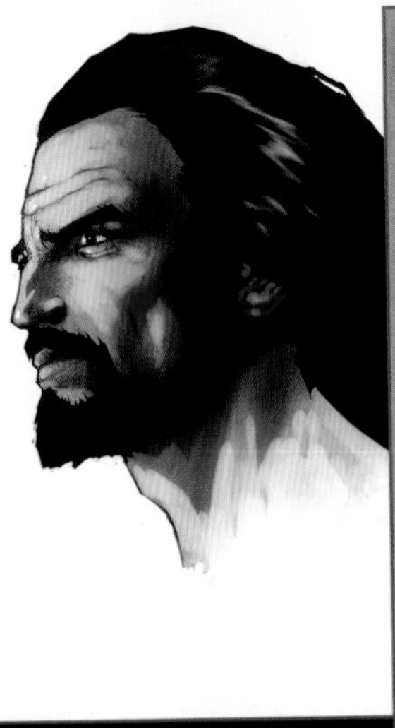

These were my first concept sketches for Vlad, largely based on what Nick Postic had already been drawing. I was told that I could change as much as I liked, but I saw no reason to mess with it really. I ditched the dragon from the tunic, but that's about it.

In retrospect, I'd have made the outer tunic more like a giant poncho, freeing up the legs a bit.

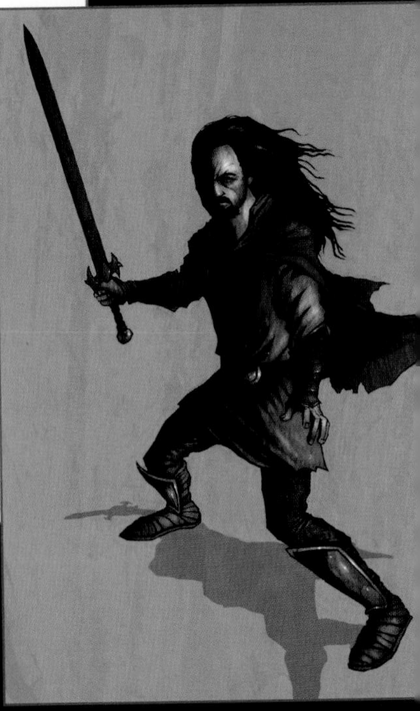

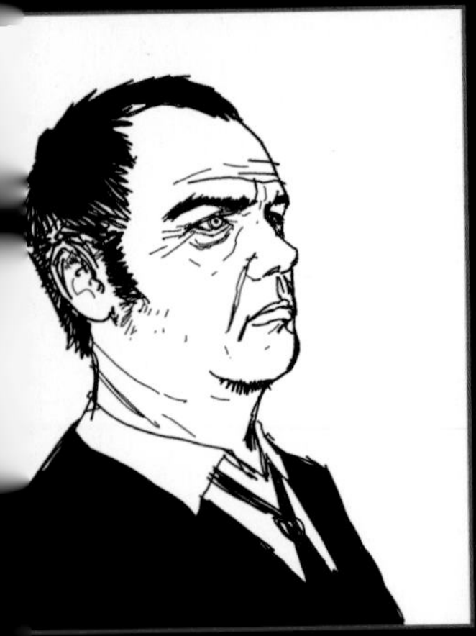

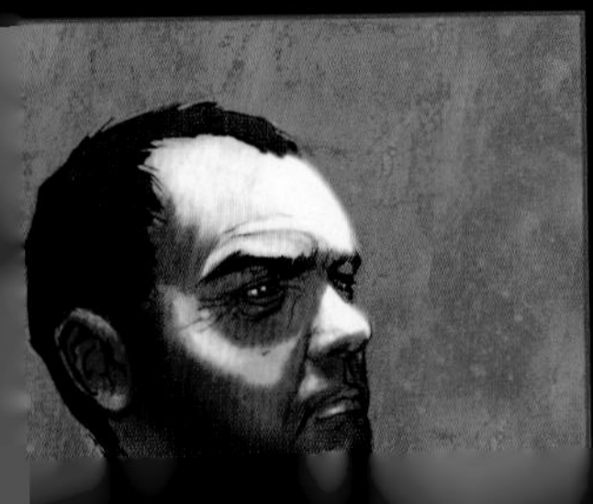

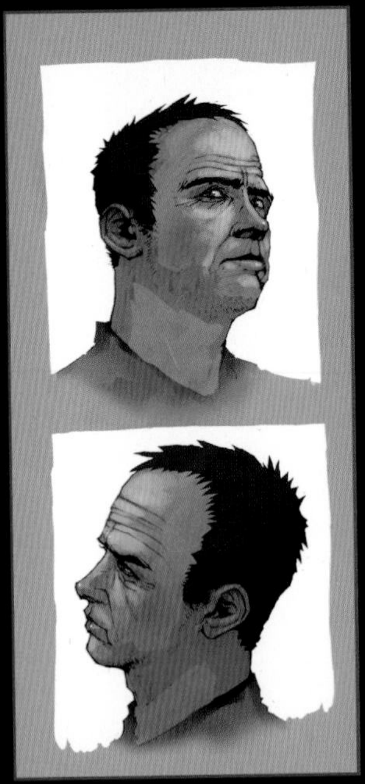

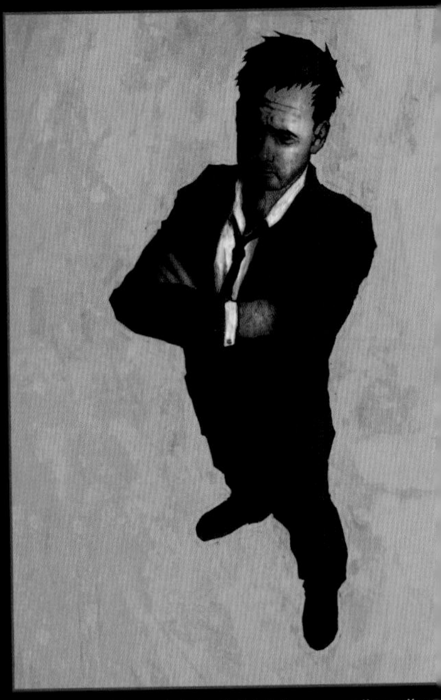

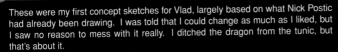

Victor was always my favourite character to draw, although I don't think I ever really nailec age- which I think was meant to be around 50. As the story progressed and Vlad cured hir radiation sickness, I think he was supposed to be slightly younger and fitter- but som

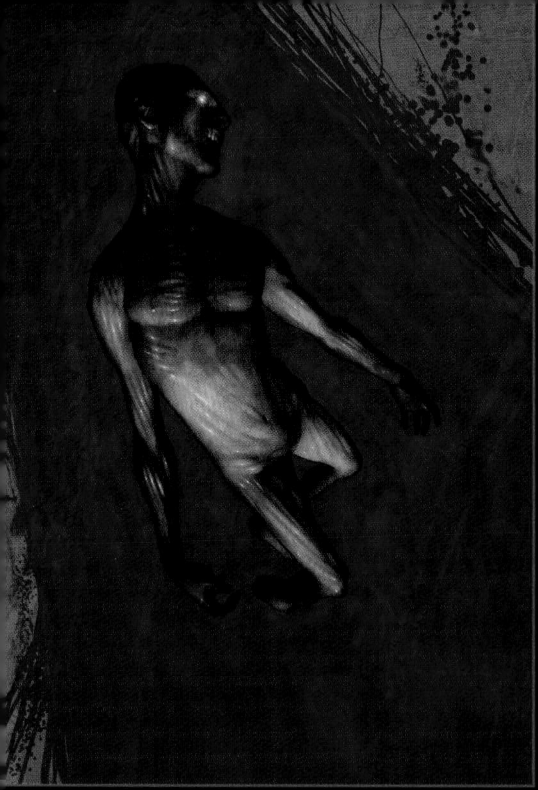

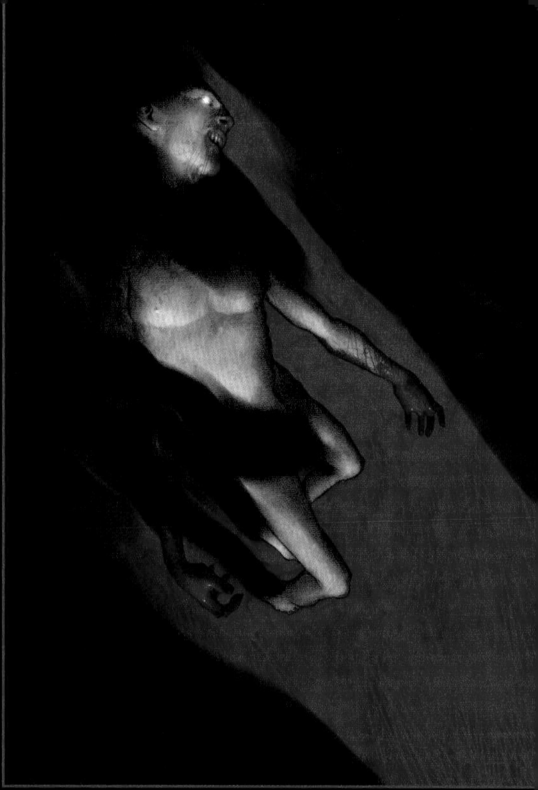

Rejected redesigns for the vamps- not that different from the originals really, but minus the cracks in the skin. I'm glad they got rejected now- even though those cracks were a pain to draw, they definitely added to the horror.

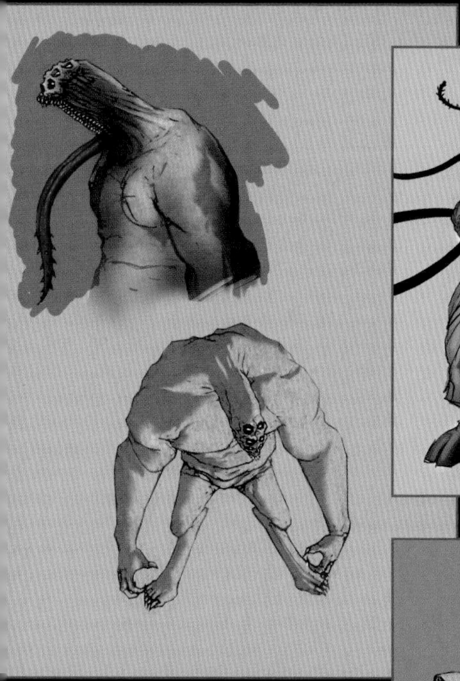

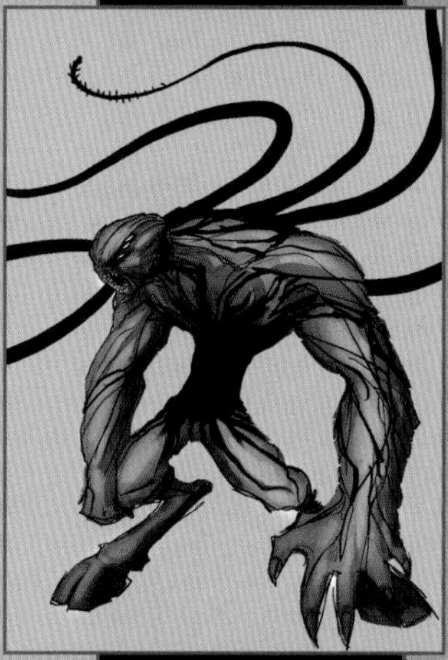

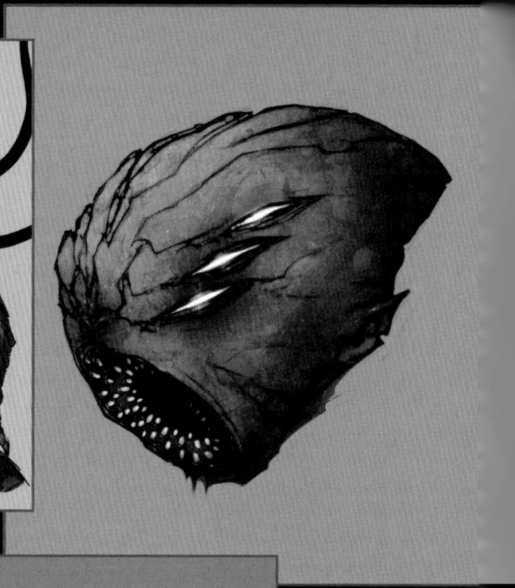

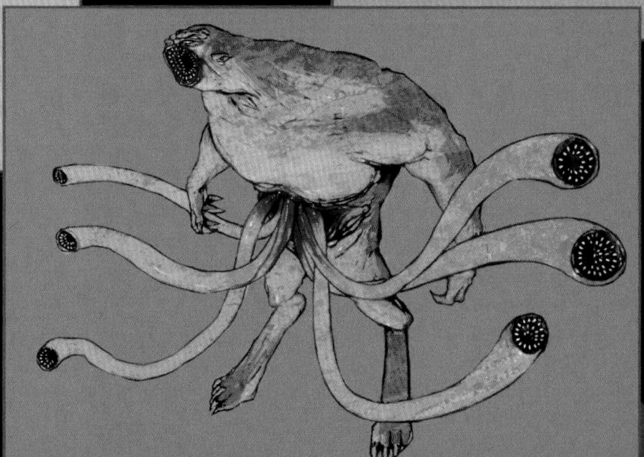

Initial concepts for the Alpha Vampire. I knew the rough body shape I was going for from the outset- it's practically the Fury, from Captain Britain. I grew up with the original b/w strips by Alan Moore and Alan Davis and I always thought that the Fury was truly terrifying- both in deed and in the way that it looked. Of course, the whole goat-legged look has since become shorthand for 'scary monster'- but I wasn't going to let that stop me...

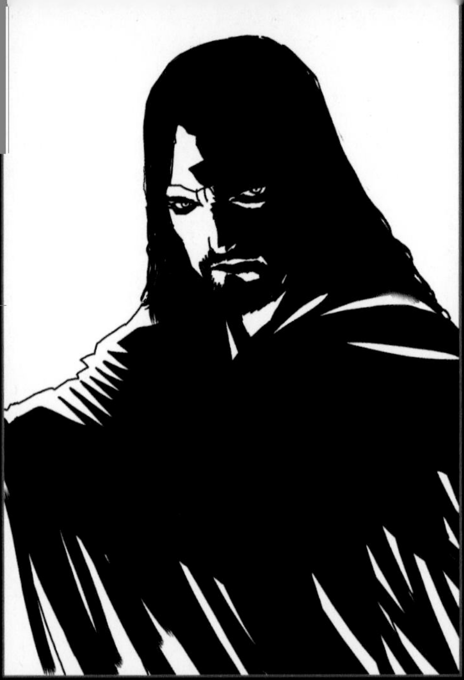

This is an early Vlad doodle that I did and consigned to the bowels of my Hard Drive- until Filip Sablik asked me if I had anything he could use for a promo cover. I laughed when he told me which previous scribble I'd done that he was thinking of using- and then drew this up for him instead. It became the retailer incentive variant for issue 1. The last laugh was on me though- I never billed anyone for it...

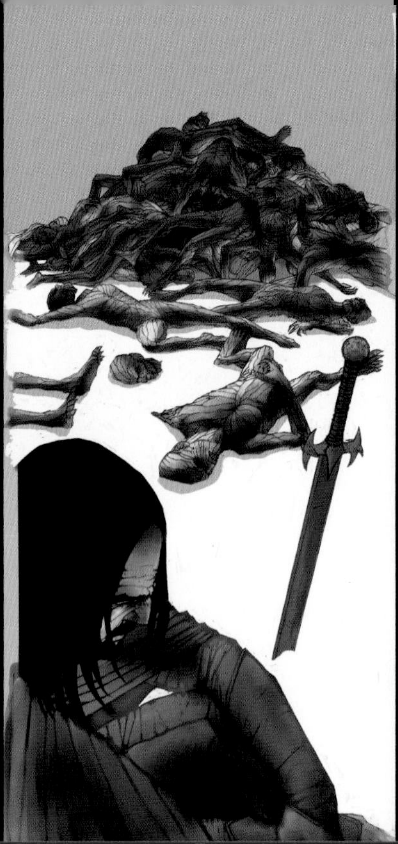

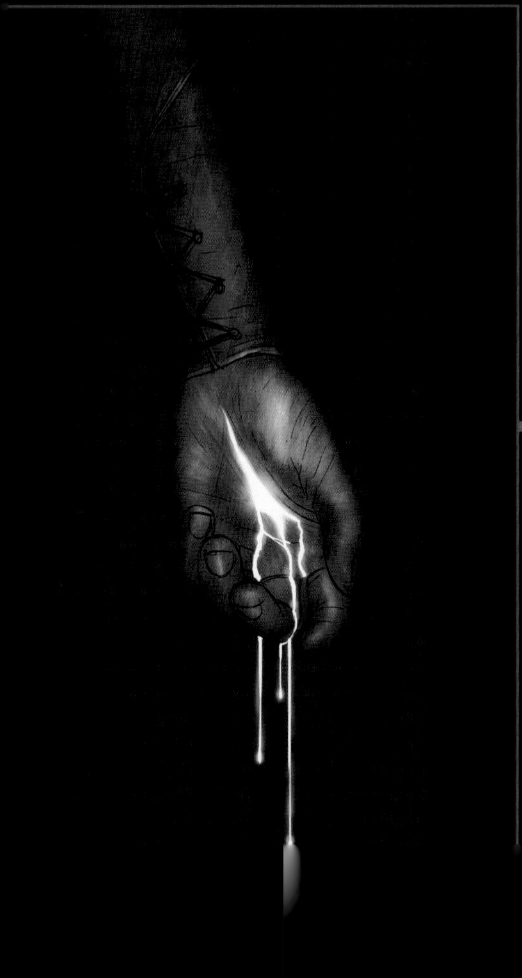

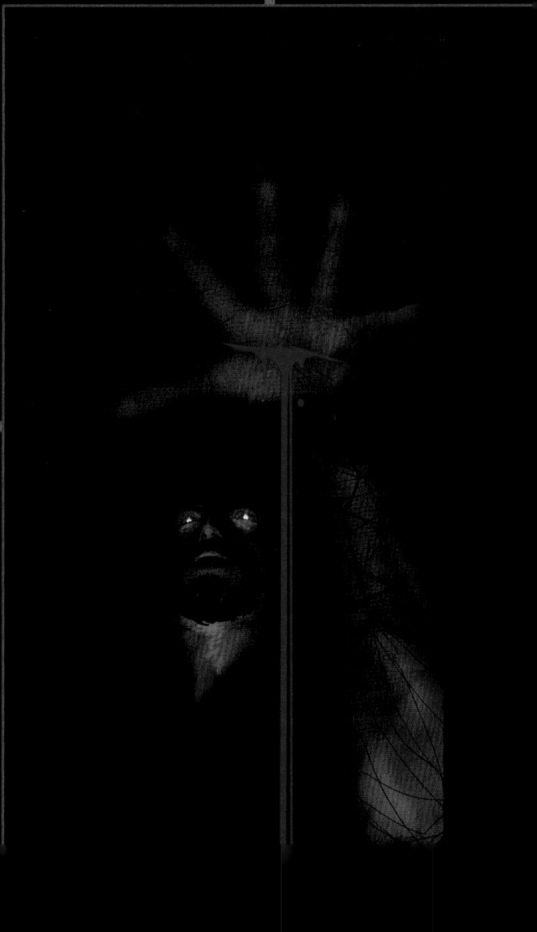

Not every cover made it onto the shelves, for various reasons. The original cover for issue 3 had Vlad sitting around, presumably contemplating something or other, after having hacked up a horde of vamps. It was one of those pieces that seemed to work really well in the rough stage, but went through multiple tweaks and redraws until I finally snapped and drew something else instead.

SPECIAL THANKS & ACKNOWLEDGMENTS

First of all, thanks to the folks at Top Cow for not only publishing *Impaler*, but for supporting it and seeing it through to the conclusion of this story arc. Matt, Filip, Phil, and Rob went the extra mile for this book, and I owe them a lot.

Thanks to Matt for turning in amazing page after amazing page, and for drawing all of the crazy things I asked him to draw. When Matt's a superstar, I'll be able to proudly point to this book and say that I worked with him way-back-when.

To my friends Li Kuo, Corey Cohen, and Rob Smith who either gave me feedback on the scripts or pimped the comic in their magazines -- I owe you guys. Special thanks also to my friends Sean Cleveland and Bryan Del Rizzo at NVIDIA, who helped me keep my computer up and running.

The Comic Stop in Redmond and Zanadu in Seattle both hosted awesome Impaler events and helped us get the book out to a lot of new readers.
For my family, thanks for always supporting my writing.

To the readers who doggedly waited for each issue, Matt and I can never thank you enough. Without you, this book wouldn't exist.

While writing *Impaler*, I listened to Iron Maiden, Korn, Judas Priest, Johnny Cash, Queensryche, Radiohead, and Rise Against. Not necessarily in that order.

--**William Harms**
mail@williamharms.com

Typically, William has already pretty much covered anything I've got to say about Top Cow and the people that made *Impaler* possible. They were all great people to work with and, even better, they taught me a lot about drawing comics while paying me to learn. Result!

Big thanks to William, for asking me to draw some quite literally impossible stuff- and for not taking it too badly when I said no. Seriously, there was always an openness to any art suggestions from me that made my life a lot less stressful and the book far more pleasurable to work on.

Thanks to Sara, Lottie and Woody, my beautiful family- mainly for not taking it to heart when I was grumpy (and I was grumpy a LOT) and for just being there when I needed them. Lottie told her teacher that I was drawing Ben 10 and, to his credit, he seemed only slightly less impressed when I told him the truth.

Finally, I'd like to thank the people that read *Impaler* and who went out of their way to tell us how much they enjoyed what we were doing. Jim Zuran, in particular, wrote me several nice emails- as well as Chris Drylie, who I met at my first ever signing at the British International Comics Show (I say signing, but nobody knew who I was, so it was more like a lengthy sit down) and who has been telling anyone who will listen that they should be buying my stuff ever since. He has also yet to send me anything weird in the post or turn up at my house in his boxers- so there's that.

As noted, William listened to some really rubbish music while writing *Impaler.* My own music collection is infinitely superior.

Fact.

--**Matt Timson**, somewhere in the UK, 2010.
http://matttimson.com

Ready for more? Jump into the Top Cow Universe with Witchblade!

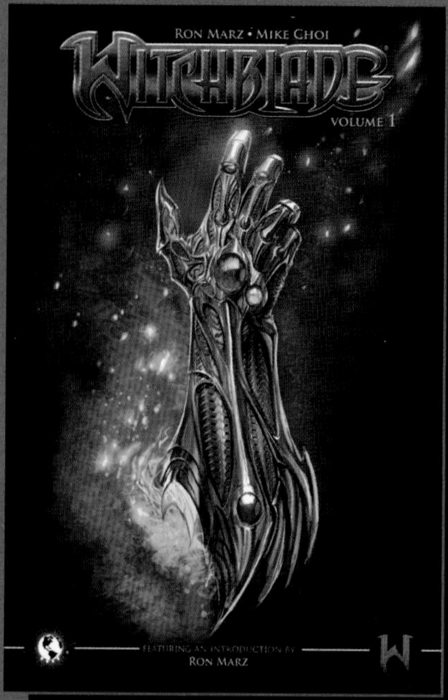
RON MARZ • MIKE CHOI
WITCHBLADE
VOLUME 1
FEATURING AN INTRODUCTION BY
RON MARZ

Witchblade
volume 1 - volume 7

written by:
Ron Marz
art by:
Mike Choi, Stephen Sadowski, Keu Cha, Chris Bachalo, Stjepan Sejic and more!

Get in on the ground floor of Top Cow's flagship title with these affordable trade paperback collections from Ron Marz's series-redefining run on Witchblade! Each volume collects a key story arc in the continuing adventures of Sara Pezzini and the Witchblade.

volume 1
collects issues #80-#85
(ISBN: 978-1-58240-906-1) $9.99

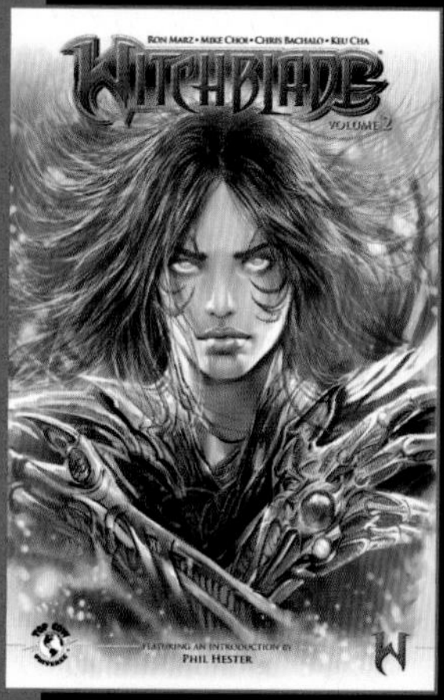
WITCHBLADE
VOLUME 2
PHIL HESTER

volume 2
collects issues #86-#92
(ISBN: 978-1-58240-886-6)
U.S.D. $14.99

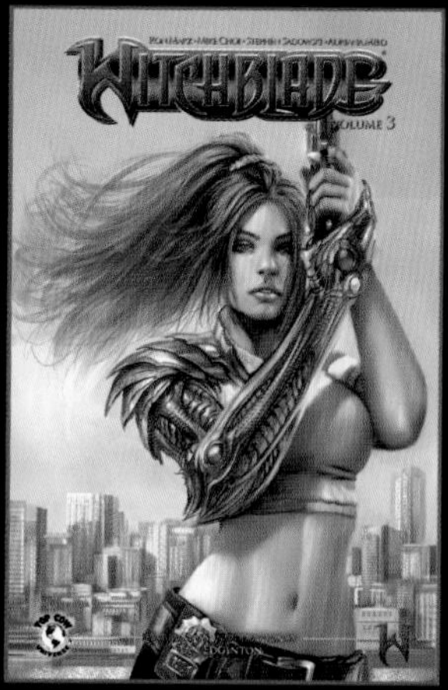
WITCHBLADE
VOLUME 3

volume 3
collects issues #93-#100
(ISBN: 978-1-58240-887-3)
U.S.D. $14.99

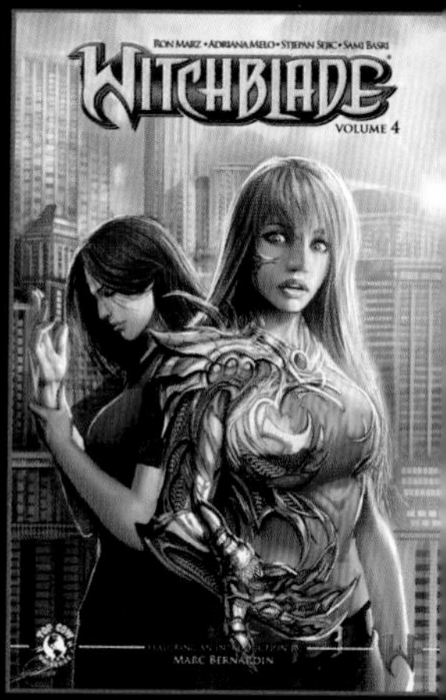
WITCHBLADE
VOLUME 4
MARC BERNARDIN

volume 4
collects issues #101-10
(ISBN: 978-1-58240-898-9
U.S.D. $17.9

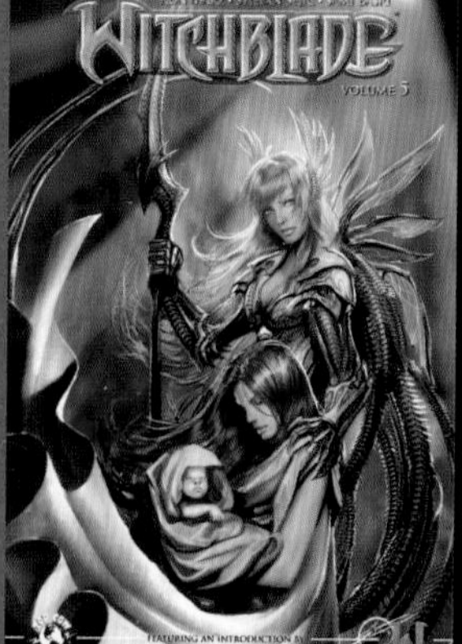
WITCHBLADE
VOLUME 5
FEATURING AN INTRODUCTION BY
ROBERT KIRKMAN

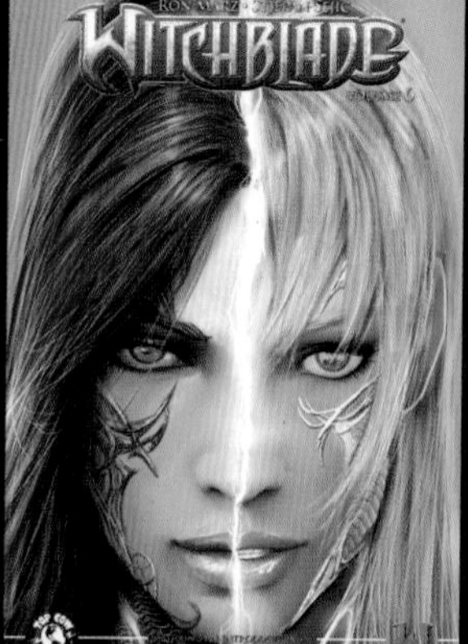
WITCHBLADE

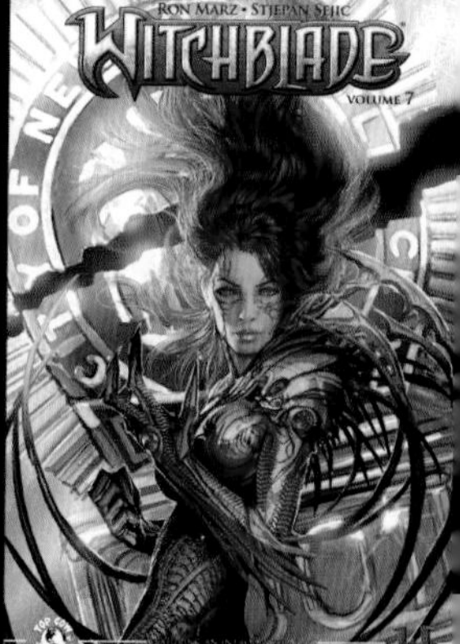
RON MARZ • STJEPAN SEJIC
WITCHBLADE
VOLUME 7

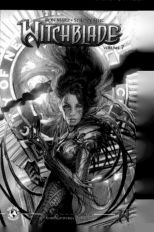

Jump into the Top Cow Universe with The Darkness!

The Darkness
Accursed vol.1

written by:
Phil Hester

pencils by:
Michael Broussard

Mafia hitman Jackie Estacado was both blessed and cursed on his 21st birthday when he became the bearer of The Darkness, an elemental force that allows those who wield it access to an otherwordly dimension and control over the demons who dwell there. Forces for good in the world rise up to face Jackie and the evil his gift represents, but there is one small problem. In this story...they are the bad guys.

Now's your chance to read "Empire," the first storyline by the new creative team of **Phil Hester** (*Firebreather*, *Green Arrow*) and **Michael Broussard** (*Unholy Union*) that marked the shocking return of *The Darkness* to the Top Cow Universe!

Book Market Edition
(ISBN 13: 978-1-58240-958-0) $9.99

The Darkness
Accursed vol.2

written by: **Phil Hester**

pencils by: **Jorge Lucas, Michael Broussard, Joe Benitez, Dale Keown** and more!

Collects *The Darkness* volume 3 #7-10 and the double-sized *The Darkness* #75 (issue #11 before the Legacy Numbering took effect), plus a cover gallery and behind-the-scenes extras!

(ISBN 13: 978-1-58240-044-4) $9.99

The Darkness
Accursed vol.3

written by: **Phil Hester**

pencils by: **Michael Broussard, Jorge Lucas, Nelson Blake II** and **Michael Avon Oeming.**

Collects issues #76-79 plus the stand alone Tales of The Darkness story entitled "Lodbrok's Hand." Features art by regular series artist Michael Broussard (*Unholy Union*, *Artifacts*), Nelson Blake II (*Magdalena*, *Broken Trinity: Witchblade*), Jorge Lucas (*Broken Trinity: Aftermath*, *Wolverine*), and Michael Avon Oeming (*Mice Templar*, *Powers*).

(ISBN 13: 978-1-58240-100-7) $12.99

Premium collected editions

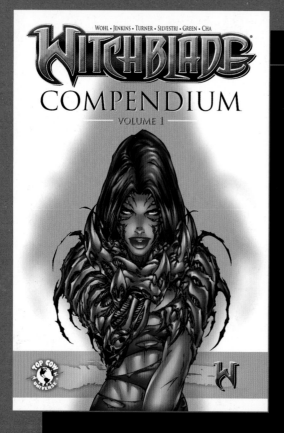

Witchblade
Compendium vol.1

written by:
David Wohl, Christina Z.,
Paul Jenkins
pencils by:
Michael Turner, Randy Green
Keu Cha and more!

From the hit live-action television series to the current Japanese anime, *Witchblade* has been Top Cow's flagship title for over a decade. There's nothing like going back to the beginning and reading it all over again. This massive collection houses issues #1-50 in a single edition for the first time. See how the Witchblade chose Sara and threw her into the chaotic world of the supernatural. Get the first appearances of Sara Pezzini, Ian Nottingham, Kenneth Irons and Jackie Estacado in one handy tome!

SC (ISBN 13: 978-1-58240-634-3) $59.99
HC (ISBN 13: 978-1-58240-798-2) $99.99

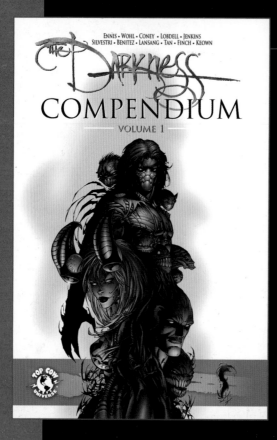

The Darkness
Compendium vol.1

written by:
Garth Ennis, Paul Jenkins,
Scott Lobdell
pencils by:
Marc Silvestri, Joe Benitez and more!

On his 21st birthday, the awesome and terrible powers of the Darkness awaken within Jackie Estacado, a mafia hitman for the Franchetti crime family. There's nothing like going back to the beginning and reading it all over again-- issues #1-40, plus the complete run of the *Tales of the Darkness* series collected into one trade paperback. See how the Darkness first appeared and threw Jackie into the chaotic world of the supernatural. Get the first appearances of The Magdalena and more!

SC (ISBN 13: 978-1-58240-643-5) $59.99
HC (ISBN 13: 978-1-58240-992-7) $99.99